The Social Life
of Materials

The Social Life of Materials

Studies in materials and society

Edited by Adam Drazin and Susanne Küchler

BLOOMSBURY ACADEMIC
An imprint of Bloomsbury Publishing Plc

B L O O M S B U R Y
LONDON • NEW DELHI • NEW YORK • SYDNEY

Bloomsbury Academic
An imprint of Bloomsbury Publishing Plc

50 Bedford Square	1385 Broadway
London	New York
WC1B 3DP	NY 10018
UK	USA

www.bloomsbury.com

BLOOMSBURY and the Diana logo are trademarks of
Bloomsbury Publishing Plc

First published 2015

© Adam Drazin and Susanne Küchler, 2015

British Library Cataloguing-in-Publication Data
A catalogue record for this book is available from the British Library.

ISBN: HB: 978-1-4725-9263-7
PB: 978-1-4725-9264-4
ePDF: 978-1-4725-9265-1
ePub: 978-1-4725-9266-8

Library of Congress Cataloging-in-Publication Data
A catalog record for this book is available from the Library of Congress.

Typeset by Newgen Knowledge Works (P) Ltd., Chennai, India
Printed and bound in India

Contents

Part 3 From substance to form

Part 4 The subversion of form by substance

Part 5 Ecologies of materials' social lives

List of figures

Notes on contributors

Andrew Barry is professor of Human Geography at University College London. His research interests centre on the political geography of materials, social and anthropological theory and the role of the natural sciences in political and economic life. His most recent books are *Material Politics: Disputes along the Pipeline* and *Interdisciplinarity: Reconfigurations of the Social and Natural Sciences* (ed. with Georgina Born).

Filipe Calvão is an assistant professor at the Graduate Institute of International and Development Studies in Switzerland. His PhD is from the University of Chicago. He has published on value, diamonds and corporate mining in the journal *Anthropological Theory* and in edited volumes.

Laurence Douny is an honorary research fellow and former postdoctoral Leverhulme Trust Early Career Fellow at UCL Anthropology. Since 2008, she has been conducting research on wild silk and indigo dyeing materials, techniques and design in West Africa among the Dogon and Marka-Dafing of Mali and Burkina Faso as well as the Hausa of Northern Nigeria.

Adam Drazin lectures in the Department of Anthropology at UCL, where he coordinates the MA in Materials, Anthropology and Design. He has worked at several universities as well as for multinational companies as a design anthropology consultant, including HP Labs and Intel; and he is external examiner at Glasgow School of Art, department of product design. This career has resulted in a diverse range of research experience. He has mainly published on the material culture of the Romanian home, and on issues of practice and training in design anthropology. His most recent publication is a paper on design concepts in *Design Anthropology* (ed. Wendy Gunn, Ton Otto and Rachel Smith), and an edited volume *Exhibit Ireland: Ethnographic Collections in Ireland*, published by Wordwell Press.

Tom Fisher is professor in the School of Art and Design at Nottingham Trent University, where he coordinates research. After study in art and design and some years running a small craft business, he earned his PhD at the University of York in Sociology, concentrating on the role of plastics in consumption experiences. His work draws on his background in craft practice and stresses the materiality of our interactions with things, and therefore their design. It has led to a book on the everyday reuse of packaging, as well as funded research on sustainable clothing (Defra) and industrial heritage (AHRC). His current work is focusing on embodied knowledge; the ethics of design and technologies; and design, culture and innovation.

David Howes is an anthropologist based at Concordia University, Montreal and the director of the Centre for Sensory Studies. The Centre provides a collabo-rative interdisciplinary platform for research in the social life and history of the senses, multisensory aesthetics, and the development of technologies for expanding the sensorium in innovative ways. A pioneer of the anthropology of the senses, Howes has carried out field research on medicine and the five senses in Northwestern Argentina, the sensory life of things in the Pitt Rivers Museum, Oxford, and the comparative study of sensory orders in Melanesia. An important further branch of his research concerns the application of sensory ethnogra-phy to market research. Howes is one of the founding editors of *The Senses and Society* journal, co-author of a widely acclaimed (and translated) book on the cultural history and anthropology of smell called *Aroma* and the author of *Sensual Relations*. He recently published *Ways of Sensing: Understanding the Senses in Society* (with Constance Classen).

Susanne Küchler is professor in Anthropology and Material Culture at University College London. She has conducted ethnographic fieldwork in Papua New Guinea and Eastern Polynesia over the past 25 years, studying creativity, innovation and futurity in political economies of knowledge from a comparative perspective. Her more recent work on the history of the take-up, in the Pacific, of cloth and clothing as 'new' material has focused on social memory and mater-ial translation, and on the epistemic nature of materials and its role in long-term social change. Over the past five years she has extended the comparative remit of this research to science based materials innovation, commodification and consumption. Working from within material culture studies, her work is ethno-graphic in orientation and is influenced by a close reading of German and French writing on epistemology and the culture of things.

Fiona P. McDonald completed her PhD at University College London in 2014 in the Department of Anthropology (Material Culture and Visual Anthropology). She is currently a researcher at New Knowledge Organization, a non-profit academic think-tank in New York City (United States). Her research on woollen blankets builds upon her graduate studies in Art History (Canada) and Māori

Material Culture (Aotearoa New Zealand) to consider the social specificity of the aesthetic transformations of materials in contemporary art, craft, and customary Indigenous regalia. Fiona is a founding member of the curatorial collective, *Ethnographic Terminalia*; a group that curates exhibitions at the intersection of art and anthropology. Fiona's areas of interest are: Indigenous material and visual culture, contemporary Indigenous art, museum studies, Māori *Taonga*, Tlingit *At.óowu*, material culture theory, ethnographic object analysis, curatorial studies, and performance theory.

Deirdre McKay is a senior lecturer in Social Geography at Keele University, and was previously at the Australian National University. Her research work has focused on place-based experiences of globalization and development, especially in the Philippines. Her books, *Global Filipinos* (Indiana 2012) and *Archipelago of Care* (Indiana, 2016) explore the affective texture of the global in the daily lives of Filipino migrants. With her colleague and collaborator Padmapani Perez (University of the Philippines, Baguio), she has only recently started exploring the social significance of materials.

Padmapani Perez is Senior Lecturer in Anthropology at the University of the Philippines, and co-owner of the Mountain Cloud bookstore. Ruel Bimuyag is an Ifugao cultural practitioner, musician, award-winning photographer and eco-guide. Based in Baguio City, he guides visitors across the Philippine Cordillera Central and collects plastic art, as well as making his own plastic crafts. Raja Shanti Bonnevie, drummer and eco-guide for the Baguio City region, is completing his Masters in Development Studies at the University of the Philippines.

Mark A. Miodownik is professor of Materials and Society and director of Institute of Making at UCL where he teaches and runs a research group. He received his PhD in turbine jet engine alloys from Oxford University in 1996, and since then has published more than 100 research papers. His current research interests include smart materials, innovative manufacturing, and sensoaesthetic materials. Prof Miodownik is a broadcaster and writer: he gave the 2010 Royal Institution Christmas Lectures, and regularly presents BBC TV programmes on engineering and materials. In 2014 he was elected a fellow of the Royal Academy of Engineering.

Urmila Mohan is a PhD candidate in the Department of Anthropology, University College London. She has a Master's degree in Art (Pennsylvania State University, United States) and undergraduate degrees in design (National Institute of Design, India) and anthropology (Victoria University of Wellington, New Zealand). She is interested in the philosophy and use of materials in art, craft and design as well as how these practices relate to sociality and identity.

Peter Oakley is research leader for the School of Material at the Royal College of Art. His research interests cover: the manufacture and retail of luxury goods, specialist manufacturing clusters and communities, the technical analysis of substances and the management, presentation and commercial exploitation of heritage. He is a Fellow of the Royal Anthropological Institute, an Honorary Research Fellow at UCL and a member of the advisory boards for the Sustainable Luxury Forum and Making Futures. He is currently conducting research on the fine jewellery and watch industries and its supply chains and on interactions between craft practice and digital technologies.

Chan Chow Wah has a Masters of Science in Social Anthropology from London School of Economics. He is an independent scholar with research interests in consumption, marketing, religion and history of Singapore and Overseas Chinese. His recent book and documentary is *Light on the Lotus Hill*, documenting a forgotten dimension of Singapore wartime history.

Graeme Were is senior lecturer in anthropology and museum studies at the University of Queensland, Australia. He has conducted extensive research on material innovation in Melanesian society as well as the significance of pattern across the Pacific. His book *Lines That Connect* was published with University of Hawaii Press in 2010, and he was co-author of *Pacific Pattern* (Thames and Hudson 2005). He has guest-edited, and published in a range of journals including *Textile, Journal of Material Culture*, and *Journal of Visual Communication*.

Sarah Wilkes is the research manager and post-doctoral researcher at the Institute of Making, University College London. She completed her PhD in the Department of Anthropology at UCL, in collaboration with industrial partners at the Institute of Materials, Minerals and Mining (IOM[3]). Her current work focuses on the ways in which perceptions of risk, health and sustainability inform the selection and use of materials in the United Kingdom. Research interests include the governance of materials, the relationship between materials and personhood, and interdisciplinary engagement between materials research and design.

Acknowledgements

This book has taken several years to come together – and the work it contains has taken even longer. The work has arisen from the ideas, suggestions and contributions of a wide range of people and networks who have been pushing the concerns of cultures of materials forward in recent years. The editors would like to acknowledge in particular the wide range of people who over the years have contributed to the study of materials at University College London. These various materials experts have included Linda Barron, Margaret Pope, Jakki Dehn, Mark Nesbitt, Sophie Thomas, Kaori O'Connor, Geoff Hollington, Glenn Adamson, Zoe Laughlin, Lucy Norris, Sevra Davis, Dinah Eastop, Camilla Sundwall, Chris Lefteri, and Victor Buchli. We would also like to thank Anais Bloch, who worked through various early drafts of the book cover.

Graeme Were would like to acknowledge the kind support of Scion Research for the work presented in Chapter 2, especially Professor Roger Newman who provided invaluable assistance and knowledge of *harakeke* and materials innovation.

Chapter 3 was previously published in *Theory, Culture and Society* 22:1 (2005), and is reprinted here with permission. Andrew Barry would like to thank Georgie Born, Monica Greco, Mariam Fraser, Sarah Kember, Mick Halewood and Celia Lury; the referees of *Theory, Culture and Society* for their comments on an earlier draft of the article; and Alan Blackwell of Crucible for his support and collaboration. Thanks also to ArQule and Camitro and, in particular, Mike Tarbit, Matt Segall, Mark Ashwell and Steve Gallion for the support, interest and comments.

Chapter 4 was previously published in the journal *Pure and Applied Chemistry* (2007) Vol. 79(10): 1635–41, and is reprinted here with permission. Mark A. Miodownik wishes to thank UCL and all members of the Institute of Making, past and present.

An earlier draft of the first half of Chapter 5 was published in the *Proceedings of the Ethnographic Practices in Industry (EPIC)* 2013 conference (Howes 2013). David Howes wishes to thank the copyright holder of this material, the American Anthropological Association, for allowing its reproduction here. In being transposed, however, it has been substantially modified and expanded. The cultural history of plastic presented in the concluding section of this essay derives in large part from his introduction to *A Cultural History of the Senses in the Modern Age, 1920–2000* (Howes 2014).

The first part of Laurence Douny's ongoing research on West African wild silk, presented in Chapter 6, was funded by the Leverhulme Trust (2009–2012) and supervised by Dr Claude Ardouin at The British Museum (1950–2011). Dr Douny is grateful to Dr Guindo and Dr Maiga at the CNRST and Mamadou Diawara and Dr Sissoko at Point Sud in Bamako; Dr Some, Dr Basile Guisson and Dr Assimi Salawu at the CNRST Ouagadougou from whom she obtained research permits and research affiliation. She would like to thank Salif Sawadogo, Hamadou Djibo and all her Dogon and Marka-Dafing informants in Mali and Burkina Faso and Violet Diallo (GAP/Bamako) for copy-editing.

Tom Fisher gratefully thanks María José Ossandón for permission to refer in detail to her blog *La Vie en Plastique*.

More than one funding body provided support that facilitated the research in this volume. Urmila Mohan's fieldwork in India was partially funded by a 2012–2013 India Travel Award by the Nehru Trust for the Indian Collections at the Victoria and Albert Museum, London. Peter Oakley's fieldwork was undertaken with financial support from the Arts and Humanities Research Council (AHRC). Sarah Wilkes would like to gratefully acknowledge the support of the AHRC, who funded the research presented in Chapter 12.

Filipe Calvão would like to thank two anonymous reviewers for their comments, SSRC-IDRF and FCT/MCT for funding different moments of this research, as well as Tracey Rosen, Susan Gal, Claudia Cruz Leo, and the Semiotics Workshop at the University of Chicago for insightful criticism on previous versions of this chapter.

Fiona P. McDonald dedicates Chapter 14 to all of the international artists that work and have worked with woollen blankets in their art. In particular, sincere and warm thanks are due to Marie Watt and Tracey Williams for sharing their material experiences so openly.

Preface: Materials transformations

Adam Drazin

Why conduct ethnographic studies of materials and society?

What disciplinary approaches are there to materials?

What anthropological approaches are there to materials?

What terms and terminologies can be used?

Why conduct ethnographic studies of materials and society?

We may be in the midst of a materials revolution, a historical moment of innovation and change in the diversity of materials available to us, and in the constitution of the materials which already surround us. Professional fields such as materials science, engineering, manufacturing and design are feeling the impact of this revolution at the moment, which could compare with the digital revolution in its implications. It is however not only a revolution in science but a social and cultural revolution.

As they have emerged into public consciousness, it is increasingly being realized how important materials are to many dimensions of policy, economics, ethics and the public sphere in general (Hudson 2011). This is for several reasons, which concern the macro-politics, the micro-politics, and the experience of materials. At a global level, certain specific materials have come to be crucial ingredients in modern technologies. Mobile phones and touchscreens, for example, depend upon iridium and other very specific substances. Many such materials have very limited sources in the world, or even a single source. Frequently, these sources are located in zones of political and economic disturbance, or places where there is a risk of war or revolution. The world's contemporary dependence on certain materials heralds repetitions of historical cycles of conflict. If we recall how in recent years global conflicts have been linked to global dependence on, and interests in, oil and petrochemical materials, then why should not similar conflicts happen in future around other comparable materials? Materials usage is not politically or economically neutral and especially in material monocultures.

Materials do not only have macro-politics and geopolitics, but micro-politics. They are one of the media through which corporate involvement in everyday life can be felt. Corporations are beginning to own certain kinds of substances, those which it can be claimed have been either 'created' or 'discovered'. It is not only products and things which are 'owned' in our lives, but increasingly the stuff itself of which things are made. Some companies (as David Howes notes in this volume) are also tightening their grip on materials through their branding of, and intellectual property ownership of, certain sensations and senses.

Moving away from private corporations, materials have also become more of a focus for NGOs and social movements. The aspiration for something called sustainability has grown ever more powerful in everyday life and made people more aware of materials. As more people profess to consider and examine their worlds in terms of sustainability, they perceive more clearly the materials and substances of which the world comprises.

In terms of individual experience and imagination, this moving territory, ranging from uniform 'grey goo' to exciting rainbows of possible substances, can be problematic. A putative materials revolution means that a person can no longer be certain of what things are made from. If you have ever washed something at the wrong temperature, printed the wrong ink onto the wrong paper, used the wrong kind of flour in a recipe or melted new kitchen implements and then felt that this was a mistake on your part, then you will have experienced a changing materials world. Our capacity to fulfil tasks and live up to our responsibilities to others can depend upon knowing how substances behave. Materials innovation reveals and challenges those doxic material mappings we carry around with us and makes us reconsider experience.

In materials innovation, there is a particular gap between the conception of a material, existing as raw 'stuff', and the moment when it comes to be a part of life as something used. Materials, new or old, can be seen to 'succeed' or 'fail' in this sense (Küchler, this volume). Very many materials have not yet succeeded, the kinds of materials that are exciting laboratory oddities. In some ways, we are experiencing a political divide around materials. On one side are those who favour monocultures of mass-produced, known materials. On the other side is a strange coalition of different groups who celebrate materials diversity through science, art, laboratory work, crafts, design, historical discovery, localism or simply playfulness.

The subject of materials is a pervasive one, not one which can be easily relegated to specific domains of life, or contained behind certain boundaries. People are constituted in materials. Information is constituted in materials. Objects are constituted in materials, some more evidently and some less, from televisions to touchscreens to jeans to wedding rings to bricks. In this sense, the study of materials transcends the study of any individual material. It is a field that reaches into questions of ontology and being, epistemology and knowledge.

However, materials have historically proved an evasive topic of study for social science. Often, materials have seemed un-social, the raw stuff from which people would be able to shape cultural and social life, but in themselves not cultural. Materials have been subject (and victim) of the worship of pure nature. In this volume, we relocate materials. In social terms, they are no longer 'raw'.

There is therefore a need for an academic ecosystem of diverse ideas and approaches around materials. Social studies of materials and society, as are to be found in this volume, are just one of the diverse ways in which we need to look at materials. They amount to a socially empirical approach. There is the risk of being over-dependent on laboratory-based and studio-based approaches to materials, which conceive of them as having inevitable intrinsic properties that will determine social and cultural implications or effects. We here celebrate socially empirical studies, and especially ethnographic studies, because they are the only way in which we can begin to observe what actually happens around materials, test whether our ideas apply and see just why materials matter. It is important to ask what is it that materials actually do?

Throughout this book, different authors present their own observations and studies of certain materials. What they also do is explore different ways of thinking about materials. There are a wide range of ways in which one can think about materials, and we need to find more such approaches. Through this book, hopefully every reader can begin to ask for themselves whether they are confident they know what materials are, and what their own approach is. And if they do not yet know, they can be helped to see some possible answers for themselves.

What disciplinary approaches are there to materials?

A number of disciplines have responded to the prospect of a materials revolution by outlining more focused approaches to what they are and what they do. Such approaches have particular characteristics, and show something of the variety of ways in which materials can be conceived and approached epistemologically.

We cannot attempt any kind of comprehensive bibliography here, just a few windows into different relevant areas of work.

Materials science and engineering is evidently a key field, where a scientific perception and analysis of materials is prevalent and well developed. There are a number of different approaches within this discipline. In Cambridge, one influential approach is provided by the team coalescing around Mike Ashby (Ashby and Johnson 2009), and popularized and promulgated with particular software tools known as CEU EduPack. Within engineering, there is a particular attention to the chemical composition of materials and structure at different levels (atomic, nano-, crystalline, etc.). Materials science often groups materials by category. The categories may in some sense overlap, or be sorted into macro- and micro- categories, but have a utility and commonsense nature about them. Hence 'stones', 'foams', 'metals', 'ceramics', 'plastics' could be deployed. One can also consider more abstract categories such as 'natural materials', when it is difficult to distinguish such materials as wood, resin, rubber, or shell, and such categories reveal the grey areas of engineering's approach where more flexibility is required. The field also has difficulty deciding how to incorporate many phenomena that other disciplines would consider very important as materials, such as textiles.

The capacity exists within engineering to define and measure materials' properties and to map and locate materials according to such properties as acoustic qualities, density, tensile strength and so forth. In this sense, practically anything that can be quantitatively measured can be seen as a property. Another implication is that practically anything physical in the world can fit into the schema. From an engineering point of view, you can take any observed situation and reduce it to its constituent materials and their properties. No particular aspect of a situation is more or less of a material, unlike within many cultural paradigms where certain things at certain times are seen as 'materials' more. There is also a strong degree of comparability, and in some cases even substitutability, of materials in engineering work. It is possible to begin to see materials as 'the answer' to a utilitarian problem. If you need a material for a task, which needs to have a certain density, strength, and thermodynamic properties, then through a quantitative analysis of these properties, one may produce a selection of possible alternatives.

While the greatest, significant contribution of products such as CEU Edupack has been to classify and categorize properties, it is very explicit that the people who have developed and use it do not consider this kind of 'intrinsic properties' approach to be sufficient in itself. Most engineers acknowledge the need to mitigate the more positivist tendencies of engineering. The quest for finding the 'right' material or materials is not a journey, for them, which necessarily has a 'right' answer, but rather a journey in which one can avoid wrong answers and deploy measurements and modellings to get a much better-engineered result. Hence Ashby advocates taking several approaches in materials work, among them Synthesis, Similarity and Innovation. By this, he means that one should experiment with, compare and contrast, artistically experience and play with materials, as a part of their exploration. Mark A. Miodownik (this volume) is also one of a number of engineering voices who advocate much broader, and socially informed, approaches.

Mainstream engineering approaches to materials have provided especially powerful ways to model sustainability in materials. The definition of what is 'sustainability' here must be very specific (see Wilkes, this volume), often seen through an analysis of the measured energy implications if a particular thing or product is engineered in a particular way. An analysis of the energy implications of using a material must take account of, among other things, transport, lifespan, origins and production. This 'universalizing' approach to the energy implications of a material is exceptionally powerful and is an important weapon in making our world more environmentally attuned.

Within design (which is as diverse a field as is engineering, ranging from industrial design to service design, to arts, to graphic design), an entirely different set of paradigmatic approaches applies. The design literature is full of large, glossy books, which are not so much analyses as catalogues of materials to which a designer can turn for ideas or inspiration (Lefteri 2006; Howes and Laughlin 2012). Unlike in engineering, the physical image or presence of materials comes to be very important and an appreciation of the aesthetic properties of materials. It is impossible to produce anything remotely comprehensive, and so there is a balance between presenting materials that are in some sense typical of a category (e.g. a ceramic) and those that are somehow 'innovative' materials.

Many designerly materials would not from an engineering point of view be considered as materials but rather as composites. Hence materials such as textiles, various kinds of sculpted cardboard or layered wood are also materials from a design point of view. These types of thing-manifested materials expose the fallacy of the idea that a complete distinction can be made between form and substance. They are convergent. Likewise, design concerns itself equally with the 'experience' of people who use and work with designed products and services. Materials often 'speak for themselves', and there is a resistance to 'explaining' them in terms for example of abstract properties. Hence experience is ever more as an entry point into materials and categories of materials (Karana et al. 2014). Where an engineer may distinguish the material as thing from the material properties, using the one to explain the other, in design this distinction may be less clear.

Both engineering and design are especially concerned with certain macro-categories of materials, which are not definitive but ways of considering significant issues in contested ways. Such categories may include sustainable materials, natural materials, bio materials, innovative materials, smart materials. The persistent tropes of naturalness, artificiality, and smartness, help to trans-late the implications of the incipient materials revolution into design-suggestive social or cultural terms.

Like engineering and design, philosophy has begun to address the implica-tions of the putative materials revolution. The most common suggestion is that experience of materials is changing at an ontological level. In the past, in a world where materials were only rarely invented or discovered, where many materials were locally sourced and the possibilities for mixing and reinventing them was likewise relatively slow, you could be fairly sure of knowing the properties of any particular material you encountered. This predictability rendered materials as in some sense reactive. Their properties would be what Leibniz would call passive, appearing in pre-determined and pre-intended uses in reaction to human action. For a number of reasons, however, we can no longer depend on the predictabil-ity of materials. The conception of materials as active (Bennett 2010), as agentic, and as much more causal in social and epistemological situations, can be seen as a 'vitalist materialist' perspective:

> Is it not possible to imagine matter quite differently: as perhaps a lively material-ity that is self-transformative and already saturated with the agentic capacities and existential significance that are typically located in a separate, ideal and subjectivist realm? (Coole 2010: 92)

Coole and Frost (2010) explore the range of philosophical presentations of this phenomenon, which comprises one of the contemporary challenges to the notion of the Kantian subject (Poe 2011). If materials are something which can help constitute subjectivity, then this reverses some of the philosophical assumptions of the past two centuries. Materials come to be active ontologically, and in political participation.

All three of these disciplines – Engineering, Design and Philosophy – are lack-ing in empirical observations of materials in everyday human situations, because they depend upon experimentation, studio work and the academy. The immense literatures within archaeology, art, and craft (which, with apologies, we cannot broach here) each take a much more hands-on approach to specific materials.

Anthropological approaches meanwhile are the main concern of this volume's contributors.

What anthropological approaches to materials are there?

As well as setting out ethnographic studies of materials, the contributors to this volume present a range of new epistemological approaches to materials, largely from an anthropological perspective. Their work is however based on a longer-term tradition of studies of materials in social science. Historically, a number of approaches are particularly worth mentioning.

Leroi-Gourhan (1943, 1945) provides the starting point for a modern cultural appreciation of materials and matter, and reveals both positive aspects and difficulties with an anthropology of materials. Leroi-Gourhan is concerned with the question of the universality of technical tendencies in objects, being strongly concerned with archaeology and a material culture approach to society. Leroi-Gourhan's method involves the conundrums of how to approach social questions through things which are material, which exist in anthropology both as social artefact and as social data. Through an exploration of the 'technical' domain, he proposes one is able to conceive of the interrelation of human groups with environments and produce subjective modellings of operational sequences, which produce particular material and social forms.

Leroi-Gourhan's ideas are very contemporary in the ways in which they deal with the social problematics of materials. Leroi-Gourhan's notion of 'matter' (*la matière*) correctly clouds any clear distinction between conceptual and material. His approach is also admirably processual. However, in spite of his intentions there arises still a certain dualism, in which a need arises to deconstruct notions of nature and environment. In Leroi-Gourhan's terms, materials still fall somewhere between the category of the environmental or natural, and the category of the technical or resource. There remains the notion of materials as raw, unprocessed, awaiting the human hand as the magic ingredient that is to render them somehow cultural.

Through the mid-twentieth century, within the Anglo-American tradition of anthropology, the study of materials declined a little, as semiotic and linguistic approaches in anthropology, alongside an emphasis on production within economic anthropology, gained the ascendancy to the detriment of some other aspects of material culture. The revival of material culture interests from the 1980s at first occurred with an emphasis on objects and goods, more than materials (Hahn and Soentsen 2011). Wagner describes the 1990s, for example, as a period of 'marginalization of materials' (2001; cited in Hahn and Soentgen 2011: 24). From the 1990s, however, a range of work brought concepts back on the radar which opened the door to a better appreciation of materials, especially work on properties and embodiment. One important earlier example in the Scandinavian tradition is Fredrik Barth's work (1990), which provided detailed localized ethnographies demonstrating the ways in which making with different materials can be generative of meaningfulness. Barth discusses materials as ways to significantly rework structures and categories of meaning in embodied acts.

The French praxeological tradition of examining the notion of technical action, begun by Leroi-Gourhan, also remained very active and unfolded through several generations of critics in journals such as *Techniques et Culture*. Pierre Lemonnier's work (2012) has in particular placed emphasis on the role of materials within the understanding of social action, techniques and skills. This school of anthropological approach has always advocated ways of approaching cultural and social contexts that take account of materials intrinsically as a part of modelling action. Hence materials are situated as one of the foci of anthropological and ethnographic activity, and one of the lenses through which one begins to perceive culture itself.

From the late 1990s, the work of Michael Taussig and Marilyn Strathern, in very different ways, proved beneficial to exploring materials. Through an emphasis on properties, both of these thinkers advance and problematize intersections between notions of knowledge and experience, between global and local. For Taussig (2008), an understanding of localized conceptions of what properties do, is one of the ways to resituate anthropological understandings of 'experience' as, rather, understandings of potentially oppressive socioeconomic forces of globalizing capitalism. This argument is most coherently advanced in his work on indigo, the substance and the colour. The glorious colour of indigo, he argues, has a literally magical subversive capacity, and in many ways the Western world works to suppress its dangers.

Marilyn Strathern has also helped to shift anthropological conceptions of materials. While we cannot in a short space summarize her ideas in themselves, we can consider some of their implications. One of the fundamental questions that Strathern's work addresses is 'What makes a person?' Rather than considering such entities as given, she points out how persons can be dependent upon the convergence of substances, properties and property relations in society (Strathern 1999). The science of new reproductive technologies (Strathern 1992) is one example of the prior anticipation of persons through perception of

materials. Like Taussig then, Strathern models one way in which material properties and property relations intersect and are evidenced in social effects. Second,
she addresses the problematic inclination for material aspects of social life to
be seen to represent universalizable qualities, while the quality of diversity is
ascribed to human groups (Leroi-Gourhan's ideas, among others, imply this
difficulty). By contrast, Strathern's work has enabled anthropology to scrutinize
how notions of universality and of diversity are themselves culturally negotiated.
Hence, she draws attention to questions about when cultures see themselves
as pluralistic or monolithic, and how a diversifying world of properties may relate
to reconceiving society.

A range of work through the 1990s and since 2000 moves attention from
properties and more towards materials themselves. Tilley (1999) is one of
these thinkers. He develops arguments to reconsider the cultural effectiveness
of materials when they are categorized as types of matter and conceptually
interconnected in metaphorical relationships. Rendered as metaphors, materials come to be not only ways of doing but ways of thinking and understanding,
becoming a part of the architecture of ontologies and cosmologies. A second
pillar of Tilley's work, also developed by other archaeologists and anthropologists (see Bradley 2000) challenges the notion of materials as separable from
things that are artefactual or artificial. There is a long tradition in anthropology of deconstructing the notion of the natural, especially within rethinkings of
gender. Tilley brings this critique into material culture studies, by challenging
distinctions made between, for example, different stones in an archaeological
landscape – those which previously were seen as artefactual or monumental,
and those which were seen as not worked upon by people and hence natural. By contrast, Tilley considers a landscape or environment which comprises
in materials with which people engage in different ways. This leads towards
a phenomenological position on culture (Tilley and Bennett 2004).Taking a
more phenomenological approach challenges the idea that biographical
approaches are adequate for a study of materials, and undermines some
of Leroi-Gourhan's initial work in the field. Recent studies do not necessarily
appreciate materials by asking where they come from, what their social journeys are, or what happens first and what happens next. If it can be deceptive
to divide the natural from the artefactual, then of what relevance is the domain
of the technical? Similarly, and perhaps counter-intuitively, this kind of work
moves in a different direction from some work on properties by people such
as Strathern and Taussig, because it begins to undermine the relevance of
notions of exchange relationships around materials. In this sense, the anthropology of materials has fundamentally moved to critique the notion of 'the
social life of things' (Appadurai 1986) being the key paradigm through which to

approach the material world. When one focuses on materials before objects, different concerns, tensions and problems emerge.

Tim Ingold (2012, 2007) has done perhaps more than anyone to put materials per se back on the map of social science, as subjects of inquiry in themselves. Materials are an integral aspect of what Gosden refers to as 'Ingold's ecological perspective', looking at 'the rhythms that exist in different areas of life which help create and grow things within a series of echoing forms' (2006: 430). In this work, notions of social life as experiential, and the idea of flow, are integral. Ingold retains a sense of environment as universalizable in description, such that similar materials in different places matter, coupled with a localist poetics. In a 2012 article, he argues that the study of materials in anthropology will rebalance a past emphasis in the discipline on discrete material object forms, which has among other things helped to undermine the appreciation of persons as material entities. Re-awakening our sensibilities to the fact that we experience the world as a knitted fabric of textures, colours, and properties which are embedded in a materials consciousness, Ingold's work has opened the space of debate about *how* social scientists can, and should, appreciate materials. The contributors to this volume, in different ways, respond to this call.

In brief, at the time of writing, an anthropologist, or other social scientist, has a choice of intellectual tools to engage with materials. One can look first at techniques, often with the implication of an emphasis on acts of making in the world; one can discuss material properties as social and cultural phenomena, in which substances and materials are often the means by which material properties, social property, and intellectual property, are conveyed, exchanged and demonstrated in politicized networks and frameworks; one can consider material metaphors and explore the experience of materials and convergent categories; and one can draw on notions of flow, experience and phenomenology in ethnographic work to aspire to a more cosmological approach to materials. The long and the short of it is, however, that one must first conduct some kind of empirical research, to observe materials, substances, properties and senses. The role of the anthropologist is often to 'ground' theory and knowledge through convergent acts of observation and interpretation.

What terms and terminologies can be used?

This history of ideas has resulted in a specific set of terminologies, which it is important to outline. Each discipline works with materials in an utterly different environment, and each anthropologist has wrestled with local and particular words and terms for materials; so the authority of particular materials 'languages' can depend on where you are standing. Nonetheless, it is important to propose the ways in which we can communicate because, in exploring the kinds of terms that are professionally used, one also begins to perceive what the issues and points of difference may be.

When we talk of material stuff in general, the word *matter* is appropriate, and does not distinguish much between types of matter. *Materials*, meanwhile refers to slightly more specific categories of matter. They may be distinguished in a number of different ways: by chemical atomic composition, chemical or crystalline structure, origins, or the ways in which they are used in a particular place. The recognition of materials may be a question of etymology not chemistry, but nonetheless it is the notion of discreteness among types of matter which is often important. The term *substance* particularly tends to be used for material when a material is in a dialogue with the notion of *form*.

When we talk of *material properties*, this then means the ascription of the quality of having material *effects*. We have ascribed this ability to the substance of which a thing comprises. Recent debates have focussed on discussions as to whether properties primarily are a function of the relationships around things, or are intrinsic and essential to things. The notion of material properties, as a subset, then particularly focuses on the material substance.

Effects can of course take many different forms. Gell (1998) in particular placed an emphasis on effects, meaning the cognitive and social impacts arising from an encounter with a material thing. The idea of effects thus is useful partly because it is not very specifically defined but rather denotes a particular idea of how change happens between entities and in their engagement at discontinuous moments, rather than continuously. The notion of effects is handy for describing situations where change is seen to be connected to particular happenings or events.

The word *properties* tends to imply that there is a sense of inevitability about the effects or uses of materials, as if cotton must always be clothes, or plastic always kitsch, which is not correct. Alternatively therefore, we can choose to deploy the term *tendencies*, to describe and connote the sense of possibility or probability which surrounds properties. Leroi-Gourhan (1943) distinguishes tendencies (*tendances*) of materials from the facts (*faits*) of materials, to describe how materials are understood as doing things actively in the world, or may be considered as neutral and reactive in this respect. An active tendency of glass is to conduct light into a building and also to acquire dirt and become more murky unless cleaned. Those are active tendencies, and the glass causes the light to be a certain way. It also may shatter and create many sharp edges, but this latter tendency is a passive possibility, if you happen to want a sharp edge. Tendencies can themselves be described as intrinsic or extrinsic to a thing – for example, people with a scientific education see light as an extrinsic or reactive property. Light is in the atmosphere, and some things may reflect it, and have the property of shininess. Others may ascribe the lightness to the object itself, representing this light property as intrinsic to a thing, such that a mirror might be described as a light or bright object.

Strathern's work on properties (1999) indicates how the term typically situates the specific qualities of a thing or material in a wider set of social relations. It is not enough in many cases to specify that a particular sensory quality exists; rather there is the need to explain where such properties come from. Material properties and property relations are here intermingled for the purposes of the examination of many social environments.

The terms *senses*, *sensoriness,* or *sensoriality* are also frequently useful in this domain. This terminology comes to be useful within a paradigm which emphasizes perception and experience, either as social phenomena, or as the prime methodological tools by which a researcher comes to examine the material world. Phenomenological approaches are especially useful here.

In practice, then, one may encounter or use the terms materials, properties, and senses, within this field – and yet placing more emphasis on each of these three terms tends to carry with it a different set of paradigmatic assumptions.

The book

In the chapters that follow, we elaborate on these various themes. By examining particular interdisciplinary approaches, and a range of specific instances of materials, we aim to pull apart what this territory of the study of materials and society comprises. We set out social and cultural interpretations and understandings that arise from a focus on materials, and we criticize and problematize those that do not fit, with reference to grounded, observed examples. If a materials revolution is impending or occurring, we hope this book will point to some possible responses to the challenge and assist materials innovators, designers, engineers, artists, archaeologists, makers, anthropologists and others to rise to the choices that we face.

References

Appadurai, A. (ed.) (1986), *The Social Life of Things*. Cambridge: Cambridge University Press.
Ashby, M. and K. Johnson (2009), *Materials and Design: The Art and Science of Material Selection in Product Design*. London: Butterworth-Heinemann.
Barth, F. (1990), *Cosmologies in the Making*. Cambridge: Cambridge University Press.
Bennett, J. (2010), *Vibrant Matter: A Political Ecology of Things*. Durham, NC: Duke University Press.
Bradley, J. (2000), *An Archaeology of Natural Places*. London: Routledge.

Coole, D. and S. Frost (2010), *New Materialisms: Ontology, Agency and Politics*. Durham, NC: Duke University Press.

Gell, A. (1998), *Art and Agency*. Oxford: Clarendon Press.

Gosden, C. (2006), 'Material Culture and Long-Term Change', in C. Tilley, W. Keane, S. Küchler, M. Rowlands and P. Spyer (eds), *Handbook of Material Culture*, pp. 425–442. London: Sage.

Hahn, H. P. and J. Soentgen (2011), 'Acknowledging Substances: Looking at the Hidden Side of the Material World', in *Philosophy of Technology*, 24: 19–33.

Howes, P. and Z. Laughlin (2012), *Material Matters: New Materials in Design*. London: Black Dog.

Hudson, R. (2011), 'Critical Political Economy and Material Transformation', in *New Political Economy*, 17: 373–397.

Ingold, T. (2007), 'Materials against Materiality', in *Archaeological Dialogues*, 14(1): 1–16.

Ingold, T. (2012), 'Towards an Ecology of Materials', in *Annual Review of Anthropology*, 41: 427–442.

Karana, E., O. Pedgley and V. Rignoli (eds) (2014), *Materials Experience: Fundamentals of Materials and Design*. Amsterdam: Butterworth-Heineman.

Lefteri, C. (2006), *Materials for Inspirational Design*. Hove: Rotovision.

Lemmonier, P. (2012), *Mundane Objects: Materiality and Non-Verbal Communication*. London: Left Coast Press.

Leroi-Gourhan, A. (1943), *Evolution et Techniques I: l'Homme et la Matière*. Paris: Albin Michel.

Leroi-Gourhan, A. (1945), *Milieu et Technique*. Paris: Albin Michel.

Poe, A. (2011), 'Review Essay: Things-Beyond-Objects', in *Journal of French and Francophone Philosophy*, XIX(1): 153–164.

Strathern, M. (1992), *Reproducing the Future: Anthropology, Kinship and the New Reproductive Technologies*. London: Routledge.

Strathern, M. (1999), *Property, Substance and Effect: Anthropological Essays on Persons and Things*. London: Continuum.

Taussig, M. (2008), 'Redeeming Indigo', in *Theory, Culture and Society*, 25(3): 1–15.

Tilley, C. (1999), *Metaphor and Material Culture*. Oxford: Wiley-Blackwell.

Tilley, C. and W. Bennett (2004), *The Materiality of Stone*. Oxford: Berg.

Wagner, M. (2001), *Das Material der Kunst: eine andere Geschichte der Moderne*. München: Beck.

Part 1

Introduction

Chapter 1

To live in a materials world

Adam Drazin

The atoms of men have already spent infinity

as part of something else and all your human fudge

is the passing of a thread through the surface of a light.

(Jack Underwood, 'Death Says')

Imagining a materials world

The importance of materials in the social imagination has risen and fallen historically at particular times, and especially in reaction to enlightenment ideas of knowing and dominating a material world through the power of mind and body (Küchler, Chapter 15, this volume). The enlightenment and industrial revolution eras tended towards homogeneity of a few materials in society, based on abstracted measurements and functions, while by contrast medieval alchemy and the Romantics each celebrated a diversity of materials and material transformations. The modern technical capacity to turn lead into gold at a molecular level, for example, would be at a conceptual level no surprise to a medieval alchemist. Ours is therefore not necessarily the first era when matter has been seen as potentially 'vibrant' or 'living' (Bennett 2010). In the following chapters, we flesh out the reasons why materials demand special attention at the current social moment in history and explore what ethnographic or socio-cultural studies of a material look like. These studies provide examples of the ways in which society tries to find ways to perceive and scrutinize materials, examine the cultural implications of changes in materials uses and shifts in the kinds of materials used, outline how notions of use itself have changed (Küchler, this volume) and give examples of the networks and structures that can arise around a specific material.

This introduction argues that a paradigm shift of knowledge can occur, in which one sees the world as comprised of materials more than of objects (Brown 2004). This perceptual act I consider to be the 'materials world', a sub-set of the more commonly used term 'material world'. I argue that the materials world, as well as being deliberately evoked in academic acts or when learning about materials in places such as materials libraries, comes to be evident at particular moments in everyday life. There are times in many ethnographically observed contexts when a transformation occurs between perceiving surroundings as an agglomeration of forms or seeing them as an agglomeration of substances.

Tim Ingold draws on James Gibson's work to describe a world of materials, which conceives of flows and material properties coming to the fore:

> Supported by the ground, the inhabitants of Gibson's account are not so much composites of mind and body, participating at once in the material world and the world of ideas, as immersed in a world of materials comprising earthly substances and the aerial medium. (Ingold 2011: 116, citing Gibson 1979: 16)

Materials in practice have no absolute ends, only transformations (Hahn and Soentgen 2011: 30) in which some aspects always remain while others change. A materials world is one in which all is potentially a resource, a world of potentially endless making and resistance to making. The materials world is hence fundamentally uneasy, and to imagine it is often an act of problematization as much as explanation. It is not necessarily a question of existing or even becoming in the world in a fluid sense, or that materials form a part of cosmology. Some communities such as hunter-gatherer communities may be best described as existing in such a state of becoming, with a highly developed capacity for materials knowledge and perception of their surroundings, as Ingold evokes. There may also be places such as craft studios where acts-of-making can be contained and controlled. However, in many instances the materials world is unexpected, and in an ontological sense can be deeply disturbing. Many materials demand some kind of social control because of their uneasiness. Materials are experienced at best like exciting curiosities, slightly disfigured, and at worst like gaping wounds in the fabric of social life, when the perceived separation of the noumenal and the phenomenal (Küchler, this volume) collapses. Materials as social phenomena happen not only when wood becomes a table, or paper becomes money, but when your table is wood, your money is paper, and your body is flesh.

Materials libraries and the materials world

'The world is a materials library', commented Zoe Laughlin as she showed us, a group of anthropologists, around the library at the Institute of Making in London. She was implying that the experience of visiting her library should not be simply a visit, an experience that begins and ends at the door. It should be a lasting personal change, enabling an enduring potential paradigm shift in one's knowledge and perception. Rather than the library being an echo of the world, into which one goes in order to find answers, it is here rather a lens through which one perceives the world differently and potentially changes it.

At the time of writing there are a growing number of materials libraries in London, in the United Kingdom and in the world. Miodownik (this volume) details many. They do not all have Zoe Laughlin's philosophy, but they are all vehicles for thinking about materials: what materials are, why they are important and how we come to know them. Each has its own philosophy in other words. In the London area, institutions that incorporate what might be termed a materials library, and which I visited in 2011–2014, include the Institute of Making, the sustainable materials library at Kingston University, the design materials library at Central St Martins and the economic botany collection at Kew Gardens. Many museums meanwhile have a strong consideration of kinds of materials in the ways their collections are organized, such as the Victoria & Albert Museum, the British Museum, Science Museum and the Horniman Museum with its large textiles collection, to mention but a few. Several commercial enterprises present themselves as materials libraries in London shops, as well as online.

The idea of a 'materials library' promises a great deal. Like the original Alexandrian conception of a 'library' as a bringing together of all knowledge, one has the impression that somewhere there must exist a large, imposing building or room, within which samples of the entirety of creation's substances has been brought together. You can imagine finding every kind of substance across the globe and through history in a materials library – adobe clays and reinforced concrete, silicon wafers and plastic polymers, liquid mercury and silk and walnut wood and flesh and bone and water and . . . and . . . and. . . .

The ideal materials library does not exist of course, perhaps because it is the world itself. It is rather like Borges' story of a map, which, in becoming an absolute representation of the world, is at last the same size as the world. Even if one considers an individual object, the perception of the substance from which it is made, as independent from the thing itself, is an act of fragmentation. Substance and form are not separate. Brown (2004) compares objects in this fashion to windows, shapes through which one begins to glimpse some part of what things are actually made of.

But nonetheless the ideal materials library is being evoked in a range of institutions and places, each with its own kind of formulation, self-conception, history and physical organization. Visiting a materials library, incorporating the moment when you encounter the curator and are brought into a space, is a moment of discovery of the library alongside the materials themselves. Visiting such a place produces many questions, and I will describe some of my own such visits.

In October 2012, the Institute of Making was in the process of moving its materials collection, but Zoe Laughlin had drawn out a set of materials which were intended to show our visiting group of anthropologists what the library contained. The display area being constructed for the library was planned in a way to deliberately reduce the possibility of categorizing the samples, so that it would be difficult to reduce them to 'types'. The Institute proposes that we can make great strides in knowledge by taking an experimental approach to materials, engaging physically and playfully with them. In this way, and not by trying to pre-define certain uses or even presuming that pre-determined properties are limiting, we may find all sorts of new uses for materials, things they can do, as well as new structures and combinations of materials. The Institute was thus planning to use open shelves for its exhibits, and a system of electronic tags to track down samples as they move around. The library catalogue is not according to substance, use, appearance, or property, but simply numbered in order of acquisition. Other information about the material is to be found in the catalogue under this simple numbered sequence.

A visit to the Economic Botany Collection at Kew is an entirely different experience. With a group of students, I entered a modern, concrete building and descended a ramp into the noticably cooler, temperature-controlled collection space. A huge warehouse-size hangar greeted us, with row upon row of collection shelves (see Figure 1.1). This looks like a proper materials library. At the end of each row, a large circular handle enabled the curator, Mark Nesbitt, to move the huge sets of shelves and enter in between. He explained how the Economic Botany Collection is not a materials library in the 'strict' sense. It originated in the aspiration to explore how plants from across the world might be exploited commercially. The hundreds of shelves house specimens that take many forms. Old victorian jars, labelled in spidery handwriting, accompany plastic trays, bundles of leaves and flowers, large bulbous black growths and long pieces of wood or bark. The items in the collection, which could be called specimens or materials or samples equally, are organized mainly by botanical genus. This means that for some parts of the collection, they look similar – a genus of plants

Figure 1.1 In the Economic Botany Collection, Kew, with Mark Nesbitt. Arrays of collected samples demonstrate the concept of 'materials'. Photo by Adam Drazin.

where most members take the form of trees means a row of comparable wood samples. In other parts, a plant genus may include tree forms, small shrubs, or flowers, and may have a bewildering diversity of forms.

Three key points need to be made here. First it is not clear what a 'materials library' is in an abstract sense, because they are all different, although you do know it when you see it. They are attempts to 'materialize' what a library is, and simultaneously an experience of knowing. Second, it is not completely evident what a 'material' is. Third, and importantly, materials are more evident in the evocation of transformations than of stasis. Transformations here occur of different kinds.

Materials libraries then are 'discovered' as much as 'made'. Many institutions have historically held collections organized, intentionally or unintentionally, according to the kinds of substances they comprise. Clothing collections and museums comprise fabrics, sometimes according to type. Design and art exhibitions may be divided up into products of stone, ceramics or wood. Archaeology commonly works with categories of substance. Hence the Kew Gardens economic botany collection has only recently come to be seen as a 'materials' library. Likewise, when Jakki Dehn in Kingston began to collect

Figure 1.2 In the Sustainable Materials Library, Kingston, with Jakki Dehn acting as a human 'mediator' to the collection. Photo by Adam Drazin.

together samples of sustainable materials, her aim was primarily to help students think about and work on sustainability (Figure 1.2). Subsequently, this collection too came to be recognized as a 'materials' library, but the term 'materials' in that instance makes no sense without the qualifier 'sustainable'. One exception might be Margaret Pope, currently of Central St Martins, who has been a pioneer in this field, deliberately establishing and maintaining a materials collection for designers when she was at the Royal College of Art beginning some decades ago.

The negotiability of the term materials is likewise related to the perceptual paradigms of discovery and making. Everything comprises materials, and at the same time in any particular moment certain things are recognizable as materials while others are not. For many engineering contexts, fabrics, for example, are not evidently materials. A material may be cotton, for example, while the weave of the cotton is not the material itself but the structure. By contrast, in a design school such as Central St Martins (Figure 1.3), items such as corrugated cardboard, netting or chipboard comprise materials in the sense that they are resources for design work and design thinking. Some things, in some contexts, are seen as composites or mixtures of two or more materials, while in other contexts they are themselves seen as a unified material.

Figure 1.3 In the Design Materials Library, Central St Martins, London. The materials invite physical engagement. Photo by Adam Drazin.

Hence different materials libraries present different things as 'materials'. The fact of the existence of this thing called a 'materials library' is itself a defining framework for what lies within. Asking 'what is this material' is a question that must run in parallel with 'what is this library', or, 'what is knowledge of this material?' I suggest that the growth of these types of collections globally – London is only one place in the world where this phenomena is developing – is indicative of a widespread shift in the ways that professional cultures are perceiving and relating to material culture.

If both materials and libraries are so evasive to define, how is it that these places actually manage to put them on display? What do we see or experience when we see a material? Often, we see a transformation – by which I mean here a material demonstration of a change. For example, some exhibits manifest a material through a negotiation on uselessness and usefulness. If you want to take an object and present a material, then a broken object does the job much better. Fragmentation is also achieved in 'samples' and 'swatches', such as rows of square pieces too small to be used for anything.

Transformation can be addressed in different ways. In Kew, at the Economic Botany Collection, individual exhibits are often arranged in arrays or sequences. For example, the notion of 'rubber' may at first seem to be adequately presented by a piece of rubber. However, it is more effective to present several pieces: a ball of raw rubber as historically collected in the Amazonian forest, followed by pieces of processed rubber and jars of sap, followed by artefacts fashioned from pieces of rubber, such as early hot water bottles. Some of these artefacts represent the kinds of experimentation people undertook when exploring the range of possible uses of rubber – for example, rubber wall tiles, which never emerged as viable commercial products. In this sequence, neither a hot water bottle nor a large hard black ball of stuff really communicates the idea of rubber. The sequence of processing and transformation, through which you can imagine the material changing form, and to a certain extent substance, is much more effective in conveying rubber. In this kind of context, if rubber exists, it does not wholly exist as a thing but rather as the idea of a material process. The process is one which is particular to that material, with material properties which only become apparent in processualized moments of action and reaction. To a certain extent, in this area, the material-as-process has referents and placedness. The processing of rubber comprises a global and historical journey evoking specific sites.

This means that materials do not necessarily have consistency, even of substance. A fibre such as cotton may undergo significant processing from the moment of harvesting from the plant, to taking form as clothes. It has not only changed in terms of the structure of the fibres, but has been washed and treated in ways which affect the substance itself. And yet it remains the material 'cotton' throughout.

Another mode of manifestation is by transformation between forms, in a way which expresses the meta-transformation between form and substance. For example, the idea of cork is represented in the Institute of Making through pieces of cork, which are 'raw' bark from cork oak trees and from which corks for bottles have been punched (Figure 1.4). The implicit transformation in this object conveys the idea of 'cork' as material. It combines a sense of the work of processing, with a transformation of utility, a commentary on the natural, as well as a transformation between form and formlessness. On the one hand, you have a lump of something that is not really 'cork' per se, but rather is a piece of tree bark from a cork oak. On the other hand, you have a bottle top. Straddling these two forms and in between them you can apprehend the substance as an alternative to form. Trees are cut down and bottle tops briefly used, but materials persist.

Figure 1.4 In the Institute of Making Materials Library. A sample that transforms between 'corks' and 'cork oak bark' demonstrates the material 'cork'. Photo by Adam Drazin.

In some sense, the act of going into a library and coming out is being constructed as an act of transformation between form and substance. Within the library, materials exist. Outside the library is a world which by implication has form. But as a learning experience, the purpose of going into the library is to be enabled to perceive and understand this world which has shape in a different way. As well as deepening knowledge of particular materials, their properties and behaviours, and as well as perhaps 'finding' a material you can use, one is also educating oneself through the capacity for a knowledge paradigm shift.

Materials libraries can be more about knowledge paradigms than about getting to know materials. In this sense, they are about ways of getting to know the world through materials, which necessitate getting to know the world as materials. One expectation people have in visiting libraries is that they will acquire knowledge: knowledge of specific, discrete kinds of materials, easily-identifiable, separable, fungible materials, which have definable and measurable properties which can be learned about. And, that they will acquire skills, the ability to better match certain kinds of materials to certain kinds of uses. Of course, in visiting libraries you do acquire knowledge and to a certain extent new skills. However, the curators of many such libraries do not themselves, surprisingly, subscribe to a single paradigm of a world which you can simply get to know and understand. Counterintuitively perhaps, the person who engages in knowing the world as comprising materials is not necessarily a skilled figure, a person characterized by their skills in knowing materials or in making but rather a figure who becomes schooled in knowing the problems of materials better.

Hence the work of evocation of a 'materials world' is difficult and not necessarily what you might expect. It is however important work. The problem in some ways can be seen as the opposite of what confronted people dealing with the digital revolution around new information technologies since the 1990s. Appreciation of the digital in sociocultural terms used to be severely hampered by immaterial parallelism – ideas of cyberspace, or parallel domains of experience, somehow unrooted from material existence. Notions of an overdetermined 'digital world' led to idealist utopian and dystopian interpretations about how digital technologies might liberate people from social and material bounds. In fact, digital technologies are profoundly material (Miller and Horst 2012) but are easy to imagine as immaterial. Studies of materials face the opposite problem in many ways. Imagining the materials world is difficult, because one simply cannot see the wood for the trees except through deliberate acts of distantiation.

What notions of transformation can we use to help us to perceive and study materials? One might think that Heidegger's (1978) discussion would be useful here of the difference between a tool that is *present-at-hand*, lying on a table, and *ready-to-hand* when it is being used. As the tool is taken up, a perceptual shift occurs where the tool comes to be unconsciously a part of the embodied craftsperson. Heidegger is illustrating a perceptual shift by reference to tools, hence rendering the material world as tool-like. Hahn and Soentgen (2011) consider this kind of appropriation as important to appreciating what materials do in society.

While transformations between ready-to-hand and present-at-hand are relevant, the materials world can also present a somewhat deeper problem. If we want to work with wood, we can use a saw to experience and make the wood; or we can use a screwdriver to engage with the metal of screws. How are we to perceive the screwdriver or the saw as themselves materials? I do not wish to attempt to 'explain' the materials screwdriver in terms, for example, of the fungible way it uses materials with particular properties or in terms of our prior knowledge of metals and wood or that by using the thing we experience it in an embodied way. A different order of anthropological thinking is required here to account for materials. We live at a time when the screwdriver may shortly no longer be made of metal and wood, but different materials. The things that are currently put together using screws may be made of materials that do not require screws but attach differently.

These kinds of changes are happening all the time. I myself am currently having to force myself to use the range of colourful silicone cooking utensils in the kitchen, which seem to me things that should immediately melt if I place them in an oven or in contact with a hot pan. I feel more secure with metal utensils. I experience difficulties washing clothes, as the types of textiles and their combinations proliferate. To be able to perceive and understand the material, as well as form, can be tricky.

Such materials shifts are happening in textiles, biomaterials and in other domains. What we wish to do in this book is to heighten our ability to problematize the screwdriver and its context through imagining the materials world. It has always been to a certain extent inadequate to conceive of material things as tool-like; it is doubly inadequate to see them as forms. We wish to, not so much propose other ways of understanding, but in the main to try to elaborate on this materials problem. The imagination of a materials world is not necessarily an act of explanation but can be an act of problematization, a challenge to the inevitability or given-ness of the *composition* of the world. What is the problem of materials exactly, in instances where the material comes to the fore?

I now present the bones of an approach to a social science of materials (or, more specifically, an anthropology of materials), which means recognizing their transformational aspects. I also outline how the chapters of this volume illustrate and help us constitute the imagination of the materials world.

The study of materials and society

This book suggests that an 'anthropology of materials' comprises the empirical observation and interpretation of the sociocultural implications of those moments when a transformation between form and substance is manifest.

This suggestion means moving away from some alternative propositions. Materials need different kinds of approaches from objects or things. The book proposes that the anthropology of materials should not be exclusively, or even predominantly, about moments of making. We wish to move away from approaches which would simplistically elide acts of knowing and of making (which often overlap, but need not be similar), and of approaches which consider the material world itself only in terms of praxis or embodiment. Our work takes a materialist approach, but does not consider there to be one materialist approach (certainly not only a Marxist materialism, a vitalist materialism nor only an approach to materialism orientated towards consumer society discourses), but a plurality of potentially conflicting materialisms, which nonetheless encompass praxis and discourse as subdomains, since both practice and discourse have material form. The implication of this is that explorations of materials and materiality are best employed in social science as vehicles to problematize ideas of knowing and doing rather than knowing and doing being vehicles to understand the material world better.

The social life of materials implies a wholly different phenomenon from the social life of things (Appadurai 1986). While the social life approach is one of the most significant contemporary approaches within material, it is aimed primarily at understanding objects rather than materials. The social life of materials is much less about biographies, birthless and deathless as materials are, and rather about types of transformations (see Frow 2004). The 'life' of materials concerns questions about how materials are 'vitalist' (Bennett 2010), what they do and how they have effects, how they have meaning, how they are known and what social and cultural forms happen through and around them.

This volume is divided into subsections that explore what happens around moments of transformation between form and substance.

On materials innovation

The first section presents some historical overviews and theoretical viewpoints on materials from different disciplinary points of view. We begin with Graeme Were's study of *harakeke*, or New Zealand flax, which sets the scene for what a social study of a material may look like. The story of *harakeke* (or, New Zealand flax) incorporates many elements that can be seen to typify why materials are interesting. For more than a century, *harakeke* has been the subject of attempts at innovation, of technical change and of cultural contestation. *Harakeke* has been the focus of repeated attempts to use and develop its fibres in ever-more interesting and exciting ways. It is a potentially organic replacement for fibreglass, ideal to make, for example, a surfboard. It is also a face cream or a piece of clothing. It is also a traditional 'treasure' of Maori culture, something claimed as traditional property and collective intellectual property. The chapter demonstrates how binarisms, such as modern versus traditional, culture versus science and success versus failure, can be simply dissolved or seem irrelevant in the face of a social study of a material. Were situates the notions of innovation and discovery within long-term historical frameworks, moving beyond them to an analysis that draws on Gell (1998) to examine the agencies involved in and around New Zealand flax. He proposes a type of analysis and understanding that develops the 'material expressivity' of a material.

Following this 'typical' materials and society study, Andrew Barry's chapter then draws on human geography to expand on some alternative ways in which one can consider this phenomenon of what might be loosely termed a popular chemistry, a culture of materials that is beyond professional scientific circles. Barry offers here one of the prime paradigms that we can use to study materials by considering pharmaceutical molecules as 'informed materials'. He thus opens up a range of new possibilities for the social study of materials, bringing into the equation the ability to work not only with actually existing pharmaceutical substances, or the social relations around them, but the various ways in which the conceptualization of those relations happen. In the understanding of materials, he proposes, we should in most cases not see ourselves as inventing materials. Rather, we should consider the work as discovery or innovation (the same notion that Were situates culturally and historically in Chapter 2). Barry's critique of invention (which is extended by Küchler in the conclusion) highlights the large philosophical baggage that the idea implies, and he shows how if we talk of invention, or innovation, we in doing so infer presuppositions as to what relations between people through things comprise. If we recognize at least some materials as 'informed', they are seen to be part of a potentially immense scaffold of knowledge and communication between people.

If Andrew Barry offers us an alternative voice from within human geography, Mark A. Miodownik offers us one from engineering. For some years, Miodownik has been a strong advocate for more profound academic attention to the study of materials in society and culture. His contribution here is to begin to frame the problems of materials. He specifies two of the most important challenges that materials present us with, which are both essentially extensions of his central point that materials do not definably exist except in terms of the scalability of matter. First, we have the problem of how to know materials, whether through forms of scientific empiricism based on deduction and experimentation or through artistic empiricism based on experience. We know materials not in one way, but through conflicting knowledge paradigms. Within materials science, materials emerge somehow in the panoply of different scalarities within the structure of substances – if one is studying crystalline structures, then the 'material' is about how crystalline structures and atomic compositions interact; while if one is studying molecular forms, the 'materials' may seem to comprise the range of ways similar molecules may be structured. Hence even for a scientist, or perhaps especially for a scientist, materials do not exist in a reliable fashion.

Second, Miodownik highlights the problem of multiplicity and complexity. The sheer breadth of the topic of materials is astounding, from every aspect of the material world, from steel girders to jeans to the foam on baths, to scents and senses, to just experience. And every aspect of materials descends into ever-more complicated subdivisions, such that one has no sooner started to study concrete than one must study concretes. Materials comprise one of those topics that grows and proliferates at a pace faster than one is able to study it. We will always feel as if we are lagging behind. But this is no reason to deter us; rather it is what makes materials interesting to study. By way of signposting the methodological ways forward, as well as sociocultural studies of materials, Miodownik advocates materials libraries and artistic work as ways to help understand materials.

In the last chapter of our introductory section, David Howes brings us back to anthropological territory. One of the implications of Were's and Barry's arguments in particular is that we find it increasingly difficult to maintain distinctions between professional and popular knowledges developed around materials, and Howes' chapter travels the contemporary territory between these two, from product development testing centres through the commercial networks to consumption. The spread of notions of experience and of the senses into commodity branding and sales signifies a move towards understanding of goods as conveyers of material properties.

Howes' argument as regards the sensory turn in anthropology provides a brief outline of one of the most significant approaches to materials that anthropology has to offer. In Howes' work, people are veritable vehicles of sensation, entities that move through the world soaking up experience. This emphasis on the sensory aspects of humanity, an emphasis that is not necessarily a universal but also produced by contemporary corporate and scientific cultures, contrasts with the kinds of emphasis that Were evokes of knowledge and agency. By throwing light on the science of sensory evaluation, Howes unpacks fixed ideas of material properties, and especially challenges the idea that intrinsic properties in materials are their most important features. Instead, he develops the 'extrinsic properties and associations' around materials. In doing so, he evokes the 'metaphysics of association', which Barry discusses for informed materials, and yet Howes places much more emphasis on the social context than does Barry. 'Sensory experience is social experience' is one of the main lessons we learn.

All four of these theorists in our introductory section are seeking alternative knowledge paradigms in order to think about materials. At first, they may appear very similar, because they share the same target. All are critiquing the idea of materials as fixed, definable, with measurable and specifiable properties and open to a process of 'invention'. Of course, no one questions that it is certainly possible to work with materials in a positivist, scientific fashion, but these thinkers are questioning whether such an approach is adequate. Where they differ is in the alternative approaches which they advocate. With differing emphasis on agency, knowledge, making and doing or experience, together these thinkers offer a wide spectrum of possibilities to advance our critical approaches to materials in society. The implications of their work is that in response to the complexity of the materials world we begin to consider more widespread, historically informed network-type analyses of the assortment of transformations and relationships that occur around materials – networks that can be infused with material knowledges and experiences of properties. These four chapters situate our approach to materials as strongly concerned with various dimensions of embodied cognition: knowing, remembering, communicating and imagining.

Exploring transformations from substance to form

The notions of making and craft are at the heart of a lot of contemporary work on materials. Some authors posit craft as fundamentally moral and potentially an economically and politically redeeming activity (Sennett 2008). While we think too much emphasis on making and crafting can be limiting to understanding materials, in the sense of being unbalanced, it is certainly important.

Laurence Douny's chapter gives us some insights into the wide-ranging implications of the consideration of the world as a kind of immense resource of materials for potential acts of making. Douny is an anthropologist who has been working for some years on various different materials within West African life and is known for her provocative thinking about the cosmological pervasiveness of materials. In Dogon areas of West Africa, the study of silk reveals how silk and the properties of silk infuse many states of being. As a material, something called silk can be found in many different locales – gathered from the environment as cocoons, within a range of stages of making processes and in finished artefacts. Understood as a carrier and conveyer of a particular kind of power (*daoula*), silk material is at the heart of many processes of social becoming. The silk is not only subject to techniques of making but enables those techniques as well, and Douny proposes that a focus on the *properties* of silk, its visual *sheen*, can help us to transcend these dualities. This comprises one of the most complete studies in existence of the idea of 'sheen' and its social relevance. The ways in which the sheen of silk comes to be a part of clothes and artefacts constitutes 'material aphorisms' or truths. The material comes to constitute moral values and legitimize social relations.

For many people, perceiving the cultural nature of silk in West Africa may be easier than perceiving how plastics in their own homes may be subject to very similar, and equally glorious, cultural processes. Tom Fisher is a well-published expert on plastics within design and design history. His arguments about plastics are comparable to Douny's, in that he suggests that 'they provide the material ground for a plasticity out of which individuals may fashion themselves'. While the process of 'becoming' may be different from West Africa, the sentiment is similar. Fisher's arguments for the constructiveness of plastics are in some ways controversial, for they run against the current of arguments about plastics' association with inauthenticity, which McKay (this volume) also discusses. The celebration of 'plastic utopianism' in a 'plastic age' rings very true.

The third chapter on transformations from substance to form, and on ways of making, also concerns fashion. Urmila Mohan's work defies any idea that fashion culture must be the domain of the purely human, or is secular. Materials in her work can be essentially, profoundly religious. Here she studies a workshop environment in which people make clothes for iconic deities in a temple in Northern India. Far from being a passive template on which social relations, identities, consciousnesses and beliefs are imposed, the materials used are here constitutive of such phenomena. Mohan develops Warnier's (2001, 2009) notions of material consciousness and material religion to understand this situation.

These pieces of research all indicate moments of transformation from substance to form, within the wider constitution of social and cosmological orders. The materials are considered important in very different ways in each case however: for example, an actual materialized power in Dogon areas, contrasts with a 'dematerializing ontology' in Hindu India, which downplays the material as a separate phenomena from spirituality.

All three studies challenge some of the common assumptions of what materials are and show how cultures of materials differ. Some approaches would situate materials as significant purely for how they facilitate making, or craft, and as objects for people to work their magic upon through intentional acts. By contrast, these three studies are more cosmological than they are ontological, representing materials rather than people as the prime conveyers of ideas. The social relations surrounding the materials (Sennett 2011) are pre-eminent in this research, beyond individual work, and it shows how materials can produce an exaggerated sense of value around objects.

Exploring the subversion of form by substance

The central section of the book examines moments of less certainty, in which the truths that materials convey are not channelled into the made forms that people and communities necessarily intend. Rather, they examine those times when legitimate forms are undermined by their deliberate or unexpected reversion into substances, and social orders can seem similarly challenged.

Peter Oakley, an anthropologist at the Royal College of Art in London, examines the promotion of a 'new' material, fairtrade gold, a gold proposed as materially constituted in a different fashion from other kinds of gold. However, Oakley shows how a material can present many contradictory meanings and paradigms. Some of the contradictions around gold may occur among different groups, while other contradictory thoughts can be held consecutively by one person. At the same time, at another level, the immanence of gold presents an integrity that resists attempts to categorically differentiate gold into types.

Oakley's work demonstrates how an inherent tension exists in the treatment of gold in particular. Fairtrade practices of tracing provenance come into conflict with the historically established practices of gold traders who use mass-balancing methods in perceiving gold. The attempt to rethink or reimagine gold ultimately fails against what people are used to doing with gold, revealing a gulf of thought and action.

Deirdre McKay (et al.)'s work also evokes a sense of uneasiness as the concept of *plastik* in the Philippines is made evident in plastic artefacts that aspire to be art. McKay emphasizes how value is here not only being imparted by the agency of makers, or by skill, or by the form of artefacts but also by the undeniability of the material of which things comprise. Far from being a material that can be taken for granted, plastic is shot through with uneasiness wherever it appears, questioning authenticity, art, value, individual identity and class identity. As a material that epitomizes certain aspects of Filipino identity (just as Fisher suggests for modernist identities), plastic is a problem as the material of poverty, problematic in attempts to aestheticize it or use it in art and problematic in its deployment for middle-class or classless purposes. Plastic beads are here also disturbing in that, through use of plastic, the material itself comes to the fore. Rather than being beads, these objects suddenly comprise evidently of 'stuff'.

Different materials will lead social research in very different directions. If one material leads to an ethnography of identity, another leads to religion, and yet another to power. Filipe Calvão's discussion of diamond-trading rooms in Angola means consideration of global macro-issues, the 'imagined representations of the global market', witnessed within small rooms. Diamond trading is founded on assumptions of how the intrinsic material properties of a diamond have value. In practice these truths about diamonds are negotiated, accessed through certain technologies and terminologies, and implicated in trades that, ultimately, are about a lot more than a particular diamond. Calvão reminds us of how global orders such as capitalism may themselves depend on how particular materials are valued and perceived. To consider 'diamond' as a substance with particular properties and in particular terms, in spite of the variability of individual diamonds, is to help produce a potentially global set of hierarchies and orders. It is no small statement to assert that diamond is a potentially valuable substance.

These three studies are all evidence of what ethnography may do, and observe, which other methodologies may not. This is hard-won fieldwork, for which these researchers invested time, work and patience to place themselves in the situations and among the communities which they describe. Literally years were spent on these pieces of fieldwork.

Materials are, in all three of these studies, rendered as somehow foundational of a social order and of a particular way in which the world 'should' be. At the same time, however, the properties of a material itself are in point of fact not reliable and consistent, but negotiable. Those moments in which things are scrutinized for their substance are, in point of fact, often destabilizing. Such acts of scrutiny are of wider relevance. The issues of tracking and tracing are presenting themselves to us ever more frequently, for example, in food scares in which one slab of beef is not the same as another, but the modes of acquisition and purchase of meat depend on material commensurability. It is profoundly disquieting that what you thought might be one material might suddenly turn out to be something else entirely.

Since, as we have seen, materials do not exist in a universal sense, but as a cultural, perceptually scalable and comparative category of understanding of the world, the different approaches indicated by Oakley, McKay and Calvão also present us with potential ways of defining and approaching materials. We could consider a material to be defined by its particular, unchanging properties – as with mass balancing for gold. We might alternatively consider the provenance and biography of a particular mass of stuff – such that, for example, free range organic meat might be a different material from meat from cage-reared animals, or British wool might be a different material from New Zealand wool. Alternatively, as McKay suggests, we might see a material as a cross-cutting meaningful category, interconnecting the consideration of the world as a resource for value, and artefactual forms.

In sum, what this section does in the main is show the potentially disruptive agency of materials in moments where substance subverts form and a sense of harsh reality emerges into the social consciousness.

Exploring ecologies of materials

As the first three sections of the book suggest, the study of materials necessarily comprises the study of relations and associations, which constitute the transforming and transformative life of materials. The fourth section of the book contains studies that move beyond particular transformations in particular contexts, to examine wider mappings of processes, relations and associations around materials; in which the sense of life around materials (their agency, effects, vibrancy and reactivity) build into wider social phenomena. What are the implications and contextualizations of materials' social lives? We call these 'ecologies', which is a fairly loose, metaphorical use of a biological term for the study of life-in-context. Strictly speaking, an ecology implies the sum total of living relations around one material, while if you look at the intersections of interrelations of many materials, it is a materials ecosystem.

In Chapter 12, we explore an example of a legislative and disciplinary regime that responds to an emergent materials world within the United Kingdom. Sustainability is a powerful and undeniable modern imperative, at the forefront of many peoples' concerns about materials. Whatever one thinks sustainability means, it has become a key measure to evaluate the world we live in. Sarah Wilkes' critical commentary on cultures of sustainability and regulation demands that we consider not only 'materials innovation', but what happens next? And she asks questions that are crucial for the many professionals and disciplines involved with materials at the present time. Wilkes demonstrates how sustainability is interesting not only because it can have a range of potentially conflicting meanings but also because it is part of the general attempt to conceive of the slippery and evasive notion of materials per se. Conceived of as a question about the world, sustainability proposes a materials world paradigm, and Wilkes' work synthesizes many of the issues raised in preceding chapters, and shows how these issues are not just philosophical, but actively being addressed in everyday life. The world of goods is coming to be perceived as an interconnected chemical and energy-constituted 'environment', and there is an increasing pressure to regulate and legislate for situations in which the substances that surround us may be harmful or simply out of place. Materials in 'the environment' are considered in terms of their effects on the young, the elderly, the weak and the 'exposed' and reinforce normative mappings of social power, capacity and privilege.

Chan Chow Wah meanwhile presents an alternative history of materials and the senses, which reveals the ways in which cultures of fragrance and scent intersect with colonial and postcolonial global mappings. The history of fragrance is commonly written as a unitary, global human universal, much as Howes notes in

Chapter 5. This history is in fact here revealed as a Western or European history, but the Chinese experience presents the possibility of an entirely different history. The pertinence of this alternative is testified to by the ways that Chinese companies have managed to supersede the marketing-led behemoths of Unilever and Procter & Gamble in the Chinese bath products market, through the scents in their products.

The topic of fragrance is especially interesting, because it is testament to an instance in which the properties of a material (such as soap) are demonstrated to be detachable and negotiable. Soap and scents are different materials in the industry. The possibility of a movement between form and substance, the existence of materials in other words, is what makes properties detachable. Chow Wah's work instantiates points made both by Howes and by Barry. The kinds of substance used for fragrance, which infuse soap products, are perceived to be intrinsic, semi-magical 'essences'. But these essences are chemicals, which are manufactured, traded and negotiated along their own networks. A trade in fragrance materials is also to a certain extent a trade in possibility and Platonic ideals of things, as well as a trade in the senses themselves. Moving far beyond the localism of earlier chapters, Chow Wah is also exploring a global web of materials whereby the mass-manufactured chemical 'blanks' of material properties are commandeered, shipped, reshaped and sold and appropriated en mass across many different places and social locales. The scale of such a materials-based network is immense, and its cultural implications profound.

Lastly, in Chapter 14, our final ethnographic study, Fiona P. McDonald's work concerns the mnemonics of the senses that happen around woollen blankets, providing a highly politicized reading or mapping of historical processes. Colonial encounters across the world have through history been contextually associated with blankets made from wool, and are evoked by the particular sensation of the blanket. Contemporary artists deploy the properties of such blankets to manifest, and then reappropriate, such political commentaries. She shows how it is the experience of the material, and especially the particular sensoriality associated with it, that enables people to locate themselves within history. The materials paradigm here functions to historicize and politicize the self and self-consciousness. More importantly, she stresses the capacity of materials to reveal, to clarify and to challenge social relations, especially historicized ones. The blankets that she studies, within an art context, are in some ways social life made manifest. In this sense, their political role is highly nuanced, a point which Susanne Küchler expands in more detail in the conclusion.

These three studies of materials ecologies, or of networks of the social lives of materials, build the points that previous chapters have made into understandings of wider social contexts. Materials ecologies offer for us new kinds of social forms and structures. Sets of relations and institutions based around a material or a property are closely linked to notions of social change, and related pressures towards social control, discipline and regulation. There is also the consideration that those moments when materials come to be evident in the world compel the exercise of authority and the mobilization of those people and entities who would see themselves as being in control.

In the concluding chapter, Susanne Küchler brings our discussion of materials back to the themes of innovation and invention, which Were broaches in Chapter 2. She traces the changing ways in which materials in general have been perceived and evaluated, especially within the European tradition. The moment when materials are seen as potentially 'useful' is the cultural equivalent of dynamite, and ushers in a whole new era of conceiving materials as designed, an era when the burden of utility lies not with objects, but with the substance of which they are made. Her analysis is an antidote to the euphoric optimism that sometimes surrounds materials innovation. The notion of 'materials-by-design' may indeed usher in more crafting and making, but does not necessarily imply greater sustainability nor necessarily a move away from our undeniable reliance on minerals and petrochemical materials.

Situating the study of materials and society within a history of ideas, Küchler makes us aware of the contemporary era in which we live, the cultural moment within which the putative materials revolution is happening, and she leaves us with questions that demand a response.

Raw no more: The social study of materials

All of the various studies of materials and society in this volume manage to look at particular transformational moments when materials come to be evident. While we could do a study of materials in the world in general – attempt to actually see the world in its entirety 'as a materials library' – the remit of such a study would be impossible, and its academic benefit questionable. Some focus is necessary. The remit of a good social study is typically delineated by a material and perhaps a related community, locale or activity. All of these researchers are not so much attempting to *explain* materials, as wrestle with the ways in which they are problematic. Their methodologies for this achievement are varied, including combinations of using historical approaches, looking at networks, contrasting conflictual and contradictory viewpoints, considering the cosmology and power of materials, looking at the techniques and technologies of perceiving materials, analysing materials as categories of knowledge and focusing on property and on certain material properties.

Disturbing and disruptive as they are, materials provoke responses. Materials happen at moments when the material world manifests purposelessness, inviting us to rush in with intentions to fill the void. Materials happen – are perceived – at moments of the genesis and destruction of forms that are familiar to us. And yet they have effects as if they act, and not only as 'smart' materials. Their shifting qualities manifest in every object and person the slow evidence of quick or gradual ruination, substances changing over time to subvert the consistency of the social world. In a materials world, we are all incipient creations and ruins.

As Wilkes comments, among many materials scientists, 'materials are no longer thought of as raw, physical matter' (Wilkes, this volume). It is tempting to retain the fiction that inherently uneasy materials are 'raw', acultural and unsocialized stuff. All of the authors in this volume resist this temptation and attack the myth of *rawness*. First, we challenge the mistaken notion that materials are more 'natural' than objects. This comprises an ideology of 'nature' that has been attacked and deconstructed for some decades with anthropology, most pertinently within thinking on gender (see Strathern and McCormack 1980; Bradley 2000). For those who think 'ideology' to be too strong a term, it may be more true to say that nature exists as a social fact not scientific fact, and that materials are especially subject to being constructed as 'natural', and hence acultural until appropriately processed into a particular form.

Second, we challenge the misconception that materials are antithetical to information. Andrew Barry undermines this idea most strongly by pointing out that materials are 'informed'. Chow Wah's discussion of the globalized trade in fragrances closely evokes the same discussion. In other chapters, materials are presented as things that are, in Gell's (1998) sense of the term, 'cognitively sticky'. Materials are carriers of a range of forms of information. They may, in different instances or contexts, convey data, imagination, meaning, knowledge, beliefs and truths.

A third pillar of the mythology of rawness relates to skill. Skill is an increasingly important topic of academic study, and rightly so (Grasseni 2007; Ingold 2013). However, the study of skill, crafts, and artisanal knowledge can detract from the appreciation of what materials can do. Skill is not distributed equally in a community, and it often does not function to make materials evident. Good craftsmanship often defies or conceals materials. A focus on skill, and craftsmanship can exaggerate peoples' knowledges above objectified knowledges (Bourdieu 1990), including siliconized information (Horst and Miller 2012). Skill therefore, while important, is not sufficient and entire in itself. Materials should not be considered as only resources for skills to be exercised.

The mistaken notion of the rawness of materials therefore arises from a number of specific presumptions. Traditionally, social studies of knowledge, practices and even of material culture, have each not quite taken enough account of materials. Because of this, materials have often been seen as all the 'bits left over' in social life, once you have studied ways of knowing, ways of doing, and the forms of artefacts and objects. In fact, to some degree, materials comprise all of these fields of social life, and this is beginning to be recognized.

Beyond 'things': Reimagining stuff

Those people near the top have the power to make things durable and to make things transient, so they can ensure that their own objects are always durable and that those of others are always transient . . . Only if one remains within severe cultural and temporal confines can one sustain the commonsense belief that rubbish is defined by intrinsic physical properties. Step outside these limits and one sees that the boundary between rubbish and non-rubbish moves in response to social pressures. (Thompson 2004: 295)

We can return to the problem of perceiving the screwdriver as materials. In the development of material culture, the engagement between materials and minds has traditionally been seen to be the form, or shape, of objects and artefacts. Frequently it is making and doing that have been seen as the point of articulation between minds and materials. Hence the study of 'stuff' has come primarily to be understood as production, making, crafting, creating, designing, consumption, accumulation, appropriation, of objects. We need to add to these understandings in the social study of materials, because they are not sufficient. We need to reimagine stuff in frameworks other than form and praxis, and particularly through examining transformations of stuff.

As several of us have observed, especially Miodownik and Küchler, the enlightenment provided a primary moment of intellectual fracture around how materials and minds engage. Looking back at, and reflecting on, this enlightenment moment, a great deal of social science effort has been directed to critiquing the notions of the Cartesian mind and of the material world as simply the object of human understanding and control. A significant moment in this respect was social constructivism's rise from the 1960s, and its related approaches, critiquing the idea of knowledge as a fixed body of truth, and rather highlighting processes and activities of making knowledges. Its influence has been widespread, but it has not been good for the social study of materials. In some ways, constructivism simply takes the idea of doing in all its specificity, and imports it wholesale into the project of knowing. Knowing is 'like' doing or making. As a critique of abstracted knowledge, constructivism has been very successful and influential but has also detracted from the rearticulation of minds and the material world.

A slightly different trajectory has seen from the late 1970s a range of approaches to embodiment using the idea of the body to reposition how knowing, doing and materiality intersect. One highly important aspect of this movement has been phenomenological approaches, which interpret moments of knowing as situated moments of experience. More recently, the work of Ingold (2011, 2013) has continued to focus on this area. What is emphasized in his more recent work is the ways in which making is itself a process of knowing, through experiencing. Materials can facilitate a consciousness of this engagement. As Oakley says of gold, 'the interpenetration of what is thought and what is done became startlingly apparent as FT/FM gold was found to be excluded from large swathes of manufacturing practice' (Oakley, this volume).

One can consider knowing-as-making or making-as-knowing, but we would also emphasize that there is more to materials than this and rather focus on materials as problematizing ways of knowing. The problems of knowing are not necessarily the problems of praxis, because materials themselves do perform cultural kinds of work, and they are especially kinds of informational or knowledge work.

There are many ways of knowing. By this, we do not mean only different cosmological paradigms or 'social worlds'. One can know, believe, experience, discover, invent, mean, dream, imagine, learn, question, guess or sense. Information may take many corresponding forms: knowledge, data, truth, meaning and so forth. In this volume, the researchers have adopted many tools, methods and routes towards researching materials. They look at cosmologies (Douny, Mohan, Were), networks (Oakley, Were, Wilkes, Chan), techniques of perception (Howes, Oakley, Calvão), categories of meaning (Howes, Fisher, McKay, Douny), subjectivities (McKay, Mohan, Fisher, Barry), histories (Miodownik, Were, Barry, Chow Wah, McDonald) and properties (Howes, Chan, Douny). All of these tools are ways into examining material transformations and the associated social implications.

The imagination of the materials world in these studies draws attention to the possibility of certain kinds of social transformations, implicit in the tensions that the exposure of materials reveals. As they sensorially enable appropriation, materials also can defy and undermine ownership. They are the manifestations of material properties, and the means to ascribe efficacy, and yet they challenge the boundaries of property relations. The making evident of formlessness in materials can reflect a sense of unboundedness in social terms. As a student commented during a visit to a materials library, reaching for an intriguing sample, 'materials tempt you in – like bubble wrap'. In this respect, the idea of properties and of property are frequently placed in oppositional dialogue: When the thing is seen to 'naturally' have the property, where does that leave an object's owner? The property boundaries of materials are not yet naturalized or normalized. Property relations are frequently challenged by materials (Calvão, this volume).

Materials can underlie and naturalize established social orders and hierarchies (Wilkes). But when they come to be made evident, they can expose these orders. Thompson (1979) long ago suggested that dominant elite groups are often those who are able to define what is 'rubbish' and what is not, expressing the disturbing dependence of power on rubbish. Douny makes comparable points in talking of moments when the silk and sheen of West African women's clothes shines through: 'These woven aphorisms allow women to express themselves in implicit ways that enable them to subvert or contest, but also as a self-reminder and sign of adherence to social moral values and status' (Douny, this volume).

By way of a concluding summary, the materials world can be profoundly, ontologically, disturbing and uneasy. In the extreme, materials have no births nor deaths but emergences and re-emergences in reconfigurations of matter. They have no absolute death, but become different. They can be unreliable – while forms endure, the materials comprising them decay. They challenge social mores, boundaries and hierarchies. They can be purposeless, useless and pointless. Does rock have purpose? Materials challenge property relations, relationships, ownership, identities and extended personhoods based on objects and forms. They do not possess a defined biography or 'social life' (Appadurai 1986; Kopytoff 1986). And yet, in the current moment of celebration of materials, these qualities of the materials world stand in profound opposition to the human hope for discovery, innovation, progress and social mores in materials.

An 'anthropology of materials' explores moments of manifest transformation between form and substance and their sociocultural implications. It involves particular knowledge paradigms and shifts in perspective. It explores the world seen as assemblages and compounds of properties, more than assemblages of objects, seen and appreciated culturally and locally. It looks at the interface between subjective sensory experience and the ascription of objective properties to the material world. It is cosmological, involving an appreciation of how things are constituted, and exist, as they are. It is reflexive, in that it also considers how we as humans are constituted, how we exist, and evokes how we might not exist. It necessitates a long-term viewpoint on the existence of matter. It lastly considers the significance of social and cultural ecosystems of matter, more than the constitution of an individual object as made of matter.

The following chapters, each in their own way, elaborate on aspects of these points.

References

Appadurai, A. (1986), *The Social Life of Things: Commodities in Cultural Perspective*. Cambridge: Cambridge University Press.

Bennett, J. (2010), *Vibrant Matter: A Political Ecology of Things*. Durham, NC: Duke University Press.

Bourdieu, P. (1990), 'Objectification Objectified', in *The Logic of Practice*, pp. 30–41. Stanford: Stanford University Press.

Bradley, R. (2000), *An Archaeology of Natural Places*. London: Routledge.

Brown, B. (ed.) (2004), *Things*. Chicago: University of Chicago Press.

Frow, J. (2004), 'A Pebble, a Camera, a Man Who Turns into a Telegraph Pole', in B. Brown (ed.), *Things*, pp. 346–361. Chicago: University of Chicago Press.

Gell, A. (1998), *Art and Agency*. Oxford: Clarendon Press.

Gibson, J. (1979), *The Ecological Approach to Perception*. New York: Lawrence Erlbaum Associates.

Grasseni, C. (ed.) (2007), *Skilled Visions: Between Apprenticeship and Standards*. New York: Berghahn.

Hahn, H. P. and J. Soentgen (2011), 'Acknowledging Substances: Looking at the Hidden Side of the Material World', *Philosophy of Technology*, 24: 19–33.

Heidegger, M. (1978), *Being and Time*. Oxford: Wiley-Blackwell.

Horst, H. and D. Miller (eds) (2012), *Digital Anthropology*. Oxford: Berg.

Ingold, T. (2011), *Being Alive: Essays on Movement, Knowledge and Description*. London: Routledge.

Ingold, T. (2012), 'Towards an Ecology of Materials', *Annual Review of Anthropology*, 41: 427–442.

Ingold, T. (2013), *Making: Anthropology, Archaeology, Art and Architecture*. London: Routledge.

Kopytoff, I. (1986), 'The Cultural Biography of Things: Commoditization as Process', in Appadurai, A. (ed.), *The Social Life of Things*. Cambridge: Cambridge University Press.

Laughlin, Z. and P. Howes (2012), *Material Matters: New Materials in Design*. London: Black Dog.

Merleau-Ponty, M. (2002), *Phenomenology of Perception*. London: Routledge.

Miller, D. and H. Horst (eds) (2012), *Digital Anthropology*. Oxford: Berg.

Sennett, R. (2008), *The Craftsman*. London: Penguin.

Sennett, R. (2013), *Together: The Rituals, Pleasures and Politics of Cooperation*. London: Penguin.

Strathern, M. and C. McCormack (eds) (1980), *Nature, Culture and Gender*. Cambridge: Cambridge University Press.

Thompson, M. (2004 [1979]), 'The Filth in the Way', reprinted in V. Buchli (ed.), *Material Culture: Critical Concepts in the Social Sciences*, 3(2): 292–303. London: Taylor and Francis.

Underwood, J. (2015), 'Death Says', *Happiness*. London: Faber & Faber.

Warnier, J.-P. (2001), 'A Praxeological Approach to Subjectivation in a Material World', *Journal of Material Culture*, 6(1): 5–24.

Warnier, J.-P. (2009), 'Technology as Efficacious Action on Objects . . . and Subjects', *Journal of Material Culture*, 14(4): 459–470.

Part 2

On materials innovation

Chapter 2

What's in a plant leaf? a case study of materials innovation in New Zealand

Graeme Were

In F. Dillon Bell and Frederick Young's (1842) *Reasons for Promoting the Cultivation of the New Zealand Flax*, the authors observe how a 'change has come o'er the spirit of their dream'. Bell and Young are referring to the failure of white settlers to sufficiently develop the plant New Zealand flax (*Phormium tenax*) – or *harakeke*, the Maori term the plant is commonly referred to in New Zealand. They wanted the settlers to transform the long bladed coarse green grass – recognized for the tensile strength of its internal longitudinal fibres – into an economic crop that could be used in the manufacture of naval ropes, sacking, upholstery and other fibre products. Their efforts to offer 'a premium' to the colonists to design a machine that could adequately extract the strong fibres from the leaf appeared fruitless.[1]

I begin this chapter with a story of nineteenth-century attempts at materials innovation because it underlines the 'expressivity' of *harakeke*: the potential of a material to create social effect. As DeLanda (2006) states, materials are not passive entities: instead they perform in ways that make their presence known. *Harakeke*, even after research and development, could not be controlled to make the desired object. For scientists, if the strong fibres could be extracted efficiently, the performance of *harakeke* could be calculated and the material be used as a mass object. Yet *harakeke's* non-compliance instead demonstrates, as Norman (1988) famously argues, how often well-laid plans and designs are tempered by constraints of a social, technical and logical nature.

In this chapter, I will investigate the ways in which materials enter the social world through a sociohistorical analysis of the development of *harakeke* in New Zealand industry. I will examine what drives material innovation, focusing on the historical processes and distributed agency that make materials innovation possible and demonstrate how the identity of *harakeke* is continually shifting as the world changes around it. I will question the notion of materials innovation and, at the same time, provide anthropology with a theoretical framework to analyse materials innovation in society.

Materials, innovation and anthropology

Materials are ubiquitous (Ashby and Johnson 2002). They help shape – through their experiential and agentive capacity – human thought and action (Boivin 2008; Knappett and Malafouris 2008; Miller 2005; Tilley 2004). Through their innovation and use in society and industry, materials play a significant role in social change (Ashby and Johnson 2002; Boivin 2008). The innovation of materials is important as the process makes a more efficient and effective market for industry producers as well as consumers. Materials innovation is often driven by the necessity to optimize existing consumer products by selecting suitable materials that perform better or fulfil certain requirements. It can also apply to the process of improving existing materials by altering their molecular or biophysical structure or finding new applications for well-known materials, such as plant fibres and timbers (Ball 1997). Innovation is also driven by the environments in which materials are situated. As Welz (2003: 256) states, economics is a driving factor of innovation: the capacity to innovate is a key determining factor in the competitive advantage of national economies, industries and private business. With the development of 'knowledge societies', Welz states how a 'culture of innovation' has been invented in which a plethora of policies, institutions and procedures of 'innovation management' generate new knowledges, products and services.

In my approach to materials innovation, materials are not passive entities; I will show how their capacity for transformation enables social worlds to come into being and be known (Ingold 2011; Were 2013). Materials are 'expressive' (DeLanda 2006) and as Bennett's study of their vibrancy outlines, materials lend themselves to a congregational understanding of agency rather than individualism (Bennett 2010).[2] My approach is guided by the work of Hawkins, Potter and Race (in press), who demonstrate how research and development into plastic water bottles had a huge impact in the social world: It changed consumer habits and had unintended consequences, generating an environmental waste problem due to problems in plastic bottle disposal. Scientists undertook research and development into inventing a new form of plastic suitable for use in the bottled water industry. Their work reveals how scientists experimented with polyethylene terephthalate (PET) in the laboratory in order to find a material that was robust enough to contain water under pressure, could safely contain water without contamination and that would remain opaque like glass. Their work is important to developing an agentive approach to materials because it emphasizes how materials innovation has observable effects outside the laboratory.

What is also significant about their work is how research and development into a type of PET plastic was guided by industry demands to develop a suitable material that could perform as a water bottle. The object became the guiding principle for innovation. This illustrates how materials innovation is not solely driven by activities within the hermetically sealed space of the laboratory; rather, research and development is intimately connected to issues, agendas and networks in the outside world (Barry 2005; Latour 1996; Latour and Woolgar 1979). This is emphasized too in O'Connor's study of research and development of Lycra (O'Connor 2011). In her ethnographic study, O'Connor demonstrates how the American science company Dupont led research and development into Lycra during the Baby-boomer era of the 1950s as an alternative to the rubber girdle then worn by women. The girdle was considered stiff, uncomfortable to wear, and was also prone to deterioration. O'Connor points out that a crucial factor in the emergence of the new elastane fibre for use in girdles is how Lycra came into being through executive brainstorming sessions, design meetings, consumer wear-testing, and new factory mass production techniques. Thus, not only does this study underline the collaborative and codependent nature of materials innovation; successful transmission of Lycra's qualities to the public and to industry was vital to its uptake in the global marketplace. O'Connor's study demonstrates how important intensive marketing campaigns were to its successful launch and how a new visual culture of pamphlets and adverts emerged that positioned Lycra as a superior stretch fibre for women. The effects of this material innovation were the creation of new kinds of gender identities and body images.

While these approaches foreground the processes and practices in which new materials emerge in the world and their impact on human behaviour, I will argue that materials innovation is driven by a much deeper engagement than otherwise suggested in these studies. Indeed, I will suggest that the innovation of materials provides insights into the mind at work, revealing the cognitive work of materials in world-making (Ingold 2011; 2012). Since materials innovation is a form of material engagement involving trialling, testing, brainstorming activities and so forth, I am reminded by Alfred Gell's seminal work that draws attention to the abductive quality of material culture (1998). Of particular significance to my argument, Gell states that artefacts possess the capacity to ensnare minds through their cognitive complexities: this involves a process of 'working things out' much like the context of materials innovation. Using a stylistic analysis of Maori meeting houses to develop this claim, Gell (1998: 256–258) argues that each house instantiated an engagement of mind – house building was competitive and involved thinking through how to deploy resources to develop a new house to rival others. We are told that because meeting houses were related to ancestral power, future houses were generally built in a recognizable form to previous houses – what Norman (1988) would call a design constraint – but innovated (e.g. larger, taller, etc.), and so past houses can be regarded as 'protensions towards' the ultimate meeting house. In other words, for Gell, innovation involves thinking through a set of possible transformations that can be enacted or performed on a prototype (the Maori meeting house) while working within a field of constraints (e.g. form, style, tradition, etc.).

Gell's argument is useful for developing my own approach to *harakeke* because his insights reveal how scientists engage deeply with materials to develop new products and applications. In particular, his work underlines how materials innovation – through transformation, testing and comparative analysis, objectifies and externalizes the mind at work as scientists think through uses and applications in the real world. This suggests that materials innovation cannot be understood in isolation, but involves a material engagement as innovation involves thinking about other materials and objects. Situated in complex relational and context dependent environments (Bennett 2010; Gell 1998), materials and objects are active coagents that mutually inform possibilities on the basis of their known and observable performance. In ascribing an agentive capacity to materials, I am claiming that research and development is driven in ways in which the performance of materials cannot be separated from their objecthood or their environments. As such, how a material emerges in society is also shaped by social, economic and political environments as it is by the transformational capacity of the raw material. In some cases, as Welz (2003) states, economics is the driving force for innovation, but in others, this may be tempered by availability of key resources or environmental issues (Sheller 2014). Seen this way, materials innovation involves a complex engagement between minds, matter, and their environments.

Indeed, as I will discuss, much like social networks and visual culture in which new materials like Lycra and PET plastic have emerged in society, my analysis of materials innovation reveals a comparable story of trialling, testing and transformation over 150 years, directed largely by lucrative market opportunities that reside outside of the laboratory setting and incorporate projects of colonial science, nation branding exercises and military conquest. I will show how research and development into the potential use of *harakeke* originally focused on its material substance – how the strong fibres could be extracted from the plant leaf efficiently. This research, however, was driven by the internal objective of transforming *harakeke* into an economic crop that could support the New Zealand economy; but it was also guided externally by the need to develop a strong naval rope, an object that directed research and could compete with other fibre products on the international market. After its decline in the second half of the twentieth century, I will also show how a new niche was suddenly opened for *harakeke*. Laboratory practice has been driven by the need to capture the lucrative clean green market of the New Zealand economy, and so research and development has focused on developing a suitable biomaterial (a *harakeke* composite) to match the needs of an environmentally conscious consumer and, at the same time, measure up to the required performance (of object and material). By highlighting the different pathways and relations in which material and object are inextricably intertwined in the process of innovation and design, this chapter will reveal how material substances are active agents in the wider environments and infrastructures through which materials and objects emerge in the world, and how these create new subjectivities, relationships and power relations.

In seeking to control the material expressivity of *harakeke*, I will show how the intended outcome of material scientists has been to create a range of commercial products that are intimately tied to the New Zealand landscape. This demonstrates how, as Ingold (2012) claims, materials undergo continual modulation in the course of their history as their environments shift, and which I believe has important implications for developing an anthropological perspective on materials and society.

Harakeke and manufacturing industry in New Zealand

Harakeke (*Phormium tenax*) is a plant with long spear-shaped leaves that is native to New Zealand and Norfolk Island. It is well-known for the strength of its inner fibres, which run parallel to the length of the leaf. The plant grows on hills and in swamps, from sea level to around 4,000 feet, though performs better (for commercial purposes) when cultivated close to rivers. It is propagated by either seeds or by division of its rootstock. Its rootstock spreads horizontally underneath the soil and, from it, sword-shaped leaves grow in clusters (Shaw, Bicking and O'Leary 1931).

Harakeke is considered sacred to Maori, a *taonga* or treasured possession. Recently, Maori groups have been fighting a legal battle to assert intellectual property rights over its use. Known as WAI262, or the Flora and Fauna inquiry, the 2011 outcome of the Waitangi tribunal ruled in favour of improved protection of indigenous knowledge, cultural heritage, environmental resources and language as well as new partnerships in education, conservation and cultural heritage (see Lai 2014).

The plant appears in many varieties and names, each with specific applications for weaving and other uses. Maoris extract the strong fibres from its leaves by hand using a mussel shell that they scrape along the length of the leaf. Washing, drying and twisting produces a soft, pliable and strong fibre that is able to hold dyes as well as being waterproof. The fibres are almost white in colour, flexible, soft and silky. These properties of the fibre made them ideal for manufacturing textiles and clothing as well as making floor mats, baskets, nets and ropes.

Captain Cook first brought *harakeke* fibre to the attention of Europeans having observed its common use by Maoris (Dodge 1897: 261). Europeans quickly recognized the possibilities of cultivating *harakeke* for industrial purposes. Hector (1889) and Murray (1838) include descriptions of the economic value of New Zealand flax and its use and application in papermaking and rope. Such was the enthusiasm towards this new material that Murray (1838) had some of his book printed on it to demonstrate its potential application. Later, Shaw, Bicking and O'Leary (1931) conducted a feasibility study of New Zealand flax use in the papermaking industry. Their report to the US government points to how its success would rely on its availability in large quantities. They conclude how New Zealand flax 'is a promising material for the manufacture of wrapping and writing papers' (1931: 420).

There were several reasons why *harakeke* fibre was considered to be a competitive fibre. First, when compared with other fibres, it had a high yield. A much higher percentage of fibre could be extracted from the leaves in comparison with its competitor sisal hemp. Second, the plant could be easily cultivated. Each leaf was long and the plant could easily be propagated from the roots. A third reason was its harvesting cycle. One planting could last several years, and there was no need to harvest crops, if so desired (Critchfield 1951: 177).

Commercial production and export began in the early nineteenth century, in which Maori people prepared increasing quantities of *harakeke* by hand for export (Brooker et al. 1989). According to Cruthers, Carr and Laing (2009: 104) dressed and partially dressed fibre extracted by Maori people was sold to settlers who exported the fibre, and used it to manufacture various products in New Zealand. Trading of *harakeke* flourished between 1828 and 1853 between Maoris and settlers with most of the fibre reportedly exported to Australia and Britain. Export production was transformed by the development of machinery to extract the fibres from the leaves, replacing the labour intensive hand-extraction process performed by Maoris. An invention, 'the stripper', extracted fibrous strands from the green leaf by drawing the leaves between a metal bar and cylindrical drum. According to Jones (2003), one machine could produce about 250 kilos of fibre a day – compared with the one kilo of finer fibre that one person could create. This resulted in an increase in exports from 1,062 long tons in 1831 to 5,471 tons in 1870 (Critchfield 1951: 175).

One of the greatest impediments to large-scale production of *harakeke* has been the efficiency of the technology of extraction (as outlined in the opening paragraph of this chapter). While the development of mechanized techniques of fibre extraction increased yields of *harakeke* fibre, the efficiency of the available technology impacted on the condition of the extracted fibres. This was because the mechanical stripping process – as well as removing the useful fibres – also extracted coarser fibres from the leaf (in comparison to the fibres extracted by hand), lowering the quality of the *harakeke* fibres for export and so increasing failure rates when tested under lower loads. This meant that *harakeke* fibres, tested under load, were liable to break at lower loads than other natural fibres. In contrast, the fibre dressed by Maori people was of higher quality than machine dressed fibre, but the rate of production was slower (Cruthers, Carr and Laing 2009). In a report to the State Department submitted by the US Consul, the following assessment was made of *harakeke*:

> The fiber of Phormium tenax is susceptible of a much higher degree of prepa- ration than has been bestowed upon it up to the present. This, however, is not altogether the fault of those who are engaged in its manufacture; it is for want of the necessary machinery. The hand-dressed article prepared by the natives is as fine as silk as compared with the modern machine-dressed flax of to-day. This only demonstrates the fact that the fiber may be reduced to a much finer quality, and all that is necessary to do this is an improved machine.
> (US Consular Report May 1890, cited in Dodge 1897: 265)

It appears, therefore, that the technology developed for extracting useful fibre gave the *harakeke* an unreliable identity, making it difficult for it to compete with other hard fibres in the international marketplace. According to Hector (1872: v), one solution to this problem was when New Zealand flax was renamed 'New Zealand hemp' in 1871 in order to account for its lower quality and so give it an advanta- geous position alongside other hemp fibres that were traded at the time.

To reduce the failure of *harakeke* to a singular outcome, as Bennett (2010) argues, is to deny it of it material vibrancy: its relation to assemblages of events, persons and objects. Indeed, there were also natural factors that hindered the commercial development of *harakeke* fibre. For instance, *harakeke* was beset with cultivation problems. One of the major drawbacks to the establishment of *harakeke* plantations was the long harvesting cycle of the plant. Few farmers would risk investment in *harakeke* when their first economic returns came after at least five years. Another problem was its cultivation. *Harakeke* was vulnerable to disease. In the 1920s, yellow-leaf disease destroyed plants, while other fibres that *harakeke* fibre competed against remained unaffected. Once these natural factors had been taken into account, *harakeke* fibre had to compete commercially with other hard fibres processed throughout the world, notably sisal hemp, which was of higher quality and comparable strength.

And like all market economies, the New Zealand flax industry was susceptible to periods of economic growth and decline as market conditions fluctuated. Jones (2003) states how New Zealand flax underwent three periods of substantial growth: the first two boom periods for New Zealand were 1869–1870 and 1889–1890, and the third began in 1898 when the Spanish-American War cut off the supply of manila fibre from the Philippines. This underlines the relatedness of the fibre to the material vicissitudes of other fibres in the global marketplace.

The industry boomed in the first quarter of the twentieth century when *harakeke* was used as a replacement for sisal, manila and other hard fibres used in naval ropes. In 1907, exports peaked, when 28,547 long tons were shipped abroad (Critchfield 1951: 176). The economic depression of the 1930s sent the industry into decline. As exports dwindled, the industry switched attention to domestic markets, and processing mills began to produce fibre for use as woolpacks in the wool industry. In 1936, the New Zealand government restricted the import of woolpacks made from Indian jute in order to support the domestic flax milling industry.

During the Second World War, the flax milling industry briefly blossomed due to the disruption of fibre imports to New Zealand. The New Zealand government provided financial support to the industry in order to ensure that the country had enough fibre for agricultural and military use. After the war, import restrictions remained and so supported *harakeke* production and the 15 to 20 mills that were still in operation. The mills mainly produced fibre to make woolpacks, but also for underfelt, carpets and upholstery materials and binder twine to tie up hay bales (Jones 2003). With the lifting of government protection in the 1970s, New Zealand flax could no longer compete with other natural fibres that were produced more cheaply elsewhere in the world. Moreover, the development of cheaper synthetic fibres such as polyester signalled the end of the industry and the closure of the last flax mill in New Zealand in 1985. However, Cruthers, Carr and Laing (2009: 108) claim this is an over simplification of the facts as overall world demand for fibre – both natural and man-made – actually has increased. In any case, Brooking (2004) succinctly notes, the flax industry promised so much and delivered so little.

Clean, Green *harakeke*

So far, this chapter has concentrated on the story as to how the performance of *harakeke*, through its application and use in the design of objects such as wool-packs, ropes and matting, was evaluated by a network of scientists, brokers, and farmers. It has emphasized how *harakeke* was positioned, not as a material in isolation, but in terms of its performance as an object and its relation to other types of fibre products that were available at the time in terms of its economic potential. Performance, moreover, was not just about its strength and stiffness under load but also its capacity to be cultivated quickly, processed easily, its resistance to disease and its capability to attract government subsidy. Thus, the material identity of the plant fibre – its potential application (as a hard fibre) and its reputation (performance) – had been constructed in line with market opportunities on an international scale.

Markets, however, are not static and neither are material identities. As the well-documented case of the social history of plastic in Western consumer culture testifies – how its identity as an easily mouldable material that was clean and hygienic shifted to one that posed large-scale waste and environment problems (Meikle 1997; Hawkins 2011), material identities are susceptible to shifting and refining. Indeed, as I will now demonstrate, new market opportunities and social movements have meant that new possibilities have emerged for *harakeke*. A major factor has been the emergence of a bio-based economy and the commoditization of the New Zealand landscape. The plant's association to the land has provided a space for a new identity to be created which has been capitalized on in New Zealand by material scientists, cosmetic companies and product designers.

Since the late 1990s, Tourism New Zealand has been running an international branding campaign as a green and clean country. Its '100% Pure' brand was developed by M and C Saatchi and established in 1999 through aggressive marketing in several countries. According to Medway and Warnaby (2014), places are increasingly regarded as brands: countries like New Zealand become commodities that are marketed with associated values and images. In New Zealand, the natural landscape has become a niche brand. The 100%

Pure campaign aimed to combine New Zealand's brand essence – its distinctive landscape – with a real point of difference that no other destination in the world could possess (Morgan et al. 2002: 351). In brand marketing, it is the positioning of the brand image that is more important to the ultimate success than its actual characteristics. The outcome of this branding process was that New Zealand became recognized internationally for its green values. This has acted as a powerful marketing tool to attract international tourism, develop economic productivity and raise environmental sustainability (*Greening New Zealand's Growth* 2011). The notion that New Zealanders share green values has been pivotal for creating a new space to support renewed efforts to research the potentials of *harakeke* as an economic plant. While the New Zealand flax industry of the nineteenth and twentieth century positioned the material as a coarse fibre, material scientists began to develop a new generation of sustainable materials known for their clean and green credentials. In other words, place branding has helped drive materials innovation.

Scion, a Crown Research Institute based in Rotorua, New Zealand, is currently leading research and development into *harakeke* and other native plants through the production of a range of environmentally sustainable products that have minimal impact on the environment. Their aim is to develop a range of biomaterials that help support a new bio-based economy in New Zealand and support the image of a clean green country.[3] Their vision is: 'Prosperity from trees' or 'Mai i te ngahere oranga' (Maori). The Annual Report 2013 states: 'Scion's purpose is to drive innovation and growth from New Zealand's forestry, wood product and wood-derived materials and other biomaterial sectors, to create economic value and contribute to beneficial environmental and social outcomes for New Zealand' (Scion Annual Report 2013). In addition to these vision statements, the chairman and CEO of Scion state how 'Scion is also dedicated to increasing the benefit to New Zealand from forest ecosystem services and improved environmental sustainability' (Scion Annual Report 2013: 5).

The Scion website fashionably adopts the language of environmentalism and sustainability. Its 'Manufacturing and Bioproducts' webpage points to key developments in 'wood and fibre technology', 'industrial biotechnology' and 'packaging' and is an example of a materials-focused approach to innovation. It states how 'the world is witnessing a major shift towards materials, chemicals and fuels made from renewable resources'. Scion, it states, 'offers New Zealand's leading research capability in utilising industrial biotechnology to create new materials, energy products and green chemicals'. The website goes on to state, in relation to wood and fibre technology, how the world is increasingly seeking to use renewable and sustainable materials to meet consumer needs and as a consequence, new applications for wood and plant fibres are rapidly emerging.[4]

I visited Scion in June 2011 to investigate further why scientists had decided to conduct research on *harakeke*. In particular, my interest was raised by media reports of one of the products Scion had developed – a surfboard made using *harakeke* fibre. According to the Scion scientists, *harakeke* was selected because it offered an environmentally friendly alternative to glass fibre, which was made from petrochemicals. Scientists had selected *harakeke* because of its biophysical properties: its strength and stiffness were considered ideal for surfboard design. Scientists combined *harakeke* with synthetic resins to produce a lightweight, strong composite structure that made the board waterproof. The surfboard could also be coloured, due to the fact that *harakeke* fibres can be dyed.

Scientists outlined three main reasons for thinking that *harakeke* could perform as a suitable substitute for fibreglass in the design of the surfboard. First, scientists had observed its strength and stiffness (since they were aware that it had been used as naval ropes up until the Second World War). Second, *harakeke* was environmentally friendly – it grows wild in New Zealand, and, at present, there are government programmes to promote its cultivation. And finally, the surfboard demonstrated that it was possible to make a water-resistant composite material using biomaterials. The natural fibre was combined with synthetic resins and forms to make a lightweight, strong composite structure that made the board waterproof and also gave it a unique decorative effect, owing to the fact that *harakeke* fibres could be dyed. It was explained that by adding organic nutrients – or diallers as they are termed in the materials industry – the life of composite materials could be prolonged or cut short the time a product takes to decay in the environment and so address or conform to environmental and waste regulations.

Scion had developed the surfboard (as well as a series of other prototype models of eco-products) to demonstrate how biomaterials could potentially be marketed in the design of eco-products. These bespoke biomaterials – with time built in to them since their rate of decay is known – appear to have obvious environment benefits. But because extracting the *harakeke* fibres was a complicated process, as outlined at the beginning of this chapter, scientists could not scale up production to the model of mass production they desired and so the surfboard was considered to be commercially unviable.

Instead, the 'operational realism' (Barry 2005) of *harakeke* (as a hard fibre) meant that efforts appeared to be orientated towards developing products on a model of small-scale production. *Harakeke* biocomposite could not be produced commercially in manufacturing industry, but it could assume a craft potential as it conformed to small-scale models of production required for handmade products. This was made evident when Scion formed a partnership in 2010 with David Trubridge – a prominent New Zealand designer working with sustainable materials – to create household lamps made using a specially developed composite material from bioplastic (polylactic acid) and *harakeke* fibre (Scion Annual Report 2011). Trubridge stated that in this design 'we are expressing our spreading awareness of, and connection to, Nature.' (Scion Highlights of the Financial Year 2010/2011). The product's value is clearly in Trubridge's innovative use of *harakeke* and the plant's unique place in the cultural and natural landscape of New Zealand.

Harakeke oil extraction and environmental branding

While research and development continues to explore the potential of *harakeke* in a bio-based economy, its unique and natural association to the '100% Pure' New Zealand landscape has created another niche within the green cosmetics industry in New Zealand. The oil extracted from the plant's leaves and its seeds have been successfully used in healing and soothing ointments and creams. This material transformation has positioned *harakeke* as New Zealand's answer to aloe vera. These cosmetic products, as I will demonstrate, render the actual material substance (*harakeke*) unrecognizable (since the raw materials are reduced through processing to creams or liquids) and in so doing, rely on a visual culture of labelling and promotion that situates the products in the New Zealand landscape. An analysis of two corporate marketing websites of popular cosmetic companies will reveal how *harakeke* products build on the success of the 100% Pure New Zealand brand and demonstrates how development of *harakeke* has been guided by its potential as a cosmetic product.

Living nature

The website of Living Nature (http://www.livingnature.com/pages/*harakeke*) brands itself as '100% natural' and 'uniquely New Zealand'. The natural cosmetics company produce and market a range of products including skin care oils and cream, shampoos and conditioners for the hair, and face, eye and lip care cosmetics. The products are packaged simply displaying the Living Nature logo, a circular design similar to a Maori curvilinear *kowhaiwhai* rafter pattern. Its mission is rooted in the land and the unique plant resources New Zealand offers:

> featuring the uniqueness of our plant resources and earning export income; on the world by being a model of ethical, honourable business and solving inherent 21st century problems in a way that inspires the human spirit.

Their website goes on to assert how the company has 'harnessed the purifying, healing and nourishing power of New Zealand's unique native botanicals like *Harakeke* Flax Gel, Totarol, Manuka Honey, Manuka Oil, Hallo Clay and Kelp'. Their green credentials are underlined further with the following statement about their commitment to the environment. Their facility 'uses energy from a New Zealand power supplier that generates renewable energy from wind and water (hydro) and we harvest our own filtered rainwater. Our packaging is fully recyclable, meets the highest EU environmental standards and is 100% free from harmful phthalates and Bisphenol-A (BPA). Paper and cartons are sourced from renewable, managed forests and, like our inks, are free from dioxin and elemental chlorine'.

Further information on the website presents Living Nature as a pristine environment that thrives on its unique environment. It asserts that because of the isolation of the islands that emerged over 80 million years, 80 percent of the plants found in New Zealand are unique to the region and found nowhere else in the world. It states how these unique plants are specially sourced on the basis of their bioactive ingredients from the most potent plants known for their healing, purifying and nourishing qualities.

Plants in the New Zealand landscape are marketed as bodily transformative. A number of indigenous plants are presented as 'hero ingredients' and the resulting cosmetics 'hero products'. *Harakeke* leaf sap is categorized under this. The sap is extracted from the plant's older leaves to make a natural gel product that helps hydrate the skin. The product description mentions the traditional uses of *harakeke* by Maoris as well as by early European settlers for rope and linen. The website has a close-up image of *harakeke* leaves behind which in soft focus is pictured a middle-aged woman with clear white skin. The image is emblazoned with the slogan '*Harakeke*: Nature's Super Skin Hydrator'.

Place is important in the promotion of product and its authenticity. The website ascribes provenance, pointing how the gel is sourced from Te Araroa on New Zealand's East Cape. It provides further details about extraction process, stating how the gel is physically removed from the base of the mature leaves so that the main rootstock and younger leaves are preserved. The company uses the *harakeke* leaves for the gel and the seeds for making soap. A short film provides visual testimony of the source for the gel, located at the base of each leaf.

Primal Earth

The cosmetics company Primal Earth (http://www.primalearth.co.nz/) produces natural plant-based skincare products that utilize New Zealand's natural environment to market the efficacy of their products. Their slogan 'Powered by Plants' accompanies a range of products including shaving creme, face creme and moisturizer in earthy green packaging. The cosmetics company utilize *harakeke* and Mamuku fern, highlighting their use as natural skin lotions and healing properties. The Primal Earth oath states: 'Just New Zealand naturally active ingredients that work.' It adds: 'This range is powered by plants. No harsh chemicals. Look and feel great, without irritating your skin. Made in New Zealand, by Kiwi's.'

The company website features three images of plants (*harakeke*, aloe vera and Mamuku fern) situated in New Zealand's natural landscape with no signs of human intervention. In their promotional material about the different properties of plants, the website states:

> *Harakeke* is a striking plant that features dominantly in the New Zealand landscape. It is native to New Zealand and a handful of Pacific Islands. *Harakeke* is renowned for the clear polysaccharide gel exudates produced on the surface of leaves at the base. This gel is often referred to as the New Zealand *Aloe Vera* gel. We use it extensively in our products for its skin soothing and hydrating properties. It is a superior natural alternative to petro-chemically derived synthetic gels.

The positioning of *harakeke* as New Zealand's answer to aloe vera builds on the plant's existing identity as a herbal medicine. Unlike the other cosmetic companies that market *harakeke*, the website does not include details of how the gel is extracted, its provenance or any historical reference points relating to the importance of *harakeke* to New Zealand (Maori and white settler) identity.

These natural products that are produced from the *harakeke* plant therefore serve to underline how products are successfully marketed internationally for their association to a natural, unique and pristine environment, much in the same way Lycra had to sold to consumers through adverts, pamphlets and so forth (O'Connor 2011). This branding builds on the clean green image that has been constructed and transmitted by the 100% Pure New Zealand campaign. It foregrounds visual representations of the New Zealand landscape to assert its New Zealand identity in distinctive ways that add value to the product (cf. Ball 1997). It also demonstrates how material innovation has been driven by available demand for renewable products in the green cosmetics industry and the wider environment in which the New Zealand landscape was transformed into a recognizable and understood brand that transmitted a set of green values and visual images.

Concluding comments

To summarize, while Maoris have for generations utilized *harakeke* fibre for their own ritual and social practices, colonial scientists and biomaterial experts have been unable to map their own model of mass production onto the fibre for the product they are designing. It appears that even when *harakeke* is repositioned as an alternative to mineral and petrochemical based products, *harakeke* is still not compliant to the kinds of outcomes that the scientists so desired through their products. That is, the operational realism of the fibre material meant that products like the surfboard and the woolpacks were deemed uneconomic and inefficient to produce and support once positioned alongside other products readily available and easily extractible in the global materials industry, resulting in their failure of uptake. This demonstrates that even though the material had the potential to innovate design and meet the needs of an environmentally conscious public, in its object form, the *harakeke* did not meet commercial expectations. In Gell's terms (1998), this suggests that *harakeke* lacked 'coherence' in its object-form and thus failed to perform to expectations.

This story of innovation has also demonstrated how materials are intimately tied to cultural and political environments into which they emerge, and how in turn these influence users' and consumers' perception and performance of materials. The national branding of New Zealand as a green and clean economy has helped open a niche for the plant fibre and drive research and development into the *harakeke* plant as an alternative to petro-based materials. Its operational realism has opened opportunities for a craft-based industry due to the lack of investment to find a technical solution to extract the strong fibres. In effect, it has meant that scientists have looked for other properties of the plant, such as the gel, which draws on the known curative properties of *harakeke*. This illustrates how the material expressivity of *harakeke* shapes social worlds and guides research and development in innovative ways.

Materials innovation, I have hoped to emphasize, is not simply about discovery. Rather, as I have demonstrated, it involves a deeper engagement as materials provoke connections that shape their substance and form, which in turn, informs their use and application in society. As Ingold (2000) rightly reminds us, this is why materials and culture permeate each other and do not exist in separate domains of experience.

Reports

Greening New Zealand's Growth, Report of the Green Growth Advisory Group. December 2011. Ministry of Business, Innovation and Employment: Wellington.
'The Utilisation of New Zealand Hemp Waste'. *Bulletin of the Imperial Institute* XVII (1919): 485–488.
Scion Annual Report 2011. Downloaded from: http://www.scionresearch.com/__data/assets/pdf_file/0003/35526/Scion-Annual-Report-2011-web.pdf (accessed on 17 March 2014).

Scion Annual Report 2013: Highlights. Downloaded from: http://www.scionresearch.com/__
        data/assets/pdf_file/0017/42443/ScionAnnualReport2013-Highlights.pdf (accessed on 17
        March 2014).

Notes

1. Hector (1872) describes how in 1844, a company was formed in England that sent
   out specialist machines and technicians to New Zealand. The enterprise, according
   to Hector, failed as the machines 'proved unsuitable for the purpose' (1872: iii). Many
   other attempts were made to extract the fibre; experimentation with different types of
   machinery resulted in the fibre failing to meet the quality of other fibres. These projects,
   as a consequence, ended in financial disaster.
2. Although Ball (2012: 362) asserts how materials are computational and 'the material
   structure itself is the machine'.
3. See Kotler and Simon (2003) for an analysis of the impact the materials industry has on
   the economic productivity of a country.
4. See http://www.scionresearch.com/research/manufacturing-and-bioproducts/wood-
   and-fibre-technology (accessed 17 March 2014).

References

Ashby, M. and K. Johnson (2002), *Materials and Design: The Art and Science of Material
    Selection in Product Design*. Oxford: Butterworth-Heinemann.
Ball, P. (1997), *Made to Measure: New Materials for the 21st Century*, Princeton, NJ: Princeton
    University Press.
Ball, P. (2012), 'Material Computation', *Nature Materials,* 11 May, 362.
Barry, A. (2005), 'Pharmaceutical Matters: The Invention of Informed Materials', *Theory, Culture
    and Society,* 22(1): 51–69.
Bell, F. D and F. Young (1842), *Reasons for Promoting the Cultivation of the New Zealand Flax*.
    London: Smith, Elder and Co.
Bennett, J. (2010), *Vibrant Matter: A Political Ecology of Things*. Durham, NC: Duke University Press.
Boivin, N. (2008), *Material Cultures, Material Minds: The Impact of Things on Human Thought,
    Society, and Evolution*. Cambridge: Cambridge University Press.
Brooker, S. G., R. C. Cambie and R. C. Cooper (1989), 'Economic Native Plants of New
    Zealand', *Economic Botany,* 43(1): 79–106.
Brooking, T. (2004), *The History of New Zealand*. London: Greenwood Press.
Critchfield, H. J. (1951), 'Phormium Tenax – New Zealand's Native Hard Fiber', *Economic
    Botany,* 5(2): 172–184.
Cruthers, N., D. Carr and R. Laing (2009), 'Research Note. The New Zealand Flax Fibre
    Industry', *Textile History,* 40(1): 103–111.
DeLanda, M. (2006), 'Material Expressivity', *Domus,* 893: 122–123. *Lebbeus Woods*. 5 January
    2009. http://lebbeuswoods.wordpress.com/2009/01/05/manuel-delanda-matters-4/.
Dodge, C. R. (1897), *A Descriptive Catalogue of Useful Fibre Plants of the World*. Washington:
    Government Printing Office.
Gell, A. (1998), *Art and Agency: An Anthropological Theory*. Oxford: Clarendon Press.
Hawkins, G. (2011), 'The Politics of Bottled Water: Assembling Bottled Water as Brand, Waste and
    Oil', in T. Bennett, and C. Healy (eds), *Assembling Culture,* pp. 177–189. London: Routledge.

Hawkins, G., E. Potter and K. Race (in press), *Plastic Water*. Cambridge, MA: MIT Press.

Hector, J. (1872), *Phormium Tenax as a Fibrous Plant*. Wellington, New Zealand: Colonial Museum and Geological Survey Department.

Ingold, T. (2000), *The Perception of the Environment: Essays on Livelihood, Dwelling and Skill*. London: Routledge.

Ingold, T. (2011), *Being Alive: Essays on Movement, Knowledge and Description*. Oxford: Routledge.

Ingold, T. (2012), 'Towards an Ecology of Materials', *Annual Review of Anthropology*, 41: 427–442.

Jones, J. (2003), *Harakeke Flax*, Alpha 127. Wellington: The Royal Society of New Zealand.

Knappett, C. and L. Malafouris (2008), 'Material and Nonhuman Agency: An Introduction', in C. Knappett and L. Malafouris (eds), *Material Agency: Towards a Non-Anthropocentric Approach*, pp. ix–xix. New York: Springer Books.

Kotler, P. and F. Simon (2003), *Building Global Biobrands: Taking Biotechnology to Market*. New York: Free Press.

Lai, J. C. (2014), *Indigenous Cultural Heritage and Intellectual Property Rights: Learning from the New Zealand Experience?*. London: Springer International.

Latour, B. (1996), *Aramis, or the Love of Technology*. Cambridge, MA: Harvard University Press.

Latour, B. and S. Woolgar (1979), *Laboratory Life: The Construction of Social Facts*. London: Sage Publications.

Medway, D. and G. Warnaby, (2014), 'What's in a Name? Place Branding and Toponymic Commodification', *Environment and Planning A*, 46: 153–167.

Meikle, J. L. (1997), *American Plastic: A Cultural History*. New Brunswick: Rutgers University Press

Miller, D. (ed.) (2005), *Materiality*. Denver: Duke University Press.

Morgan, N., A. Pritchard and R. Piggott (2002), 'New Zealand, 100% Pure: The Creation of a Powerful Niche Destination Brand', *Journal of Brand Management*, 9(4/5): 335–354.

Murray, J. (1838), *An Account of the Phormium Tenax, or, New Zealand Flax: Printed on Paper Made from Its Leaves (Bleached) with a Postscript on Paper*. London: Relfe and Fletcher.

Norman, D. A. (1988), *The Psychology of Everyday Things*. New York: Basic Books.

O'Connor, K. (2011), *Lycra: How a Fiber Shaped America*. London: Routledge.

Shaw, M., G. Bicking and M. O'Leary (1931), 'The Paper-Making Properties of Phormium Tenax (New Zealand flax)', *Bureau of Standards Journal of Research*, 6(3): 411–420, Research Paper 285.

Sheller, M. (2014), *Aluminum Dreams: The Making of Light Modernity*. Cambridge, MA: MIT Press.

Welz, G. (2003), 'The Cultural Swirl: Anthropological Perspectives on Innovation', *Global Networks*, 3(3): 255–270.

Were, G. (2013), 'On the Materials of Mats: Thinking Through Design in a Melanesian Society', *Journal of the Royal Anthropological Institute*, 19(3): 581–599.

Chapter 3

Pharmaceutical matters: The invention of informed materials

Andrew Barry

In comparison to physics and biology, chemistry appears to be a science lacking in theoretical interest. Unlike physics, it does not claim to be concerned with the investigation of fundamental forces and particles. Unlike biology, it does not concern itself primarily with the properties and dynamics of living materials. Indeed, as Bernadette Bensaude-Vincent and Isabelle Stengers note in their *History of Chemistry,* the discipline is often considered merely a 'service' science. In one common view, although chemistry did once play a leading role in the development of scientific thought, in the twentieth century that role seems to have been displaced by other fields. To be sure, chemistry is a large field embracing a huge range of important topics and problems, but it apparently no longer possesses the status that it once had in the hierarchy of scientific disciplines: 'Chemistry may seem to be a kind of applied physics, whose focus is not on the progress of knowledge but technico-industrial utility' (Bensaude-Vincent and Stengers 1996: 245). From this perspective, chemistry is doubly uninteresting. First, the direction of its development is determined by purely instrumental considerations. Second, the discipline no longer aspires to address any fundamental questions. At best, contemporary chemistry simply makes it possible for some of the fundamental scientific developments of the twentieth century (quantum mechanics and genetics, in particular) to find fields of application. At worst, it remains tied to a naïve and outdated ontology of atomism and mechanism. The received view that chemical thought is theoretically limited is not new. In his *Creative Evolution*, Henri Bergson had drawn a sharp contrast between the limitations of physics and chemistry and the philosophical importance of the sciences of life: 'Those who are concerned only with the functional [as distinct from the creative] activity of the living being are inclined to believe that physics and chemistry will give us the key to biological processes' (Ansell-Pearson 1999: 149; Bergson 1998: 36).

In this chapter, I make four intersecting arguments, which contest this received view. First, I argue that chemistry is of general interest to social theory not because of its larger theoretical claims or ethical implications but rather because, as Bensaude-Vincent and Stengers argue, it is an industrial, applied and empirical discipline. Indeed, part of the theoretical interest of chemistry is that it indicates the importance of research that is not primarily guided by theory but is attentive to the singularity of the case. Second, focusing on a specific case of R&D in pharmaceutical chemistry, I develop Bensaude-Vincent and Stengers' claim that one of the key features of chemical R&D is that it is concerned with the invention of what they term *informed materials*. The chapter argues that molecules should not be viewed as discrete objects, but as constituted in their relations to complex informational and material environments. Third, drawing on the philosophy of A. N. Whitehead and the sociology of Gabriel Tarde, I suggest how we might make a distinction between the concept of invention, used by Bensaude-Vincent and Stengers, and the concepts of discovery and innovation. While we may or may not agree with Bergson's claim that chemistry does not provide an account of the creative activity of living materials, I argue that chemical R&D is not merely innovative, but is itself creative or inventive, in Tarde's sense of the term. Chemical R&D does not, among other things, discover or synthesize new molecules or new molecular structures, but, as Bensaude-Vincent and Stengers argue, it invents informed materials. Fourth, I argue that an important feature of contemporary pharmaceutical chemistry is, to use A. N. Whitehead's terms, the invention of new methods for the invention of such materials. Although the materials produced by chemists have always been informed, the development of contemporary pharmaceutical research has fostered new forms and levels of informational enrichment. My suggestion is that the chemical molecules invented by chemical R&D are now so rich in information that the informational content of invented materials becomes easier to recognize. In part, the conduct of contemporary pharmaceutical R&D is of general interest precisely because it makes the informational content of invented materials more clearly visible. In sociology, as in chemistry, the general interest of the example derives from an attention to its specificity.

Chemistry

In their history, Bensaude-Vincent and Stengers do not deny that there is some truth in the received view of chemistry as merely a service science. But they offer two correctives, both of which suggest a richer account of the history of chemistry. First, they note some of the ways in which chemistry has continued to produce surprising and fundamental results in the twentieth century. They point, in particular, to Prigogine's work in far-from-equilibrium physical chemistry and his analysis of self-organizing systems. Contemporary chemistry, in their view, points to the limitations of those approaches that seek to deduce from first principles but instead recognizes the possibility of learning from the contingent.

> What are the properties of a substance if one is interested only in deducing them without learning? And how does one learn from them if not by painstaking experiments of which they are an integral part or deciphering the temporal configuration of all the processes at work? (Bensaude-Vincent and Stengers 1996: 264).

In this view chemistry is not so much a positivist science, but a discipline that points to a new form of empiricism. It produces substances, the properties of which *cannot* be derived from general laws.[1]

Second and relatedly, their history indicates that the 'technico-industrial utility' of chemistry cannot be understood simply as a process of application. On the one hand, once outside of the laboratory chemists confronts environments or open systems, which do not correspond necessarily to the closed environments of the laboratory (Bensaude-Vincent and Stengers 1996: 249). In these circumstances, the relation between the field of application (factory, urban environment, field) and the laboratory is necessarily one of translation rather than application or diffusion (Latour 1988, 1999). On the other hand, in so far as chemistry has played a critical part in the development of new materials it has also given rise to a different notion of matter. Matter is not merely reshaped mechanically through chemical R&D but is, according to Bensaude-Vincent and Stengers, transformed into *informed material*:

> Instead of imposing a shape on the mass of material, one develops an 'informed material' in the sense that the material structure becomes *richer and richer in information*. Accomplishing this requires a detailed comprehension of the microscopic structure of materials, because it is playing with these molecular, atomic and even subatomic structures that one can *invent* materials adapted to industrial demands. (Bensaude-Vincent and Stengers 1996: 206, my emphasis)

Bensaude-Vincent and Stengers' argument raises two immediate questions, to which they do not provide an answer in this text. First, what is implied by the idea that such materials are invented? What is at stake in using the term 'invention' in describing what happens to chemical substances in the laboratory rather than, for example, the term 'discovery'? Second, how are we to make sense of the idea that materials can somehow become 'informed' or, as they suggest, 'richer and richer' in information.

Invention

What is an invention? In *The Laws of Imitation*, Gabriel Tarde provides us with a starting point for a social theory of invention. For Tarde, invention was not the opposite of imitation, nor was the relation between invention and imitation analogous to the sociological distinction between agency and structure. Rather, invention involved the novel composition of elements that were themselves imitations: 'All inventions and discoveries are composites of earlier imitations . . . and these composites are, in their turn, destined to become new more complex composites' (Tarde 2001: 105). In Tarde's ontology there were no fundamental elements from which composites were invented. Even those objects that were often taken to be fundamental – such as chemical atoms and human individuals – were only fundamental from the point of view of specific scientific disciplines.[2]

As a composite, the properties of any invention were not reducible to the elements from which it was composed. At the same time, as Tarde argued, the process of invention provided a direction to history, although one that was neither linear nor predictable. Anticipating the conclusions of more recent economists and sociologists of technology, Tarde recognized that the process of invention was contingent, irreversible and path-dependent. In this way, Tarde conceived of inventions as events, not as mere moments in the progressive evolution of technology or the manifestation of the movement of societies from one form to another: 'To establish social science it is not necessary to conceive the evolution of societies . . . with a formula comparable to the type of itinerary planned in advance that the railroad companies propose to and impose on tourists' (1967: 93).

Some of Tarde's comments on invention seem to imply that he viewed individual genius as being of critical importance to the inventive process. Yet his account of invention was not psychological, nor did Tarde have a romantic conception of the individual creator. On the one hand, his account was based on a generalized social psychology of belief and desire, in which the notion of society applied as much to non-human as to human entities (Alliez 1999). On the other hand, Tarde recognized that what he termed scientific geniuses (such as Cuvier, Newton and Darwin) mobilized the action of many obscure researchers whose contribution was often ignored (Tarde 1999: 66). Invention, in Tarde's account, was accomplished not by an individual agent, but by lines of force that came to traverse the individual person. Moreover, for an invention to become irreversible depended on the extent of its subsequent imitation by others.

Tarde's conception of invention provides a corrective to two commonplace ways of conceiving of technological invention, in general, and the inventive practice of chemistry, in particular. In one view, chemical research and development is driven by social and economic forces. It is a service science, after all. In this way, the products of chemical innovation (such as molecules) become shaped by a social and economic dynamic that was external to them. In Tarde's terms, this form of socioeconomic analysis operates with an excessively restrictive conception of society. In effect, the activity of chemical substances is simply rendered inert, excluded from the active realm of the social. In a second view, the chemist works to *discover* new materials. Indeed, the idea that new molecules are discovered is one apparently implied by pharmaceutical chemists themselves who write of research and development as a process of 'drug discovery'.[3] In this account, the fundamental properties of the finite set of chemical elements that make up the periodic table provide a set of given possibilities out of which effective drug molecules can subsequently be synthesized. This view resonates with the nineteenth-century notion that nature exists as a repository of potential inventions that are simply there waiting to be realized or discovered by the scientist or engineer (Macleod 1996). For Tarde, such an account fails to recognize that an atomic element or a molecule is never just an element in isolation. Inevitably, the chemist, in discovering a new molecule, invents a new composite element. Invention leads to the actualization of the virtual rather than the realization of the possible (Deleuze 1988: 96–97).

Although Tarde does provide a starting point for a social theory of invention, his own historical analysis fails to recognize the significance of the industrialization of science and engineering that occurred in the late nineteenth century (Noble 1977). In this respect, his image of invention was indebted to romantic notions of individual creativity. A. N. Whitehead's later remarks on the history of nineteenth-century science in *Science and the Modern World* are more suggestive. For Whitehead, 'the greatest invention of the nineteenth century was the invention of the method of invention' (Whitehead 1985: 120). This oft-quoted comment seems remarkable in a book that is primarily concerned with issues in the history and philosophy of science rather than the sociology and history of technology. Yet it makes perfect sense in the context of Whitehead's philosophical project. In *Science and the Modern World,* Whitehead had little to say about the kinds of problem that traditionally preoccupy philosophers of science such as the relation between theory and evidence or the nature of scientific method. His concerns were metaphysical, not epistemological, and at the heart of his philosophy was that 'the ultimate metaphysical principle is the advance from disjunction to conjunction, creating a novel entity other than the entities given in disjunction' (Whitehead 1978: 21). As for Tarde, Whitehead's was a metaphysics of association. For Whitehead, the nineteenth-century invention of the method of invention made the production of novel associations a matter of systematic research and development. While fields concerned with the invention and investigation of materials such as chemistry and metallurgy have arguably played a merely supportive part in the development of many of the most well-known developments in twentieth-century scientific theory, from the point of view of the history of invention their role is absolutely critical.[4] To view such fields of science as merely instrumental, or simply driven by an economic logic, would fail to recognize their inventiveness. The notion of informed material, put forward by Bensaude-Vincent and Stengers, points to one way in which such sciences have been inventive and to one way in which atoms and molecules come to exist, to use Tarde's terms, as 'complex composites'.

Informed materials

How can we understand the idea that materials can be informed? Two views were commonplace among chemists in the late nineteenth century. First, in comparison to physics, which sometimes dealt with metaphysical abstractions, chemists prided themselves on the practical craft of their discipline. In this period, 'chemistry's greatness consisted precisely in its not transcending the facts learned from its practice' (Bensaude-Vincent and Stengers 1996). Chemistry was a discipline grounded in the controlled environment of the laboratory. Meeting the 'converging interests of academic research and industrial production', the chemistry laboratory both produced new entities and provided the space within which they could reliably be witnessed (Stengers 1997: 95).

Second, many (although not all) chemists viewed the discipline as a science of atomic elements and molecules. This identity was displayed clearly in the periodic table, a diagram that is still to be found on the walls of the present-day laboratory. Conceived in this way, chemistry appeared to make two assumptions. One was that atoms have given and invariant identities, an assumption that was (partially) undermined with the discovery of radioactivity at the beginning of the twentieth century. The second was that chemistry is a science of combinations between these invariant entities. Despite the fact that chemists write of things such as carbon, water and iron all the time, such atoms and molecules are never studied in isolation. The chemist is interested in the fact that the properties of atoms and molecules vary considerably depending on the form and circumstances of their association with others.

For A. N. Whitehead, the discipline of chemistry had a particular importance in the exposition of his philosophy of organic mechanism. For Whitehead recognized that the image of matter as being composed of distinct atoms and molecules had come to inform contemporary understandings of reality. In this commonplace view, a molecule is thought of as something like a stone – a kind of stuff 'which retained its self-identity and its essential attributes in any portion of time' (Whitehead 1978: 78; Stengers 2002). Whereas Bergson wished to distance himself from what he viewed as the limitations of chemical thought, Whitehead's own criticism of this commonplace view drew some inspiration from chemistry. In his account, however, the identities of atoms and molecules were not distinct, nor were they invariant. Rather than starting out from the first assumption (the invariability of atoms and molecules), Whitehead began from the second (the variability of their associations). Viewing chemistry as a science of associations or relations, Whitehead argued that a molecule should be considered a historical rather than a physical entity. In his view, a molecule should not be understood as a table or rock but rather as an event: 'A molecule is a historic route of actual occasions; and such a route is an event' (Whitehead 1978: 80). Seen in these terms the endurance of a molecule through time cannot be taken for granted. Molecules certainly endure, but it cannot be assumed that they remain the same: 'Physical endurance is the process of continuously inheriting a certain identity of character transmitted throughout an historical route of events' (Whitehead 1985: 136).

Chemistry should not be understood then as a science of combinations between given elements that are nonetheless be considered distinct and immutable. Rather, the identity and properties of atoms and molecules are transformed through their changing associations. The properties of a hydrogen atom bound within a water molecule are different from the properties of a hydrogen atom bound within a hydrogen molecule. The properties of a water molecule are quite different at temperatures above and below 0°C. The properties of a metal vary considerably depending on whether it contains trace impurities of other elements. In displacing the notion of the object by the notion of the actual occasion or actual entity, Whitehead suggested a different account of atoms and molecules. For Whitehead, actual entities, including molecules, are not bounded at all, but are extended into other entities, while folding elements of other entities inside them. As became clear with the development of quantum chemistry, apparently distinct atoms and molecules entered into the internal constitution of others through their association. This recognition was a central part of Whitehead's metaphysics: '[An] actual entity is present in other actual entities

. . . The philosophy of organism is mainly devoted to the task of making clear the notion of "being present in another entity"' (Whitehead 1978: 50; see also Deleuze 1993: 78; Halewood 2003).

For chemists, the fact that molecules have changing properties depending on their associations is an everyday reality. The molecule that is isolated and purified in the laboratory will not have the same properties as it has in the field, the city street or the body (Barry 2001: 153–174). The challenge, for the chemist, is to multiply the relations between different forms of existence of a molecule both inside and outside the laboratory (Latour 1999: 113–114). It is impossible to establish an identity between the molecule in the laboratory and a molecule elsewhere, but it may be possible to establish a relation of translation. The problem is particularly difficult to address in thinking about the properties of drugs. Bensaude-Vincent and Isabelle Stengers note the challenge faced by chemists engaged in pharmaceutical research:

> The pharmacological chemist can certainly pursue the dream of an *a priori* conception of molecules to be synthesized for their pharmaceutical properties, but it is still the case that 60 to 70 per cent of medicines today are of natural origin . . . From this field the chemist takes the active molecules, which he isolates, purifies and copies, and modifies at leisure. But it is also 'on the field – on the ailing body' – that medicine designed in a laboratory must operate. Humanity delegates active chemical substances to act not in the aseptic space of a laboratory but in a living labyrinth whose topology varies in time, where partial and circumstantial causalities are so intertwined that they escape any *a priori* intelligibility. (1996: 263)

Bensaude-Vincent and Stengers pose the problem of the relation between the 'aseptic space of a laboratory' and the 'living labyrinth' of the body as an ontological one. Molecules necessarily do have different identities and effects in the laboratory and the body. But, for pharmaceutical research, the gap between the laboratory and the body is equally economic, regulatory and legal. Although pharmaceutical companies may be able to identify potential drug molecules through a variety of methods, there is no guarantee that active molecules will work effectively and safely as drugs in living bodies.[5] During development many active molecules fail whether because they are poorly absorbed or metabolized, or are subsequently shown to have toxic effects. Moreover, in the context of the growing concern of consumers, regulators have become more cautious about drug approvals and 'increasing post-marketing surveillance has led to an increasing number of withdrawals'.[6] The withdrawal of Bayer's Baycol™ is a well-known recent example.[7] In these circumstances, research and development costs have escalated. Pfizer, for example, the world's largest drugs company, has warned that its $5 billion annual research budget will yield only about two major new drugs per year. The average pre-clinical trial development cost of new chemical entities is said to be $30 million per molecule. Perhaps 90 per cent of such molecules fail such trials. The cost of generating a single approved medicine is claimed to be over $600 million.

For pharmaceutical companies the costs of clinical trials and the even greater costs of withdrawing drugs after they have been marketed poses a clear problem: How is it possible to maximize the chances that a drug will be both effective and safe prior to the conduct of such trials and, thereby, to increase the productivity of pharmaceutical R&D? How can reliable relations be established between the 'aseptic space of a laboratory' and the 'living labyrinth' of the body without the presence of real bodies? In brief, how can innovation be speeded up?[8]

Bensaude-Vincent and Stengers indicate one solution to the problem. Pharmaceutical R&D can be directed to the extraction and purification of active molecules from naturally occurring substances. This practice can give rise to a series of legal and ethical questions concerning the ownership of intellectual property, for example, regarding indigenous knowledge of the medicinal properties of plants or the ownership of viruses that are present in particular populations (Pottage 1998). Such an approach is of continuing importance, but it is only one possible research strategy open to pharmaceutical companies. A more general understanding of pharmaceutical R&D is suggested by the notion of informed material.

One way of understanding the idea that a material entity (such as a potential drug molecule) could be informed or 'rich in information' would be to say that the material *embodies* information. In this view, the design process builds information into the structure of the molecule. But this view would not make sense if we understood the molecule to be simply a discrete and bounded entity. For if molecules were simply discrete entities, how could one then distinguish between a molecule that embodies little information and the 'same' molecule with the same structure of elements that embodies a great deal of information? In Whitehead's and Stengers' terms, it is possible to give a different and more precise meaning to the idea of a material object being rich in information. This would acknowledge that material objects (such as molecules) exist in an informational and material environment, yet this environment cannot, as Whitehead argued, be considered as simply external to the object. An environment of informational and material entities *enters into* the constitution of an entity such as a molecule. Nor can this environment be perceived from a viewpoint that is external to it. The perception of an entity (such as a molecule) is part of its informational material environment (Fraser 2002; Whitehead 1985: 87).

Thus defined, the notion of an informed material makes sense of what pharmaceutical actually do. Pharmaceutical companies do not produce bare molecules – structures of carbon, hydrogen, oxygen and other elements – isolated from their environments. Rather they produce a multitude of informed molecules, including multiple informational and material forms of the same molecule. Pharmaceutical companies do not just sell information, but neither do they just sell material objects (drug molecules) either. The molecules produced by pharmaceutical companies are more or less purified, but they are also enhanced and enriched through laboratory practice. The molecules produced by a pharmaceutical company are already part of a rich informational material environment, even before they are consumed. This environment includes, for example, data about potency, metabolism and toxicity and information regarding the intellectual property rights associated with different molecules. In this way, pharmaceutical laboratories have similarities to other laboratories. As Karin Knorr-Cetina argues laboratories: 'invent and recreate . . . objects from scratch . . . creat[ing] new configurations of objects that they match with an appropriately altered social order' (Knorr-Cetinà 1999: 44).

Drug discovery

Consider the case of a medium-sized pharmaceutical company called ArQule, which, towards the end of the 1990s began to transform itself into a 'drug discovery company' – a company oriented towards the development of new chemical entities. Although ArQule was unusual in some respects, its approach to drug discovery is indicative of broader shifts in the conduct of contemporary pharmaceutical R&D. These centred on the introduction of new technologies, including high-throughput screening, combinatorial chemistry, genomics, and computer modelling (Bailey and Brown 2001).[9] In this way, elements of the drug discovery process, which had hitherto been based on craft laboratory skills, became increasingly industrialized (Augen 2002; Handen 2002). At the same time, the introduction of new technologies involved alliances between companies working in distinct areas of technology, and also the formation of so-called virtual pharmaceutical companies that managed such alliances (Cavalla 2003: 267).

ArQule made its name as a pioneering company in combinatorial chemistry, a set of techniques that made possible to produce a huge number of potential drug molecules cheaply and quickly.[10] Instead of being the product of specific synthetic pathways of the kind associated with traditional synthetic organic chemistry, combinatorial chemistry enabled new molecules to be mass produced (Hird 2000; Thomas 2000: 69–88).

Synthetic chemistry: A + B + C -> AB + C -> ABC (an individual compound)

Combinatorial chemistry: $A_n + B_n + C$ -> $A_nB_n + C_n$ -> $A_nB_nC_n$ (combinatorial library of 10,000–1,000,000 compounds)

For the traditional organic chemist the problem was to find the most efficient way of synthesizing a given molecular compound (ABC) from a finite set of building blocks of existing compounds (A,B,C, D . . .), which were either readily available in the laboratory or could be purchased from chemical suppliers. Indeed, the discovery of solutions to particular synthetic problems was central to the field of organic chemistry, as it was once taught in University courses. In the laboratory, organic chemists had to deal with the all the difficulties of translating formal solutions to synthetic problems into practice. As Bensaude-Vincent and Stengers explain: 'organic chemistry texts usually present the classic, conventional reaction chains. But to the student or researcher falls the problem of directing the actors in a play, so to speak, and creating the situations they need to achieve the desired goal' (1996: 159).

By contrast, combinatorial chemistry performs synthesis through mass production. Through combinatorial chemistry a large number of different but chemically similar building blocks (A_a, A_b . . . A_n) can be reacted with sets of other building blocks (B_a, B_b . . . B_n) and (C_a, C_b . . . C_n) to produce huge numbers of synthetic compounds. In this way, molecules come to exist not as the product of individual synthetic pathways, as was previously the case, but in conjunction with a multitude of other molecules produced through combinatorial pathways. Physically, molecules produced through such techniques are dissolved in standard solutions and stored, for example, in arrays of test-tubes. These arrays collectively form what in the industry are termed *libraries* of compounds (Beno and Mason 2001). The metaphor of a library of molecules is appropriate because not only do such mass produced molecules have a material existence but they also are held in an informational form in catalogues and databases. Without further research, individual molecules produced through combinatorial chemistry have little commercial value. In practice, combinatorial chemistry companies, such as ArQule, sold whole libraries of molecules to those larger pharmaceutical companies that had the resources to investigate and exploit them.

But although combinatorial chemistry, in conjunction with high-throughput screening techniques, reduced the costs of producing and analysing the properties of new molecules, it did not solve the problem of how to determine whether they would work in living bodies. According to industry reports combinatorial chemistry companies faced the problem that the new technology was not yielding the kinds of dramatic improvements in the productivity and efficiency of drug discovery that had been anticipated by investors and partners. The danger was that ArQule would end up simply providing the bulk material for drug development, but not playing any significant role in the subsequent informational enrichment of its product. It would not be able to engage in either what researchers term 'lead generation' (developing a set of molecules which have the potential to become drugs) or 'lead optimization' (refining this set). In these circumstances, ArQule's strategy was to reinvent itself as a 'drug discovery company' and, at the same time, to attempt to create a new form of informed material. Value could be realized by enriching molecules with information.

In broad terms, ArQule's attempt to do this had two elements. One was to integrate elements of the existing 'drug discovery process'. To work as a drug, a molecule did not merely have to be potent but it also had to be absorbed by (and eliminated from) the body, it had to be non-toxic and metabolized neither too slowly nor too quickly. Traditionally, major pharmaceutical companies had performed tests for these properties in sequence. First, potential drug candidates were tested for potency against specific targets, then the other properties of those molecules that were likely to be potent were investigated. ArQule's aim was to perform them in parallel thereby dramatically reducing the time taken to optimize the design of a potential drug molecule.

> In the traditional drug discovery process, physico-chemical properties, selectivity, potency and ADMET (absorption, distribution, metabolism, elimination, toxicity) parameters are evaluated in a sequential manner, extending the time required to identify a lead candidate and increasing costs. Key information provided by ADMET profiling is historically obtained *at the end of the discovery process*. Adverse results at this step can eliminate compounds that have already progressed for many years, at a substantial cost (ArQule 2001) . . . [Instead, the] sequential process with late failures must be replaced by a multi-parameter filer at every stage of the drug discovery process. (Hill 2001)

This strategy was called Parallel Track™ drug discovery: The trademark is an indicator that this method of invention itself had a market value and public visibility. As a brand, ArQule did not address itself to consumers (Blackett and Robins 2001) but rather to the network of potential investors, collaborators and researchers necessary to maintain an innovative company.

The second element of ArQule's approach to the problem of drug discovery involved a proliferation of the forms of existence of molecules. Molecules increasingly existed in ArQule not merely as material and informational objects in laboratories and libraries but also as the objects of computer modelling. To be sure, computational methods had already established a place in the drug discovery process, however, this place had been a limited one.

> [In drug discovery a] team must come up with a drug which will interact with a novel target for therapeutic intervention in an important disease. The team will have access to data on related targets and existing drugs which interact with them. They may have a crystal structure of a target protein. And using a library of computational tools, with their inherent sets of chemical rules, the team can make an informed assessment regarding the shape of molecules that might interact with the target. In modern companies, they will then be able to enumerate a focused library of possible actives using these methods. But this is where their 'simulation' ends. (Beresford et al. 2002)

ArQule's approach was to extend the use of computer models to the simulation of ADMET. Through computer models, the libraries of molecules generated through combinatorial chemistry could be subject to what pharmaceutical researchers called *virtual screening* (Manly et al. 2001). In this way, it would become much easier, and cheaper, to deal with the size of library generated by combinatorial chemistry. In principle, huge libraries of molecules could be enriched through computer modelling, reducing the need for costly laboratory experiments. In practice, however, the development of computer models that might be of use to the laboratory chemist is far from straightforward. Models themselves can be derived, in part, from general quantum mechanical principles. But, as Bensaude-Vincent and Stengers argue, chemistry can rarely rely on general principles, perhaps particularly in the case of the pharmaceutical industry. Necessarily, the development of computer models relies on data derived from earlier laboratory and clinical trials on molecules that may be more or less different from the molecules that the chemist is interested in. However sound the theoretical bases of models are, their reliability depends on the quality and breadth of the data sets on which specific calculations are based.

In discussions between chemists, the term 'chemical space' has particular importance. Why is this term so significant? One reason is that it provides a way of thinking about the distance between the properties of the molecules they are interested in and the properties of the molecules that have been used to derive the models. The quality of the models depends on the volume of chemical space they are able to operate within with some degree of reliability. As one team of chemical modellers explained:

> Any primordial models in the past were invariably poor in their predictability because they were based on a very small data set of tens of compounds. (Beresford et al. 2002)

In this way, the concept of chemical space is both important and difficult to operationalize. It is not a Newtonian space, governed by particular coordinate axes that exist independently of the entities that exist within the space. Rather, chemical space is a relational space, the coordinates of which are governed by the particular medical chemical process under investigation. Two different molecules that exist in close proximity to each other in relation to one specific process, for example, may be distant from each other when viewed in relation to a different process. Different pharmaceutical companies, research teams or projects may temporarily occupy different regions of chemical space. But, at the same time, they are likely to conceive of the structure of chemical space in quite different ways.

While computer modelling can be used to select molecules from the libraries generated through combinatorial chemistry, modelling also generates and tests molecules that may not necessarily have any material existence at all. Molecules can be synthesized on screen – even more easily than through combinatorial chemistry. As well as combinatorial libraries it is now possible for pharmaceutical companies to hold virtual libraries of molecules that have never been synthesized. However, it should not be thought that such computational experiments are necessarily less real than those tested in a traditional laboratory. For some pharmaceutical researchers and managers all techniques are viewed more or less instrumentally in terms of how quickly and efficiently they yield molecules with a potential to become drug molecules. Others point out that computational experiments are closer to external reality than traditional laboratory experiments as they are likely to be based on data derived from trials on living bodies, whereas laboratory experiments will be conducted in standard solutions.[11] Linguistically, researchers establish equivalence between experiments conducted through computer models by computational chemists and experiments conducted using chemical materials by laboratory chemists. The former experiments are *in silico*, the latter are *in vivo* or *in vitro* (Leach and Hann 2000). For the chemist, it would not make sense to say that experiment that takes place through a computer model is simply a representation of the kind of experiment traditionally carried by the organic chemist or biologist in the laboratory. *In silico, in vivo* and *in vitro* experiments are all considered as distinct events that constitute their own objects, relations and forms of measurement, and have their own strengths and weaknesses. The problem for a pharmaceutical research group is to translate between the different forms of experiment and different forms of existence of molecules, so that they enrich each other. In practice, this translation is likely to be difficult.

ArQule did not produce molecules that could be sold directly to consumers. The company did not have the resources to invest in expensive clinical trials, nor the political and legal expertise with which to manage its relations with the regulatory authorities, nor the infrastructure required for marketing and distribution. In this context, measurements of the properties of molecules, in their various material and immaterial forms, are critical to the formation of the market for potential drug molecules for companies such as ArQule (cf. Callon et al. 2002: 198–199). For along with other pharmaceutical companies, ArQule had to develop new materials that were sufficiently rich in information that they could provide both the basis for claims to intellectual property and that would also be likely candidates for further development. Potential purchasers of ArQule's research did not purchase molecules but rather molecules of which the properties had, in various forms, been measured and that were, thereby, uncertainly predictive of their clinical existence. The economics of the pharmaceutical industry revolve around an extraordinary level of investment in measuring equipment – including computer modelling technology, laboratory tests and clinical trials – which produces uncertain results.

Thus specific molecules exist in the informational and material environment of the laboratory. But they also exist in a legal and economic environment of other molecules developed by other companies. Necessarily, in formulating research strategies chemists take into account the existence of prior patents.[12] This information, updated daily, is available on commercial databases. The importance of this informational environment accounts for a second sense in which chemists use the term 'chemical space', which refers to the distance between patented drug molecules and the set of molecules they are investigating. In the context of this information, chemists may seek to buy into the legal-chemical space owned by other companies through collaboration. But they may also try to develop molecules that exist just outside of the space defined by a patent,[13] or colonize unexplored volumes of chemical space, or attempt to redesign drug molecules that have been patented but which have failed clinical trials.[14] Moreover, in developing computer models chemists make use of publicly available data on patented molecules. In these ways, intellectual property law should not be considered simply part of the external environment within which pharmaceutical companies operate and drug molecules are developed. In a number of different ways, information about existing patents enters into the life of molecules, even during the earliest stages of their development. The molecules produced by the pharmaceutical laboratory are rich in information about their (global) legal and economic, as well as their chemical relations to other molecules. The pharmaceutical laboratory is not a closed system, but a space that itself includes its external legal and economic environment (cf. Mitchell 2002: 303; Strathern 2002).

Conclusions: Chemical invention

Does it make sense to describe pharmaceutical R&D as an inventive practice rather than merely a practice of discovery? Are the kinds of entities produced through pharmaceutical companies novel? Certainly, the molecules developed by pharmaceutical R&D do not exist 'in nature'. But neither can they be designed simply on the basis of fundamental chemical principles. Nor are they merely structures of atomic elements that always had the potential to be discovered or realized. As we have seen, the development of new drugs involves the multiplication of forms of existence of molecules. But, at the same time, the multiplication of forms of existence of molecules is associated with their progressive informational enrichment.

Thus, the kinds of entities that are produced by pharmaceutical R&D are not simply bare molecules. Rather they can be understood as 'societies' of different elements, as long as we understand that societies are associations of non-human as well as human entities. The idea of chemical space, which is used so frequently by pharmaceutical chemists, conveys precisely the way in which chemists understand that molecules are 'societies', in Tarde's sense of the term. As I have argued, the kinds of societies produced by pharmaceutical R&D take specific historical forms. The molecules produced in the contemporary pharmaceutical laboratory certainly are more or less purified as chemicals, but they are also enriched in new ways. They are part of increasingly dense, spatially extended and changing informational and material environments formed not just through laboratory syntheses and tests, but through virtual libraries, computational models and databases. The notion of 'informed materials', introduced by Bensaude-Vincent and Stengers, describes such novel entities very well.[15]

For A. N. Whitehead, it was a mistake to imagine that material objects (such as molecules) ever had a concrete existence. Rather than imagine that there are concrete material objects to which social meanings and uses are then added, he argued that objects themselves take historical forms. Whitehead himself was preoccupied by the problem of how, despite the historicity of things, things didn't change that much. Things endured. One of the key assumptions of chemistry is, of course, endurance. Atoms and molecules are never exactly the same as they were before, depending on their changing environments, but they also have an amazing capacity for endurance. Within the drug discovery process, the forms of existence of molecules proliferate. Molecules have characteristics and properties depending on their existence in different informational material forms (in laboratory tests, clinical trials, computer models, patent databases, etc.). But this does not mean that the identities of molecules are fluid. On the contrary, pharmaceutical research can only proceed on the basis that molecules actually endure across different sites, through different parts of the laboratory, throughout their life as products. In the pharmaceutical laboratory, the generation of enduring novel entities depends upon the multiplication of different forms of informed material.

Notes

1. In the sense given to the idea of empiricism by Whitehead and taken up by Deleuze: 'the abstract does not explain, but must itself be explained; and the aim is not to rediscover the eternal or the universal, but to find the conditions under which something new is produced' (Deleuze 1987: vii).
2. 'The final elements that every science ends up with – the social individual, the living cell, the chemical atom – are final only with respect to their particular science. They are themselves composite' (Tarde 1999: 36 cited in Alliez 1999: 10).
3. One of the leading trade journals of the industry is called *Drug Discovery Today*, and chemists speak of pharmaceutical companies as 'drug discovery companies'. The frequent use of the term 'discovery' does not mean, however, that chemists understand the term literally.
4. Whitehead noted the critical importance of metallurgy to the development of physics in the early twentieth century: 'The reason why we are on a higher imaginative level is not because we have finer imagination, but because we have better instruments. In science, the most important thing that has happened over the last forty years is the advance of instrumental design. This advance is partly due to a few men of genius such as Michelson and the German opticians. It is also due to the progress of technological processes of manufacture, particularly in the region of metallurgy' (Whitehead 1985: 143).
5. I leave aside here the critical question of the politics of clinical trials and the relations between pharmaceutical companies and regulatory agencies. For further discussion of these issues, see Abraham (1995).
6. *Financial Times*, nd., 2001.
7. In August 2001, Bayer voluntarily withdrew Baycol from the US market because of reports of sometimes fatal rhabdomyolysis, a severe muscle adverse reaction (Food and Drug Administration 2001).
8. Macdonald and Smith (2001: 947) give an indication of the pressures placed on pharmaceutical R&D for increased productivity in the late 1990s: 'In 1998 GlaxoWellcome embarked upon a new enzyme-inhibitor programme [featuring] an aggressive timeframe of seven years, from the start of medicinal chemistry through to drug launch. This period, dominated as it was by the constraints of the clinical programme [i.e. of testing on human patients], translated into a lead-optimization phase [i.e. the period in which likely potential drug molecules are identified prior to clinical trial] of no more than 12 months'. See also Peakman et al. (2003).

9. While the ethical and political implications of genomics have been a key focus for research in the social sciences the development of genomics has seldom been placed in the context of other related trends in research and development. At the same time, elements of the drug discovery process, which had hitherto been based on craft laboratory skills, became increasingly industrialized (Augen 2002; Handen 2002).

10. Later commentators indicate that combinatorial chemistry became, for a period, an industrial fashion, just as genomics was later in the 1990s: 'The launch of combinatorial chemistry onto an unsuspecting pharmaceutical industry in the early 1990s resulted in several frantic efforts as companies tried to maintain a competitive edge through the generation and screening of compounds in unprecedented numbers and at an unprecedented rate' (Everett et al. 2001: 779). The importance of speed in the commercial development of chemistry is not new. Synthetic chemists have often been concerned with the question of the speed and productivity of reactions and the whole field of catalysis derives from this concern.

11. In a pharmaceutical laboratory, potential drug molecules will generally be tested in solution. The solutions used by different laboratories need to take standard forms in order for results of different experiments to be comparable (Cambrosio and Keating 1995: 82). Such standard solutions can never correspond to the more complex and variable conditions found in a living body. For examples of the presentation of results of computational experiments, see http://www.documentarea.com/qsar/a_beresford2002.pdf.

12. See, for example, *The Investigational Drugs Database,* which 'is a daily updated, enterprise-wide competitor intelligence and R&D monitoring service. It provides validated, integrated and evaluated information on all aspects of drug development, from first patent application to launch or discontinuation. Subscribers include most major pharmaceutical and biotechnology companies the world over. In addition, more and more companies servicing the pharmaceutical and biotechnology sector are subscribing. Chemical companies, CROs, consultants and media providers find the IDdb3 invaluable in locating lucrative new business partners', http://www.iddb3.com/cds/solutions.htm.

13. A patent is likely not to apply to one molecule but to a set of molecules with similar structure (the 'scaffold') and similar biological activity.

14. This strategy is termed 'drug rescue' by researchers. On the relation between the dynamics of innovation and the occupation of technological space more broadly, see Barry (1999/2000).

15. Scott Lash argues that information should be understood as more than merely a collection of signals or data: 'The constant bombardment by signals, the ads of consumer culture and the like does not constitute information. It is chaos, noise. It only becomes information when meaning is attached to it. Information only happens at the interface of the sense-maker and his/her environment' (Lash 2002: 18). Lash's analysis of information has parallels with my analysis of chemical material. The molecules produced through the industrial process of combinatorial chemistry can be thought of as material forms of noise that need to be filtered before they become useful. Individual molecules only become progressively informed in the assemblage of pharmaceutical research.

References

Abraham, J. (1995), *Science, Politics and the Pharmaceutical Industry: Controversy and Bias in Drug Regulation*. London: UCL press.

Alliez, E. (1999), 'Tarde et le probleme de la constitution', introduction to G. Tarde, *Monadologie et Sociologie*. Paris: Institut Synthélabo.

Ansell-Pearson, K. (1999), *Germinal Life: The Difference and Repetition of Deleuze*. London: Routledge.

ArQule (2001), Arqule corporate website, http://www.arqule.com.

Augen, J. (2002), 'The Evolving role of Information Technology in the Drug Discovery Process', *Drug Discovery Today*, 7(5): 315–323.

Bailey, D. and D. Brown (2001), 'High-Throughput Chemistry and Structure-Based Design: Survival of the Smartest', *Drug Discovery Today*, 6(2): 57–59.

Barry, A. (1999/2000), 'Invention and Inertia', *Cambridge Anthropology*, 21(3): 62–70.

Barry, A. (2001), *Political Machines: Governing a Technological Society*. London: Athlone.

Barry, A. and D. Slater (2002) 'The Technological Economy', *Economy and Society*, 31(2): 175–193.

Beno, B. and J. Mason (2001), 'The Design of Combinatorial Libraries Using Properties and 3D Pharmacophore Fingerprints', *Drug Discovery Today*, 6(5): 251–258.

Bensaude-Vincent, B. and I. Stengers (1996), *A History of Chemistry*. Cambridge, MA: Harvard University Press.

Beresford A., H. Selick and M. Tarbit (2002), 'The Emerging Importance of Predictive ADME Simulation in Drug Discovery', *Drug Discovery Today*, 7: 109–116.

Bergson, H. (1998), *Creative Evolution*. Mineola, NY: Dover Publications.

Blackett, T. and R. Robins (2001), *Brand Medicine: The Role of Branding in the Pharmaceutical Industry*. Basingstoke: Palgrave.

Callon, M., C. Méadel and V. Rabeharisoa (2002), 'The Economy of Qualities', *Economy and Society*, 31(2): 194–217.

Cambrosio, A. and P. Keating (1995), *Exquisite Specificity: The Monoclonal Antibody Revolution*. Oxford: Oxford University Press.

Cavalla, D. (2003), 'The Extended Pharmaceutical Enterprise', *Drug Discovery Today*, 8(6): 267–274.

Deleuze, G. (1988), *Bergsonism*. New York: Zone.

Deleuze, G. (1993), *The Fold: Leibniz and the Baroque*. London: Athlone.

Deleuze, G. and C. Parnet (1987), *Dialogues*. London: Athlone.

Everett, J., M. Gardner, F. Pullen, G. F. Smith, M. Snarey and N. Terrett (2001), 'The Application of Non-Combinatorial Chemistry to Lead Discovery', *Drug Discovery Today*, 6(15): 779–785.

Food and Drug Administration, Center for Drug Evaluation and Research (2001), 'Baycol Information', http://www.fda.gov/cder/dru/infopage/baycol/default.htm.

Fraser, M. (2002) 'What Is the Matter of Feminist Criticism?', *Economy and Society*, 31(4): 606–625.

Halewood, M. (2003), *Materiality and Subjectivity in the Work of AN Whitehead and Gilles Deleuze: Developing a Non-Essentialist Ontology for Social Theory*. Unpublished PhD thesis, University of London.

Handen, J. (2002), 'The Industrialization of Drug Discovery', *Drug Discovery Today*, 7(2): 83–85.

Hill, S. (2001), 'Biologically Relevant Chemistry', *Drug Discovery World* (Spring): 129–130.

Hird, N. (2000), 'Isn't Combinatorial Chemistry Just Chemistry?' *Drug Discovery Today*, 5(8): 307–308.

Knorr-Cetina, K. (1999), *Epistemic Cultures: How the Sciences Make Knowledge*. Cambridge, MA: Harvard University Press.

Lash, S. (2002), *Critique of Information*. London: Sage.

Latour, B. (1988), *The Pasteurization of France*. Cambridge, MA: Harvard University Press.

Latour, B. (1999), *Pandora's Hope: Essays on the Reality of Science Studies*. Cambridge, MA: Harvard University Press.

Leach, A. and M. Hann (2000), 'The *in Silico* World of Virtual Libraries', *Drug Discovery Today*, 5: 326–336.

Levere, T. (2001), *Transforming Matter: A History of Chemistry from Alchemy to the Buckyball*. Baltimore, MD: Johns Hopkins University Press.

Macdonald, S. and P. Smith (2001), 'Lead Optimization in 12 Months? True Confessions of a Chemistry Team', *Drug Discovery Today*, 6(18): 947–953.

Macleod, C. (1996), 'Concepts of Invention and the Patent Controversy in Victorian Britain', in R. Fox (ed.), *Technological Change: Methods and Themes in the History of Technology*. Amsterdam: Harwood Academic.

Manly, C. J., S. Louise-May and J. Hammer (2001), 'The Impact of Informatics and Computational Chemistry on Synthesis and Screening', *Drug Discovery Today*, 6(21): 1101–1110.

Mitchell, T. (2002), *Rule of Experts: Egypt, Techno-Politics, Modernity*. Berkeley: California University Press.

Noble, D. (1977), *America by Design: Science, Technology and the Rise of Corporate Capitalism*. New York: Oxford University Press.

Pottage, A. (1998), 'The Inscription of Life in Law: Genes, Patents and Bio-politics', *Modern Law Review*, 61(5): 740–765.

Shapin, S. and S. Schaffer (1985), *Leviathan and the Air-Pump: Hobbes, Boyle and the Experimental Life*. Princeton, NJ: Princeton University Press.

Stengers, I. (1997), *Power and Invention: Situating Science*. Minneapolis: Minnesota University Press.

Stengers, I. (2002), *Penser avec Whitehead: une libre et sauvage création de concepts*. Paris: Seuil.

Strathern, M. (2002), 'Externalities in Comparative Guise', *Economy and Society*, 31(2): 250–267.

Tarde, G. (1967), *On Communication and Social Influence*. Chicago: Chicago University Press.

Tarde, G. (1999), *Monadologie et Sociologie*. Paris: Institut Synthélabo.

Tarde, G. (2001), *Les Lois de L'imitation*. Paris: Seuil.

Thomas, G. (2000), *Medicinal Chemistry: An Introduction*. New York: John Wiley.

Whitehead, A. N. (1978), *Process and Reality*. New York: Free Press.

Whitehead, A. N. (1985), *Science and the Modern World*. London: Free Association Books.

Chapter 4

Toward designing new sensoaesthetic materials: The role of materials libraries

Mark A. Miodownik

The development of materials was traditionally driven both by aesthetic and technological goals. At the end of the nineteenth century, things changed dramatically. Scientists started being able to analyse composition, detect structure and make a link between structure and properties. The subsequent twentieth-century revolution in new materials changed almost all aspects of human activity. However it was not without serious side-effects, the first of which has been that the materials science community has largely separated itself from material culture. The second is the decreased interest in the use of the sensual and aesthetic properties to guide materials development. This chapter discusses these issues and suggests that materials libraries offer a new way to address the divides in the materials community and also nurture a more innovative materials culture.

The materials that define our clothes, homes and cities are largely chosen by fashion designers, product designers and architects from the vast array of materials in production. There is a growing recognition that this task is becoming more and more difficult, requiring as it does a knowledge and understanding of materials technologies, the diversity and complexity of which are growing at increasing rate. Individual materials experts tend to have specialized areas of expertise of particular technologies and processes, for example, a knowledge of silicone rubbers; their properties, processing, advantages, disadvantages, suppliers, etc. But it is becoming simply impossible for individuals, and even organizations, to have such in-depth knowledge across the spectrum of materials (Institute of Materials 2012).

Materials libraries have emerged as one solution to this problem. Like a library of books, these are repositories of knowledge, but instead of books, they contain the materials themselves. Physical access to samples of materials is the crucial aspect of these libraries, because many aspects of materials are currently unquantifiable, and so a hands-on sensory interface is seen as a vital part of the design process. This function is usually fulfilled through the provision of samples and swatches of materials from the manufacturers (Laughlin 2012). Materials libraries are new approach and have only been in existence since 1997, but nevertheless are now a global phenomenon from New York to Beijing (Laughlin 2012).

Materials libraries take many forms including independent organizations (see the list of resources below: Materials ConneXion 2012; Materia 2012; Modulor 2012; Materio 2012; Materialbiblioteket 2012; Materioteca 2012; Inventables 2012), university based resources (Rematerialise 2012; Institute of Making 2012; Materials Lab 2012; Materials & Products Collection 2012; Materials Resource Center 2012; New Materials Resource Center 2012), and in-house facilities of commercial companies (see Laughlin 2012). Apart from a commonality of purpose, these libraries share very little else. Unlike traditional libraries, which have had hundreds of years in which to refine and agree on standards, formats and taxonomy, the materials library as a formal concept is barely 15 years old. Some libraries exist primarily as a searchable database, with a much smaller physical archive of samples. In these cases the physical materials serve as a proxy for the whole wealth of materials technologies, but arguably their main role is to contextualize the language of the materials database underpinning the library, which contains the majority of the information. These databases typically describe materials in non-technical terms so that a wider range of users can perform useful searches. The language of such search terms is still extremely variable across the materials libraries and typically consists of words that allude to tactile and perceptual interface as 'warm', 'textured', as well as more functional properties such as 'fireproof'. Some materials libraries exist as a specialized reference library on a particular topic, for instance Kingston University's materials library (Rematerialise 2012) specializes in renewable and recyclable materials, while the Materials ConneXion exists to serve the design and architecture community. The further development of materials libraries is certain to continue, both as useful knowledge interface between materials producers and materials users, and also as a shop front. They provide a potential solution to an increasing problem, that of increased specialization and complexity, and the need for central repository to access information about existing materials. However this virtue is also paradoxically the obstacle to their success: they attract a wide variety of users from car designers to artists, from structural engineers to clothes makers, but each type of user 'talks' a different materials language. Some require facts such as a material's strength or corrosion resistance, while others need to know perhaps about a material's ecological impact or want to understand how a material feels, smells or sounds. These disparate ways of viewing materials have proved hard to condense into a coherent whole. In order to understand why materials are viewed in such a wide variety of ways it is useful to consider the history of their development.

The development of materials science

In ancient societies materials were developed without knowledge of the laws of thermodynamics, crystal structures, phase diagrams or any other of our modern theories of material science. Nevertheless our ancestors discovered and developed most of the major materials we have today: metals, concretes, pigments, ceramics, composites and glasses (Seymore 2005; Smith 1981). Although each ancient civilization pushed forward materials technologies, they did so empirically. A deductive theory of materials was not fully developed until the twentieth century. The roots of this approach are to be found in the Renaissance of Europe in the fifteenth and sixteenth centuries. The practice of alchemy grew, and, although shrouded in the occult, it instilled a thirst in its adherents to discover the hidden principles behind the transformative nature of some materials processes, and the apparent immutability of materials such as mercury and sulphur. Among other things, these experiments yielded new pigments, mordents and binders, which were then used by Michaelangelo, Titian and other Renaissance artists. Thus development of materials was driven both by aesthetic and technological goals (Ball 2001).

The openness to new modes of thought about the natural world, which was initiated in the Renaissance ultimately led to the rejection of Aristotelian principles of intuition and dogma. By doing so, natural philosophers discovered a huge wealth of new phenomena, such as electricity. It was an extremely fruitful period in which concept of a 'scientist' was born (although the name 'scientist' was coined much later). This new approach is encapsulated by Santiago Ramón y Cajal (1897):

> The intellect is presented with phenomena marching in review before the sensory organs. It can be truly useful and productive only when limiting itself to the modest tasks of observation, description, and comparison, and of classification that is based on analogies and differences. A knowledge of underlying causes and empirical laws will then come slowly through the use of inductive methods. Another commonplace worth repeating is that science cannot hope to solve Ultimate Causes. In other words, science can never understand the foundation hidden below the appearance of phenomena in the universe. As

Claude Bernard has pointed out, researchers cannot transcend the determinism of phenomena; instead, their mission is limited to demonstrating the how, never the why, of observed changes. This is a modest goal in the eyes of philosophy, yet an imposing challenge in actual practice.

But the discoveries of the Enlightenment period, and the new attitude of taking-apart the natural world, in order to discover its mechanisms, provoked strong reactions by various parts of Western society. In particular, a Romantic movement grew up, which in its most extreme form, was opposed to the active deconstruction of Nature. This attitude is typified the following passage from the poem *Lamia* by Keats (1884):

Philosophy will clip an Angel's wings,

Conquer all mysteries by rule and line,

Empty the haunted air, and gnomed mine –

Unweave a rainbow, as it erewhile made

The tender-person'd Lamia melt into a shade

In this poem Keats comments on Newton's theory of light, which he regards as 'unweaving' the poetry of a rainbow and so as an attack on the fundamental mysteries of the Universe. In the same period Mary Shelley wrote the novel Frankenstein, which was a reaction to the newly discovered phenomenon of static electricity, which Galvini had recently showed could provoke a severed frog leg to twitch. This Frankenstein theme, in which scientific discoveries are viewed as leading to the downfall and degradation of the human spirit, is another Romantic theme, and continues to modern times.

The philosophical split between the Romantics and Rationalists deepened in the nineteenth century, as the Industrial Revolution took hold. The defining material of that century, steel, allowed engineers to give full rein to their dreams of creating suspension bridges, railways, steam engines and passenger liners. In doing so, engineers used steel as a material manifesto to transform the landscape and to sow the seeds of modernism. The industrialization of the countryside, towns and cities showed that science had the power to transform society, but more than that, it gave status to engineers as powerful architects of cultural change.

The scientific project of cataloguing the phenomena of world led also to the development of a large body of deductive theory, which not only yielded new understanding about observed phenomena, but predicted new phenomena. This was particularly important for materials technology. As the discipline of

Chemistry progressed in nineteenth century, it became possible to systemati-cally explore materials properties. The establishment of the periodic table was a good example of this: it predicted the existence of certain elements, which were then discovered. This caused among other things new pigments to be created such as Cobalt Blue and Cadmium Yellow, which ultimately gave rise to artis-tic movements such as Impressionism and to the Colour Theorists (Ball 2001). But while it might be supposed that the discovery of new pigments might have initiated a new closer relationship between the arts and sciences, in practice it heralded an end to the collaborative exploration of materials. After this, materials discovery and development was largely to become a scientific activity.

The twentieth century is often referred to as the age of silicon, in reference the materials breakthrough that gave rise to the silicon chip and digital comput-ing. But this is to overlook the kaleidoscope of new materials that revolutionized twentieth-century living. Architects took the new mass-produced sheet glass and combined it with structural steel to produce skyscrapers that invented a new type of city life (Hughes 1991). Product designers and fashion designers took the new plastics and transformed the home and fashion (Ashby and Johnson 2002). Polymers were used to produce celluloid and in doing so ushered in the biggest change in visual culture for a thousand of years, the cinema. The development of aluminium alloys and nickel superalloys allowed us to fly cheaply and changed the rate at which cultures collided. Medical and dental ceramics allowed us rebuild ourselves and change the social context of disability and age (Kemp and Wallace 2000). New composite materials, such as fibreglass and carbon fibre reinforced plastics, literally changed the shape of sporting equipment (Gordon 1982).

Thus the twentieth century witnessed a materials revolution in which the new discipline of materials science played a central role in transforming architecture, product design, urban design, fashion, transport technology, medicine and the visual and performing arts. However the arts/science split in materials, has led a situation where now the scientists, technologists and industrialists (the materials science community) involved in the development of new materials, move in both academic and social circles widely separated from designers, architects, media, crafts people and artists (the materials arts community).

This status quo may not be desirable for a number of reasons. First, the materials arts community are not playing their full role in determining the focus of publicly funded materials research (at the moment it is the military and indus-trial sectors that collaborate most closely with materials science departments). Second, the cultural sector has a long history of posing interesting problems that benefit the arts and push science forward. A contemporary example could be the need in the digital media community for haptic materials that transform their properties in response to digital stimuli so that virtual touch and haptic feedback can become a (virtual) reality. Such new materials could also have impact on architecture, jewellery, product design, the special effects industry as well as art (Ede 2001). Third, materials have an immense cultural significance and the further introduction of new materials by an isolated science community holds the prospect of a further deepening of the rift between scientists and society.

Psychophysical properties

Materials science as a discipline is the study of the structure of materials. It is a central tenet of materials science that a particular structure will always yield a particular set of properties, so control of structure yields the control of properties (e.g. strength, toughness, etc.). Materials science became possible because scientific instruments were developed to enable the observation of structure at different scales, first through the optical microscope, then through electron microscopes, atom force microscopes and a myriad of other techniques. These observations then give rise to a body of theory that can predict how to improve properties. In this way theory, simulation and experiment all inform each other to provide a framework of the systematic development of new materials.

The close relationship between materials science and engineering, promotes this innovation. The disciplines share a common language in mathematics, and have agreed standards. Materials testing and the establishment of mathematical definitions of properties such as strength and toughness were developed precisely because engineers wanted quantitative information about the materials they were using to build. The Kirkaldy mechanical testing laboratories in London, were the first such foray into developing this common language, which is now standard practice. Large databases have now been developed, which are an effective translation between the language of crystal structure, chemical bonding, nanostructure and microstructures that materials scientists study, and the language of fracture toughness and elasticity that engineers need to design buildings and machines (see Granta Design in list of resources below).

The relationship is particularly strong in sectors where performance improvement is the only key to commercial survival, such as the electronic and aerospace industries. The design of a jet engine, for instance, involves engineers and materials scientists working at all length scales to deliver the required increase in performance. The ability to hand information up and down the scales in a form useful to each practitioner has been the key innovation to the reduction of the cost of flying and to the increase in safety. This separation of approach and profession, as a function of the scale of structures is illustrated in Figure 4.1, which represents

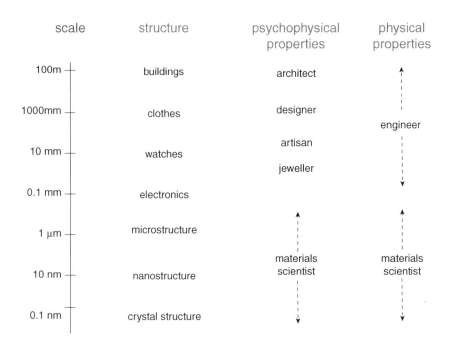

Figure 4.1 Figure showing scale, structure, psychophysical properties and physical properties.

a schematic of how the psychophysical and physical properties of structures are designed and used by different professions and at different scales.

The situation is very different for structures whose performance is not based solely on the physical parameters but also on psychophysical properties of materials (sensual, aesthetic and culturally influenced). These are structures such as buildings interiors, urban spaces, clothes; in other words, structures in which human comfort, inspiration, and satisfaction are important. These structures tend to be designed by the materials art community because of their expertise in understanding needs and desires of people. Unlike the aerospace industry, however, there is no systematic methodology for development of materials with such properties. There is no body of research linking structure to psychophysical properties of materials, except in the case of pigment design.

Part of the reason for this is that many of the psychophysical properties of materials are clearly subjective, and so are outside the realms of materials science. The aesthetic appeal of wood interiors for instance, is by definition a matter of taste, which depends on the culture of the person as well and the intended role of the structures. Nevertheless some materials are perceived to be warm (woods) and others cold (metals), and these associations have been quantified (Laughlin et al. 2011; Wongsriruksa et al. 2012). The smell, taste, sound of materials do not just have their origin in a shared cultural outlook but rather in our shared biology. Metals are good conductors of heat and so conduct heat away quickly, making them seem cold to the touch. Woods are thermal insulators, so the reverse is true. Thus the interface between humans and the material environment is mediated by the senses, the colour, smell, sound, touch and taste of materials. These psychophysical properties are also unusual because they have a psychological and cultural component. For instance, the colour blue, is not perceived as a fixed hue in the brain, the perception of blue is relative to the colour context (Purves and Lotto 2003). Similarly, the taste of a material depends on action and association of the context of eating: a potato can taste like an apple, in the absence of smell (Kosslyn and Koenig 1992).

The broad relationships between physical properties and psychophysical properties has been studied by Ashby and Johnson through property mapping (Ashby and Johnson 2002). For instance the acoustic properties of materials may be characterized as a combination of pitch and brightness. The former being defined by the physical parameters, modulus and density, the latter being defined by the damping coefficients of the material. Using these attributes, a property map is built up that clearly clusters materials that will sound 'bright' if struck, like glass or bronze, or muffled, like lead and rubbers. The usefulness of such an approach to the materials arts community is clear, in that it becomes a way to categorize and select materials for their acoustic properties using existing materials science databases (Ashby and Johnson 2002; Granta Design).

This approach also provides an insight into how to modify psychophysical properties. The modern designer, artisan or architect no longer has to rely on empirical methods to develop new materials with particular combinations of physical and psychophysical properties. While a musical instrument maker in the seventeenth century had no choice but to rely largely on trial and error, a materials scientist can use the wide range analytical tools to determine the internal structures of the materials and so correlate them with the psychophysical properties. Thus mirroring the approach employed so successfully to understand the physical properties of materials (see Table 4.1). An example of the successful application of such an approach is the work by Derby and Ferguson to develop new mokame gane techniques (Derby and Ferguson 1998; Ferguson and Derby 1998).

The role of materials libraries

What role can materials libraries play in this new materials design paradigm? First, a materials library provides a repository of materials, which allows the systematic investigation of both the quantitative and qualitative aspects of psychophysical properties. We have used our materials library for several such studies on the taste and touch of materials (Laughlin et al. 2011; Piqueras-Fiszman et al. 2012; Wongsriruksa et al. 2012). Second, the materials themselves provide a language to interface the materials arts and science communities since generating physical encounters with matter provides an often forgotten way into technical discourse and interdisciplinary discussion. For instance, allowing a materials library user to cut ice using simply a wafer of aluminium nitride, provides a non-mathematical sensual way to discuss the thermal conductivity of materials. In other words, the sheer extraordinariness of some materials demands explanation of the science that underpins them (Miodownik 2005), and so can initiate research collaborations. The materials library also provides a natural interface to discuss the ethical and cultural impact of new materials technologies, such as nanotechnology and rapid prototyping. The presence in the library of samples of materials produced using these technologies, immediately showcases the present state of the technology and removes the mathematical barrier to discussion between the materials art and materials science communities. As the materials scientist and art historian, Cyril Stanley Smith, commented:

> The great success of the logical analytical reductionist approach to understanding over the last four centuries and the utility of the application of its principles has not negated the evidence of history that the sensual-emotional-aesthetic capabilities of the human being also have validity. The problem is to find the proper nonexclusive role for each. (Smith 1981)

Importantly, as 'interfaces', materials libraries enable us to begin the journey of exploring society itself, and the ways in which materials come to be active and activated within culture. Through this kind of activity, we can begin to move our understandings away from an exclusive focus on what materials are, towards a more inclusive range of questions about why and how they matter.

Conclusions

The underlying assumption with the current materials paradigm is that materials scientists need microscopes and sophisticated analytical equipment to develop new materials with novel physical properties because they know that without this, little progress could be made. The situation is no different for developing new psychophysical properties of materials. There is very little activity in this area because the materials science is largely estranged from the materials arts community who are expert in the psychophysical properties. Nevertheless the development of materials libraries largely by the materials arts communities has provided a forum and archive of materials with which to systematically investigate the psychophysical properties. They also provide an instinctive, aesthetic and tactile interface between materials science and the materials arts community.

Materials libraries and resources

Granta Design. Software tools, materials data, and materials database solutions for industry and education. Based Cambridge, also Germany and United States, www.grantadesign.com.

Institute of Making. (2012), A materials library based in UCL specializing in connecting materials science to the wider materials community, www.instituteofmaking.org.uk.

Inventables. (2012), Online hardware and materials store for designers. https://www.inventables.com/.

Materia. (2012), A Dutch materials library that acts as knowledge centre for developments and innovations in materials, and their applications for architecture and design, www.materia.nl.

Materialbiblioteket. (2012), A Swedish materials library dedicated to supporting the Scandinavian community of architects, industrial designers and product developers, www.materialbiblioteket.se.

Materials and Products Collection. (2012), A materials library based in Central Saint Martins College of Art & Design, that brings together a range of innovative materials representing current trends in design and manufacturing, http://www.arts.ac.uk/library/collections/csm/.

Materials ConneXion. (2012), A global materials consultancy and library of innovative and sustainable materials, www.materialconnexion.com.

Materials Lab. (2012), A materials library based in the University of Texas that stimulates and supports the integration of materials in the design curriculum, http://soa.utexas.edu/matlab/.

Materials Resource Center. (2012), A materials library based in Rhode Island School of Design to explore materials and discover new methods and processes, http://library.risd.edu/materialslibrary.html.

Materio. (2012), A French materials library that is an independent information centre on materials and innovative products, www.materio.com.

Materioteca. (2012), An Italian materials library, www.materioteca.it.

Modulor. (2012), A German materials library supplying materials for professional design, www.modulor.de.

New Materials Resource Center. (2012), A materials library based in the California College of the Arts, with a role to inspire designers to focus on the materiality of things, http://libraries.cca.edu/material-resource-center.

Rematerialise. (2012), A materials library based in Kingston University specializing in recyclable materials, www.kingston.ac.uk/rematerialise.

References

Ashby, M. and K. Johnson (2002), *Materials and Design: The Art and Science of Material Selection in Product Design*. London: Butterworth-Heineman.

Ball, P. (2001), *Bright Earth – The Invention of Colour*. London: Penguin.

Derby, B. and I. Ferguson (1998), 'Modern Materials for Mokume Gane', *Materials World* (April 1998): 213–214.

Ede, S. (2001), *Strange and Charmed: Science and the Contemporary Visual Arts*. Lisbon: Calouste Gulbenkian Foundation.

Ferguson, I. and B. Derby (1998), 'Diffusion bonded mokume gane decorative metal laminates', *Journal of Materials Science and Technology*, 14: 510–517.

Gordon, J. E. (1982), *The New Science of Strong Materials or Why We Don't Fall Through the Floor*. London: Penguin.

Hughes, R. (1991), *The Shock of the New – Art and the Century of Change*. London: Thames and Hudson.

Keats, J. (1884 [1820]), *The Poetical Works of John Keats* (reprinted from the original editions, with notes by Francis T. Palgrave). London: Macmillan.

Kemp, M. and M. Wallace (2000), *Spectacular Bodies: The Art and Science of the Human Body from Leonardo and Now*. Exhibition Catalogue, London: Hayward Gallery.

Kosslyn, S. M. and O. Koenig (1992), *Wet Mind: The New Cognitive Neuroscience*. Cambridge: The Free Press.

Laughlin, Z. (2010), *Beyond the Swatch: How can the Science of Materials Be Represented by the Materials Themselves in a Materials Library?* Unpublished PhD Thesis, King's College London.

Laughlin, Z., M. Conreen, H. J. Witchel and M. Miodownik (2011), 'The Use of Standard Electrode Potentials to Predict the Taste of Solid Metals', *Food Quality and Preference*, 22 (7): 628–637.

Miodownik, M. A. (2005), 'Facts not Opinions', *Nature Materials*, 4 (July): 506–508.

Piqueras-Fiszman, B., Z. Laughlin, M. Miodownik and C. Spence (2012), 'Tasting Spoons: Assessing How the Material of a Spoon Affects the Taste of the Food', *Food Quality and Preference*, 24(1): 24–29.

Purves, D. P. and R. B. Lotto (2003), *Why We See What We Do: A Wholly Probabilistic Strategy of Vision*. London: Macmillan Press.

Ramón y Cajal, S. (2004 [1897]), *Advice for a Young Investigator* (2004 Reprint; ISBN 0–262–18191–6). Cambridge, MA: MIT Press.

Seymore, R. (2005), 'Creating the Future', *Materials World* (December): 22–23.

Smith, C. S. (1980), *From Art to Science: Seventy-Two Objects Illustrating the Nature of Discovery*. Cambridge MA: MIT Press.

Smith, C. S. (1981), *A Search for Structure: Selected Essays on Science, Art and History*. Cambridge MA: MIT press.

Wongsriruksa, S., P. Howes, M. Conreen and M. Miodownik (2012), 'The Use of Physical Property Data to Predict the Touch Perception of Materials', *Materials and Design*, 42: 238–244.

Chapter 5

The science of sensory evaluation: An ethnographic critique

David Howes

There is a class of scientists who specialize in the analysis of the sensory qualities of commodities – the colour, sound, smell, taste and feel of things. Their work has not attracted much scrutiny in material culture studies or social studies in science to date. The original name for this area of research was 'organoleptics'. Its origins, at least in the United States, can be traced back to the 1930s when the Arthur D. Little industrial consulting firm devised a 'Flavor Profile Method' and 'Hedonic Index' for use by commercial food and beverage companies, and the first panel on 'Flavor in Foods' was presented at the 1937 meeting of the American Chemical Society. The field was given a major boost during World War II, when the US Army found that industrially produced troop rations, which had been designed for their nutritional value, were 'not performing their role because the men didn't like how they tasted and looked' (Shapin 2012: 179). Various studies were commissioned to find out how to make the food more acceptable (Lahne 2015; Pangborn 1964).

The title of 'organoleptician' has since been dropped, replaced by 'sensory professional'. The sensory evaluation of food products remains central to the practice of these professionals (a practice that goes under the name of 'sensory evaluation' or simply 'sensory science') but the scope of the products that now fall within their purview has expanded significantly to include everything from personal care to household cleaning products and home decor to automobiles.[1] Sensory professionals have also lobbied hard to expand their role within the companies they work for, seeking to convince management that the application of sensory evaluation techniques is crucial to every stage of product development, from conception to consumption. They like to use the language of driving, as in 'sensory properties drive consumer acceptance and emotional benefits' (Kemp et al. 2011), and it has had the desired effect. The science of sensory evaluation now forms an integral part of what Steven Shapin has called the 'aesthetic-industrial complex.' It is one of the 'sciences of subjectivity' that, as he suggests, 'are world-making' (Shapin 2012). But what sort of world are these professionals making out of our senses?

The science of sensory evaluation rests on a fundamental paradox. On the one hand: 'Most sensory characteristics of food can only be measured well, completely, and meaningfully by human subjects' (Poste et al. 1991) as opposed to scientific instruments. On the other hand, it is considered important that human subjects behave as much like scientific instruments as possible: 'When people are used as a measuring instrument, it is necessary to control all testing methods and conditions rigidly to overcome errors caused by psychological factors' (Poste et al. 1991: 1). In a similar vein, Meilgaard, Carr and Civille (2010) affirm that the key to sensory analysis is:

> to treat the panellists as measuring instruments. As such, they are highly vari-
> able and very prone to bias but they are the only instruments that will measure
> what we want to measure so we must minimize the variability and control the
> bias by making full use of the best existing techniques in psychology and
> psychophysics. (2010: 1)

The controls in question include creating a sampling environment that is as sensorially neutral as possible with regard to such factors as temperature, colour and odour and ensuring that 'irrelevant' sensory factors, such as the size of the samples, do not impinge on the panellists' judgement. Furthermore, assessors are trained to evaluate products 'monadically' – that is, to assess one sensory charac-teristic at a time: the use of blindfolds, nose clips and 'ear defenders' is advised to ensure that panellists maintain the desired focus (Kemp et al. 2011: 2.2.1.5 and 3.2). Focus is also enhanced through isolating one panellist from another by having them perform their tasks in individual booths or cubicles (for illustrations of the design of such cubicles, see Meilgaard et al. 2010: 24–30). In addition, asses-sors are commonly instructed not to discuss samples before evaluation since this might create expectations, which are considered one of the most serious potential sources of error; and to work in silence, since 'comments or noises made out loud e.g. urgh! or Mmmm! can influence sensory judgments' (Kemp et al. 2011: 2.2.1.2). Panellists are otherwise instructed to disregard their 'subjective associations' since the objective is to 'provide precise, consistent, and standardized sensory measure-ments that can be reproduced' (Poste et al. 1991: 15).

There are basically three kinds of tests used in sensory evaluation experi-ments. 'Discriminative tests' are used to determine whether or not a difference exists among samples. 'Descriptive tests' are employed to identify sensory characteristics that are important in a product and give information on the degree or intensity of those characteristics. 'Affective' or 'hedonic tests' are used to measure how much a panellist likes a product sample based on its sensory characteristics. There is at least one kind of test missing from this repertoire, as we shall see presently.

Finally, the variability of responses is controlled for through the use of standardized questionnaires and standard numerical scales (e.g. Meilgaard et al. 2010; Stone et al. 2012), as well as through statistical analysis of the results of the experiments and the plotting of such results in the form of graphs and tables. Only those results that are 'statistically significant' are considered 'meaningful'. In other words, while sensory evaluation experiments are concerned with assessing the *qualities* of products, it is the *quantification* of sensation that (really) counts. There are some cautionary voices: 'Statistical analysis is not a substitute for thinking', hence, 'Just because one obtains a graphical display or a series of tables with associated statistical significance does not mean it has any meaning or external validity' (Stone et al. 2012: 2). Nevertheless, such cautions go largely unheeded, and in the final analysis the interpretation of results boils down to tabulating responses and pinpointing averages so that any trace of the 'subjective associations' of individual panellists can be eradicated from the overall picture of a product's sensory qualities.

To an outside observer, it might appear difficult to distinguish between the protocol of a sensory evaluation test and the protocol of the sensory deprivation experiments of the 1960s (see Zubek 1969). It is indeed remarkable the degree of sensory restriction to which the sensory professional is subjected in the interests of producing results that are 'precise, consistent' and, above all, reproducible (Poste et al. 1991).

A survey of the articles published over the past five years in the *Journal of Sensory Studies*, one of the leading journals in the field, reveals that many of the papers are concerned with the development of sensory lexicons. The construction of these vocabularies is important both to the standardization of communication among sensory professionals working in different countries, and the communication of sensory product attributes to the consuming public. While coffee and meat are the most studied products, one study concerned the development of a sensory lexicon for the description of the flavour, aroma, texture and appearance characteristics of dry dog food products (Di Donfrancesco et al. 2012). No dogs were consulted for this study. The lexicon was entirely based on the perceptions of a five-member highly trained descriptive sensory panel of *Homo sapiens*.

The papers may otherwise be grouped according to whether they use trained panellists or so-called naïve panellists, whether they use forced-choice, projective mapping or some other scaling method and whether they are unimodal (e.g. Jeguirim et al. 2010), multimodal or cross-modal (e.g. Piqueras-Fiszman and Spence 2012) in orientation.[2]

A good example of multimodal product profiling, which is by far the standard, is provided by a paper on 'The Perception of Creaminess in Sour Cream' (Jervis et al. 2014). This paper starts from the observation that creaminess perception in dairy products is complex, and above all tied to fat content, which in turn determines liking. This poses a challenge for those manufacturers who wish to introduce low-fat and reduced fat products since, despite their health benefits, such products lack the sense appeal of their full-fat counterparts. The experiment involved the use of an 11-point creaminess rating scale and a 9-point hedonic scale. It unfolded over a series of seven sessions that sought to hold different sensory modalities constant and in this way measure the contribution of each modality to the perception and liking of the array of sour cream products tested. In an initial session, all of the modalities were engaged and the results of this session were used as a baseline. Subsequent sessions involved visual inspection only, visual inspection and physical stirring only, blindfolds and stirring only (to focus attention on the haptic), blindfolds while tasting (to isolate in-mouth texture and flavour), blindfolds and nose-clips while tasting (to control for sight and flavour) and nose-clips only while tasting (to control for flavour). In the result, it was found that olfaction of milk-fat associated flavours has the greatest impact on creaminess perception, followed by visual assessment of flow while stirring. With this information in hand, sour cream manufacturers can know which factors have to be 'accounted for' in order to maximize consumers' perception of creaminess and liking.

In another paper (Oberfeld et al. 2009), which attracted considerable media interest (Oberfeld-Twistel 2013), researchers at the University of Mainz related how they invited panellists to taste wine under different ambient lighting conditions: red, blue, green and white. The colour of the wine itself was occluded by serving it in black opaque glasses. Among other things, it was found that blue and green ambient lighting made the wine taste spicier than under white light, and that red ambient lighting made the wine taste as much as 50 per cent sweeter than under blue or white light. General liking and willingness to pay a higher price were also found to be augmented when the illumination was set to red or blue rather than green or white. It was the same wine in all cases (a dry white Riesling). This study is of interest for its methodological innovation. It did not just focus on the product, the way most sensory evaluations do. It modelled an environment. And it did not just treat the senses monadically (i.e. by concentrating on a single sensory characteristic) or additively (i.e. toting up the scores to arrive at a 'complete' sensory profile of a product). Rather, it allowed that the senses might be interactive. In the result, it was found that the red ambient light, which was not a property of the product (the wine), but rather the environment, decidedly influenced the perception of the product's flavour, and so on with the other colours.[3] Hence, the wine's taste must be recognized as contingent on its context of consumption, *but* it is precisely context that the design of the sensory evaluation laboratory (except in the case of this study) is designed to rule out. Ergo the majority of the studies published in the *Journal of Sensory Studies* are valid to the extent that the products concerned are consumed in the laboratories in which they were tested. But who wants to drink wine alone in a booth in a sensory research laboratory?

Sensory professionals are to be admired for the sensory and social sacrifices they make to test and 'perfect' (or bring what is called 'quality control' to) the products we consume. However, there are serious questions concerning the validity and applicability of the findings of sensory science outside (and even within) the laboratory that still need to be addressed.

Summing up, it is difficult to imagine a more asocial or, practically speaking, more asensual environment and protocol than the environment and protocol of a sensory research laboratory. This is due to the assumption that, as Meilgaard et al. put it: 'We must minimize the variability and control the bias [of panel-lists] by making full use of the best existing techniques in psychology and psychophysics.'

The senses in everyday life

What if the methodology of some other discipline, besides psychology and psychophysics, such as anthropology, were incorporated into the practice of sensory science? Anthropology has, in fact, begun to make inroads into the field due to the rise of the subdiscipline known as the 'anthropology of the senses' or 'sensory anthropology' (Howes 2003). It is exemplified by the work of Sarah Pink (2004, 2009), John Sherry (2006), Timothy Malefyt (2014), Jake Lahne and Amy Trubek (2014), and the Concordia Sensoria Research Team (CONSERT), among others. The principles of this mode of inquiry may be summarized as follows:

First, sensory anthropology understands acts of perception to be cultural as well as biological and psychological processes.

Second, it takes the study of product perception out of the sensory research laboratory and into the street, the home, the bar or whatever the 'natural environ-ment' of the consumer may be. The meaning of a product is in its use, and not its physical structure (abstracted from any context) alone.

Third, its methodology is one of participant sensation, or feeling along with one's informants, as opposed to subjecting them to some predetermined proto- col and list of questions the way a sensory scientist would.

Fourth, the focus of sensory anthropology is on eliciting 'the native's point of view', or rather, because one doesn't want to privilege the visual over other senses, the native's 'ways of sensing' (Howes and Classen 2014) – that is, the practices (including technologies) which frame a given group's perception of the world.

Fifth, sensory anthropology postulates that 'the senses interact with each other first', in culturally conditioned ways (Howes and Classen 1991: 258). Hence, the focus is on analyzing the relations and transfers *between* the senses rather than viewing them as independent channels or separate silos.

Sixth, 'as we sense, we also make sense', in Phillip Vannini's felicitous expres- sion (Vannini et al. 2012). This formulation plays on the polysemy, or double meaning, of the word 'sense'. This word includes both sensation and signifi- cation, both feeling and meaning in its spectrum of referents, which should be conceived as forming a continuum.

The polysemy of the word sense is lost on sensory scientists. The signifying (or 'symbolic') and also social dimensions of perception are occluded by their research protocols. By limiting the sorts of tests they use to the discriminative, the descriptive and the hedonic, they prevent themselves from ever investigat- ing what could be called the semantics of perception (but see Alcántara-Alcover et al. 2014). A semantic test, such as an anthropologist would be the first to util- ize, would seek to 'determine the meanings or mental associations stimulated by a given product's sensory characteristics' (Howes 2003b: 119).

In addition to highlighting the issue of sense-making, as will be discussed further below, research in the sensory anthropology of consumption has shown that consumers may be more or less discriminative in a particular sensory regis- ter, depending on how it is weighted or valued in their culture or subculture. By way of example, consider Sarah Pink's study of 'the sensory home', which was informed by the methodology of 'sensory ethnography' (Pink 2009).

The sensory home

In this study, which was commissioned by Unilever, Pink (2004) compared atti- tudes toward household cleanliness and practices of housework in Spain and the UK. Her informants included students and retired people, as well as single and married women (or 'housewives') of middling age. She asked her informants to take her on a tour of their house or flat and recorded their actions and words on video. The tours typically involved poking her head in cupboards, and being invited to 'smell this', or 'feel that', in addition to conversing with her informants (thereby breaking the silence that normally prevails over the assessment of products in the sensory research laboratory).

For the Spanish subjects, 'dust' referred to matter that had infiltrated the home from the outside world, and was classified as dirt to be eliminated. For the British subjects, dust referred to the flakings of persons and matter such as paint or plaster inside the home, and people were more tolerant of a certain build-up. It was not dirt as long as it did not smell or appear tacky. One young man stated that when the floor of his apartment started to feel sticky it was time for cleaning.

Pink found that the practice of cleaning house sometimes involved people 'dancing uninhibitedly' to their favourite music while wielding a broom or mop. Thus, housework had an audio component, a kinaesthetic component (which involved more than just scrubbing) and it also involved setting out scented products, like incense and essential oils as a finishing touch. In other words, cleaning did not involve eliminating odours so much as enhancing the existing smell of the home. Significantly, Pink found that all of her informants compared themselves (often negatively) to what they suspected a 'real housewife' would do, thereby incorporating a social dimension into what might otherwise be seen as a very private practice.

Pink's study of 'the sensory home' brings out how consumers do not necessarily use products 'as directed' but rather 'negotiate' social meanings through them and in so doing construct identities for themselves. Consumption is a creative process, Pink argues, wherein products do not 'drive' or 'trigger' responses in a straightforward fashion but rather are selectively deployed to construct 'worlds of sense' within which people can feel 'at home'.[4]

The interplay of the senses

As noted previously, sensory evaluation tests frequently involve the construction of barriers between people, between the senses, and between the 'subjective associations' of the assessor and his or her response to the sensory characteristics of the product tested. This is accomplished through training and through the architecture of the sensory research laboratory with its individual booths and 'neutral' atmosphere. Assessors are instructed to discriminate, describe and express their preferences, but not associate. Do these firewalls work? They might be made to work in the context of the laboratory, though they would hardly work in everyday life, but even in the laboratory it is dubious that the play of associations between the senses can be forestalled. In one of the studies we reported on in *Aroma: the Cultural History of Smell* (Classen et al. 1994: 194) involving a test of facial tissues, it was discovered that respondents found pine-scented tissues to be 'fresher' but also 'rougher' than unscented facial tissues, even though there was no actual difference to the texture of the tissues used in the two samples. The reason is obvious: the respondents did not dissociate the scent of pine from the feel of pine needles, which are, of course, prickly. This is because, 'As we sense, we also make sense' (Vannini et al. 2012).

In another study reported on in *Aroma*, respondents in a Chicago shopping mall were asked: What odours make you feel nostalgic?

> People born in the 1920s, '30s and '40s said that such odours as rose, burning leaves, hot chocolate, cut grass and ocean air made them feel nostalgic. Persons born during the 1960s and '70s, in contrast, grow nostalgic at such scents as Downy fabric softener, hair spray, Play-Doh, suntan oil, Cocoa Puffs, and candy cigarettes. (Classen et al. 1994: 202–203)

The trending evidenced by this survey, when the responses are grouped by decade of birth, are significant: there has been a shift away from 'natural' odours towards 'artificial' ones, and many of the latter come already trademarked. This pattern brings out nicely the extent to which the sensorium is an historical formation:

> It is not only in clothing and appearance, in outward form and emotional make-up that men are the product of history. Even the way they see and hear is inseparable from the social life-process . . . The facts which our senses present to us are socially preformed in two ways: through the historical character of the object perceived and through the historical character of the perceiving organ. (Horkheimer quoted in Levin 1997: 63, n. 1)

A study conducted a number of years back by the Concordia Sensoria Research Team brings out further the sociality of sensation and the indissociability of the senses. We asked: What accounts for the popularity of Corona, the best-selling imported beer in Canada? Preliminary research suggested that part of the answer must have to do with gender. Men are, notoriously, far more avid drinkers of beer than women, and in the case of most brands the ratio is 5 male drinkers to one female drinker. In the case of Corona, however, the ratio is more like 3 to 2. This means that its popularity among women is key to its success. So we set out to investigate why women prefer Corona. Our quest took us to a range of bars and restaurants, many with a Mexican theme, where we talked with both men and women about their preferences. This displacement was essential, since in anthropology one wants to encounter subjects on their own ground and elicit the categories they use to order the world.

We did not go in with a predetermined set of questions. Instead we let the questions emerge in the course of interaction. Some subjects said that they had encountered Corona while on vacation in Mexico. For them, drinking Corona when back in Montreal was a way of injecting some festivity or 'vacation spirit' into the drudgery of everyday life. More typically, however, those subjects who drank Corona regularly said they liked it because it is 'light'.

Technically, Corona is not a 'light beer'. It has the same alcohol content and carb levels as regular, domestic beers. This response, then, is an example of consumer-added meaning (and value). We needed to discover what motivated this categorization. What was it about the sensory characteristics of Corona that could explain this 'misperception' (which is not a misperception at all, of course, from the native point of view)?

The design of the Corona bottle struck us as one of the factors contributing to the perception of the beer as 'light'. Corona comes in tall, slender bottles that are clear and translucent. By contrast, most domestic beers, such as Molson Canadian, come in short, stubby, brown-coloured bottles that even look more weighty, more dense than the former. Furthermore, the colour of Corona is light, like sunshine, compared to the golden colour of Molson Canadian. From our conversations with our research subjects, it appeared that they were condens-ing – or 'associating' – a number of different sensations into one: the bright (or 'light') tint of the beer and the translucency (as well as slenderness) of the bottle was identified in their minds with lightness of taste (or, put another way, absence of heaviness). This impression was borne out by the gestures people used to describe their taste experience. When men talked about what they liked in a beer they would pat their stomachs whereas the women would rub their thumb and fingers together. The latter gesture suggested that what women most appreciate in a beer is a refined or delicate taste, whereas men are more interested in a full (and filling) flavour. Indeed, those men who preferred domestic beers claimed that Corona 'has no taste' (by which they meant body) whereas those men who drank Corona with their female friends dissociated themselves from more 'heavy drinkers', as they styled their male counterparts.

The Corona study has implications for the study of the perception of creami-ness in dairy products discussed earlier. It suggests that greater attention should have been paid to the interaction of the modalities involved in the trial (instead of holding them constant), and that the meaning or 'sense' of fat in everyday life for the test subjects (and the general populace) also needed to be explored. In other words, even though full-fat products can be demonstrated to have higher acceptance on account of their 'intrinsically' fuller taste or palatability, the matter does not end there. Also pertinent are the extrinsic associations that fat as a 'material symbol' evokes. The 'fatness' both of bodies and substances has recently become a topic for anthropological investigation (Forth and Leitch 2014), and this has led to a more nuanced understanding of both its (increasingly ambivalent) cultural construction and its effects.

'Sensory experience is social experience'

A study of consumer perceptions of Vermont artisan cheese conducted by the team of Jake Lahne and Amy Trubek (2014), the former a trained sensory scientist, the latter a sensory anthropologist, can shed light on this question of so-called extrinsic properties and associations. They theorize sensory perception as a learned and active *practice* (rather than passive reflex). Sensations are held to arise 'neither from the food nor from the consumer, but from the encounter between them, that is, it is neither taste nor taster, but *tasting*' (Lahne and Trubek 2014: 130, citing Hennion 2005). This shifts attention from the search for (putatively) universal, objective sensory qualities of food to the recognition that the sensory qualities of food 'emerge' for a particular consumer in a particular context.

The emphasis on context is carried further by Lahne and Trubek's insistence that 'sensory experience *is* social experience'. This is reflected in the way their preferred methodology involves holding focus-group discussions around a plate of cheeses instead of relegating participants to individual cubicles and inviting participants to recall past experiences instead of simply check off boxes. The sorts of questions Lahne and Trubek ask may be characterized as conversation-starters. They include questions about the participants' own consumption practices, about what makes a cheese 'artisan' in their estimation, and challenges like: How would you convince people who've never tried that cheese to give it a try? Is there anything besides taste that is very important about this cheese? In this way, participants are encouraged to explore the subjectivity of their own responses, instead of screening out any trace of subjectivity so as not to appear biased. Interestingly, none of the participants felt that their responses were any the less valid for being subjective, and their subjective judgments about subjectivity became part of the findings. This is in stark contrast to the objectification of taste (through the privatization, bureaucratization and pacification of the senses) in the conventional sensory science research laboratory. The context Lahne and Trubek created *activated* the senses instead of restricting and objectifying them.

Lahne and Trubek found that the sensory experience of Vermont artisan cheeses, for those who customarily consume them, 'stems from a mix of intrinsic, organoleptic properties and extrinsic socially embedded properties', but the two are 'mutually constitutive', and so it is not fruitful (or entirely possible) to disentangle them (Lahne and Trubek 2014: 132). The extrinsic properties include such things as the social context in which a cheese was first encountered by a participant (e.g. a wedding, a family meal), the memories that attach to the cheese in consequence and information about the conditions of production of the cheeses sampled (e.g. the cheesemakers' animal husbandry practices, ethos of workmanship, scale of operation, sustainability, etc.). For example, one respondent remarked on the 'grassy', 'earthy' flavours in a particular cheese possibly due to knowing that the animals were permitted to graze instead of being exclusively fed grain; another sensed the 'care' a cheesemaker put into his cheese. Lahne and Trubek also recorded instances of participants modifying their perception and judgment of a particular cheese in response to what other participants had to say.

Alice: I would say it's tangy, and it has a nice – the flavors change from when you first bite it to . . . the aftertaste.

Ben: A little citrusy, maybe?

Alice: Yeah . . . I would maybe even say nutty, like it's . . . I don't know . . . like it rolls around in your mouth and the flavors change. (Lahne and Trubek 2014: 135)

Summing up, Lahne and Trubek argue that 'through an active, iterative, and social practice of sensory perception, consumers integrate their past personal experiences, socially transmitted and valued information about producer practices, and the material properties of the cheese into a single instance of sensory experience' (Lahne and Trubek 2014: 130).

The Lahne and Trubek study is unusual in the annals of sensory science for what could be called the free-range character of the focus-group discussions (though the use of focus-groups is not uncommon) and for introducing a 'social theory' of sense experience. Its publication in the journal *Appetite* is a reflection of how the field of sensory science is changing, opening up to new methodologies and theories. One can nevertheless imagine the questions and objections that a conventional sensory professional might put to the authors, such as: What would a blind taste test involving artisan and generic cheeses reveal about which 'tastes better'? Why was there no attempt to plot liking in relation to fat content? Aren't the participants all pre-selected[5]? Aren't the questions somewhat leading questions? How can any generalizations be made on the basis of such contingent results? However, these objections can be turned around: Lahne and Trubek freely admit that their results are contingent on context but would point out that sensory evaluation experiments are no less contextual, despite their appearance of objectivity, on account of being staged in a lab.[6] Furthermore, they could point to the all too frequent practice of using the employees of the company that is conducting the study as stand-ins for 'the ordinary consumer' (see Resurreccion 2008), and ask: How representative is that? More seriously, as Lahne (2015) has argued, the research protocols of sensory science are fitted, and even 'overfitted', to industrial production where products are standardized and therefore 'portable across contexts' (e.g. a batch of Coca-Cola) in contrast to artisan production, where products are 'unfinished', often quite variable and tied to locale. There is risk involved in artisanal production, whereas variation is virtually eliminated in industrial production (Lahne 2015; see further Paxson 2013). Hence, the protocol doesn't fit the product, or vice versa .

In Lahne and Trubek's study, social context does not simply refer to the exchanges between the participants in the focus group but also extends to the geographic region or terroir of Vermont. Part of what makes the artisan cheeses 'taste better' is that they embody 'the taste of place' (Trubek 2008). But the taste of place is not a function of geography alone, Lahne and Trubek insist. It also has to do with what they call 'cultural saturation' – that is, the ubiquity of Vermont artisan cheese in Vermont, such that it is impossible for a Vermonter not to be aware of artisan cheese, and many consumers have in fact developed 'personal connections' to such products and their producers.

Generic cheeses, and processed cheeses such as Cheez Whiz, lack such personal connections and indeed are designed to be 'portable across contexts'. The same is true of most of the standardized commercial products, hatched in laboratories, which saturate our existence as consumers. These products have the effect of standardizing our perceptions, shaping our tastes to conform to those of their designers and manufacturers. But this does not prevent us from personalizing, or, as it were 'domesticating' them through incorporating such products into our everyday lives. Cheez Whiz is a case in point: it has been discovered by consumers to have many uses never imagined by its manufacturers (Green 2000). Consumption is always a matter of context in the final analysis. The meaning of goods is in their use – that is, in the sense we make of them and not simply the design characteristics (Howes 1996).

The implication of these observations is that rather than dismiss the Lahne and Trubek study for being too parochial, sensory science needs to develop new, more historically and culturally grounded methods for *understanding* (not just assessing) the sensory qualities of the full range of commodities, materials and substances that pervade our everyday lives, both those that are artisanally produced and those which are mass produced. The anthropology and history of the senses has a vital role to play in generating such an understanding by attuning us to the 'social preformation' of the senses and the extent to which 'as we sense we also make sense' (Howes and Classen 2014; Vannini et al. 2012). Perception is not a passive process, a physiological reflex, it is an active, 'world-making' activity (Classen 1993; Shapin 2012), which is nevertheless contingent on the materials at hand. A number of highly stimulating studies that illustrate this point have emerged in recent years, having to do with such materials as aluminium, the 'material of mobility' (Fallan 2013; Sheller 2014) and lycra, the fibre that 'shaped America' (O'Connor 2011). By way of closing, I would like to offer a sensory history of perhaps the most ubiquitous material of the twentieth century: plastic. Plastic was at once the substance that characterized the physical world of the twentieth century and provided a material base for much of its cultural expression.

The plasticity of the material world

The term 'plastic', in fact, covers a variety of synthetic or semi-synthetic substances, from the celluloid used in film and cheap jewellery to the vinyls employed in records, raincoats and exterior siding. However, plastic became the umbrella term for all these creations of the chemical industry. Technical advances resulted in plastics that were amazingly durable, as well as low cost. 'Plastic is forever' touted one industry pioneer, 'and a lot cheaper than diamonds' (cited in Miekle 1993: 9).

Over the course of the century the material became a familiar component of ordinary life. A family celebrating Christmas in the United States in the 1970s, for example might have a plastic Christmas tree decorated with plastic ornaments and featuring plastic Barbie dolls and Lego blocks as presents. In a famous line from the 1967 movie *The Graduate*, a recent college graduate who is uncertain about his future is told by his businessman father: 'I want to say one word to you. Just one word . . . There's a great future in plastics. Think about it' (cited in Miekle 1993: 3).

Like its material uses, the sensory properties of plastic were multiple. Easy to shape, colour, and texture, plastic might approximate anything. It could be made to look like wood or it could be made to look like glass, it could resemble flowers or it could mimic gemstones. Nonetheless, on close inspection, it always retained something 'plasticky' in its look and feel. Plastic itself had no imitators; for who would imitate such a cheap and indeterminate substance?

Due to its mutability, plastic engendered a notion of the malleability of the material world. The French philosopher Roland Barthes wrote of plastic in the 1950s that it embodied 'the very idea of . . . infinite transformation' (1972: 79). Plastic's mutability coincided with twentieth-century desires to reshape not only the physical environment but also society, and even the human body through cosmetic and surgical procedures. Limits set by nature or by custom no longer seemed to hold in a plastic world. Anything could take on a new form.

While plastic was embraced by the twentieth century for its malleability and low cost, however, it was despised (at least by the educated classes) for its 'inauthenticity'. Over the course of the century, in fact, the word plastic came to be a synonym for fake. Social critics saw plastic as a sign and symptom of a society in which simulations had a greater appeal than reality. When the businessman in *The Graduate* affirmed that there was a great future in plastics, the line was not intended to serve as an indicator of commercial acumen, but as an indictment of the superficiality and materialism of Western culture.

It was not only the look and feel of the twentieth-century industrialized world that breathed artificiality, however, but also the taste. Convenience foods – from the quick meals served up by fast food restaurants to the prepared foods stocked at the supermarket (such as the frozen 'TV dinners' made to be warmed and eaten while watching television) – became increasingly popular during the century. The new processed foods also had new artificial flavours and colours, many of them derived from petrochemicals just like most plastics (see Classen, Howes, and Synnott 1994: 187–200). In their song of 1972, 'Plastic Man', The Kinks sung disparagingly of a 'plastic man' who 'eats plastic food with a plastic knife and fork.' Many processed foods, of course, were packaged in plastic, if not canned or boxed. The contents of the supermarket thus seemed, from one perspective, to represent one more triumph of modern technology and, from another, one more of the shams of contemporary life.

Notes

1. For a survey of these parallel developments in the management of sensation in other fields of mass production-consumption besides food, see the discussion of 'giving products sense appeal' in Howes and Classen (2014: 139–141); Sheldon and Arens (1932).

2. Cross-modal investigations are new to sensory science, and many of the studies in this vein in the *Journal of Sensory Studies* have as one of their co-authors the maverick experimental psychologist Charles Spence. Spence directs the Cross-Modal Research Lab at Oxford University and is a frequent collaborator with Heston Blumenthal, the proprietor of

The Fat Duck restaurant. Spence's focus on cross-modal relations, or what we call 'intersensoriality' (Howes 2011: 177–179) is at the forefront of the critique of the compartmentalized understanding of the sensorium that traditionally prevailed in the brain sciences, and the emergence of a more integrated vision, which comes close to the interactive understanding of the sensorium that is fundamental to research in the anthropology of the senses (see Howes and Classen 2014: ch. 6).

3. In the online summary of their conclusions, the authors of the Mainz study write:
    Ambient lighting influences how wine tastes, even when it has no effect on the color of the wine in the glass. Our results show that the context has a stronger influence on the taste perception than formerly believed. These findings can be relevant for the architectural designing of restaurants and wine shops.How can the effects of ambient color be explained? The simple hypothesis that whenever a certain light color makes a person feel comfortable he or she likes the wine better could not be affirmed. The emotions elicited by a certain light color do not seem to be the cause of the effects.

    An alternative explanation could be an influence of color on cognition, for example by making us more accessible and responsive for a certain taste. Likewise, associations could play a role. (Oberfeld-Twistel 2013)

    As examples of the role played by associations, Oberfeld et al. propose that green may connote 'immature' and red may connote 'sweet'. The Mainz study departs from the vast majority of research in sensory evaluation by acknowledging the significance of context, recognizing the senses as interactive and refusing to reduce the explanation of the observed effects to the mobilization of the emotions alone: cognition (or what we would qualify as sensuous cognition) also plays a role.

4. Pink does not discuss how this information was operationalized by the study's sponsor, Unilever.

5. The participants were 'pre-selected' in the sense that they were recruited by means of advertisements that solicited 'consumers of Vermont artisan cheese who were interested in participating in a research study on their opinions' (Lahne and Trubek 2014: 131; see further Lahne, Trubek and Pelchat 2014).

6. The subjectivity of perception is made to appear objective through what Bruno Latour (1987) calls the process of 'inscription' – that is, all of the graphs and tables that 'represent' the object of study. But this objectivity is a product of the process of inscription itself. It depends ultimately on a *visualization* of taste.

References

Alcántara-Alcover, E., M. Artacho-Ramirez, T. Zamora-Alvarez and N. Martinez (2014), 'Exploratory Study of the Influence of the Sensory Channel in Perception of Environments', *Journal of Sensory Studies,* 29(4): 258–271.

Barthes, R. (1972), *Mythologies*. London: Paladin.

Classen, C. (1993), *Worlds of Sense: Exploring the Senses in History and Across Cultures*. London: Routledge.

Classen, C., D. Howes and A. Synnott (1994), *Aroma: The Cultural History of Smell.* New York: Routledge.

Di Donfrancesco, B., B. Koppel and E. Chambers IV (2012), 'An Initial Lexicon for Sensory Properties of Dry Dog Food', *Journal of Sensory Studies,* 27(6): 498–510.

El-Ghezal Jeguirim, S., A. B. Dhouib, M. Sahnoun, M. Cheikhrouhou, N. Njeugna, L. Schacher and D. Adolphe (2010), 'The Tactile Sensory Evaluation of Knitted Fabrics: Effect of Some Finishing Treatments', *Journal of Sensory Studies,* 25(2): 201–215.

Fallan, K. (2013), 'Culture by Design: Co-Constructing Material and Meaning', in K. Aukrust (ed.), *Assigning Cultural Values*, pp. 135–163. Frankfurt: Peter Lang.

Forth, C. and A. Leitch (eds) (2014), *Fat: Culture and Materiality*. London: Bloomsbury.

Green, J. (2000), *Clean Your Clothes with Cheez Whiz: And Hundreds of Off-Beat Uses for Dozens More Brand-Name Products*. Los Angeles: Renaissance Books.

Hennion, A. (2005), 'Pragmatics of Taste', in M. Jacobs and N. Hanrahan (eds), *The Blackwell Companion to the Sociology of Culture*, pp. 131–144. Malden, MA: Blackwell.

Howes, D. (ed.) (1996), *Cross-Cultural Consumption*. London: Routledge.

Howes, D. (2003a), *Sensual Relations: Engaging the Senses in Culture and Social Theory*. Ann Arbor: University of Michigan Press.

Howes, D. (2003b), 'Evaluation sensorielle et diversité culturelle', *Psychologie Française,* 48(4): 117–125.

Howes, D. (2005), 'Hyperaesthesia: The Sensual Logic of Late Capitalism', in D. Howes (ed.), *Empire of the Senses: The Sensual Culture Reader*, pp. 281–303. Oxford: Berg.

Howes, D. (2011), 'Hearing Scents, Tasting Sights: Toward a Cross-Cultural Multimodal Theory of Aesthetics', in F. Bacci and D. Mellon (eds), *Art and the Senses*, pp. 161–182. Oxford: Oxford University Press.

Howes, D. (2013), '"The Race to Embrace the Senses" in Marketing: An Ethnographic Perspective', in *Ethnographic Practice in Industry Conference [EPIC] 2013 Conference Proceedings*, pp. 5–30. Washington, DC: American Anthropological Association.

Howes, D. (2014), 'Introduction: "Make It New" – Reforming the Sensory World', in D. Howes (ed.), *A Cultural History of the Senses in the Modern Age, 1920–2000*, pp. 1–30. London: Bloomsbury.

Howes, D. and C. Classen (1991), 'Epilogue: Sounding Sensory Profiles', in D. Howes (ed.), *The Varieties of Sensory Experience: A Sourcebook in the Anthropology of the Senses*, pp. 257–288. Toronto: University of Toronto Press.

Howes, D. and C. Classen (2014), *Ways of Sensing: Understanding the Senses in Society*. New York: Routledge/ Taylor and Francis.

Jervis, S. M., P. Gerard, S. Drake, K. Lopetcharat and M. Drake (2014), 'The Perception of Creaminess in Sour Cream', *Journal of Sensory Studies*, 29(4): 248–257.

Kemp, S., T. Hollowood and J. Hort (2011), *Sensory Evaluation: A Practical Handbook*. Oxford: Blackwell.

Lahne, J. (In press), 'Sensory Science, the Food Industry and the Objectification of Taste' in *Anthropology of Food*, http://aof.revues.org.

Lahne, J. and A. Trubek (2014), '"A Little Information Excites Us": Consumer Sensory Experience of Vermont Artisan Cheese as Active Practice', *Appetite*, 78: 129–138.

Lahne, J., A. Trubek and M. Pelchat (2014), 'Consumer Sensory Perception of Cheese Depends on Context: A Study Using Comment Analysis and Linear Mixed Models', *Food Quality and Preference*, 32: 184–197.

Latour, B. (1987), *Science in Action: How to Follow Scientists and Engineers through Society*. Cambridge, MA: Harvard University Press.

Levin, C. (1997), *Modernity and the Hegemony of Vision*. Berkeley: University of California Press.

Lindstrom, M. (2005), *Brand Sense: How To Build Powerful Brands through Touch, Taste, Smell, Sight, and Sound*. New York: Free Press.

Mack, A. (2014), 'The Senses in the Marketplace', in D. Howes (ed.), *A Cultural History of the Senses in the Modern Age, 1920–2000*, pp. 77–100. London: Bloomsbury.

Malefyt, T. de Waal (2014), 'An Anthropology of the Senses: Tracing the Future of Sensory Marketing in Brand Rituals', in R. Denny and P. Sunderland (eds), *Handbook of Anthropology in Business*, pp. 704–721. Walnut Creek, CA: Left Coast Press.

Meilgaard, M., B. Carr and G. Civille (2010), *Sensory Evaluation Techniques*, 3rd edition. Boca Raton, FL: CRC Press.

Miekle, J. L. (1995), *American Plastic: A Cultural History*. New Brunswick, NJ: Rutgers University Press.

Oberfeld-Twistel, D. (2013), 'Wine and Color: Effects of Ambient Light on Taste and Aroma', http://www.staff.uni-mainz.de/oberfeld/wine2.html (accessed 15 August 2014).

Oberfeld, D., H. Hecht, U. Allendorf and F. Wickelmaier (2009), 'Ambient Lighting Modifies the Flavor of Wine', *Journal of Sensory Studies*, 24(6): 797–832.

O'Connor, K. (2011), *Lycra: How a Fiber Shaped America*. New York: Routledge.

Pangborn, R. M. (1964), 'Sensory Evaluation of Food: A Look Forward and Back', *Food Technology*, 18: 1309–1324.

Paxson, H. (2013), *The Life of Cheese: Crafting Food and Value in America*. Berkeley: University of California Press.

Pink, S. (2004), *Home Truths*. Oxford: Berg.

Pink, S. (2009*), Sensory Ethnography*. London: Sage.

Piqueras-Fiszman, B. and C. Spence (2012), 'The Influence of the Color of the Cup on Consumers' Perception of a Hot Beverage', *Journal of Sensory Studies,* 27(5): 324–331.

Poste, L., D. MacKie, G. Butler and E. Lamard (1991), *Laboratory Methods for Sensory Analysis of Food*. Ottawa: Agriculture Canada.

Shapin, S. (2012), 'The Sciences of Subjectivity', *Social Studies of Science*, 42: 170–184.

Sheldon. R. and E. Arens (1932), *Consumer Engineering: A New Technique for Prosperity*. New York: Harper.

Sheller, M. (2014), *Aluminum Dreams: The Making of Light Modernity*. Cambridge, MA: MIT Press.

Sherry, J. (2006), 'Sporting Sensation', *The Senses and Society*, 1(2): 245–248.

Stone, H., R. Bleibaum and H. Thomas (2012), *Sensory Evaluation Practices*, 4th edition. San Diego, CA: Academic Press.

Trubek, A. (2008), *The Taste of Place: A Cultural Journey into Terroir*. Berkeley, CA: University of California Press.

Vannini, P., D. Waskal and S. Gottschalk (2012), *The Senses in Self, Society and Culture: A Sociology of the Senses*. London: Routledge.

Zubek, J. (ed.) (1969), *Sensory Deprivation: Fifteen Years of Research*. New York: Appleton-Century-Crofts.

Part 3

From substance to form

Chapter 6

Wild silk indigo wrappers of Dogon of Mali: An ethnography of materials efficacy and design

Laurence Douny

This chapter sets out an ethnography of indigenous materials, which, I argue, allow us to gain insights into some of the ways in which people think and conceptualize their relationships to the natural and social realms, through making and doing (Naji and Douny 2009). By drawing upon Tengu and Tommon Kan Dogon uses of wild silk and indigo in making *tombe toun* textiles (Figure 6.1), I highlight Dogon representations about the efficacy of these materials, as it is grounded in the materials' intrinsic properties, enabling Dogon people to act upon the world in particular ways. Furthermore, I propose that an examination of indigenous perceptions of these 'raw' insect and plant materials helps to uncover the cultural significance of *tombe toun*'s blue-and-white striped designs. I conduct a close analysis of local terminologies, concepts, uses, representations and manifestations as an ethnographic entry point into these perceptions and experiences. In particular, the Dogon concepts of *daoula* and *sangah* throw light on how the materials used in these textile wrappers are perceived. The designs therefore objectify aspects of Dogon social relations and the construction and self-display of material identities through production.

Material efficacy and transformation

Let me first establish something of the history of ideas behind 'material efficacy'. The term 'making' implies transformation techniques of materials into new forms of matter, and matter into objects. Within a making process that Leroi-Gourhan describes as: 'a dialogue between the maker and the material' (Leroi-Gourhan 1993: 306), 'techniques' are meanwhile defined as 'efficacious actions upon matter' (Lemonnier 1992: 4, following Leroi-Gourhan 1993). 'Technical efficacy', contested by Latour (1996), who rather situates efficacy

Figure 6.1 Dogon *gwara* dyer showing a *tombe toun* wrapper worn by old women as it contains few stripes of silk (here mixed with cotton). Photo by Laurence Douny.

in social action, is grounded in Mauss' definition of techniques as 'traditional and efficacious actions upon something' (Mauss 1936: 371). In Lévi-Strauss' (1967) work, the notion of symbolic efficacy designates the effect of ritual heal- ers' speech on individuals through the mediation of symbols found in myths. In another vein, Salpeteur and Warnier (2013: 153–154) describe autopsy practice in the Cameroon grass fields as a form of practical efficacy on the dead and the living, through which local representations about the efficacy of bodily organs and substances are revealed. While all these approaches stemming from Mauss locate efficacy in human/body actions or practice on matter, bodies, things and the invisible world, I want here to focus in particular on the *efficacy of materials* and on *indigenous representations* about them, through techniques of making *tombe toun* textiles.

Wild silk and indigo are materials made of 'matter considered in respect of its occurrence in processes of flow and transformation' (Ingold 2012: 439). These transformations that may be natural, technical, symbolic or magical (Gell 1988), occur in particular cultural contexts, through events and within networks of people, things and spirits, out of which categories of meanings and concepts of materials emerge as deep localized knowledge (see also Mohan, this volume). Following Mauss, I propose that wild silk and indigo are perceived by Dogon as living and actively possessing 'something undisciplined, wild, dangerous and, too, animated and receptive' (Mauss 1974: 166 about earth, translated by Pecquet 2004: 152). I suggest that their material efficacy, meaning the effect that indigo and wild silk materials produce on people and thus what they enable Dogon women to do socially, is determined by their inherent properties and material relations. Hence, the efficacy of these materials of 'enchantment' (Gell 1988: 5) is harnessed by Dogon women in particular ways in order to wield power and influence over rivals and fulfil their own social ambitions.

From this perspective, I propose that a study of materials helps us to understand the social implications of Dogon concepts of efficacy, as for instance the 'sheen' (*daoula*) of wild silk, 'charm' (*sangah*) of natural indigo or the 'beauty' (*sara*) of the finished wrapper. By focusing on the relationships between these materials, I argue that Dogon women's social visibility and charismatic power is mainly achieved through the *daoula* of wild silk woven aphorisms, which are materialized in the wrapper's design. *Daoula,* as a force that resides in the fibre, implies a set of magical and medicinal properties and also includes the material's strength and durability in addition of its visual 'brilliance'. The sheen that is drawn out of the fibre requires particular techniques, knowledges and overall Dogon women's mastering of the mystic power of the material, and this also applies to indigo, which serves to enframe wild silk. I conclude that the Dogon cosmological paradigm is related to local materials and is defined on the basis of their complex nature, efficacy and relationality. Thus, at an epistemological level, indigenous materials such as wild silk and indigo undeniably challenge the ways we might think about such concepts as beauty, charm and sheen.

Sheen in the natural and material world

Sheen is a visual property that certain elements of the natural world and certain objects possess by virtue of light reflecting on their surface. The sheen of textiles, the brilliance or luminescence of minerals like the gleam of metal that attracts the eye, is coded with cultural meanings and triggers an emotional response. As Ben Amos notes about Benin court art, known for its 'bronzes' (labelled as such although most of it was made of brass), their initial shiny red appearance (Herbert 1984: 277–282) would convey awe and fear as it magnifies the power of monarchs (Ben-Amos 1980: 15). Sheen, gleam or brilliance in tandem with colour and light are embedded in cultural and multisensorial experiences of the social, natural and spiritual worlds (Rivers 2003). As Saunders explains, in Meso-American cultures, natural light and brilliance that stem from minerals, feathers and shells bestowed supernatural qualities and represented sacred power and positions in the social hierarchy, as well as life and death (Saunders 2002: 215–216). In West Africa, cowrie shells serving as a currency before colonial time and sewn on hunters' shirts would not only stand as a means of display-ing one's wealth but also, in the manner of armour, would shield against evil spirits. In fact, the gloss and white luminescence of these small round shells means they have the magical property of bewildering evil spirits (as suggested about white shells by Rivers 2003: 2). While sheen can be found naturally in materials, certain materials however necessitate specific techniques in order to bring out their sheen. Physical transformation of these materials may consist of polishing and beating material surfaces, washing or exposing materials to chemical substances. For instance, the sheen of West African indigo *bazin* cloth can be intensified by beating synthetic indigo powder into the cloth with wooden mallets, rendering a special glazed or metallic dark blue sheen. Lastly, while sheen tends to be treated as a visible material quality found in the natural or material world, it should be emphasized that sheen is also regarded as an active property, which minerals like quartz possess. Roberts, for example, suggests that it allows *Bugabo* movements in the south-eastern Democratic Republic of Congo direct communication with the spiritual world in magic rituals such as in sorcery detection, healing and hunting (Roberts 2009: 29–30).

As far as wild silk is concerned, the Tengu and Tomon kan Dogon of Mali consider sheen as a set of visual and material properties that are inherent to the insect-produced fibre and that require a technical process to obtain. The sheen of wild silk, which is perceived as a material of power defined as *daoula,* is achieved through a long and fastidious process that involves boiling the cocoons in water containing potash, as a means of releasing the fibres (degumming process), and their treatment through beating (Figure 6.2), brushing, spinning and washing in order to release their 'brilliance'. Then, the sheen of wild silk is brought out through contrasting it with indigo cotton threads that are woven together in bands. Finally, the wrapper is soaked in an indigo bath in order to darken the cotton indigo stripes, the color of which faded away during weaving, and thus reinforces and enframes the visual sheen of wild silk. Wild silk threads partly absorb indigo when mixed with cotton. As a consequence, they turn into light blue, a color that is dimmed through brushing the stripes with a toothbrush soaked with soap, in order to recover the original white of the silk.

Figure 6.2 After being boiled and dried, wild silk lumps are thoroughly beaten to remove dust (remaining dried gum and potash). Photo by Laurence Douny.

The sheen of wild silk: The Dogon concept of Daoula

When compared to domesticated mulberry silk, West African wild silk clearly lacks luster. It is endowed with a coarse and lumpy texture and rather bestows a greyish or beige color (after being washed). As a consequence, woven wild silk can be confused by non-specialists with indigenous cotton or *kapok* woven fabrics. In Dogon communities, wild silk stands as an expensive and prestigious material due to its rarity and the fact that cocoons are traded over long distances, as well as the multiple costs that are involved throughout the production of the wrapper. Yet, the authenticity of the material and therefore its high value are certified by the visual sheen or brilliance of wild silk that is said to improve through time by wearing the wrapper and by washing it, in tandem with the thick texture and heavy weight of the fibre compared to plain cotton fabrics. Nonetheless, what Dogon people describe as the 'sheen' of wild silk, *daoula,* goes beyond its visual quality, and therefore aesthetic, of visual brilliance (Douny 2013). Generally speaking, *daoula* is said to be a living and active force that certain people and animals have at birth and that runs in their blood (*boli boli*). Similarly, certain objects can possess *daoula* in their materiality depending on the materials they are made of. As a kind of aura of people, animal and things, *daoula* is said to 'shine out of' an entity permanently and to produce an emotional response of appreciation in people and its own attraction.

As far as *tombe toun* wrappers are concerned, the notion of *daoula* expresses as sheen in the sense of the intrinsic, positive and permanent values of wild silk and therefore, the efficacy of wild silk that produces grades of pale blue, or light beige or white (*pea*). This visual sheen, also luminescence, is described as *kongonron so*, that is 'something [i.e. wild silk] that shines like the sun', which is considered to be the brightest existing light. Yet, the value of wild silk in its material properties does not only encompass the visual aspect of sheen but implies the durability as well as the strength of the yarns (*tawanso* or *se balla*) as well as the medicinal and magical properties of wild silk that, as I will explain in the next section, is seen as a mystic and dangerous insect product (*djina diie odjo* or *kaba ko*). Finally, producing wild silk threads requires particular techniques and knowledge about the nature and materiality of wild silk and so mastering its power. They constitute a form of heritage (*atemu*) for the Dogon people that is also acknowledged as a dimension of sheen.

Inside the sheen: The material properties of wild silk yarns

West African wild silk is a fibrous protein that is secreted by the salivary glands of a caterpillar species known as *Anaphe* or *Epannaphe* (African Wild Silk 1916; Ene 1964; Peigler 1993). Wild silk cocoons that Dogon women transform are mainly collected from the forests of Ivory Coast, Guinea Conakry and the Savannah of North East Nigeria. The saliva or fluid secretion that silk worms spin around themselves solidifies into a thread on contact with air, forming a cocoon in which they metamorphose into a moth (Figure 6.3). Hence, wild silk is perceived by Dogon people as a mystic and powerful material mainly because of the material properties that the insect-secreted substance carries, and which according to Dogon women is endowed with the medicinal power of the tree leaves the insects feed on. Dogon perception of silk is based on the otherworldly nature of the wild and remote environment that hosts cocoons and spirits in trees, caves and underground cavities. Furthermore, the insect's extraordinary and so intangible capacity to transform inside of the cocoon that it weaves around itself bewilders as much as it frightens. Lastly, the transformation of cocoons is only operated by post-menopausal women because it is believed that boiling the matter that kills the live caterpillars remaining inside of the cocoons would provoke abortion or

Figure 6.3 Inside of a *goro dialen* cocoon showing caterpillars and moths. Photo by Laurence Douny.

badly affect the health of a newborn child. Here, processing and transforming the materials incorporates beliefs about gestation as it takes place in a woman's womb, and by comparison with insect metamorphosis inside of the cocoon, a matrix for the species' development.

The most commonly found type of wild silk that Dogon women transform is secreted by the processionary moth caterpillar (*Lepidoptera* order) called *Moloneyi Druce*, the cocoons of which are imported from Nigeria by Marka Dafing traders and are easier to transform. Wild silk traders provide Dogon women with four types of cocoons called *goro ba*, *goro dialen*, *tuntun bleni* and *tuntun de*, whose weight, quality and colour depend on the food-plant that the caterpillars consume, for instance, the leaves of the tamarind tree (*Tamarindus indica*), the kola tree (*Cola acuminata*) or doka tree (*Isoberlinia doka*), all of which possess a different tannin that also slightly colors the threads. West African wild silk cocoons that are spun by different kinds of caterpillars are generally initially white/beige or light grey in colour, but they rapidly darken on the trees, especially when exposed to sunlight and rain.

Various alternatives to wild silk that are far more affordable and broadly available include plant and industrial materials. The classification of these alternative materials by order of preference resides in their degree of resemblance to wild silk in terms of strength, texture and colour. For instance, the fibre of the dried pod of the silk-cotton tree, which partially resists indigo dye, remains the best substitute for wild silk. It is followed by the fibre of the dried pods of the red flowering silk-cotton (*Bombax buonopozense*), called *tou-oule* or *tongoron,* and indigenous cotton (*Gossypium herbaceum or Levant cotton*), called *kouni kagadji,* which possesses a hard texture compared with imported varieties of cotton. Yarns produced from indigenous cotton are soaked in the decoction of its seeds (*koriden dji*) that naturally dyes cotton yarns a light beige, a colour that matches this of genuine wild silk. The last option is polyester fibre that is unwound from the padding of armchairs or car seats.

Dogon people attribute various medicinal properties to the silkworms and the matter that they secrete. First of all, caterpillars are widely consumed for their notable curative and nutritious properties, being high in protein (Ashiru 1988). Caterpillars and the larvae found in the cocoons are said to cure diabetes, tetanus and to help reduce high blood pressure. In addition, a decoction of the bits of branches on which wild silk cocoons are spun is used to purge children who suffer from an illness called *kono,* which involves the soul of the child being taken by a night bird, and that is diagnosed as a form of chronic malaria. Finally, smoke from burning the wood that touches the cocoons is wafted around the head and breathed in, as a means to cure headaches and fever provoked by evil spirits.

The metaphysical complexity of wild silk materials, including the involvement of magic, adds to its medicinal properties. For instance, Dogon hunters' shirts (*dana arco*) may be made of wild silk. The material is used for its durability and strength that make this shirt a solid and light form of armour. Its fireproof qualities are notable in the event of wild fires. Wild silk yarns are used to seal amulets and to attach them onto the shirts. Moreover, wild silk threads are dipped into the inky rinse of Qur'anic writing boards, impregnated with Qur'anic verses to be recited and then folded into leather amulets, as a way of protecting hunters against wildlife, witches, and evil spirits, but also to heal. In armed conflict, hunters who ensure the protection of civilians and very often form a part of the national army, wear these amulets so as to protect themselves from bullets and blades. Lastly, these amulets are said to attract luck, and to confer or reinforce the charismatic power of the wearer.

Wild silk also possesses two noticeable material properties of endurance: strength and visual brilliance, which can however be weakened by chemical potash, when it is excessively used for freeing the threads or if the cocoons are over-cooked. The oldest wrapper I saw was, according to the owner Fatoumata, about 70 years old. Its cotton strips had clearly worn out over time while its wild silk strips and their sheen remained intact. By touching its surface and then holding one of its corners, she explained that no other wrapper is as strong, as wild silk challenges time and the ageing body. This wrapper will be passed onto the next generation. It can be emphasized that in colonial times, wild silk was considered by the German and British colonial administrations for use in manufacturing war supplies such as parachutes, due to the tensile strength of the material. However, the experiment was abandoned, notably because of the emergence of nylon that was easier to produce and much cheaper (Ene 1964; McKinney and Eicher 2009: 47–48). Today, the materials and design of cocoons engineered by silk-producing caterpillars constitute a considerable source of inspiration and material innovation for the development of human technology, such as producing protective lightweight armours, helmets or sustainable car panels, as recent studies have suggested (Chen et al. 2012).

A last noticeable property of wild silk recognized by Dogon comprises in how its visual sheen is said to improve with time, where the majority of natural fibres used in local textile industries would fade away. As I have already mentioned, the sheen of wild silk is obtained through a long process that starts with the degumming of threads, followed by the carding and spinning of the fiber, which is itself said to get smoother during the process as it is imbued with sweat from the hand. Wild silk threads are then washed with local soap or industrial washing powder, to restore the light beige colour of newly formed wild silk cocoons.

Textile shaping through indigo dyeing: The Dogon concept of sara

'Sara' is a term which describes the visual aesthetic of wild silk indigo wrappers as revealed through its design, which enables highlighting wild silk material. Sara is the 'beauty' of the fabric, produced through weaving and indigo dyeing, that is through shaping wild silk material. In other words, sara is what is being done with or to wild silk as a means of enframing it. It consists in the treatment and design conferred on it, resulting in a wrapper that is composed of woven white wild silk and woven blue indigo cotton stripes, sewn together to form a wrapper. The role of indigo is essential in creating that particular design through contrasting 'white' silk and indigo cotton threads. By soaking the whole wrapper in indigo, the dye reinforces the color and texture of pre-dyed indigo cotton threads. These are much weaker than wild silk, and wear out and fade away much quicker. Similarly, as Renne proposes as regards black marriage cloth in the Bunu area of Nigeria: 'Indigo enhances cloth, much like gold-plating' (Renne

1995: 60). Indigo dye not only embellishes fabric but it also changes texture by conferring temporary rigidity to its cotton. Cotton is a commonly found material that does not possess any particular force and is rather considered as a material support for dyes and decoration. In the manner of a bare surface ready for inscription, woven cotton allows fashion possibilities and meanings to materialize in the fibre. A greater cultural value is here attributed to indigo dye, which confers a particular treatment to it.

Hence, *sara* is seen by Dogon people as shaping and adding value that is produced through weaving, through indigo dyeing or in other contexts through decorating a wrapper with lurex or rayon. Similarly to *daoula* as a material aesthetic located in threads, indigo dye possesses an efficacy called *sangah*. It resides in the material itself and is brought out through techniques known to the caste of *gwara* dyers, yet it remains temporary.

Indigofera's *sangah*: Material properties and the dyeing process

The quality and material properties of indigo, a plant material, are described by Dogon as *sangah* or 'charm'. This concept refers to a substance, material or thing that in terms of textile production has material properties of a limited efficacy, ephemeral values and triggers an aesthetic judgment of appreciation that therefore fades away. Natural indigo that is perceived as a living material is a medicinal plant locally grown. It is claimed by Dogon dyers to be of a higher quality than chemical indigo that is imported from Europe and China. However, natural indigo used alone takes twice as long to become fixed and it necessitates rather large quantities of dyes compared to chemical flakes that are more concentrated, yet very expensive. Therefore, natural indigo is mixed with a small quantity of chemical indigo. Beyond the fact that natural indigo enables rebalancing chemicals, Dogon dyers, called *gwara,* believe indigo dye can never be 'foreign' as it has to be made of local indigo brought into the dyer's own recipe. Therefore, in order to be efficacious, the bath and hand process must remain 'indigenous' in the sense that the origin of indigo is known and this botanical species possesses medicinal-magical properties.

Over 600 species of indigo plants belonging to the genus *Indigofera* (family *Leguminosae*) are found in West Africa. One of the most common is the shrub *Indigofera arrecta (Hochst. ex A.Rich.)*[1] (see database.prota.org; Burkill 1995), which grows perennially on arid soils and is commonly found in the Sahel and therefore in Mali. Indigo dye can also be obtained from various indigo-bearing plants such as *Striga Rowlandii*, called '*do*', which is also parasitic on Millet crops (Dieterlen 1952: 143). These two indigo varieties differ in colour and in strength.

Indigo leaves that are collected before flowering are not only used as a dye but also as a painkiller, for instance, as eye drops or as a cataplasm that heals infected insect bites and wounds that have festered and are accompanied by high fever and nightmares (Figure 6.4). The seeds of the indigo plant, reduced to powder, mixed with a fruit tree potash and some shea oil, constitute a powerful ointment that heals body pains caused by witchcraft. They are vigorously massaged into children's bodies in which the indigo's active properties are immediately diffused inside of the body.

In a similar way, the dried roots of the plant are crushed and mixed with shea butter that adults apply on their body to prevent witchcraft. Kumba recalls that in the past, immediately after being exorcised, girls would have to carry a twig of indigo in their hands at all times so as to chase away witches. The powder of the

Figure 6.4 Crushed indigo leaves made into balls are used to dye cloth and as medicine. Photo by Laurence Douny.

roots of the indigo mixed with perfume is also placed on hot charcoals as a form of incense, the smoke of which protectively envelopes the body of the victim of witchcraft or of a spirit attack.

Hence, all parts of the indigo plant are used and administered to children and adults in different ways (i.e. ointment or smoke), as various means of healing the sick body or to prevent sicknesses that are diagnosed as being provoked by witchcraft or spirits. Indigo, a living and active material, possesses the ambivalent power of healing or killing, such as by causing abortions. Pregnant *gwara* dyers are traditionally forbidden to manipulate indigo plants, while the fermentation process of the dye that takes place in the vat is seen by *gwara* as a metaphor for gestation in a woman's womb.

The process of indigo dyeing remains mysterious. In fact, fabrics are first impregnated with indigo-white, of a green-yellow translucent aspect that gradually turns blue when the fabric is removed from the bath and is exposed to the air, a process that occurs through a chemical reaction[2] akin to magic. As Taussig describes, indigo color as a magical polymorphous substance 'eludes us because it is in continuous transformative flux' (Taussig 2009: 40–41, 149). The number of soaks and therefore time needed to impregnate cloth with indigo depends upon the strength of the dye. In this way, a good quality dye will require only one dye. Consequently, indigo plant and dye are perceived as a magic material and substance that possess *sangah* or 'charm', in the sense of its dyeing capacity and medicinal properties. Its dyeing process is also seen as magical because its transformative qualities cannot be grasped. Yet in making *tombe toun* textiles, indigo's material efficacy, and visual aesthetic as a dye stemming from a cultivated plant, is much weaker than wild silk's. Indigo fades away through washing and wearing, just as cotton fragments, whereas wild silk that possesses *daoula* as a permanent sheen is said to improve through time.

The social implications and significance of materials

As obtained through weaving and indigo dyeing, the *sara* of wild silk indigo wrappers enables production of woven aphorisms through contrast with wild silk threads. The primary function of these material aphorisms is to silently express moral values and truths as well as to legitimate social order. In other words, by wearing these wrappers, Dogon women fully embody and perform cultural codes through self-display. For instance, the aphorism *sabari tono* that means 'patience in one's marriage' is composed of one large stripe of wild silk and three smaller stripes of the same material, separated by indigo cotton stripes. It describes 'a woman who has been patient in her marriage and has had three children'. The aphorism *denkelen ba* meaning the 'mother of the only child' is materialized by one stripe of wild silk framed on both sides by a larger stripe of indigo cotton. This message is designed to mock a co-wife that has only one child, whereas the wearer has many and they represent her worth. Hence, these woven aphorisms allow women to express themselves in implicit ways, to subvert or contest, but also they stand as self-reminders, signs of adherence and expression of social moral values and status.

Wild silk wrappers that carry one or several aphorisms and therefore contain large quantities of wild silk are intended for young women who are between 17 and 35 years of age, that is of marriageable age and looking for a husband, who are getting married or simply married (Figure 6.5). Here, the *sara* that is

Figure 6.5 Dogon wild silk wrappers (mixed with cotton) on young women and displaying *'batono ti ban'* (left), meaning 'the usefulness of a mother never ends', and an 'Obama' girl (right) wearing *'pin ba da fila'* (the stripe with two white extremities) and *'moyo le zama daa ben'* ('tolerance brings people together'). Photo by Laurence Douny.

the beauty of the wrapper lies in the large amount of wild silk that decorates the wrappers and attracts the eye, because of the almost redundant abundancy of sheen in stripes and through the contrast with the cotton indigo that enframes them. For instance, the aphorism *sabari tono*[3] that I have described above may appear, in this case, four or five times on the wrapper or it may be combined with other aphorisms. This wrapper, called *'gnein e toun',* celebrates the beauty of young women who want to be seen, congratulated and therefore socially visible. On the contrary, a wild silk wrapper, which contains less aphorisms woven in silk and that therefore is darker, is worn by old women (over 35 years old) and is called *baaliku toun,* 'the wrapper of old women'. It possesses *daoula* just as the wrapper for young women does but far less *sara* as it affords few motifs or aphorisms. Dogon women see themselves as old after 35, that is, after having given birth to several children, due to the lack of medical care, a considerable load of routine physical work and also because of living in a harsh environment that wears down the body. Hence, they feel that their youth as a personal worth must be celebrated while they still can.

Social visibility and value through self-display

Wild silk as the queen of textile materials assigns honour and worth to women, who often describe wearing wild silk as making them feeling important and so charismatic. The *daoula* or sheen of wild silk as a material of enchantment attracts the eye on the wearer. Sheen as a kind of 'aura' triggers emotional responses of esteem or admiration, and so it 'enchants' the viewer to a much higher degree than indigo's charm or *sangah*. Therefore, wild silk makes women inevitably visible, as opposed to wearing dyed cotton cloths that make them 'unseen', which is equivalent to being 'naked'. This is expressed as: *'tombe toun kouni banga kouwa pere kouni toun banga ire',* which means 'a woman who wears *tombe toun* is ten times more visible and expressive than a woman who wears cotton'. Here, the aphorisms forming the design of *tombe toun* wrappers are efficacious because of the power, sheen and *daoula* of wild silk material, which legitimates the non-verbal messages the stripe bears, and also because its visual aesthetic is enhanced and enframed by indigo, which itself possesses a reduced efficacy compared to wild silk.

Wild silk is a material of prestige not only because of its price and rarity but also it is overall a material of power that authoritatively *legitimizes* the wearer's thoughts and actions. Here, the cultural significance of sheen plays a role in legitimating social codes, hierarchy and moral values through self-display. In addition, sheen imparts personal worth on the older women who produced the wrapper. It confers charisma to young women, who by wearing it flaunt their social significance and status. Therefore, they show they can afford such a prestigious cloth, are married to a wealthy husband or have a caring and hard-working mother who made the wrapper to celebrate their daughter. It is worth noting that wild silk wrappers as items of prestige constitute essential elements of dowry and of bridewealth. In both cases, the wearer feels aesthetically and socially transformed, while the viewer become socially 'enchanted'.

Materials classification and their cultural representations

Due to its formidable material properties, such as endurance and magic, wild silk is perceived by Dogon as a material of power. It is obtained through long-distance trades or journeys in the bush and in caves, and it requires long boiling to be degummed. Wild silk as a unique material provides absolute healing and long-lasting empowerment of individuals who seek protection, or luck, or strive for recognition and situatedness in the social world. On the contrary, cotton is a domesticated plant material used in textile production that does not stand the test of time even when coated with indigo. Similarly to cotton, indigo is a domes-ticated plant commonly found in villages that bears medicinal properties, which are however much weaker than silk, and are said by traditional healers to be redundant since other medicinal plants can cure the same illnesses that indigo cures. Although indigo dye obtained through crushing and fermenting leaves takes over cotton by adding value to it, its properties and visual effect fade. Here, Dogon cultural representation, appreciation and classification of these materials are based on their sources, their environment, and primarily on their efficacy. This implies their inherent force or properties, the relationality that form their materiality and also includes the temporality, techniques and knowledges of wild silk and indigo.

Within a broader Tengu and Tommon Kan craft production and material system, the role that indigenous materials such as earth, wood, iron ore, silk, cotton, indigo and animal skins play in Dogon daily and spiritual life are central to the Dogon cosmological paradigm. Their roles entail the ways by which Dogon define, order and act upon the social, natural and spiritual world, through trans-forming and using materials. As explained by a Dogon blacksmith, earth, called 'the mother of humanity', is a sacred element from which everything emerges. Life-giving earth is also a prominent building and shrine-making material.

Second, wood and by extension plants are medicinal substances, intervening in healing and ritual performances. Dogon people extract medicines and food from trees, while their wood also serves as firewood and for sculpting various objects. Third, iron ore and metals are essential in making tools to cultivate the land, to, cut wood and weapons to protect. Fourth, wild silk is primarily used for its outstanding medicinal and magical properties in addition to making textiles. Wild silk entered the Dogon micro-cosmology of materials and also tradition some 260–300 years ago with the advent of Islam, inter-ethnic marriages and collaboration with the Marka-Dafing (Douny 2013). Fifth, as I have previously explained cotton is mainly used in textile production but does not possess any inherent force. Lastly, although indigo possesses medicinal properties, dupli-cated by other plant species, likewise animal skins used in leatherwork are seen as dispensable compared to the other materials listed.

Thus, a micro-cosmology of materials for Tomon and Tengu Dogon commu-nities that is dynamic, open to change and yet excludes chemical and industrial materials (similarly see McKay et al. in this volume about Filipino conceptualiza-tion of *plaštik*) is built on materials choice and preference. These are driven by necessity and meet people's worldviews within a craft production system. The materials order depends on Dogon priorities about sustaining life and requires efficacy. The making of textiles, wild silk and indigo materials are means by which social relations are established and negotiated. They enable people to locate themselves and act upon and in the world.

Towards a micro-cosmology of indigenous materials

Through an ethnography of materials, I have examined the material efficacy of wild silk and indigo in the making of *tombe toun* wrappers. I have shown that wild silk through its sheen or *daoula* acts as a statement of social prestige and personal worth, while the wrapper's design of blue and white stripes carries aphorisms that have strong visual and communicational impact due to the effi-cacy of this material. Wild silk indigo wrappers constitute an efficacious marker of social visibility, essentially due to the way wild silk legitimizes social actions and relations. In other words, the social relevance and implication of sheen rests on the ways Dogon women engage socially with sheen, which as a material of 'enchantment' triggers an emotional response of social respect. Wild silk indigo wrappers bestow not only beauty (*sara*) on Dogon women, but power (*daoula*) and also charisma.

Wild silk and indigo are both perceived as living and active materials that act upon people because of their inherent properties, including medicinal and magical, yet with very different degrees of efficacies, in the sense of being permanent (*daoula*) and so powerful, or else ephemeral and weak (*sangah*). Dogon representations and classification of materials are based on their source of origin, materiality and transformative processes, which show materials' cosmological pervasiveness.

In other words, the Dogon micro-cosmology of materials brings people and indigenous materials into a system of relations, in which materials enable people to locate themselves, relate and act upon the social, natural and invisible world through their materiality. Consequently, such concepts of materials cosmology and efficacy allow us to better circumscribe the nature, power and relationality of materials as well as their active role in shaping cultures. In the context of making, researching materials constitutes a compelling way of uncovering implicit indigenous cultural meanings about indigenous materials and their epistemological complexity.

Notes

1. The full botanical names of plants commonly record the names of botanists whose work has been involved in ascribing the plant to a genus and family. Hence 'Hochst. ex. A. Rich.' and 'Schumach. and Thonn. Benth.', which record the five botanists involved in categorizing the plants listed, are here included as a part of the Latin names.
2. The enzymic hydrolysis that results from soaking indigo plants in water enables transformation of indican into indoxyl and glucose. Then the indoxyl converts into indigo when oxygen is added by whisking the bath (Balfour 2011: 103).
3. The majority of Dogon proverbs are expressed in Malinke, the language spoken by the Marka-Dafing people of Mali and Burkina-Faso who created these wrappers and are wild silk specialists.

References

'African Wild Silk African Wild Silk' (1916), *Bulletin of the Imperial Institute of the United Kingdom, the Colonies and India,* 14: 167–180.

Ashiru, M. O. (1988), 'The Food Value of the Larvae of Anaphe Venata Butler (Lepidoptera: Notodontidae)', *Ecology of Food and Nutrition,* 22: 313–320.

Balfour-Paul, J. (2011), *Indigo: Egyptian Mummies to Blue Jeans*. London: British Museum Press.

Ben-Amos, P. (1980), *The Art of Benin*. London: Thames & Hudson.

Burkill, H. M. (1995), *The Useful Plants of West Tropical Africa,* Vol. 3, 2nd edition, Kew: Royal Botanic Gardens, <http://plants.jstor.org/upwta/3_553>

Chen, F., D. Porter, F. Vollrath (2012), 'Structure and Physical Properties of Silkworm Cocoons', *Journal of Royal Society Interface*, 9(74) (September): 2299–2308.

Database.prota.org 'Indigofera arrecta Hochst. ex. A. Rich.', <http://database.prota.org/
     PROTAhtml/Indigofera%20arrecta_En.htm> (accessed May 2012)
Dieterlen, G. (1952), 'Classification des végétaux chez les Dogon', *Journal de la Société des
     Africanistes*, 22: 115–158.
Douny, L. (2013), 'Wild Silk Textiles of the Dogon of Mali: Towards an Understanding of the
     Production, Material Efficacy and Cultural Significance of Sheen', *Textile: The Journal of
     Cloth and Culture,* 11(1): 58–77.
Ene, J. C. (1964), 'Indigenous Silk-Weaving', *Nigeria Magazine,* June 1964: 127–136.
Gell, A. (1988), 'Technology and Magic', *Anthropology Today,* 4(2): 6–9.
Golding, F. D. (1942), 'Wild Silkworms of Nigeria', *Farm & Forest,* 3: 35–40.
Herbert, E. W. (1984), *Red Gold of Africa: Copper in Precolonial History and Culture*. Madison:
     University of Wisconsin Press.
Ingold, T. (2012), 'Toward an Ecology of Materials', *Annual Review of Anthropology,* 41:
     427–442.
Latour, B. (1996), 'Lettre à mon ami Pierre sur l'anthropologie symétrique', *Ethnologie
     Française,* 26(1): 32–37.
Lemonnier, P.(1992), *Elements for an Anthropology of Technology*. Ann Arbor: Museum of
     Anthropology, University of Michigan.
Leroi-Gourhan, A. (1993), *Gesture and Speech*. Cambridge, MA: MIT Press.
Lévi-Strauss, C. (1967), 'The Effectiveness of Symbols', in C. Lévi-Strauss, *Structural
     Anthropology,* Vol. 1, pp. 181–201. New York: Doubleday.
Mauss, M. (1936), 'Les Techniques du corps', *Journal de Psychologie,* 22: 363–386.
McKinney, E. and J. B. Eicher (2009), 'Unexpected Luxury: Wild Silk Textile Production among
     the Yoruba of Nigeria', *Textile: The Journal of Cloth and Culture,* 7(1): 40–55.
Naji, M. and L. Douny (2009), 'Editorial', *Journal of Material Culture,* 14: 411–432.
Pecquet, L. (2004), 'The Mason and Banco, or Raw Material as a Power for Building a Lyela
     Home (Burkina Faso)', *Paideuma,* 50: 151–171.
Peigler, R. S. (1993), 'Wild Silks of the World', *American Entomologist,* 39(3): 151–161.
Renne, E. P. (1995), *Cloth That Does Not Die: The Meaning of Cloth in Bùnú Social Life*.
     Seattle: University of Washington Press.
Rivers, V. Z. (2003), *The Shining Cloth: Dress & Adornment That Glitter.* London: Thames &
     Hudson.
Roberts, A. F. (2009 [1992]), 'Bugabo: Arts, Ambiguity, and Transformation in Southeastern
     Congo', <http://www.anthroposys.be/robertspdf.pdf>.
Salpeteur, M. and Warnier, J.-P. (2013), 'Looking for the Effects of Bodily Organs and
     Substances through Vernacular Public Autopsy in Cameroon', *Critical African Studies,* 5(3):
     153–174.
Saunders, N. J. (2002), 'The Colors of Light: Materiality and Chromatic Cultures of the
     Americas', in A. Jones and G. MacGregor (eds), *Colouring the Past: The Significance of
     Archaeological Research*, pp. 209–226. Oxford: Berg.
Taussig, M. (2009), *What Color Is the Sacred?* Chicago: London: University of Chicago Press.

Chapter 7

Fashioning plastic

Tom Fisher

Barbie is plastic . . . but she knows. And when I need help,
always she's there . . . I know she's plastic, I know she's
useless, but she's always there.

(Giovani Madonia 2014)

A few hours after hearing this radio interview with Giovani Madonia, the owner of the United Kingdom's biggest Barbie Doll collection,[1] I opened a new tube of toothpaste, made of plastic. It was not my usual brand and promised special tooth-whitening power. When I squirted some on my (plastic) toothbrush, I saw that the toothpaste was translucent, light blue, with dark blue flecks. Looking carefully through the plastic lenses of my reading glasses, I wondered if these might be so-called microbeads. These tiny spheres of polyethylene or other thermoplastic that are used in beauty products wash down the sink into the sea, where they absorb chemicals such as PCBs and other persistent organic pollutants (Takada 2013), and may be consumed by marine life.

These examples indicate something of the range and diversity of current manifestations of plastics. They can be the component of a personal metaphysics. They are useful in our everyday habits. They can be the focus of environmental concern. Between these extremes, as illustrated by the toothpaste example, they are ubiquitous, and consequently often escape our attention. One objective of this chapter is to acknowledge plastic's disappearance as material and its simultaneous presence as 'already more than stuff', indicating something about the texture of contemporary material ecology. As Webmoor and Whitmore (2008) put it, 'Things Are Us'. Here the suggestion is that 'Plastics Are Us' – materially so if you happen to swallow some tooth-whitening toothpaste, more abstractly if you construct your psyche 'round a Barbie collection.

The chapter approaches the strange world of plastics[2] from the perspective of design, which is a practice concerned to resolve the material facts of 'things' with their 'social life' (Appadurai 1988). It sketches in some of the history of the material: key moments in its developing cultural presence, its double nature as both useful and dubious. The main objective is to think about how to balance a necessary acknowledgement of the role of plastics' shifting material forms with a clear sense of the meanings that are activated in them. This aligns with the range of perspectives from which plastics are studied, from engineering to cultural studies, which in turn matches the range of ways it makes its presence felt in our contemporary surroundings, as well as its significance in material culture. Studies of plastics include early commentaries on their potential for design and manufacture from a technical point of view (Gloag 1943, 1945; 'Plastes' 1941; Yarsley and Couzens 1941, 1956, 1968) through to culturally informed historical narratives that sought to confirm them as the materials of progressive modern innovation (e.g. Katz 1978). More recent accounts focus on the history of the plastics industry and the cultural connotations that the materials gathered in the period of intense consumerism after World War II, which Meikle (1995) and others have called the Plastic Age (Thompson et al. 2009), as well as their consequences for consumption experiences (Fisher 2013b).

Ubiquitous plasticity

Over time, plastics have become a ubiquitous, inescapable and unremarkable part of our surroundings and everyday life in the developed world. As a consequence, they have become in a sense invisible to us, while, at the same time, becoming potentially active, 'smart' by design that operates at nano-scale. The principle of synthesis behind plastics has even transferred from the chemical to the biological due to recent work in biotechnology (Ginsberg 2014), which like the example of microbeads, points towards a blurring of the distinction between animal and material. Alongside the relative invisibility that their ubiquity brings, concerns about plastics' environmental consequences have seen the development of a negative view of them in public discourse (Frienkel 2011), which is also reflected in the attention garnered from commentators and researchers in the human sciences (Gabrys 2013; Hawkins 2001). These studies pay close attention to the material facts of plastics, bringing an acute understanding of the diffusion of these inherently labile materials through human practices and in multiple relations to human and 'more-than-human' bodies in what Whatmore calls a 'sticky web of connections' (2013: 604).

Concentrating only on plastics' material, sensorial presence, however, risks leaving behind its role as a component of our imagined 'figural' world. This chapter takes this risk as one starting point, inspecting the 'fashioning' of plastic's relational materiality by using sources close to fashion practices, in clothing and music. It reviews concepts of plasticity that appear in social media related to fashion, and delineates relationships between the consequences of particular material formulations and the work they do as signifiers in culture. Culture here is meant in the sense that Raymond Williams retrieved from the high versus popular debate – a process of artful making from which forms emerge that are significant for a time and place (Williams 1974). Fashion is a form of artful making, a feature of modernity available to all, that works with 'immaterial materials' that are infinitely malleable, infinitely plastic.

The physical materials also are as malleable in their cultural manifestations as in their physical properties, and the examples of current 'fashionings' of plasticity discussed below draw on themes that can be found in the materials' history since the start of Meikle's Plastic Age. Both their material and their abstract characteristics feed into and draw from the 'structure of feeling' of contemporary life – in ways that are critical of consumer culture and ways that celebrate the fashioning of the self within it. A critical stance on consumer culture is evident from the point that the Plastic Age began to wane, and this has an ironic reading of plasticity as a component. In 1968 the Plastic Ono Band started a theme in Art Rock that aligns with the use of 'plastic' to indicate inauthentic and uncool. It is also possible to find plasticity being invoked to celebrate what it means to synthesize the self, to be fashionable, fashioned in plastic. This chapter will return to these contrasting but related examples. First, it is appropriate to think about the physical properties of the materials that have so extended themselves into the collective imagination.

Plastic materials

'Plastic' is a misleading name for a material because it identifies a property of material, the ability to be moulded,[3] to flow, and this ability is not restricted to one category of useful matter. Glass shares many of the properties of some plastics, but its high melting point, fused structure and ancient origins give it different properties and connotations. Nonetheless, the modern materials known as plastics have come to be characterized by the fact that they are processed by moulding. The properties of the materials means that things made of plastic have moved from one form to another, and if they are heated, they may do so again. They have moved from indeterminate stuff to a determinate form and in many cases they are more ready to relinquish that form than are objects of glass, metal or ceramic.

Although they seem characteristically modern, this ability to move, to be pushed about, gives plastics strong connections to materials that belong in a pre-industrial craft setting, naturally occurring thermoplastics including shellac, gutta percha, rubber, horn, tortoiseshell and whalebone that can be worked when hot. Horners turned animal product into material for lanterns (or 'lamp-horns'), buttons, combs, handles and other objects, with increasing sophistication. Horn itself was used to make moulds to produce articles in softer material, such as straw, for votive souvenirs (Schaverien 2006). In its most advanced application by the late sixteenth century, it was used to take impressions of detailed engraved dies, in a process that points towards the moulding processes used to make objects from thermoplastics from the mid-nineteenth century.

Horn objects soften and change their shape if they are heated just as the shape of some durable plastic objects changes if they are exposed to heat by accident, or if their material is recycled, as McKay (this volume) details. Apparently stable plastic objects are only temporarily halted in their flow. They are things between states, characterized as much by motion as by the stable forms they have in use. Although it was their 'protean' ability to adopt an infinite variety of forms that fascinated early commentators on plastic (Meikle 1995: 11), here the focus is on the implications of the fact they do that – their plasticity – rather than the forms that result.

Although variety is certainly one of the defining features of plastic things, I want to think about the ways in which the motion that gives formless matter determinate shape is temporarily halted. I want to dwell particularly on the cultural forces at work when their motion is stilled, which work as much on an immaterial as a material level – the ways in which 'plasticity' works on our ideas as a consequence of its presence in our physical surroundings. So one focus here is on design, since designers are among the most significant of the agents that bring about the flow of this material, and determine the shapes in which it ends up. But the scope of the chapter is both narrower than 'what designers have done with plastic' and, at the same time, broader than this since it considers plasticity as a quality that pervades contemporary culture.

Consumer product designers and engineering designers have different but overlapping concerns. Both have made use of the fact that plastics engineering can make possible integrated forms and more efficient production. Fixtures can be embedded in complex mouldings that may be formed out of more than one polymer, with a variety of textures and visual effects. Single mouldings take the place of assemblies of components integrating structure and surface, reducing both the number of components and production operations. While design engineers are concerned with physical, mechanical performance, product designers think of plastic in terms of consumers' engagement with objects through the tactility of their surfaces and the visual effects of their forms – aesthetic relationships with objects activated by culture. This engagement has both material and immaterial dimensions. We are touched by the materials and our touch is primed by our ideas about them (Fisher 2004).

So what is relevant here are some moments in the history of plastics, some factors in their cultural trajectory, and some characteristics of their properties that are played out in the production processes that are the course along which they flow. This focus on motion, on the flow of matter through production and consumption and over time, implies the forces that move it (Fisher 2012). To say that 'a material flows', is to ascribe to it a tendency do so, implying endogenous properties that make this possible, as well as external forces that activate these properties, akin to gravity without human agency. However, in both the sphere of consumption and of production, materials are no more than matter impelled by human forces. But they are matter with properties that are the grounds for their performance and in the case of plastics these properties are both physical and cultural. They allow certain sorts of design, and have accrued an unstable repertoire of abstract 'components' that can be put to use as cultural elements in the 'fashioning' of self-hood. As McKay puts it in this volume, plastics are 'co-producers of cultural categories'.

In this 'fashioning' it is possible to discern both the pre-modern sense of 'to make' and the modern sense of 'a making' that is socially acceptable and desired. As a word to describe prevailing socially acceptable ways of doing, 'fashion' coincides with Western modernity. Its use is found from the sixteenth century, describing changes in what is considered right and acceptable in manners and accoutrements that are apparently random but temporarily meaningful. Its etymology associates it with social agreement and factions. The associated term 'vogue' derives from an Old French root with maritime associations, describing the random swaying movement of the waves.[4]

The phenomenon of modern fashion has generated a rich literature that centres on fashion in clothes and its role in self-presentation (for example, Entwhistle 2000), as well as work that locates this communicative function in a social setting. In his study of *haute couture* fashion, for instance, Blumer identifies the relationship between fashion and a shared sense of the times, calling it a 'collective groping for the proximate future' (1969: 281), noting the role of particular people – designers – in the mechanism of 'collective selection'. For Blumer,

designers 'catch and give expression to what we may call the direction of modernity' (280). As the industrial designer Raymond Loewy put it, design consists of
giving form to that which is the 'most advanced yet acceptable' (Loewy 1951:
277ff). It is possible to think about fashion and design without the assumption
that modernity has a direction if we accept that designers simply develop forms
that resonate with their times. In the case of plastic, designers stop the material's
motion at forms that are significant, fashioning the material in both the old and
contemporary senses outlined above. Our understanding of plasticity is in itself a
component of this 'fashioning', as designs mesh with their context. It is possible
to see this in plastic's relationship to fashion so it is appropriate to think about
fashionable plastic, through themes that emerge from its history.

Design history and plastic authenticity

The most authoritative account of the entanglement between plastic materials
and contemporary culture is Meikle's (1995) *American Plastic: A Cultural History*,
which emphasizes the meanings that have accrued to plastics rather than their
technical details. However, as we have seen above, the two cannot be disag-
gregated and as the materials were developed, plastics production technology
meant that familiar plastics came in familiar shapes. For instance, the production
technology behind phenolic thermoset resin moulding in the 1930s favoured
'streamlined' forms, whereas the polystyrene that emerged after the Second
World War can follow sharp angles in the mould (Meikle 1995: 187–188). But
what materials are is not simply what they can do.

   As well as forms that related to production processes, the materials accrued
meanings that depended on their material nature, including their early association with the imitation of more honorific materials. The properties of cellulose
nitrate meant it was possible to make a passable imitation of a starched linen shirt
collar, or an acceptable approximation of tortoiseshell, indeed such imitation had
been the stimulus for developing early plastic materials. Negative connotations
of inauthentic poor taste were one consequence of this imitation, which persists,
as McKay's chapter in this volume shows. In the Philippines the Tagalog usage
of '*plastik*' or 'Tupperware' is to indicate a two-faced, fake person.

   However, plastics have also been associated with positive ideas. The materials have represented a progressive modernity. The first designs in plastic
that critics took to be authentic applications of their qualities appeared in the
mid-twentieth century and did not imitate any other material but played on their
capacity to be light in weight, seamless in construction and, by then, brightly

coloured. In examples such as the phenolic radio cabinets of the 1930s, the material was taken to be expressive of the modern. Meikle calls this strongly positive construction on plastics post-1945 a 'plastic utopianism' that invoked ideas of the mastery of nature through the application of polymer science (Meikle 1995: 104–118 and 228–230).

Before Meikle, Sylvia Katz produced several histories of design in plastic (1978, 1984, 1986). The depth and reach of Meikle's work demonstrates the richness of the cultural dimensions of plastic, and the seriousness with which design history has treated it as an object of study. War-time developments in plastics production methods, and the contact citizens consequently had with the new materials, brought them to the attention of John Gloag, an early UK design historian (1943, 1945), as well as industry figures who were keen to promote the materials, notably Yarsley and Couzens who concluded each edition of their account of the current plastic industry with a piece that positioned the technology in the current times (1941, 1956, 1968; see Fisher 2013b for a more detailed comparison of the three passages). The 1941 edition proposed a future 'Plastic Man', living in a 'plastic age' (1941: 154–158); the 1956 edition identifies a fear for the future, including its materials, that accompanied anxiety about nuclear destruction. By the 1968 edition, they were able to note plastics' uptake by fashion, quoting Mary Quant: 'We were the first people to use plastic as plastic' (1968: 358). They might have made the same point by noting the 'high design' in plastics that emerged from Italy after the Second World War from firms such as Kartell (Sparke 1988).

This search for authentic 'plastic as plastic' design that would fix this fluid material into a repertoire of forms that were authentic to it had been going on since the 1950s. Meikle quotes the editor of *Industrial Design*, Jane Fiske Mitarachi, in a 1956 special issue on plastics saying that quality could only be 'designed into plastics by a frank exploitation of the things that make plastics unique' (Meikle 1995: 194).[5] The same moment produced an equivalent debate in the United Kingdom, evident in the February 1958 issue of *Ideal Home*. This appeared with a special extra 'practical guide' to plastics, its editorial engaging directly with plastics' double nature, advanced and at the same time possibly 'counterfeit, rather phoney' (*Ideal Homes and Gardens* 1958). On both sides of the Atlantic then, commentators were troubled by plastics' lack of an identity and strove to construct one.

These efforts were linked to the material's imitative origins, imitation that could be seen as a fraud against those whose social position had previously given them a 'natural' – economic – monopoly on the materials that plastics imitated. The commentary drew on a well-established rhetoric of material authenticity that derives from the writing of Ruskin, Morris and Pugin, giving imitative plastics an aesthetic association with a lack of social and physical authenticity. This challenge to an apparently natural social ordering by plastic's inauthentic dissembling existed in parallel to another established perception of them based on more metaphysical premises – they are unnatural because they are made, rather than given by nature, impure because of their origin in human reason. This theme is found up to the present in debates about materials, in which appeals to the significance of human interaction with material that is given, rather than made, have been challenged with reference to plastic.

This debate is evident in a dialogue about the concept of materiality, between Tim Ingold and Daniel Miller in 2007. The clearest differences between Miller's and Ingold's approaches centre on their discussion of particular materials, among them the plastics that make up phones. Miller (2007) criticizes Ingold's discussion of materiality for selecting only apparently natural materials (stone, wood, air) rather than more obviously 'cultural' ones, such as plastic, which he goes on to discuss in the context of mobile phones. In this, Miller could be accused of preserving the human/object, mind/matter distinction that elsewhere (2005) he states he wants to supersede by invoking these two categories of material: 'natural' and 'cultural'. In his argument, plastics are ontologically distinct from the type of materials Ingold discusses because they are 'of us', because they derive from human cognition. Plastics are made, but they are not 'things'. Plastic objects, like phones, are made of stuff, but this is stuff made out of precursor material. Plastic's origin challenges Miller's distinction, but it also breaks down on logical grounds, since to say 'that is a material' is a human act, which makes a particular relationship to matter and transforms that matter into material, whether it has acquired connotations of culture or of nature.

In a later discussion of the ecological relationship between materials and humans, Ingold stresses the significance of flows of matter – the 'leakiness' of both humans and materials – against the idea of the 'imprinting of culture on to brute material' (Ingold 2012: 438). With plastics this imprinting seems impossible since they are always already of culture. Their 'brutish' origins in oil, or latterly in biopolymers, are distant both conceptually and geographically and therefore do not signify in their identity. Plastics seem a rather good example of the 'historical' idea of materials that Ingold proposes in which 'matter is always an ongoing historicity' (ibid: 435), against the idea that there are fixed material properties and humanly understood material qualities. However, plasticity as conceived in this chapter perhaps adds a dimension to Ingold's resolution of material relations into the idea of ecology. Thinking about plasticity rather than plastics suggests that even in physical terms the materials are never 'a material', but a property or a set of potentials. As physical entities, they either pretend to be, or are taken for, other things when we encounter them in everyday settings, and they afford metaphorical plasticity, which can be mixed with or fashioned into the sense of self.

However, through their history, their identification with an inauthentic 'synthetic' origin has meant that plastics have gained a negative image. Consequently, from the 1930s, the American plastics industry made organized efforts to ensure a positive image for the materials, some of which have had a lasting engagement with design history, such as the Hagley Museum and Library at the original DuPont site in Wilmington, Delaware.[6] By 1978 the marketing section of the trade magazine *Plastics World* was describing a concerted public relations campaign by the plastics industry in the United States to rescue the reputation of 'chemicals', which had been 'the subject of attack by a generally misinformed public'. The campaign, by a consortium of manufacturers with the Society for the Plastics Industry (SPI)[7] was organized round the slogan, 'Without chemicals life would be impossible'. Its intention was to counter what Monsanto, one of the leading elements in the consortium, called 'chemophobia' (Fountas 1978).

Concerns about plastic's consequences for the environment and human health have seen the development of a negative view of it in public discourse, especially when plastic objects become visible waste (Frienkel 2011). This is identified at the extreme as 'plastiphobia' (Roberts 2010). As palpable materials, plastics have the capacity to both delight and disgust. The delight of modern consumption derives partly from the consumption of newness (Campbell 1992), and new plastics are new like no other material. The production process means that the significant investment of time and skill, and therefore money, required to make the peerless surfaces of mould tooling is reproduced perfectly on the surfaces of even cheap plastic objects. When they are old and worn, however, plastics have the capacity to disquiet us, and people may take steps to protect their plastic possessions through protective layers of more plastic (Fisher 2013a). This private concern for the ugliness that old plastics may bring to people's private spaces mirrors worries about their impact on the environment and, in particular, awareness of the plastic that ends up in the oceans.[8] This ranges from the identifiable detritus that is visible on beaches, smaller pieces of which are eaten by fish and birds and may kill them by blocking their gut, to tiny plastic beads that wash into the seas from plastic feed-stock spills and can be found in beaches all over the world along with the plastic microbeads from cosmetics that start in our bathrooms and end up in the ocean (Gabrys 2013; Takada 2013).

Cultural plasticity

Plastics now reach far beyond their use in settings where people have encountered them in the past as palpable elements of our surroundings – large non-consumer markets exist for the materials. Although 39.4 per cent of the 47 million tons used in 2011 went into packaging, 8.3 per cent into automotive and 5.4 per cent into electrical and electronic goods, the remaining 20.5 per cent was used in construction and 26.4 per cent in other applications, including agriculture (Plastics Europe et al. 2012). Nearly 50 per cent of plastics used in the EU therefore are either actually invisible – part of buildings or buried in the ground – or remain in the sphere of production rather than consumption. Along with plastics' relative lack of visibility in engineering, building and agriculture, they have become mobile in two senses. They make up the 'plastic soup'[9] circulating in the biosphere (Davison and Asch 2011; Foekema et al. 2013; Marks 2008), and some polymers can now have 'smart' properties that mean they react to their setting – they respond to stimuli from their environment. An everyday example of this is packaging that decomposes, but there are also many applications of this principle in medicine, for instance, targeting drug delivery (Galaev and Mattaesson 1999).

This diffusion and mobility coincides with the immaterial presence outlined above; a sense of plasticity that plays on the meanings the materials have accrued in the past and takes them in new directions. The 'sticky web of connections' that the materials have to us, to the environment, to our ideas about nature and culture leave a particularly curious imprint in contemporary plastic pop-culture manifestations. Here, plastics' identity is unruly, drawing from the chemophobic suspicion about the materials that has accompanied their ubiquity as well our dependence on them in everyday life. Embracing this identity has become a marker with which to fashion cultural opposition or at least critique.

Views of plastics that were built on an assumption of their lack of authenticity began to appear in public discourse in the late 1960s. Meikle notes that they cluster 'round the obscure reference to plastics in the film *The Graduate* (1997: 3, 259). The materials have appeared in everyday discourse and commentary ever since, but now often seem to be related to somewhat ironic critique, which in turn serves to construct an equivocal view of them that mirrors the love-hate relationship with plastics that is familiar in many aspects of contemporary life. Collective demonization of the plastic bag does not affect the desire for new goods. This ironic and critical stance is evident in social media.

A 2014 search of Facebook groups turns up 122 musician pages with titles that include the word 'plastic', all the way from *A Plastic Rose* to *Wrapped in*

Plastic, via Plastic Babies, Plastic Noise Experience, The Plastic People of the Universe and, of course, the Plastic Ono Band. It is hard to be certain precisely how 'plastic' is being used in each of these examples, but extending from their genealogical relationship to the Plastic Ono Band, it seems safe to assume that in all cases the word indicates a connection to the texture and aesthetics of contemporary consumption experiences. This was an explicit part of the rhetoric of the Plastic Ono Band in 1968 and in some cases is suggested through an association with a particular plastic object:

> A Plastic Rose, Plastic Animals, Plastic Bag Boyz, Plastic Dinosaurs, Plastic Flowers, Plastic Garden, Plastic Glasses, Plastic Handles, Plastic Harmonicas, Plastic Horse, Plastic Kasket, Plastic Mermaids, Plastic Panda, Plastic Rhino, Plastic Soldiers, Plastic Teeth, Plastic Toys, Plastic Tree

Plastic toys are particularly telling in this connection, given the materials' strong association with childhood – from early in its history. Yarsley and Couzens emphasized an association between plastics' qualities and childish delight in the life of 'plastic man' (1941: 154), and toys have become a defining element in contemporary 'plastic culture'. Indeed, *Plastic Culture* is the title of a recent book that reviews the genre of (mostly plastic) post-Second World War Japanese character toys that generates avid interest among collectors (Phoenix 2006). The impact of globalized production and consumption on the environment seems to hit the news particularly forcefully when the detritus at issue has recognizable form, particularly so if it is in the form of toys. The cargo load of plastic bath ducks that circumnavigated the earth is one example. Another is the container load of Lego that spilled off Cornwall over a decade ago and is still found on the beaches there.[10] Toys were famously the subject of some of Roland Barthes' musings on plastics – the problem of authenticity seemed to him particularly acute when the formative experiences of childhood were overlain with the asso-ciations of artificiality that he read out of the material (Barthes 1972: 54).

The immaterial plasticity that has resulted from the dissociation of the idea of plastic from its material foundation has a particular inflection in relation to fashion. Things have moved a long way from the 60s 'wet-look' fashion that Mary Quant called 'plastic as plastic' (Yarsley and Couzens 1968) and that depended on the material properties of PVC for that disturbingly skin-like but impossibly glossy surface. Alongside the use of 'plastic' as a signifier of an ironic stance on consumption that is evident in the names of the groups identified above, and which implies some critical detachment, it can also frequently be found used in an almost celebratory way, with perhaps an element of innocent mistranslation at times. Facebook contains a page called 'La Vie en Plastique', which has been made since 2012 by María José Ossandón, a Chilean woman, to accompany her blog of the same name.[11]

In her blog, she shares her impressions of life as a fashionable young woman, particularly tips on where to get cosmetics, as well as recipes – and there are the pictures of foods and travel that are a conventional feature of this genre of social media. However, La Vie en Plastique is distinctive in its clear connection between the concept of plastic and the richly sensual aspects of life that go along with cosmetics, clothes, travel and food as Maria experiences them. She is 'in plastic' in these decorative and sensual artefacts and the experiences through which she constructs herself as a fashionable person. 'La Vie en Plastique' is part of the fashion blogging phenomenon that Rocamora (2011) describes as a 'technology of the self' and 'a privileged space of identity construction' (p. 410) through which individuals can both reflect as in a mirror and project their sense of style to the world. Crucially for this discussion, this phenomenon is played out in a strongly visual medium, mediated by the type of ubiquitous screen that 'shows the present', as Manovich put it (2001: 99–103).

The blogs that Rocamora discusses are in the fashion system, but they disturb the production/ consumption distinction – they contradict the collective selection that Blumer (1969) identified in the process through which fashions have emerged in the past. They can be a way for nobodies to become renowned characters on the fashion stage, so they fall perhaps on the side of production. But they have strong relationships to consumption blogs too, ones like 'La Vie en Plastique', which are not just about clothes but serve to fashion the self through the fluid, plastic resources available. However, out-and-out fashion blogs, filled with images of clothes and accessories, are also not immune from the power of the metaphor of plasticity. One of the more famous fashion bloggers who Rocamora discusses, 'Susie Bubble', put up a page in May 2011 that she titled 'Plastic Candy'.[12] This is ostensibly to show off a pink plastic coat but her reflections on the page suggest it relates as much to the qualities of plasticity as to particular objects:

> For the past few weeks, whilst travelling around, I've been on a plastic candy wave. It's basically pastels coated in a glycerine-sticky-shiny sheen. It's a result of consuming too many unnatural food dyes in Japanese candy and American cereal.

Although the blog pictures are of sets of objects, not all of them clothes, which share the same sort of 'plasticky' colours, this narrative associates them unequivocally with the whole range of material properties that are characteristic of plastics. Here is the association of the materials with 'un-nature' in their origins and the sense that this compromises our bodies, though we desire them and consume them willingly. Here is the association of tasteless tackiness with the impossibly perfect gloss of new plastics – seductive, but slimy and viscous, so potentially disgusting (Sartre 1957). Recent research has shown that it is not just fashionistas who associate these qualities with plasticity. Marie Hebrok and Ingun Klepp (2014) have shown these colours to be generally associated with synthetic fabrics, and therefore with plastic.

It seems clear that what Susie Bubble and María José Ossandón are doing with this immaterial plasticity, what they are the fashioning with it, relates closely to their being in the world, to their self-concept and to the fashioned self that they project through their blogs. It is tempting to draw a parallel between the move from indeterminate to determinate form in the production of plastic goods, and this construction of modern subjectivities relevant to the material texture of the times (Berman 1982; Giddens 1991). Susie Bubble and María José Ossandón are self-consciously making themselves and the 'made' character of plastics underlines that self-consciousness.

These fashion blogs, which are not isolated examples of manifestations of fashion that refer to plastics,[13] resonate with the strong historical association that plastic materials have had to modernity. Just as the consumer culture of the period after the Second World War embraced plastic materials as signifiers of progressive modernity, the wide-eyed (perhaps false?) innocence projected in fashion blogs suggests a new strategy for being 'of the times' by being 'of plastic', embracing a plasticity. There is a sense that plasticity affords more than simply being a signifier of modernity. This is plasticity as production, plasticity as synthesis – these are individuals making, fashioning themselves with the (plastic-like) materials that are at hand – making themselves plastic. Their fashioning goes in two directions: they both fashion themselves and, in the process, help to extend the idea of plasticity beyond plastic materials, into all the materials of consumption available to them.

The sense of the fashioning of worlds through the material and immaterial qualities of plasticity borrowed from plastics that is evident in these examples seem to give credence to Ezio Manzini's stress in the 1980s on the malleability of the materials' image, its physical reality deferred by the presence of technoscientific images of their structure (1989). However, the examples introduced above do not imply technical knowledge of plastic, but processes of living through plasticity. They also imply the materials' disappearance through their simultaneous invisibility and ubiquity, and their return in this diffuse but active sense of plasticity. For all the immateriality of this sense, it is clear that its material referent will persist far into the future, and we suspect that as Jody Roberts puts it about the materials: 'Their future is as much unwritten as our own. Together we are becoming plastic.' (2013: 130).

Conclusion

The circulation of both meaning and material in the 'more than human' relations of plastic outlined above seem a long way from the pragmatics and practicalities of polymer engineering, or the origins of the materials in craft practice. It blurs the distinction between production and consumption in the ironic play with the cultural dimensions of the materials that this immaterial plasticity supports. At the same time, this play supercedes the dualities that have grown up in ideas about the materials. Plastics are not either glossy or drossy, cool or schlocky, delightful or disgusting, but they provide the material ground for a plasticity out of which individuals may fashion themselves, articulated with and perhaps critical of consumer culture. In this, they seem to be an example of material with which people think, along the lines that Ingold proposes (2012: 438).

Notes

1. *Saturday Live*, BBC Radio 4, 11 September 2014.
2. The chapter refers to a class of materials with quite different properties, 'plastics', as well as to the concept of 'plasticity', which is implied by the idea of a single material, 'plastic' – a convenient name for all those materials that have plasticity. The chapter draws out the relationship between the physical and cultural dimensions of that plasticity, concentrating on the latter.
3. The word also indicates a property of metals that can undergo 'plastic deformation', where their matter is pushed from one shape to another when cold, as well as all materials that can be formed by casting in a liquid state.
4. <http://www.etymonline.com/index>.
5. Meikle quotes from Jane Fiske Mitarachi, 'Plastics and the Question of Quality', *Industrial Design* (June 1956): 64–67.
6. The Hagley Museum and Library was endowed by the DuPont company in 1972, holding the DuPont archive. It is now a centre for the study of American business history.
7. The Society for the Plastics Industry (SPI) is an industry wide association that was set up in 1937 to represent the interests of the American plastics industry (Meikle 1995: 102).
8. A Google search for 'plastic in the ocean' in June 2014 produced 74,400,000 results.
9. http://plasticsoupfoundation.org/eng/ (accessed 25 April 2014).
10. <http://www.dailymail.co.uk/news/article-2699930/Lego-washed-Cornish-beach-17-years-container-filled-plastic-bricks-fell-sea-ship-hit-freak-wave.html#ixzz38Yt48A6X>.
11. María José Ossandón has given permission to refer in detail to her web presence in this chapter.
12. http://www.stylebubble.co.uk/style_bubble/2014/05/plastic-candy.html.
13. María's and Susie's pages are not the only social networking manifestation of this plastic fashioning. The global context revealed by Facebook shows that the concept of plasticity

resonates strongly in fashion-culture. 'Plastic Tinkerbell' is a page put up by a Hungarian woman, also sharing make-up and fashion tips. 'Plastic People', as well as being a night club in fashionable Shoreditch, is a song from 2008 by Le Peuple de L'herbe, which is a critique of consumer capitalism along the same lines as Malvina Reynolds' 1962 'Little Boxes'. This milieu is the contemporary equivalent of the cultural background against which the fashion designers that Blumer studied worked, and it has a strong connection to clothes fashion. Plastic People is also a vintage clothes shop in Tenerife and a range of t-shirts hand printed in New York. Plastic Passion is a rather arty shoe shop in Genoa. Although there seems to be nothing particularly plastic-y about its merchandise, the name reinforces the sense that plasticity is a relevant element in European fashion culture. As with María José Ossandón's web presence, there is a sense that an element of mis-translation may be present, or perhaps these slightly puzzling inflections on 'plastic' are evidence of new dimensions to the fashioning that it can afford. This may be the case with another Italian fashion retail shop called Plastic Pordenone in an unremarkable shopping mall in Pordenone, a small town near Venice. The shop sign actually reads 'Virus + Plastic', adding the idea of viral fashion to the sense of antiseptic, but cultured, alchemy that comes along with 'plasticity', both material and immaterial.

References

Appadurai, A. (1988), *The Social Life of Things: Commodities in Cultural Perspective*. Cambridge: Cambridge University Press.

Barthes, R. (1972), *Mythologies*. New York: Hill and Wang.

Blumer, H. (1969), 'Fashion: From Class Differentiation to Collective Selection', *Sociological Quarterly*, 10(3): 275–291.

Campbell, C. (1992), 'The Desire for the New: Its Nature and Social Location as Presented in Theories of Fashion and Modern Consumerism', in R. Silverstone and E. Hirsch (eds), *Consuming Technologies*, pp. 48–64. London: Routledge.

Davison, P. and R. Asch (2011), 'Plastic Ingestion by Mesopelagic Fishes in the North Pacific Subtropical Gyre', *Marine Ecology Progress Series*, 432: 173–180.

Entwistle, J. (2000), *The Fashioned Body: Fashion, Dress and Modern Social Theory*. London: Polity Press.

Fisher, T. (2004), 'What We Touch Touches Us: Materials, Affects and Affordance', *Design Issues*, 20(4): 20–31.

Fisher, T. (2012), 'Hoarding, Reusing and Disposing: The Home as a Repository for Transient Objects', in L. McAtackney and B. Fortenberry (eds) *Studies in Contemporary and Historical Archaeology in Theory* 8: *Modern Materials: Proceedings of CHAT Oxford 2009:* BAR International Series 2363, pp. 51–59, Oxford: Archaeopress, ISBN 978 1 4073 0950 7, from the event 'Modern Materials: The Archaeology of Things from the Early Modern, Modern and Contemporary World', Keble College Oxford, 16th–18th October.

Fisher, T. (2013a), 'The Death and Life of Plastic Surfaces: Mobile Phones', in J. Gabrys, G. Hawkins and M. Michael (eds), *Accumulation: The Material Politics of Plastic*, pp. 107–120. London: Routledge.

Fisher, T. (2013b), 'A World of Colour and Bright Shining Surfaces: Experiences of Plastics after the Second World War', in T. Fisher and N. Maffei (eds), 'Shininess: Bringing Meaning to Light in Design', *Journal of Design History*, 26(3): 285–303.

Foekema, E. M., C. De Gruijter, M. T. Mergia, J. A. van Franeker, A. J. Murk and A. A. Koelmans (2013), 'Plastic in North Sea Fish', *Environmental Science and Technology*, 47(15): 8818–8824.

Fountas, N. (1978), 'Tired of the Flak, The Industry Talks Back', *Plastics World*, December 1978: 39–41.

Freinkel, S. (2011), *Plastic: A Toxic Love Story*. Boston, MA: Houghton Mifflin Harcourt.

Gabrys, J. (2013), 'Plastic and the Work of the Biodegradable', in J. Gabrys, G. Hawkins and M. Michael (eds), *Accumulation: The Material Politics of Plastic*, pp. 208–228. London: Routledge.

Galaev, I. Y. and B. Mattaesson (1999), '"Smart" Polymers and What They Could Do in Biotechnology and Medicine', *Trends in Biotechnology*, 17(8): 335–340.

Giddens, A. (1991), *Modernity and Self-Identity: Self and Society in the Late Modern Age*. London: Polity.

Ginsberg, A. D., J. Calvert, P. Schyfter, A. Elfick and D. Endy (2014), *Synthetic Aesthetics: Investigating Synthetic Biology's Designs on Nature*. Cambridge, MA: MIT Press.

Gloag, J. (1943), 'The Influence of Plastics on Design', *Journal of the Royal Society of Arts*, 91: 462–470.

Gloag, J. (1945), *Plastics and Industrial Design*. London: George Allen Unwin.

Hawkins, G. (2001), 'Plastic Bags: Living with Rubbish', *International Journal of Cultural Studies*, 4(1): 5–23.

Hebrok, M. and I. Klepp (2014), 'Wool Is a Knitted Fabric That Itches, Isn't It?', *Critical Studies in Fashion and Beauty*, 5: 1.

Ideal Homes and Gardens (1958), 'Plastics in the Home', supplement to *Ideal Home*, February 1958, Vol. 77 (2).

Ingold, T. (2007), 'Materials against Materiality', *Archaeological Dialogues*, 14(1): 1–16.

Ingold, T. (2012), 'Towards an Ecology of Materials', *Annual Review of Anthropology*, 41: 427–442.

Katz, S. (1978), *Plastics Designs and Materials*. London: Studio Vista.

Katz, S. (1984), *Classic Plastics: From Bakelite to High Tech*. London: Thames and Hudson.

Katz, S. (1986), *Early Plastics*. Princes Risborough: Shire.

Loewy, R. (2002), *Never Leave Well Enough Alone*. Baltimore, MD: Johns Hopkins University Press.

Madonia, G. (2014), radio interview 'Saturday Live', BBC Radio 4, 11 October 2014.

Manzini, E. (1989), *The Material of Invention*. London: Design Council.

Marks, K. (2008), 'The World's Rubbish Dump: A Tip That Stretches from Hawaii to Japan', *The Independent*, 5 February 2008, available at: http://www.independent.co.uk/environment/green-living/the-worlds-rubbish-dump-a-tip-that-stretches-from-hawaii-to-japan-778016.html.

Meikle, J. L. (1995), *American Plastic: A Cultural History*. New Brunswick: Rutgers University Press.

Miller, D. (2005), 'Materiality: An Introduction', in D. Miller (ed.), *Materiality*, pp. 1–51. London: Duke University Press.

Miller, D. (2007), 'Stone Age or Plastic Age', *Archaeological Dialogues*, 14(1): 23–27.

Phoenix, W. (2006), *Plastic Culture*. Tokyo: Kodansha International.

Plastics Europe, European Plastics Converters (EuPC), European Plastics Recyclers (EuPR) & European Association of Plastics Recycling and Recovery Associations (EPro) (2012), *Plastics, The Facts 2012: An Analysis of European Plastics Production Demand and Waste Data for 2011*, Brussels: Plastics Europe, available at http://www.plasticseurope.org/documents/document/20121120170458-final_plasticsthefacts_nov2012_En_web_resolution.pdf, (accessed 15 October 2014).

'Plastes' (1941), *Plastics in Industry*. London: Chapman Hall.

Roberts, J. (2013), 'Reflections of an Unrepentant Plastiphobe: An Essay on Plasticity and the STS Life', in J. Gabrys, G. Hawkins and M. Michael (eds), *Accumulation: The Material Politics of Plastic*, pp. 121–133. London: Routledge.

Rocamora, A. (2011), 'Personal Fashion Blogs: Screens and Mirrors in Digital Self Portraits', *Fashion Theory*, 15(4): 407–424.

Samuel, R. (1977), 'The Workshop of the World: Steam Power and Hand Technology in Mid-Victorian Britain', *The History Workshop Journal*, 3: 58–59.

Sartre, J.-P. (1957 [1943]), *Being and Nothingness: An Essay on Phenomenological Ontology*. London: Methuen.

Schaverien, A. (2006), *Horn: Its History and Its Uses*. Adele Schaverien.

Sparke, P. (1988), *Italian Design*. London: Thames and Hudson.

Takada, S. (2013), 'International Pellet Watch: Studies of the Magnitude and Spatial Variation of Chemical Risks Associated with Environmental Plastics', biodegradable' in J. Gabrys, G. Hawkins and M. Michael (eds), *Accumulation: The Material Politics of Plastic*, pp. 184–208. London: Routledge.

Thompson, R., S. Swan, C. Moore and F. von Saal (2009), 'Our Plastic Age', *Philosophical Transactions of the Royal Society B: Biological Sciences*, 364(1526): 1973–1976.

Webmoor T. and C. L. Witmore (2008), 'Things Are Us! a Commentary on Human/Things Relations Under the Banner of a "Social" Archaeology', *Norwegian Archaeological Review*, 41: 53–70.

Whatmore, S. (2006), 'Materialist Returns: Practicing Cultural Geography in and for a More-Than-Human World', *Cultural Geographies*, 13(4): 600–609.

Williams, R. (1974), 'On High and Popular Culture', *The New Republic*, 23 November 1974: 15.

Yarsley, V. E. and E. G. Couzens (1941), *Plastics*. Harmondsworth: Penguin.

Yarsley, V. E. and E. G. Couzens (1956), *Plastics in the Service of Man*. Harmondsworth: Penguin.

Yarsley, V. E. and E. G. Couzens (1968), *Plastics in the Modern World*. Harmondsworth: Penguin.

Chapter 8

Dressing God: Clothing as material of religious subjectivity in a Hindu group

Urmila Mohan

As part of a changing Indian 'religioscape' (Appadurai 1996), the International Society for Krishna Consciousness (ISKCON) has grown from its *Gaudiya Vaishnava*[1] roots in India to become an international, missionizing Hindu group. ISKCON's unique identity is based on universalizing the worship of the deity Krishna as a means of salvation and its membership includes people from different countries, cultures and ethnicities. Materials take on a specific cultural resonance in ISKCON since the earthly world is associated with a negative materialism and the sleep-like state of *maya* (illusion) that has to be transcended. However, there is also the seeming dichotomy that materials can be used to love and serve the deity, create suitable ritualistic experiences, and transform and improve one's self. As argued by Meyer et al. (2010: 210), there is no such thing as an 'immaterial religion' since beliefs are not just internal and cannot exist without the support of things, places, bodies and practices. In this chapter, I study deity clothing as a material of religious and devotional subjectivity in ISKCON's global headquarters in Mayapur, West Bengal, India,[2] and explore how deity dressmakers and priests manipulate materials to dress the deities, embody religious beliefs and pursue their devotional goals.

'Subjectivity' is a term loosely used to refer to the inner life of the subject and to the way subjects feel, respond and experience 'and, especially, their sense of self and self-world relations' (Luhrmann 2006: 345). We live in multiple registers including that of affective, embodied intensity and of symbolic mediation and discursive elaboration. I argue in this chapter that religious subjectivity can be related to intersubjectivity and sociality through a productive intertwining with materiality, phenomenology, praxeology and cognitive studies. Merleau-Ponty's theory of subjectivity (2002) is grounded in the feeling body and its interaction with the world and others, and allows us to combine the 'lived' body with the 'acting' body with action as the basis of engagement with the world. Warnier (2001: 9–10) argues that such actions involve sensori-motor processes that combine two types of knowledge, embodied procedural and verbalized discursive, to help incorporate materials deep into the psyche of the subject and influence subjectivity. Combining these insights, I use deity clothing to explore ISKCON as a community of religious practice, that is, not just as the production of clothing artefacts but the 'learning of values and norms through participation in socio-cultural practices' (Naji and Douny 2009: 420).

The body as religious material

Devotees liken the process of 'Krishna Consciousness' to an awakening of a dormant relationship with Krishna through *bhakti* (devotion). *Bhakti* as *murti-seva* (serving the deity image) is the worship of pictures, statues or objects that embody the deity. It is aligned with notions of service (*seva*) and duty or moral order (*dharma*), and ultimately to love (*prema*). Daily temple worship in Mayapur consists of caring for these *murtis* as one would care for the deity were they personally present. The needs of the deities are seen to throughout the day (Figure 8.1). They are awakened from sleep, offered greetings, bathed, fed, dressed, fanned, praised, given naps and at the end of the day put to bed. In this highly embodied, intersubjective relationship, the deity is a person with a body and is cared for by the bodies of devotees. Remedial purificatory rituals place human bodies in the right mode to receive and worship God and so devotees follow the four regulatory principles of abstinence from meat, intoxication, gambling and non-procreative sex. Devotees also engage their senses in Krishna's glorification and service. This includes consuming *prasad* or transubstantiated food that was formerly offered to the deity, the congregational chanting and dancing of *sankirtan* and the mutually embodied gaze of deity-devotee in *darshan*.

It is generally agreed that the human body in Hinduism is transformed by transactions of giving and receiving, touching and eating and ensuing prohibitions (Holdrege 1998; Marriott 1990; Pinard 1991). As I observed during my fieldwork, this extends to cases where physical contact is not involved such as the concept of association, that is, being in the vicinity of somebody or something. One would wish to associate with an object, person or event that is sanctified and/or sanctifying, and it is worth noting that the Sanskrit word for rites of passage (*samskara*) also connotes reformation through the gathering of

Figure 8.1 Priests greeting deities in the morning with mirror and perfume, Mayapur, 2013. Photograph by Urmila Mohan.

mental impressions. This implies that transformative substances are transferred across physical boundaries even when direct contact does not take place. Drazin states in the Preface (p. xxvi) that 'the term *substance* particularly tends to be used for material when a material is in dialogue with the notion of *form*' (emphasis in original). If one accepts that the body is material then perhaps the most striking example of this is the conduction of substance through sight in *darshan*. *Darshan* in the temple is an exchange of perspectives between devotee and deity that involves an intersensory visual, tactile and olfactory empathy (Babb 1981; Eck 1985; McHugh 2007). In the context of sight, *darshan* harkens back to an extromissive theory where visual rays from the viewer's eye touch the object creating an intensity that cannot be replicated in contemporary theories of vision and aesthetics. *Darshan* is as much about seeing as being seen, and visuality is not just a physical but spiritually efficacious process. Hence, seeing the deities is a transformative experience and materials operate as substances that can mediate between the boundaries of human bodies and artefacts. Against this backdrop, how does cloth facilitate an appropriate mood of worship in a temple that will be both efficacious and satisfying for deity and devotee?

Darshan in the Mayapur temple

Life for devotees in Mayapur revolves around the physically unassuming but spiritually potent Chandrodaya temple and a daily routine of attending *aratis* (receptions for the deities) in the temple. Everyday a minimum of 1,000 pilgrims visit the temple and this number swells to 10,000 for major festivals. *Murti-seva* in the temple is based partly on the practices of the famous Jagannath temple in Puri in Eastern India and temples in the holy town of Vrindavan in Northern India. The deity images in Mayapur are of Radha-Madhava and the Astasakhis, and Panchatattva and Narasimha.[3] These *murtis* get new clothes at least three times in a year for the major festivals and have gathered a large wardrobe over time. 'ISKCON style' garments that are colourful and ornate are changed twice a day with the 'night dress' being seen at the early morning *mangala arati* and the 'day dress' being seen at the morning *darshan arati* (the word 'dress' does not have a feminine connotation and is here used to refer to the garments of both male and female deities). The deities Krishna and his female consort Radha are depicted in their *kishori* or youthful form. Krishna is a cowherd boy or *gopa* with *tribhanga* (bent in three places) dancing posture. He is dressed in a *dhoti* (a long loincloth) and a *chador* (shawl) with his signature peacock feather and flute. Radha is a milkmaid or *gopi* and is dressed in an outfit of *lehenga* (skirt), *choli* (blouse) and *dupatta* (veil). They are approached in the temple through the mood of awe and reverence expressed and embodied through material opulence. The emphasis on opulence underscores the rule-governed mode of worship (*vaidhi*) that the founder Prabhupada considered appropriate for his foreign disciples and can be observed in the ornamentation and worship of the deities.

One of the goals of deity clothing is to create an inspirational *darshanic* experience for the congregation. A senior *pujari* or priest in the temple defines an effective *darshan* as one where:

> You feel some relationship with Krishna. Because we are a preaching move-ment we want to inspire the pilgrims when they come to Mayapur. We try and create this festival mood so that they can come here and leave all their material worries, and rise above their consciousness. The temple president told me to work up to a standard of worship and *darshan* so that the pilgrims on seeing the beauty of the deity and the decorations will faint!

If it holds true that a social project that is not imposed through force alone must be 'affective' in order to be effective (Mazzarella 2009) then one could argue that the materiality of *darshan* is part of 'affect management'; that deity clothing is part of the ritual coordination of affect. Referring to the aesthetics of *bhakti* in the

Northern Indian 'Pushtimargi' sect, Jain (2007: 260) contrasts the 'sensualized libidinal involvement with the icon' to post-Enlightenment aesthetics 'predicated on an autonomous subject that has self-critically distanced itself from its sensory passions, desires, and affects, even as sensual apprehension is acknowledged as their basis'.

Dressmakers and priests who conduct the deity dressing on the altar help evoke an appropriate mood in the temple that is enjoyed by the deity and the congregation. Krishna is *Rasa Raj* or the relisher of different *rasas*, where the Indian aesthetic concept of *rasa* describes a flavourful essence or the relish of a particular experience or interaction (Schwartz 2004: 7–10). In a performative context, *rasa* belongs to the phenomenological level of human existence, but in a religious context *rasa* is also related to concepts of spirituality and transcendence. Visitors may not exactly 'faint' when they take *darshan* in the temple, but they are certainly affected by the beauty and presence of the deities and consider them *sakshath bhagwan* (God manifested). The spectacle of priestly attendance, *abhishek* (the bathing of the deity in different substances) and sumptuous *bhogs* (food offerings) for the deities, help create a mood of opulence. Such a high worship standard is believed to please the deities and make them more receptive, and devotees will use words such as 'merciful', 'responsive', and 'active' when referring to the deities in Mayapur. Whether through garments, facial decoration or altar decoration, dressing helps to elicit these different moods and efficacious responses.

Making and materializing devotional attitudes

I now proceed to two sites of clothing-related activities that could be described as situated behind the altar curtain. These are the Chandrodaya temple's sewing department where deity garments are produced and the Mayapur Academy classroom where priests are trained. Clothing is innovated by lay devotees in the temple's sewing and embroidery rooms while celibate priests conduct the dressing of deities on the altar. Dressing includes garments, ornaments, flower and leaf garlands, decorative painting and ritual applications of substances.

Mayapur Academy: Learning to take things personally

The Mayapur Academy is a school on the ISKCON campus where students are taught how to worship the deity through ritual offerings, cooking and dressing. Jayananda,[4] a senior devotee, was teaching a course on deity dressing that covered the essential elements over a period of two weeks. Most of the students were young men dressed in saffron robes that mark them as celibates or *brahmacharis*. They were taking this course to learn how to dress the deities and construct ornamental turbans for Krishna, all part of the signature 'ISKCON style' that devotees have come to expect when they attend temple services. On a table at the head of the classroom was a black mannequin bust of Krishna with wide eyes and a playful smile. Next to it was a large stone, a tray of decorative turban pieces, some golden beaded chains, a small box of straight pins and a few colourful fabrics.

Jayananda summarized the fundamentals of dressing on the whiteboard. 'Being personal' was the first precept followed by time management, artistic theory and techniques, and it referred to the belief that Krishna in his deity form is a person with senses. He followed this with a list of the senses and how each one could be used to delight Krishna. Under the sense of touch, the words 'oil massage' and 'pin=pain' were contrasted to denote pleasing and disturbing sensory experiences. The students then engaged in a turban-building exercise (Figure 8.2) around the concept of 'pin=pain'. They took long strips of foam and separated into pairs of two. One student wrapped the foam around the

Figure 8.2 Students practising turban construction, Mayapur Academy, 2012. Photograph by Urmila Mohan.

other's head and then pinned it in place using a long, straight pin. After about 10 minutes of this exercise and much laughter, Jayananda pointed out that the right technique is to insert the pin by placing one's finger under the foam strip as a barrier between the pin and the head. Jayananda further dramatized the 'P(A) IN' technique by picking up a large stone from the table and trying to push pins into it. The students concurred that an ordinary stone did not feel pain but that the deity form should be treated as-if it felt pain.

As the course progressed over the next two weeks, I along with the Bengali students learned that many details were involved in presenting the deities as 'opulent' as well as 'approachable' (Figure 8.3). While much of the richness of the garments was in their colour and embroidery, Jayananda taught the students how to enhance these using jewellery and drapery. Krishna's dancing form was animated through flowing fabrics, flower garlands and bead necklaces. The asymmetrical style of Krishna's posture, turban and dress was deemed to complement the symmetrical modesty of his consort Radha's posture and garments. Jayananda informed the class that 'Krishna's dress is more daring, confident and bold just like the single peacock feather in his turban. He is engaged but his mood is also relaxed.' Radha's symmetry created a feeling of stiffness and distance and so she had to be dressed to seem more

Figure 8.3 Student dressing mannequins of Krishna and Radha, Mayapur Academy, 2012. Photograph by Urmila Mohan.

approachable, He reminded students to enhance the *darshanic* emphasis on the gaze: 'The connection is with the eyes. If you don't bring out the sweetness of the eyes you don't have the connection!'

While emphasizing the intimacy of the gaze in *darshan*, Jayananda added that opulent dressing was needed both for Krishna's pleasure and to ensure that devotees maintain an appropriate relationship with the deity. A few days later, I waited till the students had left the classroom and pursued this line of enquiry with him. He responded with an example:

> There is one deity in ISKCON Germany whose ankle bells they (the priests outside) could hear. When they opened the altar they found the garlands between Krishna's legs. We cannot similarly dress Krishna with a garland between his feet so that he looks like he is dancing. We shouldn't pretend that there is an intimate relationship between us and him and shouldn't act as if we have it.

I asked him if the deities are material and he responded vehemently:

> No, they are not material! That's the thing. Krishna can do anything. He can take a form of stone but it is not stone. There are stories where deities have walked or come down to a *pujari*'s level because he was too old to reach him . . . the *murti* that we perceive with our material eyes is Krishna.

In Hindu worship of *murtis*, the process of ornamenting the deities is called *alankara,* which in Sanskrit means 'to make sufficient or strengthen, to make adequate' (Dehejia 2009). For Jayananda, *alankara* as opulence strengthened the deity (and the faith) by reinforcing worship as 'awe and reverence' and by creating a suitable distance between deity and devotee:

> It's about understanding that Krishna has senses and doing things so that we don't cause him inconvenience. It's not like Krishna is my friend and he will understand if it's five minutes late. No, that's not good. So when we stress that you shouldn't put pins into Krishna we mean it. I fail anybody who does it automatically, no matter how well they dressed the deity. Because that means that they have not understood that Krishna is a person.

The comment that a student was failed for putting pins into Krishna underscored that the Academy was a place where students would be assessed and sent away with grades and printed diplomas. It also indicates how ISKCON has responded to global expansion by regulating worship culture through standardized instruction. However, what is relevant to my analysis is not the rubric of formal evaluations but how sensations and emotions are used as embodied experience and knowledge. As stated earlier 'making' and 'doing' are ways of knowing. The P(A)IN exercise combines knowledge gained through embodied procedural and verbalized discursive means (Warnier 2007: 9), and helps develop a relationship between the object and subject. I suggest that the P(A)IN exercise is an act of empathy and emotional resonance between students that is then transferred to the artefact (in this case the deity) and sustained by a host of other phenomena such as sensations, emotions, verbalized and written instruction, dreams, etc., all of which come under the umbrella of 'religious experience'. The neuroscientist Gallese (2001: 46) considers emotions as one of the ways to acquire knowledge. He analyses the phenomenon of empathy through the neural matching mechanism of mirror neurons and 'as-if' body loops where emotions are neural but also triggered by observing others. In this model, emotions and actions are strongly related and sensoriality is connected to the deeper sub-personal levels of the mind. Combining Warnier's notion of an agentive subject supported by materials and Gallese's work on empathy, I argue that the P(A)IN exercise created a personal relationship between the student-devotee and the deity by facilitating an empathy and intersubjectivity that would be repeatedly enacted and developed as the course progressed.

In the sewing room: Making and doing a philosophy of materials

Deity garments for the day are highly ornate and are hand-embroidered by artisans who work only for the temple. The night dresses are simpler and are generally made from decorative fabrics to save on time and expense. The sewing room for the night dresses has a large worktable for measuring and cutting fabric (Figure 8.4), an area for storing clothing, some shelves for supplies and a small washing up area. Since I participated in many celebrations, I was able to observe dressmaking in this sewing room as a community of practice for devotees, especially women and children. Madhavi was a senior devotee who had worked in the sewing room on numerous night outfits. I asked her how she became a dressmaker and a priest:

> In my day it kind of happened automatically. You lived in the temple and you learnt on the job. You begin with doing the deity backup service by washing the brass, washing the dishes, washing and ironing the towels and handkerchiefs, washing the *arati* paraphernalia, ironing the deities clothes if they needed it. So while you are ironing the clothes or when you are helping to sew the clothes you start to understand how they go together. So by doing the backup service you start to learn. It's like an apprenticeship in a way.

Figure 8.4 Women and children working in the sewing room, Mayapur, 2012. Photograph by Urmila Mohan.

Madhavi was convinced that serving the deities had attached her to Krishna:

> Being a *pujari* just grounded me in Krishna Consciousness. I don't think I would have stuck with this if I hadn't been doing service. I know that I would definitely respect the philosophy but I don't know if I would have been as involved for so long if I didn't have the service. It has been forty years now. Now I engage others and pass it on to them.

Madhavi had a special ability to mentor young devotees and would create festival-related projects for children and teenagers. Her practical 'roll-your-sleeves-up' approach towards any new project was beneficial for my research since I was welcomed into the sewing room as an extra pair of hands that could be pressed into service. I would often interview her while she was working on her 30-year-old Swiss 'Elna' sewing machine. During one such conversation she described how doing was transformed into true devotional service:

> We engage everything in service for Krishna till we are not just engaging what we like in Krishna's service but we are doing what Krishna wants us to do. It's a paradigm shift. You are going from what makes you happy to thinking 'What will make Krishna happy'?

I asked how they knew what pleased Krishna and Madhavi considered the question:

> Things can be done automatically and it may be beautiful but if you haven't done it with your heart then it may look materially beautiful but is Krishna pleased by it? Krishna doesn't want the activity! He doesn't want this ruffle, he doesn't want that blob of paint, he doesn't want that trim. He wants the consciousness that we do it with. Yet, it's not black and white. I can throw an outfit together and there's no heart in it for me. But then if somebody else offers this dress with such devotion – if Prabhupada offers it – then surely Krishna will accept. Even if you use something that isn't real like plastic pearls or glass rubies but if you offer it with great affection then it becomes real. Krishna accepts it as real!

The belief that something 'fake' can become 'real' through the sincere devotion of the devotee and the grace of the deity was intriguing since I also encountered less transcendental attitudes about materials. For example, flowers that had no scent or shoddily made trims and fabrics were evocatively termed '*karmi* materials' to express a larger ethos of deterioration. The term *karmi* commonly refers to non-devotees or materialists trapped in the worldly cycle of actions (*karma*) and reactions, causes and effects, and credits and debits. Devotees believe that since all their actions are channelled towards Krishna and salvation, they will be freed from the eternal cycle of birth and reincarnation (*samsara*). Yet, in my observation non-*karmi* and *karmi* worlds were difficult, if not impossible, to keep separate and materials constantly challenged devotees. Madhavi described one of her trips to the city of Kolkata:

> There is one *saree* shop selling *lehengas* with intricate embroidery work. They looked gorgeous but everything you touched just fell off. They were not made to last. It used to be that if you had a Benares brocade *saree* and if the silk was finished you could take it to a man who weighed it and gave you the money for the silver. So that way the wealth was sustainable if you like. It maintained some value. But now all the opulence is plastic, sequins and glass. You pay upwards of Rs 15,000 for a *saree* and the minute you buy it, it's completely worthless. So these are the changing values of the age of *kali* – everything has to be instant and as ostentatious as possible. Ostentatious is in your face. It's nouveau riche, people who have to prove themselves because they want to be part of the upper echelons of society. Whereas opulence is quiet, not always understated but regal. It's hard to describe it. It just looks classic . . . or classy. It doesn't look cheap.

Madhavi started by referring to poor quality materials in garments but then used them to critique the culture of 'in-your-face' ostentatious where speed and superficial glamour are more important. She invoked the concept of the age of *kali* when describing the degradation and devaluation of clothing materials. *Kali* is the present age in cyclical Hindu cosmology and represents the maximum loss of religio-moral order and wisdom in the world.[5] Madhavi related problems with materials to a general ethos of decline and people's desire for status without substance. Her views on materials were derived from a lifelong engagement with fabrics and used analytical categories of illusory ostentation versus real opulence. Here the mood of opulence was invoked through substantive fabrics with intrinsic value, such as the Benares silk *saree,* while ostentation was associated with garments that were garish, shoddy and had no lasting value.

On seeing the time and effort that went into making deity outfits, I became concerned about their maintenance. Madhavi lamented the fact that the silk outfits were damaged by heat and humidity, and envisioned a day when the deity's clothes would be cleaned and darned after every use. She used the theological concept of *gunas* or the three modes of material nature[6] – creation, destruction and maintenance – to articulate her distress:

> There is just no storage here. This is an example of the three modes of material nature. Passion is about creating, ignorance is about destruction and goodness is about maintenance. We are very good at making things, we are very good at leaving things to die but when it comes to looking after things we are very bad at it!

After multiple conversations with Madhavi, she summed up her views of materials and related it to the soteriological goal of Krishna Consciousness:

> So the main thing about material things is that they have no lasting power. They will all be taken away. If I have a diamond bracelet, it's easier to take off a diamond bracelet and give it than to have it ripped from my arm. So material attachments are like that. If we can give them up willingly then we can make so much advancement. But the family, the position, the fame – all such things will be taken away at the time of death. We don't really know where we are going to go in our next lives.

My conversations with Madhavi helped me move from the aesthetic implications of materials to a wider cosmology since she thought about how her dressmaking related to the practice of Krishna Consciousness. Many of Madhavi's views echoed theological concepts that I heard from other devotees but were also uniquely hers since they were viewed through the lens of her particular *seva*. She attributed her lifetime's association with ISKCON to her *pujari* work and hoped that her service would count for something. Simultaneously, she implied that materials are worthless since the attachments of material life are temporary.

From an anthropological perspective materialism is 'a culturally agreed-upon understanding of a mode of consumption that is generally regarded negatively' (Ger and Belk 1999: 184). ISKCON is rooted in both anti- and de-materialism, wherein 'pessimism about material existence is a criterion for spiritual advancement' (Goswami 2012: 100). One may regard this as a form of material 'blindness', but all cultures are to some extent de-materialized. A general marginalization of materials pervades our daily lives until the time that we have to deal with bodies that ache, cars that don't start or fabrics that wear out. As Warnier (2007: 292) states, if we were to be aware of every material engagement then we would be frozen into inaction. That 'it is precisely because they are so *essentially* obliterated and unobtrusive that material and bodily cultures are . . . so effective in reaching deep into the subjectivity of people' (emphasis in original).

Conclusion: Clothing as entry into devotion

Cloth's transformative capacity is enhanced by its ability to evoke cognitive and corporeal states such as opulence, protection and transience through actions of tying, pinning and wrapping as well as the various stages of production such as cutting, sewing, embroidering, and so on. The emotional and psychological valences of a garment's material aesthetics are created through the use of elements such as frontality, symmetry, colour, silhouette and adornment. Each of these elements through style can have specific sociocultural connotations and effects and shape intersubjectivity through the mediation of categories of interior and exterior, divine and human, and the subject and object. Through this case study, I propose that material-cum-bodily transformation is a useful paradigm to study how devotees live and engage with the world. The ontological transformation of materials and bodies through actions oriented towards divinity makes it possible for devotees to be sensorially/ materially engaged but also helps them separate from the 'material world'. Such a culture creates a specific challenge and opportunity for an ethnographer of materials and making. The altar curtain, for example, performs its function well and ensures that most devotees appreciate the deity spectacle without needing or desiring to know how it is done. To find a material entry point into spirituality, I had to go behind the altar curtain to explore sites of dressing and clothing production.

It is clear that devotional attitudes are embodied and expressed in the temple through materials such as cloth and that sociality, materiality and morality are co-produced by members of a community through practice. This is a morality that is dynamic and is acquired and transformed through interactions with bodies and artefacts. The body is both acting and acted upon, capable of transforming interactions and processes; matter is fluid and inhabitants of the world are malleable substances. I stated earlier that ISKCON is unique because it is a universalizing Hindu group with prominent visibility of non-Indian Hindus. This alone might make a case for the praxeological importance of materials where acceptance into a 'Hindu' community is no longer based on just inheriting the right substance through birth but also on acquiring it through practice. The idea that one can become an upper-caste Brahman through a complete mental and physical transformation is not just of soteriological relevance but of material import. For a community of *bhakti* or devotional love, the transformation is not just about purifying the devotee but also about forming a personal relationship with the deity through materials such as cloth.

I have argued for a materially embodied approach through a site-specific study of deity dressing practices since belief is not just about internal states or scriptural norms but is manifested and sustained by events, places and experiences. Combining a phenomenological approach with insights from materiality, praxeology and cognitive studies, I have explored how devotees form a personal relationship with the deity through their physical and mental engagement with materials, aesthetics and religious philosophy. In the Introduction to this volume, Drazin makes the point that an anthropology of materials 'explores moments of manifest transformation between form and substance and their sociocultural implications' (p. 27). What is being created through cloth is not just garments but the subjectivity of devotees whether they are dressmakers, students or congregation. A transformative world of materials makes it possible for devotees to live and relate to the deity 'as-if' they were in a transcendental space; the concept of as-if being not just an act of individual imagination but one of conceiving and sustaining relationships. I suggest that this relational, transformative quality is one of the key attributes of a material of religious subjectivity.

Notes

1. *Gaudiya Vaishnavism* or Bengali *Vaishnavism* traces its line from the fifteenth-century saint Chaitanya who is also considered an incarnation of Krishna. The term *Vaishnavism* refers to *Vaishnavas* or devotees of the Hindu deity Vishnu of whom Krishna is considered to be one incarnation.
2. The research for this chapter is based on one year of ethnographic fieldwork in the ISKCON temple in Mayapur, West Bengal, India. Fieldwork was partly funded by an India Travel Award from the Nehru Trust for the Indian Collections, Victoria and Albert Museum, London.

3. Astasakhi literally means the eight female friends and refers to the main *gopis,* or milkmaids, who serve the deities Radha and Krishna. Panchatattva refers to Chaitanya and his four associates. Narasimha is an incarnation of the Hindu god Vishnu as half-man and half-lion.
4. The names of people have been pseudonymized to protect their identity. Devotees generally have the last name Das if they are male and Dasi if they are female, both of which mean servant.
5. The four *yugas* or epochs in the macrocosmic Hindu theory of time and society are *krita, treta, dwapar* and *kali.* The *yugas* move in a cycle of repetition and progressive degeneration with the current age of *kali* representing the most chaos and loss of coherence.
6. The three modes of material nature or *gunas* refer to the qualities and properties that approximate the categories of *sattva* (truth), *tamas* (destruction) and *rajas* (creation). *Sattva guna* involves values of purity and balance and is the desired mode of life for devotees.

References

Appadurai, A. (1996), *Modernity at Large: Cultural Dimensions of Globalization.* Minnesota: University of Minnesota Press.
Babb, L. (1981), 'Glancing: Visual Interaction in Hinduism', *Journal of Anthropological Research*, 37(4): 387–401.
Dehejia, V. (2009), *The Body Adorned: Dissolving Boundaries between Sacred and Profane in India's Art.* New York: Columbia University Press.
Eck, D. (1985), *Darshan, Seeing the Divine Image in India.* Chambersburg: Anima Books.
Gallese, V. (2001), 'The "Shared Manifold" Hypothesis From Mirror Neurons To Empathy', *Journal of Consciousness Studies*, 8(5–7): 33–50.
Ger, G. and R. Belk (1999), 'Accounting for Materialism in Four Cultures', *Journal of Material Culture,* 4(2): 183–204.
Goswami, T. (2012), *A Living Theology of Krishna Bhakti: The Essential Teachings of A. C. Bhaktivedanta Swami Prabhupada.* New Delhi: Oxford University Press.
Holdrege, B. (1998), 'Body Connections: Hindu Discourses of the Body and the Study of Religion', *International Journal of Hindu Studies,* 2(3): 341–386.
Jain, K. (2007), *Gods in the Bazaar: The Economies of Indian Calendar Art.* Durham, NC: Duke University Press.
Lele, J. (ed.) (1981), *Tradition and Modernity in Bhakti Movements.* Leiden: E. J. Brill.
Luhrmann, T. M. (2006), 'Subjectivity', *Anthropological Theory*, 6(3): 345–361.
Marriott, M. (1990), 'Constructing an Indian Ethnosociology', in M. Marriott (ed.), *India Through Hindu Categories*, pp. 1–39. New Delhi: Sage.
Mazzarella, W. (2009), 'Affect: What Is It Good for?' in S. Dube (ed.), *Enchantments of Modernity: Empire, Nation, Globalization*, pp. 291–309. New Delhi and London: Routledge.
McHugh, J. (2007), 'The Classification of Smells and the Order of the Senses in Indian Religious Traditions', *Numen,* 54(4): 374–419.
Merleau-Ponty, M. (2002), *Phenomenology of Perception.* London: Routledge.
Meyer, B., D. Morgan, C. Paine and S. Brent Plate (2010), 'The Origin and Mission of Material Religion', *Religion*, 40: 207–211.
Naji, M. and L. Douny (2009), 'Editorial: Special Issue on "Making" and "Doing" the Material World', *Journal of Material Culture,* 14: 411–432.
Pinard, S. (1991), 'A Taste of India: On the Role of Gustation in the Hindu Sensorium', in D. Howes (ed.), *The Varieties of Sensory Experience,* pp. 221–230. Toronto: University of Toronto Press.

Schwartz, D. (2004), *Rasa: Performing the Divine in India.* New York: Columbia University Press.

Valpey, K. (2006), *Attending Krsna's Image: Caitanya Vaisnava Murti-seva as Devotional Truth.* London: Routledge.

Warnier, J. P. (2001), 'A Praxeological Approach to Subjectivation in a Material World', *Journal of Material Culture,* 6(1): 5–24.

Warnier, J. P. (2007), *The Pot-King: The Body and Technologies of Power.* Leiden: Brill.

Warnier, J. P. (2009), 'Technology as Efficacious Action on Objects . . . and Subjects', *Journal of Material Culture,* 14(4): 459–470.

Part 4

The subversion of form
by substance

Chapter 9

Introducing Fairtrade and Fairmined gold: An attempt to reconfigure the social identity of a substance

Peter Oakley

This chapter considers the multifaceted social identity of a particular substance[1] – gold – and how this identity is defended by groups, institutions and existing material culture in the face of challenges to its validity. This will be done through a case study of the rise and demise of a 'new material', Fairtrade and Fairmined (FT/FM) gold, created in an attempt to challenge the status quo. Campaigners' concerted attempts to increase the multivalence of gold and the results will be considered using the analytical tool of *complexity*, an approach that helps explain how specific masses of gold can be considered and treated as different yet identical.

While the focus here is a specific material, the story of FT/FM gold has much wider implications. It exposes how dominant abstract understandings of what a particular substance is, among the specialists who work with it on a daily basis and the wider population, are shielded by practices and assemblages of objects not created to be, or generally considered as, protective. It also shows how these interlock to form a pervasive network. While influence or agency is not equally distributed across this network, there is no single dominant source, a feature that helps frustrate attempts at change. The case study therefore offers a theoretical template for researchers encountering similar, potentially protective systems.

Fairtrade and Fairmined gold: From beginning to end

On 9 February 2011, the Fairtrade Foundation presented a new material to the UK's press. Hatton garden, London's jewellery manufacturing district, was chosen for the public launch of FT/FM gold by Fairtrade and the Association for

Responsible Mining (ARM), the two organizations behind the initiative. The event brought together a mixture of professional activists, representatives of small-scale miners, journalists, bloggers, managers, directors and jewellery designers and makers.

Among the presenters were celebrity jeweller Stephen Webster, Cristina Echavarria (secretary general of ARM) and Manuel Einoso Rivas (president of SONAMIPE, the Peruvian small-scale mining association). They all spoke passionately about the difference FT/FM gold would make to subsistence mining communities in Peru and elsewhere. The climax of the event was the unveiling of the first ingot of FT/FM gold ever made. The press launch was the culmination of a well-thought-out and executed publicity campaign. The event itself was timed so reporters' articles would coincide with Valentine's Day. The launch generated sympathetic coverage in the mainstream and trade media (e.g. BBC Radio 5 2011; Bishop 2011; Taylor 2011a; Valerio 2011). FT/FM gold appeared to have a bright future.

In autumn 2012, Fairtrade began a review of the FT/FM gold standard. The review was ostensibly to 'make adjustments to the existing standards using the experience gained since product first went on sale last year' (Taylor 2012). But the review took place in a climate of concern. Fairtrade had anticipated FT/FM gold could capture 5 per cent of the world's jewellery market over 15 years (Maldar 2011). The actual take-up was falling far short of projections. In addition, existing manufacturing licensees were voicing concerns about FT/FM regulations and the rising cost of premiums. Some even claimed the FT/FM system was fundamentally unsustainable in its current form.

Fairtrade and ARM had anticipated the supply of FT/FM gold would consolidate into a steady stream, but it remained stubbornly erratic. At the launch, Fairtrade claimed there would be at least 40kg of FT/FM gold available during the first year, but the first jewellers who signed up to the programme had to wait four months for any FT/FM gold to appear (Harriet Kelsall, quoted in *The Jeweller* 2011). FT/FM gold was also scarce during the run up to Christmas, so FT/FM products made no major inroads into the United Kingdom's jewellery market. During 2012, the campaign lost momentum in the United Kingdom, and the Peruvian and Columbian miners (who were now producing more certifiable gold) were faced with a lack of buyers.

On the 15 April 2013, the Fairtrade Foundation and ARM announced they were dissolving the FT/FM partnership. After 22 April, the two organizations would promote their certification programmes independently (and, it turned out, in competition against each other). Two years after its first appearance, FT/FM gold ceased to exist.

Researching Fairtrade gold

The author's first contact with the FT/FM gold initiative occurred during fieldwork for a research project on the United Kingdom's jewellery industry and its supply chains (involving gold refiners, fine jewellery manufacturers, distributors and retailers). From 2009 onwards, the project grew to include actively observing and interviewing professional campaigners and attending private campaign meetings, public events such as the press launch and debates on ethical gold sourcing held at jewellery trade shows.

The author also engaged in an unusual form of participant-observation. After having a series of articles on the ethics of gold sourcing published in a jewellery trade journal, he was repeatedly invited to give presentations and chair panels on ethical sourcing at industry events.

Alongside the fieldwork, the chapter relies on primary literature relating to the FT/FM gold campaign, gold trading and jewellery manufacturing and retailing. This includes UK jewellery trade journals, the campaign literature and internal reports produced by Fairtrade, ARM and other NGOs and global gold market surveys.

The fieldwork was conducted among elite groups: a techno-scientific elite, a managerial elite and professional social campaigners. The jewellery trade as a whole also behaves as an exclusive professional group. The methodological issues faced during the project were similar to those identified by other researchers (e.g. Gusterson 1997; McDowell 1998; Nader 1969; Rice 2010). Though a full discussion is beyond the scope of this chapter, it is worth noting that the author's previous employment as an analytical chemist and training as a jeweller repeatedly facilitated acceptance to these elites, but despite this the project still took four years of fieldwork to complete. The author's specialist expertise affected fieldwork in other ways; the observations of refining, assaying and manufacturing activities were undertaken from the position of an informed rather than naïve observer (cf. Laudel and Gläser 2007).

Though the fieldwork was undertaken among these elites, it is important to recognize that many of the products they created (objects, images, texts and regulatory systems) were meant for general consumption. The items of jewellery, promotional materials, campaign literature and FT/FM certification system were all intended to have widespread appeal and influence.

Their success therefore depended on them conforming to wider cultural expectations.

Using complexity

Fairtrade campaigners promoted FT/FM gold as a material distinct from all other gold. This was often expressed as a dualism: FT/FM gold versus 'dirty gold' (e.g. Maldar 2011; Valerio 2011, 2013). A reliance on these types of simplifications to describe the material world was criticized by Annemarie Mol and John Law in the introduction to their edited volume *Complexities* (Mol and Law 2002). Simplification's inherent reductionism, and its elision of whatever does not fit the preconceived schema, were considered by Mol and Law to impede an understanding of real situations. But how should we define complexity itself?

> There is complexity if things relate but don't add up. If events occur but not within the processes of linear time, and if phenomena share a space but cannot be mapped in terms of a single set of three-dimensional coordinates. (Mol and Law 2002: 1)

Complexity admits of disjunctions and partial overlaps, the inability to impose overarching order and what Marilyn Strathern (1991) termed 'partial connections'. Admitting complexity presents specific problems for researchers. The lack of a predetermined stable framework amplifies the issues inherent in all ethnographic research and traditional associated modes of dissemination. But complexity can be a key analytical tool, explaining how apparently unstable or irresolvable tensions can be maintained indefinitely within cultural frameworks.

Unpacking the complexity of gold

Gold is a magnificent exemplar of how a particular substance can develop and maintain a complex social identity, and how this influences and constrains the actions of actors it comes into contact with. Gold's social identity includes four key facets: elemental gold, noble gold, transcendent gold and gold-as-money. All of these share a space, namely the yellow, heavy, metallic stuff we call gold – though the extent to which each predominates at particular times depends on the perceptions of observers.

Gold as a scientific object: Elemental gold

Today, across the West, gold is considered a chemical element. This perspective is underpinned by the cultural dominance of the scientific definition of reality, in particular the discipline of chemistry as a way of 'knowing' matter (Schummer 2008). Elemental gold is characterized by apparently inherent physical properties. It is one of only two distinctly coloured metallic elements and is heavy, highly ductile and extremely malleable: a piece of gold can be stretched into wires as thin as a hair or hammered out into a sheet only a few microns thick. As gold has the lowest redox potential of any metallic element, gold objects exhibit outstanding resistance to corrosion. In reality all these scientific properties of elemental gold are comparative, expressed relative to other chemical elements or compounds. Even supposedly abstract properties, such as weight or redox potential, ultimately rest on this type of material comparison (see Busch 2011; Gooday 2004).

Elemental gold is morally neutral: its properties are undirected and merely exist as inherent and identifying features that are *observer-independent* (Searle 1995). Though they may be extreme or unusual, these properties do not make gold more or less special than any other chemical element.

Creating a mass of completely isolated elemental gold is a practical impossibility. Physically existing gold is always understood to contain atoms of other elements, though the majority of these can be removed by using a succession of metallurgical technologies (a process called refining). Determining the percentage of gold in comparison to other elements existing in any particular physical mass is achieved through specialist analytical technologies (a process called assaying).

The majority of gold bullion being offered for sale in the major gold markets has been refined to, and confirmed as containing, 99.99 per cent gold. This substance is colloquially called 'four nines gold' (Capano 2008). Through refining, assaying and the material produced as result of these activities are all conceptualized in terms of scientific principles, their history and current practice are closely intertwined with the demands and needs of trade and manufacturing. Four nines gold can therefore be considered a type of informed material, similar to the pharmaceutical compounds described by Barry (this volume).

Gold as the king of metals: Noble gold

The modern scientific belief that gold is fundamentally unchangeable usurped an older European cosmological belief that gold was the ultimate maturation of mineral matter, the end product of the gestation of metals in the earth (Dobbs 2008 [1975]; Eliade 1962 [1956]). Many late medieval and Renaissance alchemists understood the transmutation of base metals into gold as the speeding up of this natural process.

In contrast to the moral neutrality of modern chemical reactions, alchemical transmutation had strong spiritual connotations. The contemplation of transmutation was seen by many as a means of understanding the refinement or purification of the soul (Dobbs 2008 [1975]; Linden 2008 [1996]). For alchemists, gold's observable tendencies – resistance to decay or corruption by fire and refusal to mix with base or dross substances – were evidence of its elevated moral status.

Though alchemical cosmologies are no longer current, the notion that gold is somehow morally superior lingers. Commonly used English verbal analogies rely on a link between gold and desirable morals or perfection. People can be 'good as gold' or have 'a heart of gold'. The appealing visual ratio of 1:1.618 is called the 'golden ratio'. The scriptures also use gold as a metaphor for purity or moral elevation.

Gold as supernatural material: Transcendent gold

Gold can move beyond representing temporal nobility to become a materialization of divinity itself. Polished gold surfaces reflect the light as if the source exists inside the material, so burnished gold gives the appearance of being alive with a spiritual eminence (Clarke 1986; Schroder 2012). In addition, unlike other metals and all organic materials, gold does not decay, appearing to transcend the mortal world. Such incorruptibility is often considered a divine attribute (Cruz 1977).

These peculiar and visually enchanting properties have resulted in gold being the material of choice for representing spiritual space or creating objects with an overtly spiritual raison-d'etre (Bernstein 2004; Clifford 2012). The royal crown, communion chalice and wedding ring, as well as the golden palace or statue of Buddha, all play on gold's transcendence to support their status as sacred objects.

Transcendent gold can be considered an entirely alienated substance: its perception does not encompass any prior history to its existence in the encountered form, whether this be as an object or surface (as with gold leaf or gold mosaic tiles).

The price of gold: Economic gold

Gold's resistance to corrosion also supports a more prosaic aspect of its social identity: its role as a store of wealth. In addition to being durable, gold is portable and easily identified and quantified. It is scarce enough that a small amount can be used in direct trades, but common enough to be available for a good many trades. Gold can therefore become the key medium of exchange – gold can become money (Simmel 1978).

It was during the late nineteenth century that gold reached its apogee as a financial instrument. The comparability of the gold-based currencies of the Western imperial powers led to a financial system called the *gold standard* (Eichengreen 1985; Ferguson 2009 [2008]). The gold standard was replaced by fiat currencies during the 1920s, but the idea of gold-as-money clung on (Bernstein 2004; Green 1968, 1985 [1982]). When national and international regulations covering the personal ownership and the international transport of gold were relaxed in the 1980s, it led to a resurgence of gold hoarding by individuals (Bernstein 2004; O'Callaghan 1993).

Advocates have made repeated attempts to revive a role for gold in national and international finance (e.g. Lewis 2007). Despite their efforts, situations where gold can be used directly as a medium of exchange remain strictly limited. But though gold is no longer money in the strict legal sense, it still retains its place in the popular Western imagination as the ultimate store of wealth.

Adding more complexity: Immanence versus provenance

When an object is made of gold, any combination, or even all of these facets of gold's social identity can be in play simultaneously. A gold coin can be seen as an economic instrument, material evidence of the nobility (and sometimes divinity) of the ruler who had it minted and a mass of alloy with a specific ratio of gold atoms (Oakley 2013). Though these perceptions all draw on the same material features of gold, they cannot be collapsed into one another.

Despite the divergence of these perceptions, they are all essentially immanent: they exist at each and every point of contact and are open to independent reconfirmation at any moment. In contrast, FT/FM gold is constructed in terms of its circumstances of origin. This emphasis on selected aspects of the history of the constituent material – its *provenance* – adds another, irreducible dimension. Provenance is intangible. It cannot be determined by scientific assay, by direct observation or by financial appraisal, but only by trust in the authority that proclaims it.

Fair trade, Fairtrade and the ft/fm gold campaign

From fair trade to Fairtrade[tm] and corporate engagement

Concerns over how commodities[2] are sourced in the developing world are fundamental to the fair trade movement. The first fair trade networks were established by activists in Europe and the United States in order to help coffee farming cooperatives in Latin America circumvent the free trade market. They believed establishing direct connections between coffee growers in the Global South and coffee drinkers in the Global North would engender solidarity between producers and consumers (Bowes 2011; Luetchford 2008; Perla 2008).

The first fair trade networks were ad hoc, but as the movement grew it became increasingly necessary to regulate who was eligible to join fair trade supply chains (Renard 2005). In 1997 the marketing organizations across the Global North joined together to create an international certification body, the Fairtrade Labelling Organizations International (FLO). In 2002 FLO created an independent company, FLO-CERT, to certify licensees. 'Fairtrade' was registered as a brand name along with the Fairtrade Certification Mark (Fairtrade 2013).

Since the 1990s, the organization's theoretical antagonistic stance towards commercially driven corporations has coexisted with a realpolitik of direct corporate engagement. This was initiated by the Fairtrade Foundation (the Fairtrade marketing organization for the United Kingdom and Ireland), who claimed that unless Fairtrade 'mainstreamed', it would never become socially influential (Bowes 2011; Lamb 2008). Their first corporate partnership was with a major UK retailer, the Co-operative Society (the Co-op), who chose to sell Fairtrade chocolate under the Co-op's own-brand label. The subsequent growth in Fairtrade's market share and public profile (Bowes 2011; Reed 2009) convinced the movement as a whole to adopt the corporate engagement strategy.

The Co-op's directors chose chocolate as their first Fairtrade product in part due to its potential emotional impact:

> [We have] chosen chocolate as the focus for making Fairtrade mainstream because of the stark – even obscene – contrast between the pleasure from eating it and the suffering that goes into making it. (Co-operative Group 2002, quoted in Bowes 2011: 126–127)

An emphasis on the disparity between the enchantment of the product and the abject conditions of producers has become a key promotional tool in subsequent Fairtrade campaigns, including the one for FT/FM gold. In the case of gold, the strategy was underpinned by questioning notions of gold's inherent purity and claims that only FT/FM gold was really pure (see Fairtrade Foundation 2012; Maldar 2011).

Fairtrade's increasingly formalized organizational structure and growing reliance on commercial partnerships has led to internal tensions within the

movement, particularly between the European and US marketing organizations. Some members have accused their leaders of turning fair trade into a
commercial brand, compromising its founding ideals (Bacon 2010; Lekakis
2011; Renard 2005).

The FLO-ARM partnership

The FT/FM gold initiative echoed Fairtrade's beginnings in terms of the location and organization of the producing communities. The idea that responsibly
sourced gold could be certified was first proposed by ARM, a Latin American
association of subsistence mining communities that promotes responsible mining
(Echavarria 2008). They approached the Fairtrade Foundation, who petitioned
FLO to construct a standard. FLO and ARM then formed a partnership to jointly
develop the standard. The resulting product would be called Fairtrade (relating to
the FLO licensing system) and Fairmined (meeting ARM criteria) gold.

The FLO/ARM team drew on ARM's understanding of the needs of subsistence miners and FLO's experience of creating certification systems (Echavarria
2010; Madlar 2011). However, they lacked members with expertise of refining
technology, large-scale jewellery manufacturing or the global gold trading
system. Consequently, the resulting standard was severely hampered by
misconceptions and prejudices regarding these activities. But the costs and
demands of refining, the amounts of gold needed by large manufacturers
and the mechanism behind the London gold fix (the price set for large international gold trades) were all to play a major role in the subsequent story of
FT/FM gold.

The FT/FM gold standard

The standard that emerged had four main features. First, FT/FM gold had to be
bought from the miners at 95 per cent of the day's gold fix. Second, businesses
submitting a finished gold item for hallmarking had to pay a premium to have
the item stamped with the Fairtrade and Fairmined marks. The premium, paid
to the miners, was 10 per cent of the price of the finished item for FT/FM gold
and 15 per cent for FT/FM ecological gold (which was subject to further, environmentally friendly production criteria). Third, all FT/FM gold was to be subject
to a 'track and trace' system: the movements and use of all FT/FM gold had
to be recorded for the FLO-CERT auditors. Fourth, all businesses handling FT/
FM gold from mine to hallmarking had to purchase a license from Fairtrade
(Fairtrade Foundation 2012; Maldar 2011).

Determining the price of gold

The FT/FM project team based the price for FT/FM gold on the London gold fix set by the London Bullion Market Association (LBMA). Despite the key role the fix was accorded, the FT/FM team described it in very simple terms:

> The London gold fix (or LBMA fix) as it is known, is set twice a day and is the global price reference for gold trading worldwide. These decisions, taken by traders in the City of London, have a major impact on the lives of artisan miners, thousands of miles across the world. (Maldar 2011: 8)

The Fairtrade Foundation's CEO, Harriett Lamb, was equally elusive about the fix mechanism at the FT/FM gold launch: 'these people [the LBMA] set the price for gold. I don't know who these individuals are' (personal communication 2011).

The impression being given by Fairtrade was that the LBMA arbitrarily decided the daily gold price. Others, including economic researchers, describe the LBMA as part of a wider network of gold trading exchanges, including the Gold Pool in Zurich, the COMEX market in New York, and the Hong Kong Exchange (Green 1968, 1985 [1982]; O'Callaghan 1993). Together they create a global gold market, with the daily fix being as much an outcome as a driver of events. Even within the LBMA, the fix is the result of competition rather than collusion; the agreed price is the outcome of a series of competitive bids between LBMA buyers and sellers. The fix exerts its wider influence only because of the size of the LBMA's trades (sometimes large multiples of metric tonnes) (Green 1968, 1985 [1982]; London Bullion Market Association 2013).

The project team's pricing decision exposed a paradox of FT/FM gold. Apparently essentially different to all other gold, its value was to be calculated by referring to the price set for other gold. But as the FT/FM team set the price of unrefined FT/FM gold at 95 per cent of the fix (the price of processed gold sitting in bank vaults), the additional refining, assaying and transport costs (including export licenses) pushed the price of refined FT/FM gold far above the LBMA fix. The project team's assumption that the LBMA fix was *the* gold price, rather than the internally negotiated price for a closed market whose members traded large volumes of four nines gold, was to have dire repercussions.

The resurgence of economic gold

The full implications of the FT/FM pricing mechanism only became apparent as the banking crisis of 2008–2009 mutated into a sovereign debt crisis. Five years of economic turmoil led to gold's role as a store of wealth coming to the fore. The phenomenon of cash-for-gold took hold across the United Kingdom, with financially distressed families selling their gold jewellery to local jewellers, pawnbrokers and postal gold companies. In 2011 the amount of gold being sold as scrap exceeded the amount used for manufacturing jewellery in the United Kingdom (Thomson Reuters GFMS 2012). This scrap fed the surging international demand for less spiritually imbued but still highly desirable investment objects: gold bullion bars and coins.

This demand led to an unprecedented rise in the gold price. In 2006, when ARM had first proposed a fair trade supply chain for gold, the fix was below $600 per ounce (CPM Group 2006). By the time FT/FM gold was launched, the fix was approaching $1,400 (CPM Group 2011). The price eventually peaked at $1,896 in early September 2011, after which it stabilized between $1,550 and $1,800 for the following year (CPM Group 2012; Thomson Reuters GFMS 2012).

During this period gold jewellery prices rose significantly year after year, while incomes came under pressure. For many consumers, gold jewellery shifted from being an impulse purchase to a considered luxury. At the FT/FM launch and in promotional literature the Fairtrade Foundation quoted the 2005 figures for gold items hallmarked in the United Kingdom – 19 million – as evidence of the programme's potential impact (personal communication 2011; Fairtrade 2011). This was the year before the UK jewellery mass market collapsed (Thomson Reuters GFMS 2012, table on p. 88). The figure for 2012 was just over 4 million items (Birmingham Assay Office 2013, table p. 8).

The leaders of ARM appeared oblivious to the pressure the gold price was placing on jewellery manufacturers. They assumed jewellers were making huge profits, some of which should be diverted to their miners. In an interview the day after the FT/FM gold launch, Cristina Echavarria claimed that as jewellery is a designed product and jewellers have built up brand names: 'There is greater room for the jeweller to absorb this [the FT/FM] premium and not necessarily pass it on to the consumer' (BBC Radio 5 2011). This expectation was placed on the shoulders of the FT/FM licensee jewellers, who were, in most cases, small, cash-poor businesses with minimal operating profits and little brand equity (see Fairtrade 2011; Taylor 2011a, 2011b).

ARM's representatives held a similar position during the 2012 review. They claimed the 10 per cent premium should be retained, even though the actual payment now equated to 25 per cent of the gold price when the premium was set. This charge came on top of the inflated price manufacturers were paying for refined FT/FM gold over and above the now massively risen daily fix. The miners' perspective mirrors that of other Fairtrade producers. Despite Fairtrade's rhetoric and consumers' expectations of solidarity, researchers keep finding that Fairtrade producers primarily see transactions in purely commercial terms and cannot understand why retail prices are higher than the price paid for their commodities (see Fischer 1997; Lyon 2006).

The mass balancing controversy

The lack of empathy on the part of the miners was not the only contentious issue. In September 2012, a group of licensees posted an open letter condemning a proposal to include mass balancing in the revised FT/FM standard.

The FT/FM project team had initially assumed gold would be similar to Fairtrade's agricultural products (see Fairtrade 2011: 8). These have linear supply chains that are amenable to 'track and trace'. But gold is different: due to its high value, durability and recoverability, the gold industries – at both macro and micro levels – have become acutely dependent on 'mass balancing'.

The LBMA functions in part as an international mass balancing system for bullion. LBMA members holding 'open accounts' must accept whatever London Good Delivery Bars (LGD bars) they are offered when they redeem their gold; they get the same amount of gold, but not necessarily the same pieces of bullion (Capano 2008; London Bullion Market Association 2013). In this context, LDG bars come as close to the ideal of a commodity as is physically possible (Appadurai 1986). As a consequence, the LBMA can make extensive use of ownership swops to complete international gold trades rather than physically move bullion every time it is traded (Green 1985 [1982]). This eliminates the costs, risks and delays associated with transporting gold.

Mass balancing also occurs on a smaller scale in industrial refining and manufacturing processes where gold is 'trapped' in technical systems. If a factory or refinery operates a mass balancing system, clients will get the same amount of gold they supplied, but again not necessarily the same piece. The surfeit of gold needed for the process to operate is provided and owned by the factory, stays onsite and is treated as a material asset for accounting purposes.

In contrast, Fairtrade's 'track and trace' certification system required that licensees kept FT/FM gold separate from other gold stocks. Due to the limited amount of FT/FM gold in circulation it was impossible to use machinery or equipment that required large volumes of gold to operate effectively. Processes dependent on large volumes of gold, for example, chain making, electroplating or specialist alloy production never became available to FT/FM licensees. The technologies licensees were able to use, such as casting, had to be run as bespoke operations, pushing the finished price of FT/FM gold items even higher.

Industrial manufacturers had developed a high level of *path dependency* (see Busch 2011) towards the concept and practice of using interchangeable stocks of gold. While not ideologically opposed to the ideals of Fairtrade, managers and directors knew their production systems could not accommodate the FT/FM regulations and remain commercially viable. Licensees found they were restricted to a limited range of technical options compared to competitors using ordinary gold.

FT/FM campaigners fought over the proposed inclusion of mass balancing as if it were an abstraction that could be comprehensively rejected. The extent to which it manifested itself within the industry in material ways: in ownership swops of bullion, in the nature and intentions built into the machinery and even the written accounts that were used to determine the profits and viability of individual companies was not understood.

Oro Verde goes to auction

Pricing and mass balancing were not the only problems to affect the campaign. In December 2012 Oro Verde announced they would be selling their gold by auction rather than directly to FT/FM licensees. Corporacion Oro Verde was a founding partner of the FT/FM gold campaign (Maldar 2011: 15–16). Oro Verde gold comes from the Chocó region of Columbia and is extracted using panning and sluicing techniques without any recourse to mercury or cyanide (Oro Verde 2013). At the time of the 2012 review, Oro Verde's miners were the only producers of FT/FM Ecological Gold.

Though compromising to the FT/FM gold initiative, Oro Verde's decision was a practical response to wider events. Oro Verde had built a loyal client base in the United States. During 2011 Fair Trade USA (the US Fairtrade marketing organization) was petitioned to join the FT/FM initiative. But in December 2011 Fair Trade USA left the International Fairtrade Association, due to the strategy direction of the Association (including the adoption of corporate engagement). After the split, jewellers in the United States were never going to be able to call the material they purchased FT/FM gold. Oro Verde had to cope with its partners splitting into competing factions at the same time as the gold market stagnated and the FT/FM campaign failed to deliver the promised number of new licensees. Despite campaigners' optimistic claims, FT/FM gold remained an extremely niche market that threatened to leave the Corporacion with potentially unsellable stock.

Concerning complexity

Why did the FT/FM partnership crumble? The answer is complicated, but the complexity of gold certainly played a role. It was apparent that the campaign team were ambivalent about the substance they were attempting to redefine. They attempted to subvert the noble and spiritual dimensions of gold: the launch was timed to coincide with Valentine's Day and promotional material repeatedly contrasted the miners' poverty with the enchantment of gold jewellery. Campaigners directly challenged gold's spirituality: 'This idea of purity, what are we hanging this on?' (Greg Valerio, presenting at the Eco-jewellery workshop, Hatton Garden, 3 November 2010). Gold was presented as an apparently sentient and untrustworthy substance: 'Gold does not want you to know what it is doing, or where it is . . . gold is a very bad master' (ibid.; see also Valerio 2011). Yet the same campaigners always believed gold wedding rings would be a key product line for FT/FM gold (personal communications 2010, 2011).

The Fairtrade campaigners believed the inherent nobility of the subsistence miners, together with the moral superiority they attributed to the fair trade movement and their personal efforts, would redeem this duplicitous substance and imbue it with a new spiritual quality. This romantic perception of subsistence producers and fair trade contrasted with the miners' more prosaic and ruthless approach to the trade arrangement at the heart of the FT/FM system. Due to a belief in the primacy of fair trade ideals, the campaigners also suffered from unrealistic assumptions about the level of mainstream consumer support the FT/FM initiative could rely on.

The tension between transcendent gold and economic gold was not the only barrier. Provenance, dependent on distinctiveness, was antithetical to the universalizing force that underpins elemental gold. The technologies reliant on the concept of elemental gold aided in its repeated triumph in the skirmishes that resulted. Elemental gold is more than just an abstraction. It is made manifest in industrial gold manufacturing, being embedded in the physical structures and operational capacity of the machinery and the praxis of operators. It also materializes in a different guise in company accounts and operating reports, where it underpins mass balancing tallies. These elements all reinforce each other, making the resulting assemblages thoroughly inimical to the idea and practice of treating any mass of gold as a singularity.

In contrast to the strength that centuries of interlocking and reconfirming practices gave immanence, the provenance essential for FT/FM gold was utterly dependent on a single organizational structure built from FLO's standard, FLO-CERT's certifications and the Fairtrade Foundation's labelling and promotional machinery. If this system was to break down or lose legitimacy, FT/FM provenance would vanish. The damage to the Fairtrade Association caused by Fair Trade USA's succession resulted in a decline in FT/FM gold's viability. The new substance was socially unstable: each mass could potentially revert to ordinary gold as a result of a local lapse in the credibility of its provenance or a complete collapse of the certifying system.

Conclusion

FT/FM gold was a socially complex substance that carried numerous incommensurate and contradictory aspects. To the immanence of its identity as a scientific object, store of wealth and representation of nobility and transcendence (features it shared with all gold) was added the intangible, observer-dependent property of a provenance that valorized the circumstances of its extraction.

It proved possible to create FT/FM gold as an intangible entity. This was done through the campaign literature of the Fairtrade Foundation and the regulatory standard for FLO and FLO-CERT, as well as in the beliefs of the campaigners. It turned out to be more difficult to maintain as a physical substance, a situation that the miners and manufacturers who supported the initiative found out to their cost. Exploring the contrast between the stability of substances as abstract ideals and actual physical stuff is a potentially fruitful means of analysing materials from a social science perspective that has yet to be fully capitalized on; as FT/FM gold shows, the results may be counter-intuitive as well as illuminating.

The FT/FM gold story demonstrates how each aspect of gold's social identity connects with specific social institutions that reconfirm and so protect that aspect's validity. Elemental gold is made manifest by the theory and practices of the techno-scientific activities called assaying and refining; noble gold is reinforced by the use of gold in status objects old and new; transcendent gold is underpinned by cosmologies that provide a detailed exegesis for the gold objects that enchant viewers and owners; economic gold relies on the trading floors that minute by minute reassess and broadcast the level of demand for the yellow metal. Research on materials needs to encompass these networks. Each is essential for the growth and ossification of any facet of any particular material's identity rather than an excrescence that subsequently attaches to an already formed understanding.

The creation of FT/FM gold was an attempt to directly challenge what campaigners saw as social and environmental abuses associated with the gold industries. But while the campaign focused on conceptualizations, creators of physical masses of FT/FM gold found they were faced with pre-existing technological and trading systems – consisting of human actors and inanimate objects (both material and immaterial) – which could not be easily reconfigured to accept the new paradigm. The interpenetration of *what is thought* and *what is done* became startlingly apparent as FT/FM gold was found to be excluded from large swathes of manufacturing and trading practice. The protective aspect to these systems was all the more remarkable for the lack of any overall organization. This diffusion of agency and absence of guiding intention proved to be a key feature of the system's overall resilience, as there was no specific target the campaigners could attack.

While gold is an unusual, or perhaps extreme, substance, there is no reason why the same types of networks could not exist around all materials that are socially employed. Too often researchers are content to accept material properties as inherent, without considering how these properties have been developed or are maintained. The research that has been conducted sits inside particular disciplines, remaining isolated and often marginal. In food studies, work on specific supply chains has uncovered similar networks and contestations (e.g. Busch and Tanaka 1996; Cidell and Albert 2006). Researchers in science and technology studies have started to consider how chemical reagents assume an identity *qua* chemical reagents (e.g. Klein and Spary 2010). There are also cases of art and design historians focusing on the interaction between a specific material and classes of objects made from it (e.g. Baxandall 1980; Nichols 2000). But the social sciences have not yet comprehensively addressed the questions these individual studies throw up. Broader examinations of how materials come to be seen the way they are in these and other social spheres (or across many) and a more developed understanding of the role of networks in these processes would be of immense academic interest, as well as of practical benefit.

Notes

1. In this chapter the word 'substance' is used to describe a physically existing, formally mutable material with a set of recognizable and determinable properties. This definition aligns with its usage by contemporary Western scientists (cf. Soentgen 2008) and philosophers (e.g. Putnam 1975). This contrasts with use of the word as a specialist term in anthropology to describe a supernatural and sometimes intangible material that carries life-force or fertility (e.g. Douglas 2008 [1966]; Küchler 2002; Warnier 2007).

2. 'Commodity' is used here to describe one of a restricted number of raw materials with a dedicated international market rather than the Marxist sense (cf. Appadurai 1986).

References

Appadurai, A. (1986), 'Introduction: Commodities and the Politics of Value', in A. Appadurai (ed.), *The Social Life of Things: Commodities in Cultural Perspective.* Cambridge: Cambridge University Press.

Bacon, C. M. (2010), 'Who Decides What Is Fair in Fair Trade? The Agri-Environmental Governance of Standards, Access and Price', *Journal of Peasant Studies,* 37(1): 111–147.

Baxandall, M. (1980), *The Limewood Sculptors of Renaissance Germany.* Yale: Yale University Press.

BBC Radio 5 (2011), 'Up All Night: Bolivian Fairtrade Gold Gets Royal Seal of Approval', broadcast on 15 February 2011.

Bernstein, P. L. (2004), *The Power of Gold.* New York and Chichester: John Wiley.

Birmingham Assay Office (2012), *The Anchor,* Winter 2012/13. Birmingham: Birmingham Assay Office.

Bishop, K. (2011), 'Take Some Responsibility', *Professional Jeweller,* 2(3): 22–26.

Bowes, J. (2011), 'Honesty, Openness and Social Responsibility', in J. Bowes (ed.), *The Fair Trade Revolution,* pp. 125–139. London: Pluto.

Busch, L. (2011), *Standards: Recipes for Reality.* Cambridge, MA and London: MIT press.

Busch, L. and K. Tanaka (1996), 'Rites of Passage: Constructing Quality in a Commodity Sector', *Science, Technology and Human Values,* 21(1) (Winter 1996): 3–27.

Capano, S. (2008), *A Guide to the London Precious Metals Markets.* London: London Bullion Market Association and the London Platinum and Palladium Market.

Cidell, J. L. and H. C. Albert (2006), '"Constructing Quality: The Multinational Histories of Chocolate', *GeoForum,* 37 (2006): 999–1007.

Clarke, G. (1986), *Symbols of Excellence.* Cambridge: Cambridge University Press.

Clifford, H. (ed.) (2012), *Gold: Power and Allure.* London: The Goldsmiths' Company.

CPM Group (2006), *The CPM Gold Yearbook 2006.* Hoboken, NJ: John Wiley.

CPM Group (2011), *The CPM Gold Yearbook 2011.* London: Euromoney.

CPM Group (2012), *The CPM Gold Yearbook 2012.* London: Euromoney.

Cruz, J. C. (1977), *The Incorruptibles: A Study of the Incorruption of the Bodies of Various Catholic Saints and Beati.* Charlotte, NC: St. Benedict Press and TAN Books.

Dobbs, B. (2008 [1975]), *The Foundations of Newton's Alchemy.* Cambridge: Cambridge University Press.

Douglas, M. (2008 [1966]), *Purity and Danger.* London and New York: Routledge.

Echavarria, C. (2008), *The Golden Vein: A Guide to Responsible Artisanal and Small-Scale Mining.* Alliance for Responsible Mining.

Echavarria, C. (2010), *Getting to Fair Trade Gold and Jewellery.* Association for Responsible Mining.

Eichengreen, B. (ed.) (1985), *The Gold Standard in Theory and History.* New York: Methuen.

Eliade, M. (1962 [1956]), *The Forge and the Crucible: The Origins and Structures of Alchemy.* New York and Evanston: Harper and Row.

Fairtrade Foundation (2011), *20 Companies Say 'I Do' to Fairtrade and Fairmined Gold.* London: Fairtrade, available online at: <http://www.fairtrade.org.uk/press_office/press_releases_and_statements/archive_2011/february_2011/20_companies_say_I_do_to_fairtrade_and_fairmined_gold.aspx> (accessed 11 February 2013).

Fairtrade Foundation (2012), *Every Piece Tells a Story.* London: Fairtrade.

Fairtrade Foundation (2013), *History.* London: Fairtrade, available online at: <http://www.fairtrade.org.uk/what_is_fairtrade/history.aspx> (accessed 13 February 2013).

Ferguson, N. (2009 [2008]), *The Ascent of Money.* London: Penguin.

Fischer, E. (1997), 'Beekeepers in the Global "Fair Trade" Market: A Case from Tabora Region, Tanzania', *International Journal of Sociology of Agriculture and Food*, 6: 109–259.

Gooday, G (2004), *The Morals of Measurement.* Cambridge: Cambridge University Press.

Green, T. (1968), *The World of Gold.* London: Michael Joseph.

Green, T. (1985 [1982]), *The New World of Gold.* London: George Weidenfield & Nicholson.

Gusterson, H. (1997), 'Studying Up Revisited', *PoLAR: Political and Legal Anthropology Review*, 20(1) (May): 114–119.

Hilson, G. (2008), '"Fair Trade Gold": Antecedents, Prospects and Challenges', *Geoforum,* 39: 386–400.

The Jeweller (2011), 'The Question of Ethics', *The Jeweller,* 5: 76–80.

Klein, U. and E. C. Spary (eds), (2010), *Materials and Expertise in Early Modern Europe.* Chicago: University of Chicago.

Küchler, S. (2002), *Malanggan.* Oxford: Berg.

Lamb, H. (2008), *Fighting the Banana Wars and Other Fairtrade Battles.* London: Rider.

Laudel, G. and J. Gläser (2007), 'Interviewing Scientists', *Science, Technology and Innovation Studies,* 3(2): 91–111.

Law, J. and Mol, A.-M. (eds) (2002), *Complexities.* Durham: Duke University Press.

Lekakis, E. J. (2012), 'Will the Fair Trade Revolution Be Marketised? Commodification, Decommodification and the Political Intensity of Consumer Politics', *Culture and Organization,* 18(5): 345–358.

Lewis, N. (2007), *Gold: The Once and Future Money.* Hoboken, NJ: John Wiley.

Linden, S. J. (2008 [1996]), *Darke Hierogliphicks: Alchemy in English Literature from Chaucer to the Restoration.* Kentucky: The University Press of Kentucky.

London Bullion Market Association (2013), *Specifications for Good Delivery Bars.* London, accessible online at: <http://www.lbma.org.uk/pages/index.cfm?page_id=27&title=specifications> (accessed 28 February 2013).

Luetchford, P. (2008), *Fair Trade and a Global Commodity: Coffee in Costa Rica.* London: Pluto Press.

Lyon, S. (2006), "Evaluating Fairtrade Consumption: Politics, Defetishisation and Producer Participation', *International Journal of Consumer Studies,* 30(5): 452–464.

Maldar, S. (2011), *Fairtrade and Fairmined Gold.* London: Fairtrade.

McDowell, L. (1998), 'Elites in the City of London: Some Methodological Considerations', *Environment and Planning A,* 30: 2133–2146.

Mol, A.-M. and J. Law (2002), *Complexities: An Introduction'*, in J. Law and A. Mol (eds), *Complexities*, pp. 1–22. Durham: Duke University Press.

Mondzain, M.-J. (2005), *Image, Icon, Economy: The Byzantine Origins of the Contemporary Imaginary.* Stanford: Stanford University Press.

Nader, L. (1969), 'Up the Anthropologist: Perspectives Gained from Studying Up', in D. Hymes (ed.), *Reinventing Anthropology*, pp. 284–311. New York: Vintage Books.

Nichols, S. (ed.) (2000), *Aluminium by Design.* Pittsburgh: Carnegie Museum of Art.

Oakley, P. (2013), 'Containing Precious Metals: Hallmarking, Minting and the Materiality of Gold and Silver in Medieval and Modern England', in H. P. Hahn and H. Weis (eds), *Mobility, Meaning and Transformation of Things*, Chapter 5. Oxford: Oxbow.

O'Callaghan, G. (1993), *The Structure and Operation of the World Gold Market.* Washington, DC: International Monetary Fund.

Oro Verde (2013), *'Oro Verde',* accessible online at: <http://www.greengold-oroverde.org/loved_gold/> (accessed 17 February 2013).

Perla, H. (2008), 'Si Nicaragua Venció, El Salvador Vencerá: Central American Agency in the Creation of the U.S.- Central American Peace and Solidarity Movement', *Latin American Research Review,* 43(2): 136–158.

Putnam, H. (1975), 'Mind, Language and Reality', *Philosophical Papers*, Vol. 2. Cambridge University Press.

Reed, D. (2009), 'What do Corporations Have to Do with Fair Trade? Positive and Normative Analysis from a Value Chain Perspective', *Journal of Business Ethics,* 86(1): 3–26, Fair Trade.

Renard, M.-C. (2005), 'Quality Certification, Regulation and Power in Fair Trade', *Journal of Rural Studies,* 21: 419–431.

Rice, G. (2010), 'Reflections on Interviewing Elites', *Area,* 42(1): 70–75.

Schroder, T. (2012), 'Gold and Godliness', in H. Clifford (ed.), *Gold: Power and Allure.* London: The Goldsmiths' Company.

Schummer, J. (2008), 'Matter versus Form and Beyond', in K. Ruthenburg and J. van Brakel (eds), *Stuff: The Nature of Chemical Substances,* pp. 3–18. Würzburg: Königshausen and Neumann.

Searle, J. (1995), *The Construction of Social Reality.* New York: The Free Press.

Simmel, G. (1978), *The Philosophy of Money.* London: Routledge.

Soentgen, J. (2008), 'Stuff: A Phenomenological Definition', in K. Ruthenburg and J. van Brakel (eds), *Stuff: The Nature of Chemical Substances,* pp. 71–91. Würzburg: Königshausen and Neumann.

Strathern, M. (1991), *Partial Connections.* Savage, MD: Rowman and Littlefield.

Taylor, R. (2011a), 'Good as Gold', *Professional Jeweller,* 2(3): 16–21.

Taylor, R. (2011b), 'The Pioneers: Working with Fairtrade Gold', *Professional Jeweller*, available online at <http://www.professionaljeweller.com/article-9716-the-pioneers-working-with-fairtrade-gold/> (accessed 21 July 2011).

Taylor, R. (2012), 'Public Consultation as Fairtrade Reviews Gold', *Professional Jeweller*, available online at <http://www.professionaljeweller.com/article-11856-public-consultation-as-fairtrade-reviews-gold/> (accessed 11 February 2013).

Thomson Reuters GFMS (2012), *Gold Survey 2012.* London: Thomson Reuters GFMS.

Valerio, G. (2010), 'Truth or Dare . . . the Legacy of Gold Mining', *The Jeweller,* 2: 44–46.

Valerio, G. (2011), 'The Soul of Gold', *The Jeweller,* 1: 58–59.

Valerio, G. (2013), *Making Trouble: Fighting for Fair Trade Jewellery.* Oxford: Lion Hudson.

Warnier J.-P. (2007), *The Pot-King: The Body, Material Culture and the Technologies of Power.* Leiden: Brill.

Chapter 10

Subversive plasticity: Materials' histories and cultural categories in the Philippines

Deirdre McKay with Padmapani Perez, Ruel Bimuyag and Raja Shanti Bonnevie

Plastic, because it is able to subvert cultural categories, does vital political work in the Philippines. Plastic's local history among Filipino indigenous communities opens up broader questions of value, identity and art. It's plastic's Philippine particularities that make it potent and problematic, generating a set of contested local categories. These categories emerged through the experience of a partici-patory research process for the Everyday Objects exhibition, staged by the authors in Baguio City in 2012. This chapter draws on participant observations with artisans and artists, formal interviews with dealers and collectors and audi-ences responses to the plastic artefacts the team exhibited. The caveat is that this is a fresh-from-the-field take on plastic in what is still a project in progress. Exploring plastic reveals how a materials approach unpacks the makings and remakings of distinctive global subjectivities. Here, plastic both excites peoples' interest and is used by them to express their identities and political allegiances. Our preliminary exploration of plastic's cultural specificities suggests how mate-rials can be studied for the ways that they index transformations in or struggles over social and cultural categories. For a team with little training in formal mate-rial culture studies, we found materials not only good to think about but also great to elicit rich ethnographic data.

Our Everyday Objects project began with my colleague Padma's curiosity about the new brightly coloured plastic versions of traditional indigenous basket forms she was seeing on the streets of Baguio City. She then discovered that Ruel – artist, photographer, tour guide and Ifugao cultural practitioner – was collecting these new craft objects and making his own. As more and more of these objects appeared, Padma and I bid for seed funding, deciding to explore the subversive qualities of plastic through a participatory workshop with craftspeople and artists working with repurposed materials. We recruited Shanti to help out with collections and logistics. Our team then curated the results as Everyday Objects, an exhibition that ran at the BenCab Museum in Baguio City in June–July 2012 (see Figure 10.1). After collecting plastic objects, curating them and displaying them as art, mixed in with the BenCab museum's own tribal art objects, we began soliciting peoples' opinions on the objects and their reactions on being asked to consider them as art. We learned that contemporary Filipino audiences found plastic objects, presented in their historical context,

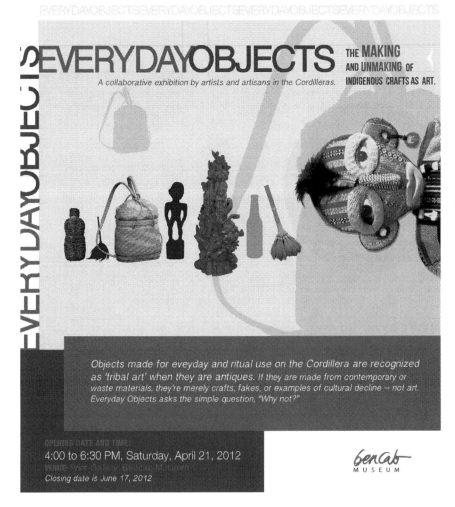

Figure 10.1 Everyday Objects exhibition postcard, 2012. Copyright Deirdre McKay.

to be surprisingly desirable and attractive. It is the material of plastic itself that brings up powerful questions of authenticity and perceived value for our audiences. Members of the Philippines' art viewing and collecting public tend to see questions of authenticity and indigenous identity as much more tied to material, rather than form. Theirs is the inverse of the views of craft producers. People who make these objects are much more interested in exploring the persistence of indigenous forms in new materials. This difference emerged because these two groups consider the ontology of plastic itself in different ways. The material of plastic itself, not the form it takes, embodies a political problematic which is distinctively Filipino.

Plastic craft and plastik, playing with Filipino categories

Google 'plastic', and you'll find the English word comes from the Greek *plassein*, meaning 'to mould', and describes a synthetic material made from a wide variety of organic polymers or, used as an adjective, means artificial or unnatural. Plastic is a subversive substance because it is not just one thing, but can be shaped, and reshaped again, into many kinds of objects. In the Philippines, the English word has been taken up and given new meanings to carry. Plastic, in the post-colonial Philippines, carries possibly even stronger messages about social class and distinction than in English-speaking countries (see Fisher, this volume, and Wilkes, this volume).

For wealthy Filipinos, plastic is the detritus of colonialist globalization. Plastic threatens the air with toxins when the poor burn their garbage, blocks the waterways and results in flooding and fills the streets when discarded by sidewalk vendors or thrown by passengers eating snacks on public buses. Metaphorically, plastic blocks national progress. In popular culture, it marks a kitsch and tacky – *baduy* – aesthetic. Most of the educated elites are reluctant to buy plastic and unlikely to decorate with it, preferring authentic Filipino natural materials. They generally prefer wood, rattan and bamboo, worked into objects by authentic artisans who have been especially commissioned by designers trained in both local heritage designs and the latest European and American architectural trends and design forms. Thus the wealthy aspire to store their fresh fruit and vegetables in metal fridges, rattan baskets or ceramic bowls. Plastic is something they accept, grudgingly, but wish to transcend.

For the poor, plastic is convenient, lightweight, durable and/or easily replaced. Its many colours cheer up their dark, poorly lit houses. Plastic containers and bags are not so badly damaged by the leaking roof and flooding that characterize rainy seasons. Plastic bags of produce hang from the walls in their kitchens while plastic jerry cans hold their cooking oil and water. Plastic's very malleability means it can be repurposed, while its light weight makes it easily transportable. Among the many kinds of plastic poorer people encounter, some are extremely versatile. Plastic can be repurposed or reworked and remoulded. So plastic sheeting can be a raincoat, then part of a roof, or the walls of a makeshift bathhouse or toilet. But pretty much the best thing about plastic for the poor is that it is usually cheap, but often free, or freely available for appropriation. Because it is widely despised and derided, bits and pieces of plastic lying about can be more or less easily liberated and repurposed to new ends. To make a plastic basket, it is much cheaper for a skilled craft producer, for instance, to use the webbing from discarded factory seconds garden chairs, pieces lifted from an export-processing zone factory, or blasting-cap wrappers from the (transnationally owned) gold mines, than it is to purchase rattan from someone who has sourced, cut and prepared it. Because poor people already have craft skills and are often underemployed, the time they have on their hands is easily put into adapting these skills to repurpose discarded plastic.

People who are both poor and members of indigenous cultural communities may have an even greater advantage here. They are often self- or seasonally employed and have more time and a wider set of skills and known forms with which to experiment on found and reappropriated materials. Everyday Objects worked with craft producers from state-recognized Indigenous Cultural Communities (also called 'tribes') in Northern Luzon who speak Kalinga, Kankanaey, Ibaloi and Ifugao languages and belong to those same ethnic groups. These peoples are often described by their shared, regional identity: Igorot. Igorots find themselves at the margins of a national Filipino imaginary dominated by the Tagalog language spoken in the region surrounding Manila. Though Igorots usually speak some Tagalog and understand more, they do not think in it or conduct daily life in it, and thus have a bit of bemused distance when it comes to Tagalog trends and slang, and, perhaps, Tagalog views on materials.

There's definitely something more to the problem of plastic in the Philippines than simply the propensity of the poor to take it when the rich have discarded it, or to throw it around and ruin the landscape aesthetic. Plastic itself indexes Filipino critiques of character and social relations, critiques that also revolve around class, solidarity and ideals for charity. In the Everyday Objects exhibition, plastic made these critiques material.

Mrs. Tupperware – plastik's etymology

Plastik as an adjective was something I first heard in Vancouver in 1994, when a Filipino migrant friend, Marlyn, describe her struggles with her Canadian employer. Marlyn was working as a nanny under Canada's Live-In Caregiver Programme and she called her employer 'Mrs. Tupperware' behind her back. Marlyn had assigned her this nickname because she was 'so *plastik* – she says I can have a writing desk, time off, overtime, but none arrives'. This nickname was a great joke, drawing on the term 'tupperware' that, in Filipino, is *sward-speak* (gay slang) for *plastik* – a Filipino borrowing of an English term to mean someone who is untrue to themselves and others. Marlyn's employer was Mrs. Tupperware, because she was only pretending to be friendly but was actually hypocritical in her relations with Marlyn.

We see here how the English word 'plastic' has entered Filipino languages in a very particular way. There's quite a bit of blogging among diasporic Filipinos on plastic that explains the Filipino (Tagalog) slang. For an anonymous blogger (languageculture.blogspot.co.uk 2008), *plastik*:

> connotes something cheap: plastic slippers, plastic shoes, plastic watch-bands, etc. It used to have that meaning too in Filipino: '*Naku, mura lang 'yang platong iyan. Plastic kasi.*' [Oh, that plate is only cheap. Because it's only plastic.] It was a cheap substitute for breakable drinking glasses, leather shoes, leather watchbands and the like.

Wealthy people have fragile, breakable glasses, durable leather shoes, and durable leather watchbands. The poor use plastic, which isn't prestigious for fragile items, but isn't durable for the items that get harder wear. It's just stuff. So the Filipino language term became a metaphor for the cheap, fake and undesirable. Thus this blogger observed that *plastik* indexes undesirable personal attributes. *Plastik* carries the notion of:

> being a substitute, '*yung pagkahindi tunay*' [not genuine] – not really glass, not really leather – [it] entered Tagalog and seems to have nudged out '*balat-kayo*', or the act, thought, feeling, sense of hypocrisy. More specifically, it dislodged '*doble-kara*' [two-faced], which describes a person's hypocrisy: saying one thing but not really meaning it; acting friendly although one really carries smoldering hatred; showing concern, love and affection although one is really just interested in the person's bankbook. It runs the gamut of situations. *Plastik* in Filipino now captures that behavior (thought, act, feeling) which is quite the opposite of what one truly feels. It carries more than the sense of being not just 'not really', but more – it also signifies 'not truly'.

Plastik carries a sense of falsity or lack of genuine intent. People say, '*Hoy, hindi ako plastik, ha!*' [Hey, I'm not plastik, eh?], to assert their sincerity in interactions with others. Very often the term *plastik* is associated with the hypocrisy the rich display in their everyday encounters with the poor. As Marlyn suggested, above, poor people use *plastik* to describe rich people giving them false respect or false promises of assistance. Another anonymous blogger at socyberty.com (n.d.) gives the following example: '*Plastik* – from plastic; meaning hypocrite, pretender, phoney Example: That *sosy* lady is a *plastik purita*'. In contemporary Filipino (Tagalog) slang, *sosy* comes from social, socialite – meaning snobby, rich or someone acting like a rich person. *Purita* comes from poor, meaning without money. Thus that lady acting rich is an insincere poor person. But insincerity can run in the opposite direction. Those merely pretending to be poor are actually undeserving of charity or donations from the wealthy.

So, in Filipino, *plastik* denotes insincerity, inauthenticity and unreliability, as well as being the cheapest, most accessible material – the material of the poor, which clogs their living areas, underpins their squatter-shacks and figures strongly in their purported preferences for bright, kitsch and easily disposable home and personal decorations. By extension, craft or art objects made from plastic may misrepresent the social position of their creator or somehow make a fool of the viewer/purchaser. Using the material itself plays on tropes of inauthenticity and resistance. Plastic, cheap and widely accessible, enables artists and artisans to call into question the stereotype of the poor as acultural, while refiguring their relationship with waste as a positive one. Plastic is, at the same time, about meaning and subjectivity; plastic is not a neutral substrate, but a co-producer of cultural categories.

Plastic, poverty and tribal art

Far from Manila and its pre-eminent position in the Filipino cultural mainstream, indigenous craftspeople play with plastic. In and around Baguio City, plastic materials now figure prominently in crafts made by Igorot artisans. The same objects, if made in rattan or wood, might be considered tribal art. *Plastik* is closely aligned to *peyk* (fake), as opposed to *jinwayn* (genuine). Something fake is not genuine tribal art, even if the object was made by indigenous Igorot producers. Igorot plastic crafts are thus playful and problematic. This play with plastic materials points to, and up-ends, a particular local history of tribal art production.

To identify genuine tribal art in the northern Philippines, dealers, collectors and curators (largely urban-based, wealthy and non-indigenous) assess the work of producers (typically rural, poor, and indigenous). Collectors and dealers apply an art-craft distinction, that is not about the skill of the producer or the aesthetic form of the object. Instead, their distinction relies on intention of the maker in not making art, but in creating an object that was used, un-self-consciously, for its quotidian purpose in traditional tribal culture. To self-consciously make something as a piece of art, or as a commodity to be sold into the tribal art value chain, makes that object not truly tribal art. In the conception of dealers and collectors, no authentic tribal person would do such a thing. Instead, the dealers' art/craft distinction relies on a notion of art that assumes a truly indigenous artist would only make something for their own ritual use, or their wider family or community. For collectors, owning tribal art remains a way of touching a history untarnished by the commodity form.

Tribal art, as a category, thus recreates geography and history to its own ends. As Fabian (1983) argued for anthropology, tribal art dealers occupy the space of interpretive intermediary, taking the place of 'here and now' in the art market and making the object of their expertise: tribal art. They do this by recognizing authentic products. Producers of art objects must be locatable in the 'there and then' of a continuing tribal past because the value of this art relies on a tribal 'other' who exists in a time not contemporary with dealers' and collectors' own. The spatial and social distance between the collector/buyer and site of craft production enables the art dealer's expert knowledge to recontextualize the object into a story of timeless ritual use for the eventual buyer/collector. This requirement for history means that dealers must claim with conviction that tribal art objects instantiate Fabian's (1983) allochrony (other-time) through material properties acquired through ritual use. On a traditional rattan backpack (*pasiking*), for example, a dealer would look for a patina created by sacrificial blood, smoke damage and worn grooves to show it had been used in authentic Igorot rituals. When Igorot artisans remake the same traditional backpack from neon-coloured plastic blasting cap wrappers liberated from a gold mine, they disrupt the fictions of cultural continuity and spatial hierarchy on which the art and antiques markets here depend. Blasting cap plastic backpacks don't acquire the same patina, and the plastic tends to break rather than get worn down.

The ways artists and artisans play with plastic thus challenge the dominant idea of cultural heritage in the Philippines. This challenge begins by undermining the tribal art dealers' and collectors' premise that market economies necessarily erode local, indigenous culture. Classifying objects as antiques or 'collectibles' leads collectors to withdraw these objects from the sphere of use and turn them into history. Acts of withdrawal or conservation are sacrifices intended to stabilize both Igorot and Filipino identities. Yet craft-art objects are important as means to assert claims for recognition of indigenous political and land rights and as component of indigenous people's livelihoods. In neither of these vital economic and political positions is it strategic for Igorot communities to portray themselves as stuck in 'other-time'. Making crafts contributes to local Igorot livelihoods, if not from cash sales into the market, then through barter, exchange and the circulation of gifts. Demand for rattan has led to such a decline in supplies that many craftspeople cannot afford to produce indigenous forms in natural materials. Thus there is great potential for Igorot migrants now living overseas to assist those at home to develop new products and access new markets for their work. However, this economic expansion can only happen if migrants themselves recognize the cultural and economic value of contemporary indigenous crafts and art. This recognition proves difficult to attain when collectors and audiences deem new materials to be insufficiently authentic or tribal and thus neither prestigious nor valuable. Crafts and tribal art producers have become caught in a heritage trap, unable to obtain traditional natural materials but expected, nonetheless, to work within the limits of a nostalgic aesthetic.

Whether craft or art, Filipino elite collector-consumers are the largest market for these objects. But the wealthy seem to worry more about certifying the authenticity of objects from disappearing cultures and the trustworthiness and character of producers who might play them as fools than the formal properties of the objects themselves. It seems there are too many *plastik* people in the tribal art supply chain and market and too many fakes made of natural materials have been sold. Wealthy would-be collectors are open to the charge of hypocrisy in not actually wanting to meet the producers of the art but rather to collect stories of their simple, tribal lives and spiritual practices. It is a comfort to the Filipino elite to believe that Igorots are poor because of their culture or their lack of education and skills, not their lack of access to infrastructure, markets and persistent state corruption. When poor Igorot producers trick dealers with fake tribal art, their poverty can also be attributed to their lack of civilization or inability to engage respectfully and equitably in a market transaction. Thus the tribal producers' identities also have a certain plasticity. With fakes, dealers refigure artisans from indigenous artists into undeserving charlatans who may even be faking their own poverty to gain sympathy and thus appropriate more money than their products are worth.

In the Everyday Objects exhibition, artists and artisans subverted the heritage trap with plastic. Their plastic crafts and art objects made no attempt to pass as authentic rattan, wood or cotton or to claim ritual use. With their self-consciously garish colours, they struggled to become art in public estimation, even in a museum exhibition context. Plastic fish traps were one of the first plastic crafts we collected for this exhibition. Gallery visitors saw them not as basketry, but as repurposed garbage – little more than recycling. But their persistent form recalls Gell's (1996) analogy between artworks and fish traps. The ways art objects may act with agency, as Gell argued, tells us about limitations on the cultural and political agency of their producers. The exhibition-space was key to these limitations. As Foster (2012: 3) observes, 'Gell's conception of art as entrapment and enchantment – his claim that art-works captivate, and thus exert a kind of (secondary) agency on people (patients)' (Gell 1992, 1996, 1998), depends largely on the underexplored aspects of exhibiting such work in museum or gallery installations'. The key point for materials studies here is that, if we find Gell's patients created by these craft objects, it isn't through the forms they take. Instead, the creation of viewers as patients lies in the action of the objects' *material composition*. It is this capacity of materials to act on viewers or owners that *devalues* these objects as art. It is plastic itself that denies their producers recognition as artists or as bearers of culture rather than craft skills.

Contributors to the Everyday Objects exhibition confronted audiences with plastic to explore just this problematic. They intended their colourful plastic versions of traditional tribal art objects to be precisely the obverse of formal tribal art: not to be sacrificed, nor to become antiques. Our participating artisans produced these objects from waste materials – baby oil bottles, plastic ties, plastic webbing and broken CD cases. They sourced plastic materials from domestic and industrial waste or liberated them from commercial enterprises. As craft producers, they sacrificed their time and effort to make use – not let go to waste – materials at hand, while trying to remain true to culturally prescribed patterns or forms that come from their indigenous heritage and which they already have the skills to produce. They intend their plastic crafts to portray their producers as creators and innovators, as canny and potent, at the same time as they sustain their indigenous ethnic identities by citing and reworking heritage forms from their communities of origin. By using plastic materials, however, these indigenous artists position themselves as 'not tribal, just poor'. Blurring the distinctions between art and craft, indigenous and 'just poor', Everyday Objects asked audiences to reconsider their own received notions of cultural authenticity and value.

The way plastic problematizes these cultural categories was revealed by what were easily among the most challenging objects for visitors to the Everyday Objects exhibition: plastic replica trade beads. Viewers described these beads as being most common, most easily found in the market, requiring the least skill in production and as fakes. To understand why, it's helpful to visit the site of their production. McKay, Bimuyag and Bonnevie travelled north from Baguio City to interview a bead-maker in Kalinga Province. The following sections draw on McKay's participant observations on that trip and from follow-up fieldwork with migrant Filipinos in London.

Plastic beads: A case-study

Repurposed plastic has been extracted from the waste stream and used to make replica trade beads by Igorots since at least the 1950s. The practice began with melting down old toothbrushes but has expanded to encompass a variety of other forms of waste. Today, strands of plastic replica beads are on sale in Baguio City. Their intended market is Igorot high school and college students who are, as part of their education, expected to take part in cultural performances. Strung according to Kalinga traditional patterns, but used by other ethnic groups to denote Igorot identity, these beads replicate strands of glass and stone heirloom trade beads. The trade beads themselves had become (comparatively recently) a definitive aspect of the material culture of the Kalinga ethnic group of Northern Luzon and serve specific ritual purposes in life-cycle events (Abellera 1981). The plastic beads thus replicate the distinctive bright colours of a set of beads made from stone, ceramic and glass used as a currency to exchange for goods and services during the colonial era (sixteenth to twentieth centuries). Among Igorots, these original beads still serve as a store of familial wealth, being valuable heirlooms passed down to the next generation. The replicas, however, are extremely useful for the expanding calendar of cultural presentations and ethnic events attached to education and local politics.

Replica beads replicate important markers of ethnic identity and social status. Among indigenous groups on the northern Philippine Cordillera Central, heirloom beads 'serve as an external diacritical mark to distinguish one ethnic group from another' (Francis 2002: 191) and to distinguish one person and their extended kin group from the next, in terms of wealth, power, political alliances and marital status. Most Kalinga heirloom trade beads date to the nineteenth century. Although Kalinga people made their own alter beads, the bulk of their collections are glass trade beads that travelled well-documented South-east Asian routes from colonial trade-bead production centres in Venice and from Vietnam and China (Francis 2002). Francis (2002: 251, note 12) reports that Kalinga craftspeople started making plastic replicas of these beads in 1969, and the practice expanded in the 1980s. By the 1990s, small multi-strand necklaces and bracelets appeared in regional markets but were worn only by children and the very poor. The expansion of replica production likely coincided with the increasing availability of suitable waste plastics in appropriate colours to be melted down and remoulded into bead form.

To collect plastic replica beads for Everyday Objects, we visited Fely, an artisanal bead-maker, at her home workshop in Lubuagan, Kalinga. In April 2012, she was making strands of replica *bongeh* (a long double-stranded necklace in a distinctive colour-blocked pattern) for cultural performances. To do so, she was melting down an assortment of plastic, including CD cases (black), plastic spoons from Jollibee fast food outlets (white), and big yellow plastic beads she had purchased in the Divisoria market in Manila. Fely was using her cooking fire, working with improvised metal tools over an open hearth. As she worked, her elderly mother and two-year-old daughter sat nearby. The little girl had a cleft palate. Fely was trying to raise the necessary money to travel to Baguio City for surgery by meeting *bongeh* orders for the festival season (April and May). Her house was a very simple wood and galvanized iron one-room structure on posts, located on a windy hillside. Water came from a public tap and there was a communal washing block nearby. With plastic melting over the fire, the small house filled with an acrid smell. In response, Fely's mother propped open the door and took her toddler granddaughter to sit on the porch. 'Some people complain that the smell is bad for our health', Fely explained, 'they say that we should stop, because it is a pollution'.

Fely herself said she had no ill effects, or none more than she did when she or her neighbours burned their plastics-rich domestic garbage. Burning is the fate of most discarded plastic in the rural Philippines – either that, or it is buried or makes its way into a nearby watercourse. Luckily, Fely's house on the windy hillside had good natural air circulation, though it would have been fairly uncomfortable in the rain and cold of the wet season. She explained that it was burning garbage that gave local bead-makers their categories for suitable plastics. She had learned how to choose plastic to melt down from the experiments of other producers and by trying out different plastics – broken buckets, cracked Tupperware, and so on – of appropriate colours when burning garbage. She told us that the best plastics for bead making were 'shiny and hard' – cassette tape cases and CD jackets were particularly useful. Mid-interview and mid-production, one of Fely's buyers arrived, looking for her order of 15 *bongeh* replica strands. She would be doubling the purchase price to resell in her market stall in Baguio City, but needed the order in a rush, expecting high demand around the cultural programmes set for college inductions in the coming new school year. As we wrapped up the interview, I purchased a *bongeh* replica of my own from Fely (see Figure 10.2), and then we departed for our Kalinga host family's christening celebration.

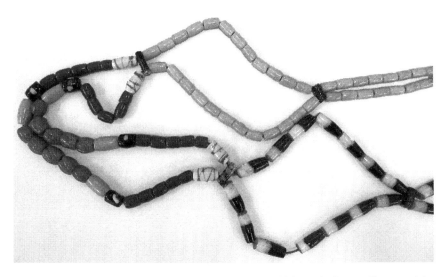

Figure 10.2 Replica Kalinga *bongeh* in plastic, Lubuagan, Kalinga, April 2012. Photograph by Deirdre McKay.

The plastic beads I bought were a topic of discussion with our host households' other guests, a group of Swiss musicians. One commented that since I didn't know what the beads meant to local people, as a non-Filipino, I shouldn't have purchased them or been wearing them. It didn't matter, she opined, whether they were real or replicas – the beads had a local ritual and spiritual significance that made them taboo for foreign visitors. Meanwhile, the beads intrigued another member of the same Swiss group, Livia. She was not concerned so much with the local meanings attached to the beads but their availability and cost. Livia had been asked by a friend to acquire some locally made beads for her Swiss-based jewellery-making business. When she learned that my beads were plastic replicas, she was disappointed; her friend, she thought, would only want real, natural materials. Both responses to the replica beads exemplify the ways that international tourism and cultural contact foster ideas of material authenticity as both viable and easily commodified. When I appeared with my new strand of replica beads, one visitor wanted to protect the local sacred from my misplaced cultural appropriation, while the other wanted to acquire that same heritage to repackage it for further value-production.

Our Kalinga host family seemed much more relaxed about my purchase of replica beads. In their home, their extensive collection of real beads was displayed behind glass in locked wall cabinets and under glass-topped tables. Plastic replica beads decorated bouquets of grass placed in big earthenware jars in the corners of their reception rooms. However, everyone in this household could tell which were real and which were replicas. Though the other visitors' responses suggested the line where plastic beads took on the cultural properties of real ones seemed somewhat malleable itself, our hosts were confident in their skills of distinction. They assured me that Kalinga spiritual practices appended ritual value and spiritual potency value to trade beads, not to plastic replicas.

The trade beads made of glass and stone were not of local manufacture, I explained to Livia, but owed their value to having been traded in, coming largely from Europe and Asia. While many beads had very high local scarcity value, dealers around the world had collected the same kinds of beads, made from the same materials and from the same sites of manufacture, elsewhere. All were available on an international market for antique beads. Her friend could thus order these same beads off the internet, at a cost reflecting their history and scarcity. A similar set of scarcity and pricing dynamics were driving the resale of heirloom strands in Lubuagan. Another anthropologist-friend had reportedly just purchased a double strand necklace of real heirloom beads in Lubuagan for about PHP 40,000 (£600/$950). The sale had been driven by the necessity of renovating the sellers' family home to accommodate an expanding extended family. Buying individual heirloom beads would be well outside Livia's price range. When she inspected the plastic replicas further, she noted that they had a nice, handmade look with pleasing irregularities and bits of soot included in them. She successfully ordered several bags of individual beads from Fely, and her friend made friendship bracelets from them, now for sale over her Facebook page. Clearly, our Lubuagan hosts did not consider the sale of replica beads to be a problem of cultural appropriation, so much as a possible opening of new markets for local artisans. Meanwhile, I found Fely's beads really travelled pretty well. Their lightweight and durable material made them both eye-catching and convenient.

Several weeks later, I was in the audience for an Igorot beauty contest held by migrants in East London. I recognized both a version of the plastic Kalinga *bongeh* on stage and some lovely examples of real Kalinga beads in the audience. I asked one contestant where she got her string of Kalinga beads, and she told me that they were her grandmother's from the Philippines. She let me hold them, and I could feel from the weight and warmth of the material that they were likely an example of Fely's craft. So, when my Igorot friends in the audience asked me 'real or fake', my answer was, '*plastik*'. The young Kalinga women in the Kalinga cultural performance that same evening were much more savvy about real/fake distinctions and the provenance of their beads. While they danced in sets of plastic beads, these were mixed with their own real strands that they had brought with them as part of their very best formal outfits. But only the real beads were part of their off-stage wear.

What my Igorot friends in London wanted to know was if I could teach them to tell the difference between *plastik* and real heirloom beads. Amy explained:

> Me, I need to know how to tell the real. Now that I'm in London and earning, we can afford to buy some sets of our own, for our dancing. But not before. It's shameful, you know? You know how it was in our place. My family, we had no beads. I think my auntie, maybe, she inherited some of our family's and then sold them. For an emergency – we've had many.

When I asked if she would consider plastic versions, she said, 'Yes, just for the representation. But I think it looks good, you know, just like those girls, to wear the real ones with your jeans and shirt, like you're still an Igorot.' What if, I asked, they were mixed together? Amy replied, 'Well, I suppose that would be ok, really. That's like how everything is for us now, being migrants and our places at home changing.' But Amy sounded reluctant to abandon the idea of authenticity as value altogether. She later showed me a plastic-bead bracelet she bought from a fellow Igorot and paid £5 for, in the belief the large central bead was a real agate. I advised her that the price was too much for plastic, and probably about £50 too little for a good agate bead. I showed her what I had learned from my hosts in Kalinga. If you check the temperature of the bead on your skin, plastic always feels warmer than glass, stone or ceramic. If you rub it against your teeth, reworked plastic is rough against your enamel, more so than ceramic or glass. If you consider its weight, it's light. If you look at how it reflects the light, plastic replicas are comparatively dull beside glass, stone and ceramic beads. Then you can examine the bead for inclusions or irregularities. An inclusion that looks like soot? That's from Fely's fire!

The materiality of plastic still plays tricks on those who aspire to status in this social field. Amy's comments remind us of two important and inter-related points. The first point is that poverty in the sense of limits on assets and value appropriated can be escaped. The second is that the diacritical markers of wealth and rank we associate with status, if not wealth *per se*, are also material ones. Materiality is part of the set of symbols learned as an aesthetic and tied to class. Amy, being newly middle class, pointed out the ways her own aesthetic for self-presentation continues to represents her origins as poor to other middle-class or elite Filipinos. She was also reminding me that I'm comfortable with fake beads because I'm a wealthier person who is able – through experience and research – to trust in my ability to discern the difference. I was not embarrassed to ask my elite Kalinga hosts for a tutorial on distinguishing plastic beads, while Amy would be. She is newly affluent and worries she has been wasting money on buying bracelets with plastic beads in the belief that her choices will help to reshape her social standing. Authenticity of material matters to Amy because she has been poor. Exploring a new and subversive aesthetic perhaps matters more to me, because I haven't.

I found myself sympathetic to Amy's response. Perhaps my 'isn't it cool' attitude to plastic crafts reads the plastic back in to the very materiality of poverty in producers' lives, admiring their ability to make something of it, to use their knowledge of indigenous forms and craft skills to transcend and refigure the garbage that they live with and in. But the aestheticization of poverty itself is no more troubling than the notion of tribal art and its idea of ahistorical indigenes living spiritual lives. Mulling over the moment when I realized I was arguing Livia into purchasing from Fely as an exercise in retrieving an authentic-but-contemporary culture, I realized I was thinking of Fely's struggle to fund her daughter's surgery, her one-room house and her deft handiwork in transforming pieces of plastic into these familiar forms. I located a value in her skills of material transformation that I felt should be rewarded – in material ways.

Making plastic into art

When placing these beads, baskets and bottles in the BenCab museum, my artist-collaborators' (Padma, Ruel and Shanthi and the rest of the workshop) practice was entirely self-aware. Padma wanted to instantiate what Kirshenblatt-Gimblett (1998: 51) calls a 'museum effect': the dual process through which museum presentation makes ordinary things special and experience of viewing such objects in the museum itself becomes a model for the experience of life beyond the exhibition. Our team was making a political statement by asking visitors to consider the broader context of their responses to plastic objects. Plastic crafts here instantiate a 'turn of the head' (Kirshenblatt-Gimblet 1998: 50) which 'bifurcates the viewer's gaze between the exotic display [of the museum exhibition] and her own, everyday world'. This turn happened in Everyday Objects precisely because plastic turned the viewer's head for her. Plastic worked its agency on the visitors/patients as an autoethnographic gesture on the part of the artists and artisans. By making tribal art in plastic, the artists and artisans turned their own gaze (and production) to meet that of the visitor, intentionally disrupting Fabian's sense of timeless othering. Plastic art thus challenges the viewer to confront received ideas about poverty and indigenous identity. Plastic art suggests that the poor can be culture-bearers at the same time as the tribal other – Igorots – can be ordinary, everyday poor people.

Our Everyday Objects exhibition thus used the materiality of plastic to reveal the network of shifting relationships in which these everyday objects were embedded (see Foster 2012: 3, paraphrasing Gell). By juxtaposing recognized tribal art pieces against utilitarian objects with multiple purposes, craft objects, and the tools used to make them, we asked audiences to confront their expectations for indigenous authenticity, temporality and value. Doing so, we made room for what might be seen as impure and/or hybrid objects (Foster 2012: 3, citing Clifford 1988) like the replica beads. All this made the exhibition into a place where people with different relations to these objects and expectations for them could come together to engage in a coeval dialogue about their forms, material and values. In the next iteration of the project, we plan to exhibit a *bongeh*-style necklace of mixed plastic and heirloom beads. For now, what we can say is that plastic, as a material, brings to the fore the problem of indigenous contemporaneity – of scarcity, trade and value. But plastic also foregrounds the issues thrown up by dynamic indigenous cultures when tradition is reinvented (Hobsbawm 1983) in not un-problematic ways to sustain people in contemporary, global economies. In a very practical way, revaluing plastic craft as art may be able to open up new potentials for diasporic community building and community-based economic development, creating new sources of income for marginalized craftspeople like Fely. The broader lesson from this case is that tradition's reinventions require not just renegotiating received ideas of authenticity and appropriation (see Aragon and Leach 2008) but also exploratory play with the physical properties and social agency of materials.

Conclusion

This chapter has shown how objects created by contemporary indigenous Filipino artisans and artists who work with plastic challenge widely recognized, if tacit, categories of identity and cultural authenticity in the Philippines. While there has been a great deal of attention to the ontology of the object (Henare, Holbraad and Wastell 2007), it is tempting to assume that ontologies of form and materials work together, rather than being in conflict. But, by setting the ontology of the material against that of the objects' form, the materiality of the object can itself works as a political commentary and blur the boundaries of established cultural categories. This is where a whole new class of problematic hybrids (see Foster and Clifford, above), like these plastic replica beads, find their particular agency. No doubt it is not only plastic but also other materials, elsewhere, that can be found to be doing the same sort of subversive work.

For materials studies, the key lesson is that materials have an agency that lies in their physical properties and cultural histories and that can work against the forms taken by the objects they make. The uneasiness generated by conflict between substance and form gives rise to political commentary. Materials' cultural histories could thus undo even the best attempts at making them sustainable or recycling them because of the cultural work they are already doing. As this case study makes clear, before launching projects to redirect plastic in the waste stream to new purposes in the Philippines, planners and designers would need to look carefully at the very particular social and cultural meanings Filipinos attach to plastic. Elsewhere, it would be other problematic materials and other histories and ontologies. In a world where stuff is increasingly not what it seems (see Fisher, this volume), mastering ontologies of the authentic and skills of distinction are necessary strategies to sustain selves and cultures in a global Age of Plastic. This is where an anthropology of materials can make its practical contribution to planning and designing sustainable futures. Beyond this, studying materials is a key methodology for ethnographic research on changing experiences of selves and 'stuff' in an increasingly global world.

References

Abellera, B. (1981), *The Heirloom Beads of Lubo, Kalinga-Apayao*. Unpublished MA Thesis. Dilman: Asian Centre, University of the Philippines.

Anonymous (2008), 'Language, Culture and Communication Skills Information' languagenculture.blogspot.co.uk, <http://languagenculture.blogspot.co.uk/2008/02/filipino-plastic.html> (accessed 7 July 2012).

Anonymous (n.d.), 'Plastic', socyberty.com <http://socyberty.com/languages/spokeningdollar-two-filipino-slang-words/#ixzz1yd9gOw8W> (accessed 7 July 2012).

Aragon, L. and J. Leach (2008), 'Arts and Owners: Intellectual Property Law and the Politics of Scale in Indonesian Arts', *American Ethnologist*, 35(4): 607 – 631.

Clifford, J. (1988), *The Predicament of Culture: Twentieth-Century Ethnography, Literature and Art*. Cambridge, MA: Harvard University Press.

Fabian, J. (1983), *Time and the Other: How Anthropology Makes Its Object*. New York: Columbia University Press.

Foster, R. (2012), 'Art/Artefact/Commodity: Installation Design and the Exhibition of Oceanic Things at Two New York Museums in the 1940s', *The Australian Journal of Anthropology*, 23(2): 129–157.

Francis, P. (2002), *Asia's Maritime Bead Trade: 300 B.C. to the Present*. Honolulu: University of Hawai'i Press.

Gell, A. (1992), 'The Technology of Enchantment and the Enchantment of Technology', in J. Coote and A. Shelton (eds), *Anthropology, Art and Aesthetics*, pp. 40–66. Oxford: Clarendon Press.

Gell, A. (1996), 'Vogel's Net: Traps as Artworks and Artworks as Traps', *Journal of Material Culture*, 1: 15–38.

Gell, A. (1998), *Art and Agency: An Anthropological Theory*. Oxford: Clarendon Press.

Hobsbawm, E. (1983), 'Introduction: Inventing Traditions', in E. Hobsbawm, and T. Ranger (eds), *The Invention of Tradition,* pp. 1–14. New York: Cambridge University Press.

Henare, A., M. Holbraad and S. Wastell (eds) (2007), *Thinking Through Things: Theorising Artefacts Ethnographically.* London: Routledge.

Kirschenblatt-Gimblett, B. (1998), *Destination Culture: Tourism, Museums, and Heritage.* Berkeley: University of California Press.

Chapter 11

Diamonds, machines and colours: Moving materials in ritual exchange

Filipe Calvão

The purest diamond is an emblematic ideation of an elusive and notoriously complex ethnographic object, the commodity. Its capricious and shifting materiality, challenging perceived notions of wants and desires, use and exchange value and rendered to consumers as a veritable icon of value fetishization, is somewhat paradoxical in that diamonds are the only gemstone that is abundant in nature. But just as much as the materiality of value is not physical but also social (Pietz 1993), there is more to the material of diamonds than the simple calculation of its material properties and qualities. At the turnover moment from rock to commodity, the materiality of a diamond – its *thingness* – remains at the centrepiece of negotiations over value. More significantly, diamonds also emerge as an unstable material by way of a ritualized negotiation. What is the matter, then, with the material life of a diamond stone?

In this chapter, I suggest that the moment when diamonds are traded provides inestimable clues to understand materials in processes of valuation. I seek to demonstrate how the value of one diamond stone (*kamanga*[1]) is produced and transformed with other circulating materials in the trading context. I approach this problem by way of ethnographic events of trading diamonds in Lunda, Angola's diamond-rich province.[2] In the region's *contuários* (also called *prontuário*, *casa grande* or office), everyday talk animates trading rooms and the economy of ritual practice complicates our understanding of sensory perception, bodily praxis and qualitative labour in processes of capital reproduction. I build from concrete instances of trading to connect the material qualities of diamonds and other things that 'leak' in-between different materials (Ingold 2011a: 4) to forms of expert knowledge or the language of 'the market' (Keane 2008). Can the social, institutional and technical process by which diamonds are evaluated change the material itself?

Materials, value and revelation

This project contributes to the field of anthropological thought on materiality, commodities and objects by 'bring[ing] the materials back in' (Ingold 2012, cf. Kuechler and Drazin, foreword to this volume). Similarly to the tension inherent in gold's multiple and immanent qualities (Oakley, this volume), I wish to locate in and through diamonds the play of unequal and asymmetrical exchanges of meaning and signs leading up to the production of value (Munn 1986; Weiss 1996, 2003). Specifically, I aim to demonstrate how materials are aligned in-between a carbon-based physical substance and the socially mediated experience of trading diamonds, thus contributing towards the definition of value and the orientation of social life more broadly.[3]

Given the 'internal instability of the commodity form and the exigencies of situated practice', as William Mazzarella points out in his discussion of the commodity-image in contemporary advertising, it becomes necessary to investigate 'the question of the relationship between the thingness of things and the meanings with which they are invested' (2003: 26). I approach this problem in the gap between technical grading and the qualitative experience of trading diamonds as a ritual spaced carved between rhetorical negotiation and the allegedly 'objective' conditions impinging on the transaction. Following Gell's discussion of substances and qualities in olfactory dream states, I suggest that awareness to the exchange of materials renders their 'context' and 'sign' 'inseparable' (1977: 33) and thus traceable for ethnographic investigation.

Theoretically, I build on studies of the political economy of language that demonstrate how linguistic and semiotic events factor into economic processes (e.g. Bourdieu 1977; Gal 1989; Irvine 1989). I also pay close attention to approaches to circulation and the semiotic properties of the commodity (Keane 2003; Kockelman 2006; Lee and LiPuma 2002; Shankar and Cavanaugh 2012).[4] The commerce of diamonds in Angola is particularly suggestive to situate this analysis, both locally and with an eye towards broader scales. In fact, international *diamantaires* are routinely invoked over the course of these negotiations and simultaneously, these moments of trading recall the performative spectacle of financial and stock exchange market trading (Abolafia 1998; Hertz 1998; Zaloom 2006).[5]

In what follows, I evoke the spatial setting of a trading room and some of the social and institutional relations permeating diamond transactions in Lunda Norte, Angola. In a second section I turn to the invocation of the market as ritual language, followed by a concluding analysis of diamonds' 'composite' materials in ritual exchange. Let us now move towards the trading room itself through the lens of one of Lunda's iconic diamond traders, or *kamanguistas*.

The trading room

Busy scribbling down some numbers from the previous diamond transaction, the trader did not bother to look up at the new group entering the room: 'Are you bringing good *kamanga* [diamond]?' he asked. 'Put good *kamanga* [on the table], can't you see [the market price] is bad?' The stone carrier unwrapped a small piece of paper and placed a rugged rock on a table cluttered with bagged diamond lots and other evaluating instruments. The trader surmised the stone, quickly examined it under the magnifying glass and positioned it on the balance plate – 2.01 carats. Some of the members of the group, presumably but not always diggers, stood up slightly from their chairs to check the weight, either to determine their initial bargaining position or to confirm the measurement given by a previous competitor in case the balance had been fixed. A calculator was passed around among the diggers, confirming the number on display or punching new ones in until finally settling on a price. The trader glanced over at their offer but was clearly not interested in the small stone in front of him, 'all *piqué*,[6] too ruined', like the many others he will see throughout the day. The main voice in the group responded firmly: 'I'm a son of the house. Accumulate [increase monetary offer]! You're the boss. You have a bank, we don't.'

In his capacity to amass large amounts of cash, Boss Tom is a 'big buyer', known locally as *Pai Grande* (Big Father), *Patrão* or Boss (originally in English). The recent renovation of his commercial space reflects Tom's concern for his public image and that of his 'house'. Unlike his brother and commercial partner, who enjoys buying diamonds in moments of 'collective effervescence' by attending to multiple groups of sellers at once and taking pride in cultivating an image of generosity and exuberance, Tom attempts to distance himself from that image and the social responsibilities accruing from a trader's expected largesse. In his own analogy, Tom is a strict but frank evaluator, playing the 'bad cop' to his brother's 'good guy' persona, and thoroughly seems to enjoy the fine-grained evaluations. The public reputation of the buyer, however, is only a stepping stone to validating the knowledge and expertise necessary to assess diamonds and thus mitigate the risks of fallibility and uncertainty associated with this economy of monetary transaction.

Over time, Boss Tom's trading post has grown from a shabby-looking, poorly lit office into one of the most influential and busiest diamond offices in Lucapa, a mining town and major hub of diamond mining and trading in the Lunda Norte province. Since my last visit, it had been turned into an upscale and air-conditioned office, furnished with sleek black chairs, an elegant leather couch and a glass coffee table with an assortment of travel magazines. His diamond business works in tandem with the family-owned retail warehouse, located on the main thoroughfare of the city in a two-story building surrounded by high walls and metal gates, which spans an entire block. On any given day, hundreds of people congregate in the vicinity of the warehouse and retail store. Far from the general public at the back, a dozen or so warehouse workers unload trucks from Luanda, stacking large pallets of frozen meat, cases of national and imported beer, sacks of flour and a wide array of other items in high towers.

Tom's trading office is a public reflection of his buying power and reputation, where he often entertains up to hundreds of diggers, their 'sponsors' (financial backers), and petty traffickers. More established diamond traders and state officials also check in routinely, sharing the latest news on the diamond market, soliciting favours, borrowing money or collecting payment for services. Having weathered the impact of the 2008 financial crisis that put a significant number of corporate mining projects on hold or made them insolvent, this was now a full-blown diamond operation, with fixed daily expenses (not including capital to acquire diamonds) of thousands of dollars, up to a dozen cars to support mining operations (transport diggers and facilitate food distribution) and an additional agent on the frontline of digging sites. To cope with growing demand, his business now has multiple evaluating rooms, arranged by estimated price range between the ground and first floors. The most valuable stones are traded directly in his office, where Boss Tom can entertain multiple groups of sellers at once, although he prefers having one group at a time to prevent conflicts and stop valuable information from leaking to rival traders.

My arrival was announced by walkie-talkie to the upstairs room. Although only a few metres away, Boss responded with a laconic 'let him in', and the senior guard unbolted the heavy metal door separating me and the main trading room. I left behind a bustling scene in the commercial warehouse, filled with retail clients loading their vehicles with supplies, a large group of loosely affiliated house employees, and a crowd of spectators. At the Boss's suggestion, I took the chair immediately to his right, across the main table, a spot usually reserved for his junior associate.

The trader's table is the centrepiece of diamond trading rooms, where beneath a fluorescent light one commonly finds a stack of white sheets of paper providing an initial colour contrast for grading purposes. To his left, Tom kept a personal laptop logged in on Skype to communicate with foreign buyers and family abroad. Behind him, atop a sturdy locked vault, was a currency-counting machine: the coveted sound of flipping crisp US dollar bills is the tell-tale sign of a successful transaction. To his right were two electronic balances, and below his desk, hidden from the curious stares of diggers, he kept a colour-grading machine, the most expensive piece of equipment in the business of evaluating diamonds, used when presented with high-grade stones of dubious colouring. Strewn across the table were various calculators (frequently used during trans-actions so as to 'talk on the machine'), magnifying glasses for close inspection of diamonds and miniature shovels to move smaller lots of diamonds onto the balance dish and place them in small zip-sealed bags according to carat, weight and colour. He often left these bags in plain sight, a customary sign of trust and clear evidence of his financial power.

Talk of the market

'The best *kamanga* comes from the mouth', I was once told. In a literal sense, the best diamonds need to be hidden away, often in the mouth. More figuratively, a good diamond is also the product and effect of intense debates: the mutual valuation of diamonds is negotiated in language use, and power relations signalled in economic transactions are established in conversation. This state-ment also indicates the proximity of the material of diamonds to the body itself, in the interpenetrable nature of bodies and commodities, materiality and language. Sellers (diggers, or someone on their behalf) are first known for deploying a barrage of bargaining techniques in order to increase the offer, monetary or otherwise, before consenting to the deal. Second, the body is therein posited as the 'material process of social interaction' where embodied practices are rendered meaningful in its proper material context (Turner 1994: 29).

Trading in diamonds is a seemingly straightforward and ordinary event of face-to-face interaction. A diamond trader (buyer) appraises one or more diamonds and the digger (seller) can accept the offer or refuse it and move on to the next trading post. In reality, however, the ethnographic moment of trading diamonds is far more complicated than what this rendition might suggest. When a diamond trades hands, there is more at stake than a simple monetary transac-tion defined by an assessment of the gemstone or the reputation of the buyer. Let us consider this problem more closely.

Importantly, representations of the market take centre stage in these nego-tiations. Traders invoke their privileged and expert knowledge of the market: 'I know the market, you have to trust'; 'my market does not work with this kind of [small] stone'; or 'the Boss of capital in Belgium says don't buy'. This knowledge of the market is often contested with responses along the same lines.[7] Rather than being bound by the experts and expertise put forth in evaluation, I take these moments of trade and talk of exchange as ritual events structured in a knowledge and speech of negotiation that anchors cultural constructs designed to interpret diverging definitions of value (Keane 1997; cf. Silverstein 2004). In my suggestion, the shifting nature of the material being traded is articulated in the tension between a 'language of the market' and the experiential and sensorial awareness of the diamond's material qualities.

While talk of the market seems dull and uninteresting, humour and joking are also injected into these conversations, providing a serious commentary on the material of the commodity, capital accumulation, or the market. These communicative strategies, including the mockery of the trader's higher standing, substantiate claims about external and intangible phenomena (again, capital or the market) brought to bear on the exchange itself. In a revealing example, when one trader asserted that 'there is problem in the world market, there is crisis of money', the attending crowd of diggers burst out laughing. Surrounded by the buyer's ostentatious and seemingly successful commercial enterprise, the group of diggers found his claim so preposterous that the supposed gravity of the argument was turned on its head by being rendered as a joke. Conversely, though rare, these jokes can lose their intended effect and become dangerous if the negotiating parties do not signal a willingness to 'play along' (Basso 1979: 43) with the temporary transformation and reversal of social roles thus entailed.

Consider the following exchange in Tom's office. The trading office was full to capacity with about 20 people, but more sellers continued to arrive. Unlike other exchanges, the large stone placed on the table sparked Tom's interest, and perhaps in light of it, he set up the negotiation by complaining about a depressed market. The group's main interlocutor questioned his complaint by trivializing his standard formula of declining markets: 'What crisis? Do we have crisis? Angola never had crisis! Crisis is *there*!'[8]

Reacting to the group's initial offer, Boss Tom pretended to return the stone as a sign of lack of interest, accusing the group of being a 'chatty bunch' (*xaxeiros*), who 'only come here to drink soda' (*gasosa*). There was laughter in response to Tom's banter, and the first moment in the negotiation was sealed. What followed included a number of recurrent elements throughout the conversation: money for work or loans, on the one hand, and the contentious origin of diamonds (with frequent references to digging sites) on the other. Pressed to reveal the stone's colour and weight, Boss Tom accused the digger of being distrustful, hinting at the possibility that the group may have tried to sell the stone to a different buyer prior to their visit. He continued: 'I'm not worried about the weight, I'm worried about the colour. It is worth little, almost nothing . . . Do you want to sell *kamanga* or do you want to play?'

This moment defined an important shift in the tone of the transaction. Jokes became scarce and recriminations were exchanged between the parties. One of the diggers who had been sitting down suddenly stood up, putting down a travel magazine he had been busy flipping through. Pointing to his wrist, as if personifying a time-is-money attitude, he complained about their wasting of time: 'Let's just negotiate'. He asserted loudly: 'You should encourage. *Kamanga* isn't easy, you don't understand . . . This is the third time we're here. How many times did we come here to receive?' Notice, too, the purported inversion of assigned social roles: Boss Tom did not know the 'price of *kamanga*', according to this digger, and it was at the digger's suggestion ('let us just negotiate') that the transaction resumed. The group remained resolute: 'We're not going to leave with the *kamanga*'. They resorted instead to their familiarity and closeness to the commercial post ('This is the third time we're here. We've taken motorcycles and everything') and their knowledge of digging, asking rhetorically if the trader had ever gone digging. The terms of sacrifice and hardship, in fact, are here reversed: finding '*kamanga* isn't easy', a digger suggested, and 'we are poor because we belong to this company', 'go[ing] for a week of hunger in the bush'.

Although the stone was 'clean' and had 'a good shape', its colour represented a 'problem' for the trader, so much so that both parties seemed unwilling to reach an agreement other than by way of taking out a loan or keeping the unevaluated diamond in the trader's premises. In this type of case, diamonds are kept sealed on consignment to ensure that the group returns to sell their production, setting a pledge of moral debt in a paperless contract.[9] In addition, some traders find ways to assess whether the group visited a rival trader prior to their arrival. Truthfully or not, however, most diggers are adamant in denying having had any previous evaluation: 'We haven't circled around with that one, I swear, this is our house'.

The trader played off on the impasse by suggesting the group seek a different appraisal: 'You guys are complicated. Go around to any *prontuário* (trading office). $1,000 (USD) is the maximum they'll pay. L colour, round, 1.95 carats. That's the stone's classification, okay?' Wrapping the stone in a piece of paper, he concluded by saying 'I'll save it with your name on it and give you a thousand dollars' (USD). Avoiding the stalemate, the trader agreed to sell but not without explaining his risk of bankruptcy, the plummeting sale price in Belgium and the need to work to set money aside in a bank. The group left with the money. It was unclear for the negotiating parties whether the money was an advance for the labor ('work money'), the group's 'contractual' relationship with the company, or monetary compensation in exchange for holding the commodity.

This exchange offers an important contrast between labor, knowledge and capital. Before agreeing to sell, the trader moves from acting indifferently to the transaction to questioning the origin and quality of the stone. Against the potential of subsoil riches and future gains, the trader counters by offering a loan (acting as a *de facto* bank). The expert knowledge required to evaluate a stone, moreover, is juxtaposed to the trader's lack of familiarity with the work of digging. Importantly, in order to convince the group of diggers to sell elsewhere, the trader delivers the stone's minute classification – colour, form, weight – thus acquiescing to his last remaining source of authority over the transaction.

These elements of ritual expertise, play and loss of control (Turner 1977) are critical in the reproduction of capital, defined less by its efficacy (e.g. the calculation of value affixed to a diamond's material properties) than by the elements brought forth to forge the ritual situation and the diamond itself. These can range from the temporary suspension of otherwise rigid social identities, the dispute over the tempo of the transaction ('let's just negotiate') or, finally, the definition of a diamond's material properties in its capacity to circulate between trading posts. In other words, these communicative modalities reaffirm the negotiating power by subverting those in control of the exchange ('Do what we tell you', a more daring digger commanded), shifting between indifference and deference, ritual drama and play, insult and joking, exoteric and esoteric knowledge. What is more, standard formulas of negotiation can be easily denounced as such, both by a process of mimetic parody (notice when the digger pressed the trader over time, pointing to his wrist – where there was no watch) or when a message proves inadequate to its context of delivery.

What is more, if the boss is said to possess a 'bank' stashed away in his vault, talk of currencies and capital is also framed in terms of accumulation, much like prices fluctuate in a geography of upward and downward movements (raise, lower, increase, decrease). Similarly, the market is a constant elliptic reference in the dialogue between buyer and seller, providing the moral predicament and pragmatic justification to contextualize any given offer (e.g. the 'crisis', 'there'). In perhaps the most deployed rhetorical device, traders personify the market and voice its momentary qualities: 'the market is bad' or, conversely, 'if the market was strong I would buy'. This remains true irrespective of diggers' or sellers' attitude and posture vis-à-vis the sale. Finally, although negotiating by invoking the external (and physically absent) properties and capacities of capital and global markets (*there* and not *here*), the outcome of these negotiations requires an agreement over what is, in the end, present and tangible: the materials in ritual exchange.

Materials in exchange

One of the idiosyncrasies of diamond exchange is that intense negotiations notwithstanding, prices are theoretically predetermined according to a chart shared regularly by the state with all licensed buyers in Angola, providing an approximate guideline for the acquisition of diamonds. Being merely indicative, the chart offers a price range per carat (based on their size, colour, clarity, cut or a combination of these) and is subject to the arbitrariness of the categories themselves. More often than not, the stone's placement within the evaluation chart is the product of intense disputes between sellers and official buyers. In fact, one slight disagreement in colour may represent a difference of several thousands of dollars or more per carat. Diggers and unlicensed buyers do not have access to official charts, and this disparity in knowledge, and the capacity to depreciate the stone rhetorically or convince a buyer of its value, often becomes one of the main driving forces behind the negotiation.[10] In what follows, I examine how specific materials, in the broad sense of resources – from machines, gifts, or colour categories – impact on the material value of diamonds and the establishment of final prices.

Take the following situation, when a 9-carat diamond showed up for sale in Tom's office. He louped the large stone through a magnifying glass, tossing it negligently over a white paper on the table, picking it up and louping it again, repeating the movement a number of times. His cigarette burned in the ashtray, untouched. He opened up the negotiation by intentionally depreciating the stone's quality: 'This is screwed.' Nonchalant, the group's interlocutor asked for a cigarette. Confronted by the seller on whether he wanted cigarettes or money, the digger quipped, provocatively, 'I still haven't asked for the motorcycle key'. Repeating his preliminary assessment, Tom pointed towards an internal 'crack . . . from side to side', refusing to engage with the digger's request for a motorcycle and cell phones. Visibly irritated, the digger responded: 'How many holes do I need to open for a *kibula* (large stone) to come out? How many holes? Tell me, how many holes?' The crack in the stone, he insisted, was 'God's fault', not his.

Like in other transactions, a calculator, 'the machine', was passed around in a muttered negotiation. The group's interlocutor sat across the table from Tom and used his loupe to examine the stone. Along with the calculator machine, the motorcycle key became a focal point of the negotiation ('Give [us] two keys and then we'll understand each other', one digger commented). All the while, other diggers punched numbers on the calculator, settling for $15,000 (USD). Rejecting the figure presented to him, Tom belittled the stone, claiming it had 'fire', or internal charcoal residues. The digger stood by the stone's colour, referencing the trader's race: 'It's your colour (white), isn't that good? If it comes out our colour, or coffee-colour . . .'.

In a first reaction, the trader was quick to dismiss the stone by suggesting it was 'ruined', tossing it over and picking it up again. While the group of diggers indulged in cigarettes and alcohol, the trader thoroughly analysed the stone from different angles, meticulously evaluating it. In the meantime, conscious of its potential value, diggers opened up the negotiation by presenting what Tom considered a number of unrealistic demands. Chief among the group's demands was a motorcycle, and convincing the trader that the stone was deemed worthy of it would exponentially increase its valuation. Rather than dismissing the seller's repetitive requests, as if testing the limits of the trader's authority, Tom contrasted them with the stone's defects. Although the 9-carat diamond was large enough for the group of diggers to have a clear perception, and act upon its sheer potential value, it was only when it became clear that motorcycle keys would not be put on the table that the group offered 'their price'. As their patience wore thin, in fact, the forceful negotiation conducted by the group's main interlocutor, and particularly his insistence on the motorcycle, a prestigious sign of material wealth, became a source of contention among the group, some of whom preferred other methods of negotiation. One digger in the group stood up and suddenly sought to expedite the negotiation: 'Let's talk on the machine [calculator]. I haven't had breakfast today . . . We're not here to tell a story but [get] price.'

After a brief exchange, the trader made a counteroffer of $4,000 (USD), mediated by the calculator machine, which was passed across the table for the diggers to see. 'This is a *kamanga* of problems', he explained. 'If it was a good stone, I'd give [a motorcycle] with pleasure . . . It's not worth buying if it means problems . . . go wash [gravel] and good things will come out'. Tom ended up raising his offer and closed the deal by giving away mobile phones in recognition of the group's allegiance to his trading post: 'Here, phones for everyone.'

The value of diamonds, as I have suggested, could not be ensured without proper market appraisal and the authority granted by technical expertise. Despite being a seasoned trader renowned for his modest evaluations, Tom knew this was a '*kamanga* of problems' and so decided to hear a definitive evaluation. We drove to the main state agency (ASCORP/SODIAM)[11] in town, where diamonds legally bought are resold and divided in lots according to official price charts. The agency's senior evaluator, a middle-aged Israeli, received us in a small office with two chairs, a computer, and practically no decorative elements other than the usual diamond appraisal paraphernalia. In silence, the evaluator proceeded immediately to loupe the stone from different angles, scratching at the surface and placing it inside an ink-based acidic solution for colour reaction. He continued to loupe the diamond, taking measures and repeatedly placing it on the balance tray as if the weight could have changed in the time it took him to examine its interior. To the trader's dismay, he appraised the diamond at about $500 (USD) per carat, significantly less than what he had just paid for the stone. Had it been clean of its crooked cleavage and *piqué* inclusions, he explained in amicable terms, it would be worth $8,000 (USD) per carat.

Significantly, material objects such as the calculator 'machine' or the myriad of gifts expected from these transactions can increase the expectations of a stone's material value or, conversely, act to deter the stone's movement. Although meant to complement the monetary transaction, gifts such as motor-cycles, cellular phones, clothes, drinks and food can sometimes be equated to the value and wealth of money proper. As one digger put it, in referring to diamonds' fungibility, 'good *kamanga* is [a] motorcycle'. In order to maintain a reputation, out of respect for established customers, or in order to forge the potentiality of future transactions, the trader is often obliged to pay for trans-portation and food, even when diamonds are not directly exchanged. Work provisions and subsistence goods are also handed out as 'support' in the form of a voucher to be claimed over time (*jeton*, or token). Though wary of custom-ers uninterested in selling diamonds and only looking to benefit from this kind of support, a trader also needs to maintain his presence as a living force in the diamond market and preserve his image of a 'big' patron (*pai grande*). As was explained to me, 'the more you retract [from buying], the more *kamanga* runs away', thus justifying the need to either provide some form of support or buy diamonds at a short margin of profit.

Alongside the calculator and other material objects, 'colour', and the machine purported to define it, emerges as a significant element in these transactions and the negotiation of gifts and monetary gains. Colour is a seemingly objective category in the grading process, more so than clarity or what is often described as the 'inner life of the diamond'[12] (Calvão 2013). The principle is somewhat paradoxical: the most sought out colour is the lack thereof (translucent 'pure white', 'D'). As one trader put it, the 'more colourless, the best colour it is'. While no one would turn down a coloured diamond (pinks are said to be rare, and some traders claim to have never seen blue diamonds), problems emerge with the classification of tones and shades of colour, leaking between categories. Is it light or full light? Pink, brown, or champagne? The entire process of evaluating a diamond is fraught with uncertainty, and colour categories partake in this economy of risk and speculation. To mitigate the uncertainty, traders occasionally make use of the colourimeter, a small yet expensive device used to determine a diamond's grading by its colour. Based on the diamond's capacity to absorb light, this remains however an unreliable measurement subject to error (Collins 1984).[13] In one specific event when the results proved inconclusive, the trader falsely explained the limits to his 'machine' according to a colour scheme ranging from D (colourless) to Z (light yellow): 'Look, it's not even K [faint yellow]. It's below K . . . Below K the machine won't say.'

In these circumstances, colour categories combine with other qualities of the stone to create what might be called 'composite' materials (cf. Drazin, this volume). For example, 'white charcoal' signifies an internal 'fluorescent' tension, 'lighting up'. By louping the diamond under water, as is customary in artisanal mining operations, any reflection indicates the presence of charcoal. Irrespective of the colour, 'strong' and 'vivid' tonalities are always valued, and some traders make a point of keeping imperfect diamonds of vivid colours to themselves, removed from circulation. In other cases, however, traders are fast to get rid of certain coloured stones. A diamond that circulates between trading posts quickly depreciates, marked by a potential internal inclusion (Calvão 2013). In some cases, traders suggest that by 'circling around (*girar*) the colour will drop.' In this case, significantly, the movement of colour is experienced in the alignment between a technical classification and the expectation of its value: given the stone's lack of quality, the prospect was that by moving from digging site to different trading post, its colour category, or perceptions thereof, would 'drop' in each transaction.

Conclusion

By situating the act of trading as communicative and social practice performed in interactions between traders and diggers, I hope to have demonstrated how the material substratum of commodity value becomes tangible as a repertoire of knowledge and labor. In the accumulative effect of utterances and discursive interactions, this 'talk of exchange' connects the setting of trading rooms to imagined representations of the global market. In other words, these discursive exchanges render visible how certain materials productively underlie social and spatial relations (*in* practices of exchange), and in turn, how they become productive features and material index of an imagined market logic (*by* the labor of exchange). This is a dynamic aspect of the ritual reproduction of capital, defined less by the calculation of value affixed to a diamond's material properties than by the elements brought forth to the ritual event itself and the temporary suspension of otherwise rigid hierarchical identities.

Other than being a semiotic object translating in social practice the abstract forces of globalization (Keane 2008), a diamond actively disentangles diverging regimes of valuation (material, semiotic, moral, or cultural) brought forth by the liminal condition of a material extracted from nature and converted as economic value. In lieu of taking the material object as abstracted from a very specific set of political, economic, and social functions, I approached diamonds and other materials – machines or technical categories – in the ethnographic convergence of economic instrumentality and ritual practice, space and time, local and global processes. The participants in these exchanges, put differently, performatively and ritually deploy the object's natural, historical and cultural significance in the mediating effect of language and enveloping social context: enacted in the authoritative translation of the 'language of the market' and surrounding materials (calculator 'machines' or other appraisal instruments), the ritual event of diamond exchange interprets and locks transformations in value. In the process, value is given shape through multiple registers of materialization, be it in the invocation of labor and natural wealth or in the utterances of space-time dialogues of exchange.

One of these registers, importantly, is the expert knowledge required to detect occult sources of value. The ability to 'talk in machines' is crucial to situate diamonds vis-à-vis a broader visual economy, namely that of divination. As one informant described, diviners in Lunda (*tahi*) 'see in their machine', so as to detect the cause of prolonged sickness. Similar to diamond evaluators, the diviner also deploys 'some jars' 'to see, look', and then voice his diagnosis. Similarly to the manipulation of jars in the visit to the senior evaluator of the state's buying agency, this knowledge to 'talk' and 'see in machines', or to let the colour machine 'say' value, echoes the expertise of diamond evaluation and contributes to situating the production of value within a broader field of material objects.

Notes

1. From the word for diamond stone (*kamaang/kamanga*) in local Cokwe-Lunda.
2. Research was based on fieldwork conducted in trading rooms in the provinces of Lunda Norte and Lunda Sul, Angola. Specific evidence for this article was collected on diamond trading practices in the urban axis of Calonda-Lucapa between 2008 and 2011. For the purpose of this article, I focus specifically on one diamond merchant, whom I call Boss *Tom*.

206 The Social Life of Materials

3. The challenge here is the commensuration of value: how, and for whom, is something deemed valuable? (cf. Comaroff and Comaroff 1992). Following Munn's pioneer work on qualisigns (1986) and Harkness and Chumley (2013), I suggest elsewhere (Calvão 2013) how opposing experiences of trading and extracting diamonds organize semiotic qualities of bodily movement (or *qualia*). Here, I wish to focus more explicitly on the material components of trading diamonds.

4. Take, for example, Kockelman's reading of the commodity as a semiotic process that gives way to an analysis of immaterial commodities (2006) or Asif Agha's proposition of 'commodity formulations' (2011).

5. In this, I follow theorizations positing the social and material world of 'things in motion' (Appadurai 1986; Bridge and Smith 2003: 3; cf. Foster 2006) so as to demonstrate the interconnected spheres of production and consumption (Mintz 1985; Smith and Mantz 2006).

6. *Piqué*, or punctured, originally from French. It designates a diamond's range of internal inclusions and spots. While the term has been replaced by more precise technical grading, it is still widely used among Angola's traders.

7. For example, when quipped by the trader with the conventional assertion that the 'market is bad', a digger simply replied that the 'market is not in the field' where diamonds come from.

8. Presumably referencing the decline in global diamond prices.

9. Boss Tom, for example, kept dozens of these stones, each lot sealed with the name of an individual standing in for the group (saying on occasion, 'I'm only taking care of your *kamanga*'). These 'contracts' project the possibility of exchange into the near future, despite no guarantees of a successful outcome as there is no formal control or obligation to sell at the home office. Conversely, this arrangement is frequently invoked by groups of diggers with a history of commercial interactions with a given trader or his company so as to ensure better dividends.

10. This is valid particularly for the case of larger stones without internal defects. With smaller stones, such as *melee* or *huit-huit* (below 0.18 carats) or *sengas* (up to 1 carat), traders tend to expedite the sale or avoid it altogether.

11. ASCORP (Angola Selling Corporation, a joint venture of private and public interests) and SODIAM (Sociedade de Comercialização de Diamantes de Angola, a public branch of state-owned Endiama) are the main agencies responsible for acquiring rough diamonds in Angola. In Lunda, they are used interchangeably to refer to the state's official buying channels.

12. Also described as *pujança* (vitality), that which catches your eye if two exact same diamonds have the same weight, colour and form.

13. Given its subjective results as well as clearly indexing the buyer's interest in the stone, this colour machine is only used sporadically with larger stones.

References

Abolafia, M. (1998), 'Markets as Cultures: An Ethnographic Approach', in Callon, M. (ed.), *The Laws of the Markets*, pp. 69–85. Blackwell Publishers: Oxford.

Agha, A. (2011), 'Commodity Registers', *Journal of Linguistic Anthropology*, 21(1): 22–53.

Appadurai, A. (1986), 'Introduction: Commodities and the Politics of Value', in A. Appadurai (ed.), *The Social Life of Things: Commodities in Cultural Perspective*, pp. 3–63. New York: Cambridge University Press.

Basso, K. H. (1979), *Portraits of 'the Whiteman': Linguistic Play and Cultural Symbols Among the Western Apache*. Cambridge: Cambridge University Press.

Bourdieu, P. (1977), 'The Economics of Linguistic Exchanges', *Social Science Information*, 16(6): 645–668.

Bridge, G. and A. Smith (2003), 'Intimate Encounters: Culture – Economy – Commodity', *Environment and Planning D: Society and Space*, 21: 257–268.

Calvão, F. (2013), 'The Transporter, the Agitator, and the Kamanguista: Qualia and the in/Visible Materiality of Diamonds', *Anthropological Theory*, 13(1/2): 119–136.

Chumley, L. and N. Harkness (2013), 'Introduction: QUALIA', *Anthropological Theory*, 13: 3–11.

Collins, A. T. (1984), 'Pitfalls in Color Grading Diamonds by Machine', *Gems & Gemology*, (Spring): 14–21.

Comaroff, J. and J. Comaroff (1992), 'Goodly Beasts, Beastly Goods', in *Ethnography and Historical Imagination*, pp. 127–154. Boulder, CO: Westview Press.

Foster, R. J. (2006), 'Tracking Globalization: Commodities and Value in Motion', in C. Tilley et al. (ed.), *Handbook of Material Culture*, pp. 285–302. London: SAGE.

Gal, S. (1989), 'Language and Political Economy', in *Annual Review of Anthropology*, 18: 345–367.

Gell, A. (1977), 'Magic, Perfume, Dream', in I. Lewis (ed.), *Symbols and Sentiments: Cross-Cultural Studies in Symbolism*. London: Academic Press.

Irvine, J. (1989), 'When Talk Isn't Cheap: Language and Political Economy', *American Ethnologist*, 16(2): 248–267.

Ingold, T. (ed.) (2011a), *Redrawing Anthropology: Materials, Movements, Lines*. Surrey: Ashgate.

Ingold, T. (2012), 'Toward an Ecology of Materials', *Annual Review of Anthropology*, 41: 427–442.

Keane, W. (1997), *Signs of Recognition. Powers and Hazards of Representation in an Indonesian Society*. Berkeley: University of California Press.

Keane, W. (2003), 'Semiotics and the Social Analysis of Material Things', *Language and Communication*, 23: 409–425.

Keane, W. (2008), 'Market, Materiality and Moral Metalanguage', *Anthropological Theory*, 8(1): 27–42.

Kockelman, P. (2006), 'A Semiotic Ontology of the Commodity', *Journal of Linguistic Anthropology*, 16(1): 76–102.

Lee, B. and E. Lipuma (2002), 'Cultures of Circulation: The Imaginations of Modernity', *Public Culture,* 14(1): 191–213.

Mazzarella, W. (2003), *Shoveling Smoke. Advertising and Globalization in Contemporary India*. Durham, NC: Duke University Press.

Mintz, S. (1985), *Sweetness and Power: The Place of Sugar in Modern History*. New York: Penguin Books.

Munn, N. (1986), *The Fame of Gawa: A Symbolic Study of Value Transformation in a Massim (Papua New Guinea) Society*. Cambridge: Cambridge University Press.

Pietz, W. (1993), 'Fetishism and Materialism: The Limits of Theory in Marx', in E. Apter and W. Pietz (eds), *Fetishism as Cultural Discourse*. Ithaca and London: Cornell University Press.

Shankar, S. and J. R. Cavanaugh (2012), 'Language and Materiality in Global Capitalism', *Annual Review of Anthropology*, 41: 355–369.

Silverstein, M. (2004), '"Cultural" Concepts and the Language-Culture Nexus', *Current Anthropology,* 45(5): 621–652.

Smith, J. H. and J. W. Mantz (2006), 'Do Cellular Phones Dream of Civil War? The Mystification of Production and the Consequences of Technology Fetishism in the Eastern Congo', in M. Kirsch (ed.), *Inclusion and Exclusion in the Global Arena*, pp. 71–93. London: Routledge.

Turner, T. (1977), 'Transformation, Hierarchy and Transcendence: A Reformulation of Van Gennep's Model of the Structure of Rites de Passage', in S. Moore (ed.), *Secular Ritual*, pp. 53–70. Amsterdam: Van Gorcum.

Turner, T. (1994), 'Bodies and Anti-Bodies: Flesh and Fetish in Contemporary Social Theory', in T. Csordas (ed.), *Embodiment and Experience: the Existential Ground of Culture and Self*. Cambridge: Cambridge University Press.

Weiss, B. (1996), *The Making and Unmaking of the Haya Lived World: Consumption, Commoditization, and Everyday Practices*. Durham, NC: Duke University Press.

Weiss, B. (2003), *Sacred Trees, Bitter Harvests: Globalizing Coffee in Northwest Tanzania*. Westport: Greenwood.

Zaloom, C. (2006), *Out of the Pits. Traders and Technology from Chicago to London*. Chicago: The University of Chicago Press.

Part 5

Ecologies of materials' social lives

Chapter 12

Sustainability and the co-constitution of substances and subjects

Sarah Wilkes

This chapter examines the role that materials play in mediating the constitution of moral persons. It draws on ethnographic research among the materials scientists, engineers and designers that make up membership of the Institute of Materials, Minerals and Mining (IOM[3]), a professional body representing the UK materials industry (Wilkes 2013). Rather than focusing on any one material, this research takes a horizontal view across myriad materials to explore the ways in which materials as diverse as PVC, concrete, carbon fibre, paper and steel jostle for market share and are dynamically and differentially categorized as sustainable or unsustainable. In this chapter I focus on attempts to classify a few of these materials as sustainable and explore how both moral persons and moral materials are constituted in the process. I argue that the production of a sustainable material is intimately connected with the construction of a sustainable producer, and vice versa.

My research participants in the UK materials community[1] are coming to appreciate materials in new ways as a result of concerns about 'sustainability'. Materials producers are increasingly recognizing that this nebulous concept can have an enormous impact on the success of their product. Since the publication of the United Nations report *Our Common Future* (Bruntland and WCED 1987),[2] there has been a move in the materials industry away from thinking about sustainability as the single issue of environmental impact and towards a more holistic and 'modern' understanding of the concept,[3] which encompasses the three pillars of economic, environmental and social sustainability. There is a growing belief among materials scientists that if they are to achieve 'true' sustainability, a concern with the physical or technical aspects of materials is no longer enough. Among my research participants the concept of sustainability seems to act as a byword for ethics, and judgments about the sustainability of their materials are intimately linked to producers' transformations into 'ethical' persons. The question of how materials are 'sorted out' (Bowker and Star 2000) into categories of sustainable or unsustainable is therefore heavily imbued with questions of morality.

This chapter focuses in part on the techniques used by the materials community to try and govern materials and thus constitute themselves as sustainable producers. Drawing on Foucault's (1985) discussion of ethics, I explore how materials producers subject themselves to moral codes to transform themselves internally. However, this chapter goes beyond the Foucauldian perspective to explore how producers can only achieve their moral vision by subjecting their materials to the same 'ethical work' that they subject themselves to (1985: 27). In governing their materials, producers also govern themselves. During an investigation of practices of governing materials, it becomes clear that 'nature cannot be forced to say anything we want it to' (Prigogine and Stengers 1984: 5). As Gregson, Watkins and Calestani (2010) demonstrate in their study of asbestos, materials have the potential to resist, inform and constrain human strategies of control. This chapter therefore draws on the work of vital materialists and waste scholars to show materials acting recursively on their producers, restricting and enabling the kinds of moral judgments that can be made about them and shaping the ethical sensibilities of their makers. It argues that 'ethics is not a solely human affair' (Verbeek 2008: 18) but rather arises from the interplay of people and the materials that they produce, use and dispose of.

The structure of this chapter is as follows: the first half of the chapter explores three of the many ways in which people try to govern materials to make them fit with their ideas of sustainability. Firstly, I look at how my research participants manage flows of information about materials in order to affect their own and their material's sustainability. Secondly, I focus on the techniques of the self that producers use to constitute themselves as sustainable producers. Finally I explore how producers govern materials to make them more sustainable.

The second half of the chapter explores the ways in which materials impact on these human strategies of control. It puts forward the argument that several different conceptions of sustainability exist across the UK materials industry, and the kinds of issues that these conceptions prioritize vary. These understandings of sustainability, and the ethical sensibilities of producers, are informed by their 'lived experience' (Kleinman 1998: 358), of which the particular affordances of their specific materials are an important part. Finally, in a comparative case study of PVC and oxo-biodegradable plastics producers, I focus on the ways in which the affordances of the materials that these producers deal with on a daily basis constitute their lived experience and thus affect their understandings of sustainability.

Making knowledge mobile

In order to make moral judgments about the relative sustainability of materials, people require more, and different kinds of, information about materials. My research participants spoke about the difficulties involved in assessing the sustainability of material in a generic way if you don't know the specific context of extraction, production, use and disposal. Understanding the relative sustainability of a material or product therefore requires us to know its story or biography. As a result, in order to make decisions about the sustainability of materials it is commonly thought that we depend upon transparency in the supply chain. Industry cannot achieve the ethical and equitable production and use of materials without a 'transparent and self-regulated' community of suppliers and consumers (Tsoukas 1997: 828).

During a conversation with Jack, a designer at a small clothing company, I was particularly struck by his complaint that a 'lack of information' is his 'greatest handicap' in choosing sustainable materials. Jack argues that 'it is not until we have all the data in front of us, that we can really start to appreciate the causality of our actions'. He describes the 'black box areas' of fragmented information that he 'kept walking into', which resulted in 'confusion about sustainable textiles'. Lauding the benefits of 'the process of understanding as much as possible', he links this directly to both 'good business practice' and 'good environmental practice'. This involves 'managing our supply chain efficiently, with effective timing so that everything is running smoothly and on time, so we don't have to rush things with air transportation'. He suggests that gaining knowledge about the supply chain causes them to change their behaviour, to act differently, which has implications for the sustainability of their products:

> For me, I feel the most important environmental consideration is understanding what it is that we are doing, and in that respect, trying to do things differently. Now that could be as subtle as buying fabric from a factory that is closest to where we are getting [our product] made, as opposed to an existing supply chain because we are trying to reduce energy. But the crux of it is doing something differently, and we do things differently because we understand what is going on.

Jack implies that once acquired, information about the supply chain cannot be ignored and has immediate and positive effects on their decision-making process. In a discussion about responsible sourcing, Paul, marketing manager for a multinational materials producer, also comments on the profound effects that information about the supply chain coming to light can have on a company. He remembers one brand that is 'now one of the global leaders in responsible sourcing, but only because they virtually lost the whole company because they were having children sew their footballs' and a television programme on the topic created a 'knee-jerk reaction' from consumers. This resonates with Marilyn Strathern's argument that in the Euro-American tradition some types of knowledge are 'constitutive', and these potent causative agents can have an 'immediate social effect' (1999: 75).

Paul also describes the process whereby the very act of instituting a 'box-ticking exercise' like a sustainability questionnaire can actually 'push responsibility through the supply chain'. Even though he describes this as the result of a 'policy' and part of a 'process', his comments suggest that the act of reporting, and the knowledge it produces, engenders 'responsibility' and ethical behaviour. At the end of this process, 'hopefully the consumer then will know that the mines that mined the [material] for the car that he's driving around weren't staffed by 10 year old boys'. This is reminiscent of Foucault's 'practices of the self' (1985: 29); in subjecting themselves to a set of moral practices, these manufacturers constitute themselves as responsible people. Paul also implies that by asking his suppliers questions, he is ensuring that they behave responsibly. This suggests that the flow of information between supplier and user is somehow positive and generative in itself.

Jack implies that a willingness to share information is indicative of the trustworthiness of his suppliers, and that receiving information from them also has moral implications for his company:

> I would always say if you have a choice of going with one company that seems to have more environmental credentials than another, but the one that doesn't have environmental credentials has more transparency, so that you can actually engage with the process more, I would always go with the latter. Because in doing so you're effectively taking responsibility for what it is that you're doing – who you're investing in – as opposed to having blind faith that because this person has accreditation, they're doing something that maybe they are not.

In stating that he would rather work with a 'transparent' company than have 'blind faith' in one with 'credentials' that they may not live up to, Jack stresses the importance of visibility for validating trust. It's only when he can see everything that he can trust his suppliers. This belief in the value of transparency is a recurring theme in my fieldwork and illustrates a key point made by Strathern that 'in the information society, with its commitment to evidence-based policy, ensuring that knowledge travels begins to carry political and moral burdens'

(2004: 27). In her examination of higher education evaluation techniques, Strathern argues that this auditing process relies on the assumption that increased visibility or transparency will axiomatically increase the moral standing of an organization: 'if procedures and methods are open to scrutiny, then the organization is open to critique and ultimately to improvement' (2000: 313). Among my research participants, attempts are made to encourage the free flow of information between supplier and user and producer and consumer, and to ensure visibility in the supply chain, with the expectation that this will guarantee moral robustness.

Within Science and Technology Studies, scholars like Pickering (2003) and Knorr-Cetina (1999) have critiqued the assumption that knowledge has some 'magical' property that allows you to accomplish anything and exert rational control on the world (Pickering 2003: 102). However, as anthropologists we must pay attention to the commonsense assumptions of our informants. Drawing on Daniel Miller and James Carrier's (1998) theory of virtualism, I would argue that this belief in the efficacy of knowledge can have material effects. Whether we consider materials knowledge to be an intangible abstraction or a concrete practice, it has undeniable material consequences, even if they are not the ones expected. 'Information' led Jack to reduce his energy use, and beliefs about the efficacy of free-flowing knowledge led him to change his zip supplier and choose one merino wool over another, therefore impacting on material flows of energy, materials and money.

Internal transformation and technologies of the self

The first part of this chapter explored the idea that the management of information about materials can lead to both ethical conduct and more sustainable materials and processes. The sustainability of a material also cannot be divorced from judgments about the motives or mentality of its producers. Determining the relative sustainability of a material obviously relies to an extent on its physical performance during use and disposal. However, a material's social, economic and environmental impact also depends on what happens behind the closed doors of factories and other extraction and production sites. Assessing the sustainability of a material therefore requires a degree of trust in producers' descriptions of these processes. Since the sustainability of a material is thought to depend on the actions and the motives of the people who produce it, a sustainable material requires an 'authentically' sustainable producer.

During my research I found that it was not uncommon for one producer to express doubt about the motives of another producer in adhering to environmental assessment schemes or sustainability frameworks. As I discuss in greater detail elsewhere (Wilkes 2013), there was a perceived difference between producers who espouse an outward-facing, superficial, shallow version of sustainability and those for whom achieving sustainability involves a deep, internal commitment. This became apparent during one discussion between a multimaterial group of materials producers. For example, branding expert Baron argued that there is a 'massive difference' between those producers that have 'truly embraced' sustainability, and those who are merely 'paying lip service' or 'being *seen* to be sustainable'. Fellow branding researcher Arun theorized that we are currently seeing a move from the 'light green business philosophy of adding a hessian pack to make products comply with concerns' to a 'deep green philosophy that places nature before humans' and argued that this move requires the internal transformation of industries and individuals. Metallurgist Bill added that 'if the idea of sustainability is intrinsic in your culture, you'll be more successful at achieving it'. Baron agreed that for a sustainability policy to be implemented effectively you need to get everyone in the company, including those people on the shop floor, to 'think in the right way'. This was one of a number of conversations that suggest that 'true' sustainability requires an internal transformation that can only be achieved if motivations are genuine.

When speaking to PVC producer Lewis, who adheres to the sustainability frameworks The Natural Step (TNS), he argues that the internal transformation of both individuals and companies can be affected by a sustainability philosophy. Lewis describes the impact of TNS on the trajectory of his material, his company, his colleagues and his lifestyle choices. PVC is a material that has received a lot of 'hostility' over the last few decades with regards to its sustainability and was most notably the subject of a single-issue campaign by Greenpeace from the 1990s onwards. Greenpeace campaigns outside PVC factories spurred questions from some employees families as to the virtue of the product they were making. Lewis sat through years of meetings where nobody challenged the Greenpeace position on PVC, and he described his experiences of meetings with retailers at that time as feeling like the 'naughty boy in the class'. However, the industry today looks very different; PVC windows have been given an A and A+ rating from the Building Research Establishment's (BRE) Green Guide,[4] and one manufacturer has been held up as exemplary case study of a 'sustainability journey' (Brennan and Smith 2008: 19).

The turning point for Lewis was when he first came into contact with Forum for the Future, the charitable organization that holds the UK licence for TNS. Forum for the Future were brought in to arbitrate between Greenpeace and the Vinyl Institute at a critical moment in discussions with retailers, who were deciding whether or not to deselect the material. As a result of this meeting, TNS began working with the PVC industry in 1999. At the time of their first report, the TNS team were not uncritical of the material, and noted that there were a number of 'substantive challenges' to making PVC sustainable, but commented that alternative materials 'cannot be assumed to be any more or less sustainable given current manufacture' (Everard, Monaghan and Ray 2000: 2).

Partnering with TNS had a dramatic and positive impact on his company's working environment. Employees became 'fully steeped' in the journey of their industry towards sustainability, with many of them undertaking training 'in their free time'. Staff were encouraged to contribute ideas on issues like 'what could be done on carbon neutrality', and Lewis suggests that their faith in their industry was restored. This created a very different working environment:

> You've no idea how fantastic that was in terms of creativity. There was just a real buzz, with people just thinking, 'This a great opportunity for *us* to come up with some really good ideas'. Many of them were doing it in their spare time. It gave employees empowerment, if you like.

Lewis characterizes his encounter with TNS as a revelatory moment, 'a real moment' in his career, and describes the transformative effects this process had on him personally:

> I live and breathe TNS, I really do, fundamentally. It has changed my life massively. Even down to things like choice of car: I've got a Prius, and I've still got it, it's six years old.

In the case of PVC and its producers, the TNS sustainability framework had a drastic impact on the ethical sensibilities of people involved in its production. Lewis suggests that having a sustainability framework to structure his thinking helped him to act more sustainably.

Controlling materials and processes

Authentic motives and genuine immersion in a sustainability philosophy are thought to be crucial for achieving 'true sustainability'. However, Lewis also emphasizes the importance of the physical transformation of his material in this process. One of the key tenets of the Greenpeace campaign was that PVC was 'inherently unsustainable' as a result of its chlorine content and heavy metal stabilizers. According to Lewis, a key moment in the fortunes of PVC came during a meeting with Jonathon Porritt, founder of Forum for the Future, when he questioned what was 'wrong' with PVC. When the response came from the Greenpeace representative that 'it uses heavy metals in manufacture' and that 'there's all this PVC that's ended up on landfill sites', Porritt questioned what the retailer response would be 'if they [PVC manufacturers] were not to use heavy metal stabilizers?' and asked, 'Can PVC be recycled?'

Once the *inherent* unsustainability of the material had been refuted, this paved the way for a number of changes in the UK PVC industry. This process resulted in quite substantive changes to the material itself. A year later, in the year 2000, a consortium of PVC producers (ECVM, the European Council of Vinyl Manufacturers) came together to commit to a series of industry-wide voluntary commitments to 'waste management, innovative recycling technologies, stake-holder engagement and responsible use of additives' (Vinyl2010 2011; VinylPlus 2013). At their biannual conference in 2010 they had successfully phased-out two of their three heavy-metal stabilizers (cadmium and bisphenol A) from PVC and had reduced lead stabilizers by 50 per cent (Vinyl2010 2011), and they had also managed to develop technology for the recovery and recycling of 270,000 tonnes of PVC. One speaker at the conference described it as 'a new PVC' and argued that the material had 'changed significantly' over the last 10 years (PVC 2011). Lewis's account makes it clear that the physical transformation of their product was a turning point in the internal transformation of his industry.

This example shows that in governing their materials, producers also govern themselves, and during this process of self-realization, some very real changes are effected in the technical and behavioural characteristics of the materials and products that we produce and use. The first part of this chapter shows that sustainability in materials and their makers is dynamically produced, and is affected by attempts to govern information, people and materials themselves. The following sections explore the ways in which specific materials resist these attempts at control in particular ways.

Industrial patterns of attention

According to Honess, Coleman and Brimacombe (2008) sustainability 'can never be defined as "all things to all people" – there is a certain inevitability of it always being "different things to different people"'. In a similar vein, during his presentation at a conference, metallurgist Bill comments that 'we've all seen the definition, and work with it' but it's 'difficult to apply in practice' (Innovation

Towards Sustainable Materials, ITSM, 2011). When it comes to sustainability, 'one of the three things we all agree on [is] that there are different priorities in different sectors and parts of the supply chain' (ITSM 2011). Other speakers at the same event expressed a similar sentiment, with one mining expert commenting that 'what's fashionable here in London may be very different in the rest of the world: here, carbon and environmental impact are very high on the agenda', but in India 'HIV, keeping staff in jobs, water and political problems' are more immediate concerns (ITSM 2011).

This recognition that understandings of sustainability are culturally specific is a sentiment commonly expressed by sustainability professionals. An ungenerous observer might argue that this allows companies to 'redefine or selectively view social problems to fit with the technologies they have'.[5] However, in both academic literature and public debate, sustainable development is accused variously of being imprecisely defined, impractical and internally contradictory (Luke 1995; Watts and Ford 2012). As a result of the broad and all-encompassing nature of the concept, both producers and users of materials struggle on a daily basis to implement sustainable development and make the nebulous and generalized moral axioms of policy makers and heads of state intelligible, particular and practicable.

As I discuss in detail elsewhere (Wilkes 2014), my research participants find themselves confronted with extremely difficult trade-offs between, for example, unemployment and carbon emissions. They explain that it is not the case that they don't care about, for example, carbon emissions, the health of a material or factory conditions. In the dynamic of daily decision-making, they are constrained by finite limits, particularly of time and money, and they inevitably have to prioritize some aspects of sustainability over others. As a result, several different conceptions of sustainability exist across the different communities that make up the UK materials industry, with each community prioritizing different issues.

Over the course of my fieldwork I was involved in a number of multimaterial sector discussions and meetings with sustainability professionals at the IOM[3]. Round table discussions at these meetings, in conjunction with participant observation at industry-specific conferences and interviews with different materials producers, allowed me to build up a picture of where industrial priorities lay. For example, in conversations with architects and civil engineers, it became evident that they were primarily concerned with the environmental impacts of materials, and particularly the reduction of carbon emissions involved in making and using materials. Duncan is a materials specialist at a civil engineering firm, and when I asked him about sustainability, his immediate priority was to lower the carbon footprint of a building, so much so that he nearly forgot to mention the conditions of production of a material:

> Sustainability is such a complex topic, we try and talk about it as four aspects of it: the climate change impact of it, the resource depletion aspect of it, whether it's a healthy and safe material and . . . [the ethics of production?] yes, thank you, responsibly sourced. I think there is a priority system – if we are going to do the right things in terms of how we build and manufacture things and reduce our climate change impact, then the priority is to use materials with a lower immediate carbon footprint and to build things that will reduce the carbon emissions that we are producing now. So in terms of the priority, that's a pretty urgent thing to do I'd say. So that's why the carbon impact of something up front gets quite a high ranking in terms of the priority.

Duncan tells me that his priorities are also influenced by the fact that any material he uses has to perform during the use phase of a building, and that performance contributes to the building's overall environmental impact. He distinguishes between the priorities for an industry where the product doesn't consume energy, and one where the use phase contributes to the overall impact of the product:

> With something like gold, which is only purchased as a luxury good, it's all about perception then – it doesn't have any energy saving benefit, doesn't have any performance in use in terms of environmental impacts. So in the end, the social impact of it, I can see why that is the big priority. Whereas something like aluminium, which is used in so many functional applications, has a big influence on how well buildings perform, for example. It uses a lot of energy in extraction and quite a lot in its reprocessing, so there, that becomes the priority.

This conversation suggests that the physical properties of the materials that producers use, and the nature or application of the product a producer is making, can impinge on their ethical stance and the concerns they prioritize. Using a more detailed comparison of the priorities of two producers of different types of plastic, the following section will explore the idea that the particular ethical sensibilities of these producers are formed in the process of making and using specific materials.

A vignette: pvc and oxo-biodegradables

Within the plastics industry there seem to be very different ideas about what kinds of qualities constitute a sustainable material. To return to Lewis, he is clearly very proud of the changes they have made to their material and industry. However, he also makes it clear that he has always had a devotion to his material, even at the height of the Greenpeace campaign. He describes what he sees as its inherent environmental and social benefits:

> In my own heart, I believed we had a fantastic product. And, I say that with absolute conviction, because all of the [other] polymers were largely 100% from oil. Here, we were producing a polymer pretty magically in terms of half of it coming from salt, which is an abundant natural resource on this planet. If we were going to continue consuming in the way we are today, in terms of salt supply, we could do that for the next 10,000 years.

He also asserts the critical importance of his material to maintaining human health:

> I think things like medical bags, blood bags and all the rest of it . . . well if you didn't use those, what are you going to use? There wasn't really any alternatives to PVC for blood bags, so if you're going to phase it out, what are you going to use there instead?

We discussed why PVC should not have been targeted in the same way as other products of chlorine chemistry like CFCs, PCBs, DDT[6] and mustard gas. Lewis states:

> All of those four substances have the propensity to be widely dispersed in nature in terms of their use, because they are largely produced, apart from PCBs, to disperse. And the other issue there is they have this persistency element, which means potential bioaccumulation in the food chain.

PVC, however, 'uses a huge amount of chlorine, but actually it's quite different to these things'. Lewis argues that this is because the material is not 'biodegrading, and therefore it's not really shedding itself into the environment'. He explains that it's because of this resistance to biodegradation that you don't get bioaccumulation in the same way:

> Bacteria actually are not digesting [it] because it is a macromolecule, so the molecule itself is just so big that you haven't got this bio-magnification, bio-accumulation.

Lewis states that this material's 'persistence is actually a strength in terms of sustainable development, enhancing the amount of service to society that may be delivered by a pool of atoms'. This material is promoted as safe and sustainable as a result of its very resistance to biodegradability. This durability is largely thanks to the technical properties and structure made possible by the addition of chlorine, which makes it fire-retardant and allows it to be separated out from other plastics for recycling.

The sustainability credentials of this plastic are couched in terms completely contradictory to those of oxo-biodegradable plastics. Lewis sees durability, stasis and the stability of his material over time as positive qualities. By contrast, Stephen, a shareholder in an oxo-bio company, expounded the sustainability benefits of materials with short lifespans, which could be safely disposed of. During a sustainability seminar at a plastics industry trade fair, he describes this polymer as a 'controlled-life plastic' and states:

> The advantage of oxo plastics as opposed to, for example, compostable plastics is you can actually tell it when to start degrading, it has a programmed service life. So in the case of a bread bag, you can tell it to degrade in 6 months, in the case of a shopping bag, 18 months, and in the case of a bag for life maybe 5 years.

Oxo-biodegradable (oxo-bio) plastics are traditional plastics in the sense that they are made from petrochemical resources, but they are manufactured with a additive that causes them to break down at a designated point in their lifecycle. They are marketed in a way that positions them as analogous to natural materials: the manufacturer states that they 'harmlessly degrade' at the end of their 'useful life' and can be bio-assimilated by microorganisms 'in the same way as a leaf' (manufacturer's website).

He argues this material is also distinguished from other biodegradable and oxo-bio plastics because it has been certified to international standards for ecotoxicity: 'no known harmful heavy metals or other toxic or hazardous substances' are released when it breaks down. Stephen suggests that his material is a solution to the 'problem' of traditional plastics, whose strength and durability normally makes them such a useful and economic material but can be a major problem when disposal is required. He warns that:

> Whilst most of us think that plastic is fantastic, it can also last for many decades, and if it gets out into the environment, as some of it surely will, this is a problem.

Stephen paints a picture of this 'problem' of the visible, dispersed and long-lasting effects of plastic waste. He describes its accumulation in the environment over decades, its ingestion and incorporation by wildlife, and the 'plastic soups of waste floating in the Pacific Ocean, covering an area greater than the size of Texas'. He positions his material as the solution to this 'disfigurement of the landscape'.

These two producers of different kinds of plastics both make claims for the sustainability of their material. As a result of the radically different physical characteristics of their material, however, they see sustainability as completely different things. For Lewis, the durability of his material in the use phase makes it efficient, safe and socially valuable, whereas for Stephen, the degradability of his material at end-of-life makes it innocuous and environmentally beneficial.

Arthur Kleinman has formulated a theory of the ways in which ethical discourse informs moral practice. He characterizes ethical discourse as the 'abstract articulation and debate over codified values' (1998: 363). Moral practices, however, are constituted at the 'local level of lived experience' (363) where our 'movements meet resistance and find directions, and our subjectivity emerges, takes shape, and reflexively shapes our local world' (359). This is not to suggest that ethical discourse is the precursor to moral experience; protagonists of ethical discourse are, of course, 'grounded in particular moral places and processes', thus moral experience informs ethical discourse (365). Scholars like Peter-Paul Verbeek and Kersty Hobson have adopted this kind of practice-based approach to ethics that takes into account the ways in which moral persons are produced at the same time as moral objects. As Hobson has argued in her study of the role of recycling bins in encouraging environmental behaviour, things do not just '"script" certain practices' and 'transfer' proper behaviour but rather 'solicit practices that forge specific socio-material relations' (2006: 325). Hobson states that 'ethics are neither abstract values, nor scripted into technologies, but are worked up and through the objects they refer to' (2006: 330). Following Hobson and Verbeek, I would argue that 'technologies shape us as specific moral subjects' since they 'help to shape human perceptions and interpretations of reality, on the basis of which moral decisions are made' (Verbeek 2008: 23).

I would argue that this is precisely what happens when materials producers struggle to make sustainable development policy a reality; their implementation of it is, necessarily, guided by their engagement in everyday life. This engagement involves interactions with particular materials and their affordances, as well as with the perceived dangers and priorities that occupy their industry's attention. In the process of making and using specific materials, the particular institutional logic of these companies and the ethical sensibilities of their employees are also produced. Because of the nebulous nature of sustainability as a concept and the different lived experiences of producers, different conceptions of sustainability and kinds of moral person are produced.

Conclusion

For reasons that I discuss in greater detail elsewhere (Wilkes 2013), this chapter takes a deliberate methodological choice to focus on multiple materials, in contrast to some of the other chapters in this volume. It provides less detail on individual materials in order to provide more detail on the relationships *between* them. This broader focus allows for observation of the dynamic struggles between different materials and producers, where some materials periodically gaining ascendancy over others. I would argue that an anthropological approach to multiple materials adds a new dimension to this field of study.

This chapter shows that the sustainability of materials is thought to require 'traceability' and 'transparency' in the supply chain. What we know about materials affects their success in the marketplace. This observation invites further questions about the relationship between knowledge and the social efficacy of materials, which I cannot deal with here due to constraints of time and space. As I discuss elsewhere (Wilkes 2014), this speaks to existing anthropological literature on knowledge transmission (Barth 1990; Harrison 1995; Strathern 2004) that explores how the management of knowledge can lead to changes in the status of people. New research that examines how the 'stickiness' of an object or material, cognitively and meaningfully, can be affected by information about its biography has the potential to add to this literature by examining how knowledge practices can impact on the trajectories of materials as well as their makers.

In examining the interplay between the UK materials community, their strategies for sustainability, and the affordances and resistances of their materials, this chapter also examines the ways in which ethical materials and their producers are co-constituted. The data presented here demonstrates that there is a link between the morality of a material and its maker. 'True' sustainability is determined by the performance of the product itself but also by the ethics, actions and motivations of the producer. When the sustainability of a material is assessed, the credentials of the producer come under scrutiny, and vice versa.

The idea that the world is not plastic and resists our attempts to control it is not a new one. What this chapter contributes to existing literature is an understanding of how both individuals and social groups are constituted through the process of materials resisting attempts at governance in specific ways. Industrial patterns of attention are developed and communities are formed through interactions with specific materials. Because materials are often ignored in anthropological studies,[7] I want to emphasize their role in the co-constitution of moral persons and sustainable materials. However, materials are not the only disciplinary apparatus that play a part in this process. As Latour comments, morality is a 'heterogenous institution that is constituted from a multiplicity of events' and that depends in part on 'technical apparatuses' but also on 'a good many other forms of organisation' (2002: 254). People, institutions, tools for knowledge production and transfer and manufacturing processes are some of the actants that play a role in the dynamic and relational process whereby materials such as steel, copper and PVC come to be seen as sustainable. The social value of a material is relationally constituted and cannot be understood in isolation from other materials, people, tools and practices.

Notes

1. I use this term to designate both producers and users of materials affiliated with the IOM[3].
2. Commonly known as the Brundtland Report.
3. Bill, metallurgist, personal communication.
4. The BRE *Green Guide to Specification* is an accredited system for comparing the environmental impacts of building materials using Life Cycle Assessment (LCA).
5. Peter, sustainable chemist, personal communication.
6. CFCs, PCBs and DDT refer to Chlorofluorocarbons, Polychlorinated Biphenyls, and Dichlorodiphenyltrichloroethane, respectively.
7. Miller (2007) asserts that *the material* is already the focus of material culture approaches. While I agree with this assertion, I would argue that *materials*, as a plural entity developed in relation to a scientific discipline of the same name, are less well studied.

References

Allwood, J. (2012), 'Materials Efficiency: Providing Material Services with Less Material Production', *Transitions to Material Efficiency in the UK Steel Economy*. Lecture, London, 31 January 2012, London: The Royal Society.

Barth, F. (1990), 'The Guru and the Conjurer: Transactions in Knowledge and the Shaping of Culture in Southeast Asia and Melanesia', *Man*, 25(4): 640–653.

Bensaude-Vincent, B. and R. Newman (2007), *The Artificial and the Natural: An Evolving Polarity*. Cambridge, MA: MIT Press.

Bowker, G. and S. Star (2000), *Sorting Things Out: Classification and Its Consequences*. Cambridge, MA and London: MIT Press.

Brennan, J. and C. Smith (2008), *Norsk Hydro ASA: Sustainable PVC at Hydro Polymers?* INSEAD, available at: <http://www.insead.edu/facultyresearch/centres/izic/ecsr/research/documents/NorskHydroASA.pdf> (accessed 23 June 2012).

Brundtland, G. and World Commission on Environment and Development (WCED) (1987), *Our Common Future,* online pdf available at: <http://www.un-documents.net/our-common-future.pdf> (accessed 23 June 2012).

Carrier, J. and D. Miller (1998), *Virtualism: A New Political Economy*. Oxford: Berg.

Everard, M., M. Monaghan and D. Ray (2000), *PVC: An Evaluation Using The Natural Step Framework*. Gloucestershire: The Natural Step and The Environment Agency.

Foucault, M. (1985), *The Use of Pleasure: A History of Sexuality Volume II*. New York: Vintage.

Gregson, N., H. Watkins and M. Calestani (2010), 'Inextinguishable Fibres: Demolition and the Vital Materialisms of Asbestos', *Environment and Planning A*, 42(5): 1065–1083.

Harrison, S. (1995), 'Anthropological Perspectives: On the Management of Knowledge', *Anthropology Today,* 115: 10–14.

Hobson, K. (2006), 'Bins, Bulbs, and Shower Timers: On the "Techno-ethics" of Sustainable Living', *Ethics Place and Environment,* 9(3): 317–336.

Honess, C., N. Coleman and L. Brimacombe (2008), *Measuring Sustainability.* Conference presentation, London, 12 December 2008, online pdf available at: <http://www.iom3.org/conference-proceeding/steel-sustainability> (accessed 13 June 2012).

Innovation Towards Sustainable Materials (ITSM) (2010), Conference, 10–11 November 2010, London: Royal Society.

Kleinman, A. (1998), 'Experience and Its Moral Modes: Culture, Human Conditions and Disorder', *Proceedings of the Tanner Lectures on Human Values*, 13–16 April 1998, Stanford University.

Knorr-Cetina, K. (1999), *Epistemic Cultures: How the Sciences Make Knowledge.* Cambridge, MA: Harvard University Press.

Latour, B. (2002), 'Morality and Technology: The End of Means', *Theory Culture and Society,* 19(5–6): 247–260.

Luke, T. (1995), 'Sustainable Development as a Power/Knowledge System: The Problem of "Governmentality"', in F. Black and M. Fischer (eds), *Greening Environmental Policy: The Politics of a Sustainable Future.* Oxford: Palgrave Macmillan.

Miller, D. (2007), 'Stone Age or Plastic Age?', *Archaeological Dialogues,* 14(1): 23–27.

Pickering, A. (2003), 'On Becoming: Imagination, Metaphysics, and the Mangle', in D. Ihde and E. Selinger (eds), *Chasing Technoscience: Matrix for Materiality*, pp. 96–116. Bloomington, IN: Indiana University Press.

Prigogine, I. and I. Stengers (1984), *Order Out Of Chaos.* Westminster, MD: Bantam.

PVC (2011), Conference, 12–14 April 2011. Brighton: Brighton Dome.

Reducing the Impact of Textiles on the Environment (RITE) (2010), Conference, 6 October 2010. London: Central Hall Westminster.

Strathern, M. (1999), *Property, Substance and Effect: Anthropological Essays on Persons and Things*. London: Athlone.

Strathern, M. (2000), 'The Tyranny of Transparency', *British Educational Research Journal,* 26(3): 309–321.

Strathern, M. (2004), *Commons and Borderlands: Working Papers on Interdisciplinarity, Accountability and the Flow of Knowledge.* Oxford: Sean Kingston Publishing.

Tsoukas, H. (1997), 'The Tyranny of Light: The Temptations and the Paradoxes of the Information Society', *Futures,* 29(9): 827–843.

Verbeek, P. (2008), 'Obstetric Ultrasound and the Technological Mediation of Morality: A Postphenomenological Analysis', *Human Studies,* 31: 11–26.

Vinyl2010 (2011), *Vinyl2010 10 Years: Reporting on the Activities of the Year 2010 and Summarising the Key Milestones of the Past 10 Years,* online pdf available at: <http://www.pvc.org/en/p/vinyl-2010-progress-report-2008> (accessed 17 November 2012).

VinylPlus (2011), *Introducing VinylPlus: The New 10-year Voluntary Commitment of the European PVC Industry.* Brussels: VinylPlus, online pdf available at: <http://www.vinylplus.eu/uploads/Modules/Publications/vinylplus-leaflet_v20_final.pdf> (accessed 17 November 2012).

Watts, J. and L. Ford (2012), 'Rio+20 Earth Summit: Campaigners Decry Final Document', *Guardian,* 23 June, available online at: <http://www.guardian.co.uk/environment/2012/jun/23/rio-20-earth-summit-document?newsfeed=true> (accessed 23 June 2012).

Wilkes, S. (2008), *Materials Matter: An Anthropological Study of Materials Libraries,* MA Thesis. London: University College London.

Wilkes, S. (2014), *In Search of Sustainable Materials: Negotiating Materiality and Morality in the UK Materials Industry*, PhD Thesis. London: University College London.

Chapter 13

The peony and the rose: Social change and fragrance marketing in China's bath market

Chan Chow Wah

In 2007, Liushen, a Chinese soap and body wash brand (Figure 13.1), overtook Lux as the best-selling beauty soap and body wash brand in China. This is a very rare achievement considering that in Asia the brands owned by global giants such as Unilever and P&G usually dominate the market.

Utilizing market reports of the China bath market set against the political and social development of post-Cultural Revolution China, along with

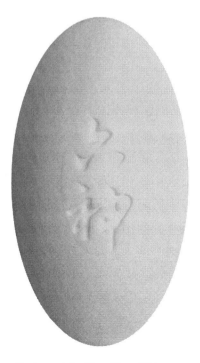

Figure 13.1 Liushen soap. Photograph by Chan Chow Wah.

interviews with Chinese consumers, I use the case of Liushen to focus on the relationship between fragrance preference and social change. I propose that collective fragrance preference in a society can be appropriated as a barometer of social change.

I present fragrance as an 'informed' material (Barry, this volume) and a product of relationships, connections and networks, embedded in the historical imagination of consumers. This perspective encourages a pluralistic approach to understand the success of a brand not just within narrow confines of 'good marketing'. The social landscape that paved the way for Liushen's success also illuminates the limitations of the 'linear' history of fragrance espoused by the fragrance industry.

Smell: The neglected sense

Medical scientists have not quite understood the human mechanism of smell, and cultures do not have the vocabulary to describe smells in any complete or absolute sense (Moeran 2005). Among the general public, discussions of fragrances are communicated through references to other senses or through metaphors. Our sense of smell can be argued to be the least understood of our senses. Yet every culture has its order and hierarchy of senses and symbolisms.

Classen (1993) has documented the decline of olfactory culture in the West as society evolved towards a visual-centric culture from the second half of the seventeenth century. The changes in the sensory landscape of the West are best reflected in the transformation of the rose, from an earlier focus on its scent to a later focus on its visual qualities. Fragrance consumption in the West has moved from public and collective to become private and personal. This shift is also reflected in the restriction of smells and olfactory symbolism in the modern West, especially as human senses have acquired a gendered association where men see and reason, while women 'sniff things out' in a more embodied sense. Fragrances as a material, within this history, began to be more closely feminized.

Classen's research explains several phenomena that we continue to observe to this day and begins to account for anthropology's lack of attention to smell. With feminized associations, fragrances continue to be linked with a 'real men don't do this' attitude, and even male scientists may blush and titter when given a smelling strip used to evaluate fragrances (Turin 2006). Meanwhile, participant observation, the anthropologist's most well-known research methodology, is also a product of the West's visual-centric culture.

Despite our lack of understanding, almost everyone interacts with fragrances on a daily basis as most consumer products are infused with fragrances produced by a multibillion dollar fragrance industry. In fact, Moeran (2005) has predicted that 'technology is bringing smell back into our daily lives and that it will be more pervasive'.

Bath products as fragrance barometer

With the exception of air-fresheners, body sprays and perfumes, consumers encounter and consume fragrances as part of a product. Generally, the choice of fragrances in a product reflects the existing fragrance associations of consumers in a particular market. The fragrance becomes part of the product's attributes and is even the primary communicator, as evidenced by peoples' tendency, in their role as consumers to smell products before purchase. In the case of soaps and body wash, fragrance is the only dimension of the product that lingers on the skin of the user and remains detectable by both the user and people around the user.

The largest product categories for fragrances are fabric care, such as detergents and fabric softeners, and personal care products such as soap, body wash and shampoo. Soaps and body wash are classified as bath products and stand out as the categories that have the widest direct contact with end consumers. The purchaser of soaps and body wash in Asia, following the paradigm of the market research reports, is usually a woman, but the entire family uses the product almost on a daily basis and even several times a day. As such, the purchaser needs to choose a product that is acceptable by the entire family, including male members. Due to its wide and regular contact with the general population in a market and country and the ability of its fragrance to linger on the skin, soaps and body wash are a good indicator of fragrance appreciation or preference in a society.

The fragrance industry

Fragrances infused into consumer goods are produced by the flavour and fragrance industry. Each company usually has a flavour and a fragrance division. The former produces flavours for use in food products while the latter produces fragrances for consumer and industrial products that are not meant for use as food. The industry in 2011 was worth about 22 billion USD, and the top four companies controlled 55 per cent of the global market.[1]

The major fragrance houses employ perfumers, whose global number is estimated to be about 500, a population less than the number of astronauts.[2] They produce fragrances from a pallet of raw materials that include both natural and synthetic raw materials,[3] that are either 'natural identical' or 'non-natural identical'.[4]

With thousands of fragrance creations, the fragrances are classified into families. When new fragrance profiles become popular, the fragrance families are updated to incorporate new subgroups. Each fragrance company has its own classification methodologies that may differ from company to company.

An independent methodology is the fragrance wheel developed by Michael Edwards and adopted by retailers to communicate fragrance profiles with customers (see Figure 13.2).[5] Using this as an example, fragrances are classified as Floral, Oriental, Woody and Fresh. While floral, citrus and woody notes are obvious and nature-inspired, the 'oriental' category illuminates the strong Western bias in the fragrance industry. Oriental notes refer to heavy blends of

Figure 13.2 Michael Edwards' fragrance wheel. Use with permission from Michael Edwards. Note the original is in colour.

resins, opulent flowers, sweet vanilla and musk that conjure up the Near East, or more specifically the Western imagination of the Middle East.

To a large extent, the fragrance industry 'smells' the world from a Western perspective and adopts a linear history of fragrance tracing its beginning in ancient Egypt and through the Greek and Roman periods, and Renaissance Europe to today's modern fragrance culture (Moeran 2005).[6] This linear history fails to take into consideration the olfactory culture of non-Western societies.

Chinese olfactory culture: The forgotten peony

In ancient times, Confucius was said to have been inspired by the orchid fragrance, and used it as an analogy for unrecognized talents. Archaeological excavations from third-century BCE Han tombs have unearthed fragrance holders with gyroscopic principles (Michaelson 1999).

A millennium later, the seventh-century Tang dynasty's extensive trade routes offered their aristocracy a wide pallet of local and imported raw materials to perfume their environment and themselves. Their fragrance pallet included camphor, lime, frankincense, cloves, patchouli, sweet basil, musk deer (Benn 2004), vanilla and aloe wood (Michaelson 1999).

In the tenth century, the Song dynasty organized imperial examinations open to all subjects. At times, candidates were even tested on their ability to compose poetry and to paint, and in one examination the candidates were said to have been tested on their creativity to paint a visual interpretation of a poem. The poem mentioned the scents of flowers, and the top candidate creatively used butterflies to convey the floral scent, while others painted flowers. By the fourteenth-century Ming dynasty, incense and incense-holders had become indispensable objects of a scholar's study, and coexisted with visual-centric literati pursuits such as calligraphy and painting.

Chinese social symbolism of fragrances

The Chinese character for fragrance is *Xiang* (香) and is used in idioms and invested with social meanings. Members of literati families are said to be someone from a 'family living in the mist of fragrances emitted from their book collections' (书香世家). The fragrances referred to are herbal, from the herbs used as insect-repellent to protect the books, and the phrase is used to mean an educated and cultivated person. In Southern Chinese tea culture, there is even a distinction between fragrance and flavour. When tea is prepared, it is poured into a smelling cup (闻香杯) to appreciate the aroma before the same tea is poured into an appreciation cup (品茗杯) to be drunk from and to appreciate its flavour.

The 'Patriotic Princess' (帝女花) is one of the most popular Cantonese operas, written in 1957 in Hong Kong. It still has a huge following in the Chinese community around the world, especially among the Cantonese. The opera revolves around Princess Chang Ping, a Ming dynasty princess who committed suicide with her consort on their wedding night as an act of political resistance against the Manchurian invaders. As the newly-weds slowly die of arsenic poisoning, they sing of how the scent of the princess's fragrance will continue to linger around their suicide site (双枝有树透露帝女香). The lyrics use fragrance as an analogy that the sacrifice of the princess will be remembered for generations after her death.

These examples highlight certain differences between Western and Chinese olfactory cultures. Chinese olfactory culture is gender-inclusive, which I suggest continues to this day. Men and women's appreciation of fragrance and the ability to articulate them is considered a mark of refinement, and apart from their olfactory value, fragrances have also acquired ascetic, social and moral values.

This Chinese olfactory culture is in contrast to the West, where the rise of its visual-centric culture developed at the expense of other senses, diminishing both the role of smells in modern Western culture and its olfactory symbolism (Classen 1993). This contrast raises an important question as to why Lux and its Western fragrance connotations have prevailed for about two decades in China, a culture with a rich olfactory history and heritage. The East-West contrast exposes the inadequacy of a linear history of fragrances. The 'Egyptian to modern perfumery' history is one fragrance genealogy that exists alongside other fragrance genealogies such as the Chinese, Indian and other cultures.

Bath fragrances

Globally, the sale of soaps and body wash is undertaken by marketing companies. This is usually done by creating a brand to differentiate their products and to present them as singular and incomparable (Foster 2008).[7] Companies such as Unilever and P&G become so successful that their brands, like Lux and Palmolive, are sold in many countries around the world. Almost every country will have local companies who promote their respective brands, competing among themselves and with international brands. Each brand usually has three to four variants, and each variant is available as a soap or body wash. Variants are differentiated by adding fragrances, cosmetic ingredients and colour. Fragrances play a unique role as the only material that lingers on the skin after use, and potential buyers often smell the product to decide on a purchase.

When a new product is planned or an existing one is being relaunched, the company issues a brief, explaining the product's concept and the fragrance requirement. Fragrance houses submit fragrance proposals by translating the brief into olfactory creations. While fragrance houses may offer different inter-pretations of a brief, only one fragrance will be selected per variant.

As an example, if customers in the industry ask for a citrus fragrance for their bath product, there are many possibilities for perfumers to create a citrus fragrance: sweet citrus, sour citrus, citrus with bitter peel notes, floral citrus, citrus with cologne touch, etc. The perfumers have much room for creativity but ultim-ately, the fragrance must smell attractive to potential and existing customers, and have some resemblance to their notion of citrus. Beyond that, perfumers are free to include any resonations they feel will make fragrance more attractive to customers.

Upon receiving fragrance submissions, the companies will conduct consumer tests to identify the winning fragrance. This winning fragrance is infused into the products and marketed to consumers. During the purchase process, most people evaluate a bath product by smelling it. If the fragrance profile is perceived to have associations with the product claims and the potential customer likes the fragrance, a purchase happens. Otherwise, the product is rejected. The collect-ive actions of consumers in the longer term determine the success or failure of the final product.

The importance of fragrances in product communication becomes even more apparent in cases when a producer uses the same soap or body wash base for all the variants, differing only in the fragrances. From the company's perspec-tive, a good fragrance must smell attractive and be able to communicate the product attributes to potential customers. From the customer's perspective, the product's fragrance profile is the main indicator of product quality and benefit. In the context of cross-cultural marketing, the fragrances play an additional role of investing the product with a cultural content (Chua 2003).

The peony blooms

In 2007, Liushen (六神) surpassed Lux to become China's largest beauty soap and body wash brand by retail share.[8] Since 2007, Liushen has maintained and strengthened its position as the number one beauty bath brand. Their retail share has grown from 5.5 per cent, to 6.2 per cent in 2010, while Lux fell from 5.4 per cent to 5.1 per cent during the same period (Euromonitor International 2011a).

Liushen is owned by Shanghai Jiahua United Company (上海家化联合股份有限公司) whereas the global giant Unilever owns Lux. Liushen's defeat of Lux, and its achievement in becoming the top-selling, and therefore most popular brand of beauty bath products in China, is an unusual phenomenon in China and Asia. In Asia, with the exception of Japan and South Korea (Euromonitor International 2011a, 2011b), and now China, Lux or one of the global brands usually captures the largest share of the beauty soap market. Very often, local competitors attempt to emulate Lux or one of the leading foreign brands by offering similar products at a lower cost and sometimes at a lower quality. Their choice of fragrances reflects either imitations of foreign brands or popular fine fragrances from the West (Europe or United States).[9]

In contrast, Liushen products and fragrances are marketed as inspired by traditional Chinese medicine, promising 'oriental charm' and 'cherishing traditions' (珍视传统). Liushen has been competing against Lux, targeting '20-35 years-old urban married women with junior high school or above education, including general labors [sic] in the society and first-line/middle management whose income are distributed between 25% and 75% of the whole population'.[10]

Liushen's positioning as local and its focus on traditional Chinese medicinal knowledge is unusual in China, where consumers generally favour foreign brands. Foreign brands are usually perceived to be of a higher quality (Fong 2004) and deemed as more appealing or prestigious.[11] Product safety concerns are another obstacle for local brands. Despite these obstacles, Liushen was able to emerge as the most popular beauty bath brand in China.

Cultural branding theory

Sales professionals often attribute the rise of Liushen to good marketing strategies, while consumers explain that Liushen is a familiar brand, but both reasons are insufficient to account for Liushen's success. Good marketing cannot explain why some brands are more successful than the others and does not take into consideration the social contexts in which the brands were promoted and the ways in which brands are being consumed and appropriated by consumers. As in Foster's value chain analysis, adding value via the expert labour of the marketer is inadequate (Foster 2008). Familiarity on the other hand is no guarantee of success as Liushen only surpassed Lux in 2007, ending its reign of nearly two decades. Both explanations, marketing and familiarity, fail to take into consideration the meaningful use to which consumers put the product (Foster 2008).

I propose that social change in China was instrumental in Liushen's ascent to become the top brand, and I draw on Douglas Holt's cultural branding model to present my argument (Holt 2004). Cultural branding proposes that brands become iconic when their product addresses cultural contradictions experienced by consumers at a particular point in time. Cultural contradictions emerge whenever an individual's ideology and real-life experience diverge, when individuals feel they live in a world that is different from how they like it to be or how it should be. These cultural contradictions are usually experienced at a collective level and occur during times of social change. During periods of cultural contradiction, products, through their marketing strategies, address the contradictions by offering consumers an imagined 'populist world' that resonates with their ideology. Over time, as conditions in a society changes, new cultural contradictions arise. Brands stay relevant by offering new populist worlds to address the new cultural contradictions. Brands that succeed thrive while those that fail lose their customers.

Social change therefore presents a challenge to existing brands while offering opportunities for new brands. In the case of Liushen, the Chinese cultural contradiction lies in the Chinese belief of their rightful place among leading nations of the world against their self-perception of backwardness and the ways they believe China has and still is being denied that status. Liushen's products inspired by Chinese heritage offer a gateway to a populist world addressing their cultural contradictions.

Locating Chinese consumption against the decline and rise of China

To understand the social context of consumption in China and the nature of cultural contradiction that Liushen benefited from, I will present (somewhat briefly, it must be acknowledged) recent Chinese history from the perspective of Chinese consumers.

The First Opium War between Great Britain and Qing China from 1839 to 1842 was a tragic historical marker for the Chinese. China had to sign the first of many unequal treaties, and Hong Kong Island was ceded in perpetuity to Great Britain among other demands. To the Chinese, this was a humiliating event marking their decline and the advert of foreign intrusion and imperialism. Other major events included the Eight Nation Alliance's (八国联军) occupation of Beijing and their entrance into the Forbidden City during the Boxer Rebellion in 1900, the Second Opium War and the destruction of the Summer Palace in 1860. During these campaigns, many treasures were looted and taken out of China.

To this day, emotions continue to run high whenever these treasures emerge in auctions outside of China (e.g. an auction by Christie's of artefacts from the Summer Palace: see BBC 2009) and there is even a social movement to buy back stolen artefacts (see, e.g. Yingzi 2008). This movement is not just a China-based initiative but includes the participation of overseas Chinese as well. The most prominent example is Macao businessperson Stanley Ho, who bought artefacts looted from the Yuan Ming Yuan during the Second Opium War and donated them to the Chinese government (see Lim 2007).

By 1912, the Qing dynasty had collapsed, but the new Republican govern-ment fared no better. At the end of the First World War, German concessions in China were awarded to Japan instead of China, although both were part of the Allied forces. In 1937, the Second Sino-Japanese War erupted and dragged on for seven years, until the Japanese surrender in 1942. The infamous Nanjing massacre, the extreme loss of life, the suffering and the Japanese refusal to apologize for the war, continue to be sore issues. Immediately after World War II, Nationalist and Communist factions began the Chinese Civil War, and China was finally united as the People's Republic of China in 1949 under Mao Zedong. From 1966 to 1976, China experienced another period of turmoil during the Cultural Revolution (Fong 2004).

In September 1978, Deng Xiao Ping came into power and initiated a series of reforms (改革开放) to integrate China with the rest of the world. During this period, Special Economic Zones were established in coastal cities and foreign investments (notably) were welcomed.

Yang as social aspiration

Deng's reform brought about economic growth and opportunities for the Chinese unprecedented since 1949. Socially, the Deng era is characterized by a desire to make money and to modernize through consumption (Pan 1986). China's open-ing up brought about economic growth but also the perception that the country and the Chinese being backward or *tu* (土). The concept of *yang* (洋) became the defining aspiration among Chinese consumers who aspired to be modern. *Yang* refers to foreign and is associated with being modern and can include ideas of being fashionable, progressive or civilized.

The pervasiveness of Yang aspirations is best reflected by Yan's (1997) account of an elderly couple's 1993 visit to McDonalds at Tiananmen on China's National day. The trip was a treat from their daughter and the memorable visit was completed with a taxi ride and photo sessions. Their adventure took place slightly over a year after Beijing McDonalds opened. It was at that time the largest McDonalds restaurant in the world and a place where Chinese consumers experienced American culture. Every year domestic tourists arrived in Beijing to visit famous monuments such as the Forbidden City and the Great Wall of China, and after the opening of McDonalds, it was added to their itinerary.

This McDonalds visit reminded the couple of their earlier Beijing visit in 1949, the founding year of the People's Republic of China, when they also had a picture taken. Proud of their visit, they sent the two photos taken 44 years apart in the same location to their hometown newspaper. Their hometown newspaper team obviously viewed the two photos from the perspective of the 'tu-yang' discourse, and went on to title their story 'Forty-four years: From Tu to Yang' (Yan 1997).

Similar cases appear in many other ethnographies: homes have not been seen as modern due to the lack of Italian design (Guldin 1996); young factory girls want a taste of 'Western wind' (西风) or a cosmopolitan lifestyle (Ngai 2003); eating at McDonalds is a way to gain status (Yan 1997); and going abroad forms part of a strategy to achieve social mobility (Fong 2004).

Lux entered the Chinese market in 1986, about a decade after Deng's reforms, and into a social climate characterized by the pursuit of yang (Euromonitor International 2011a). As a foreign brand, Lux symbolized modernity for Chinese consumers addressing their aspirations to 'be advanced, modern, developed, progressive or capturing of the western, cosmopolitan or global (Croll 2006)'. Not surprisingly, within a few years of its arrival, Lux became the number one beauty bath product in China and held this position for almost two decades until the rise of Liushen in 2007.

Filial nationalism and filial consumption

When Chinese consumers consume foreign brands and products, their consumption is located within a consumer discourse of tu and yang, but the motivation to be yang or modern is also driven by a desire or an obligation for China to rise and to be 'equal among nations'.

Even Chinese consumers who love everything Western and perceived China to be inferior still believe in their obligation to help bring China into the imagined community of wealthier societies, a phenomenon Fong (2004) labelled 'filial nationalism'. There is a love-hate relationship, or Chinese-foreign dilemma (Barme 1995), between Chinese consumers and Western countries, especially the United States and United Kingdom, who are their cultural source of modernity. However, they are also the countries, in Chinese opinion, responsible for the decline of China and even for preventing her rise. Barme (1995) goes further to suggest that 'it represents the coming of age of Chinese narcissism, and it bespeaks a desire for revenge for all the real and perceived slights of the past century.'

The desire for China to be equal among nations, to be part of the 'imagined community of wealthier societies', and the personal obligation to play a part towards this dream is in contradiction to the strong desire for Western goods and their ability to confer social status as a symbol of *yang*. This cultural contradiction is resolved by mining the past to construct a new Chinese modernity and the trend is propelled by the growing Chinese economy, as well as by increasing Chinese pride and nationalism.

A new Chinese cosmology

Deng's reforms laid the foundation for successful economic growth, rising income and living standards. These economic changes, along with recent political events, such as the Hong Kong Handover in 1997, Macao Handover in 1999, China's admission into WTO in 2001, and the 2008 Beijing Olympic Games, led to aspirations for national revival and supremacy (Barme 1995).

By the turn of the twenty-first century, the economic, social and political developments in China gave the Chinese a sense of pride that China has finally risen from, or at least is rising from, the humiliations inflicted by the Opium Wars and from the time when China was known as the 'Sick Man of East Asia' (东亚病夫). Now, China is considered to be more or less 'equal among nations'.[12]

This Post-Deng era attitude is contrasted to two earlier periods: the Cultural Revolution (1966 to 1976) and the Deng Reform era (1978 to 1997). During the Cultural Revolution, a new identity was forged through the destruction and disassociation with the past, with calls to 'destroy the four olds': ideologies (old ideas, old culture, old customs and old habits) (Roberts 2003). This attitude was materially manifested in the destruction of material culture that represented the old, such as antiques and works of art, and in the destruction of institutions such as temples, monasteries and ancient monuments.

Moving out of the Cultural Revolution and into the Deng's reform era was a period characterized by 'loss of confidence' (Croll 2006) when anything Chinese was considered *tu* while everything foreign, especially European and American, was considered *yang*. In the post-Deng era, the pride and confidence of the twenty-first century motivated Chinese consumers to embrace their cultural heritage and to mine the past for the construction of a new modern Chinese identity. The most visible manifestation of this is the rise of the *Hanfu* movement (汉服运动) since 2003 (Wong 2006), which has since spread to the Chinese diaspora.[13] Supporters dress themselves in clothing styles selected from periods of ethnic Han rule in China, especially the Han, Song and Ming dynasties, that they feel reflect Chinese culture and heritage (Figure 13.3). Considering the Manchurian rule from 1644 to 1912 as foreign, *Hanfu* enthusiasts reject the more visible *qipao* (旗袍) as inauthentic Chinese costume.

The *Hanfu* movement is a good example of mining the past to create a new modern Chinese identity. *Hanfu* dress offer customers a wide range of styles, colours and designs who accordingly to their personal preferences, disregarding the symbol, materials and colour codes imposed on the population by the respective Chinese dynasties (Clunas 2007). More significantly, Chinese female graduates who dress in *Hanfu* for their graduation are enacting an entirely new phenomenon, since the former imperial examinations system only admitted male candidates (Miyazaki 1976). Fortunately though, there have so far been no calls to revive the practise of foot binding (Gernet 1962) that used to form a part of elite Chinese women's fashion since the tenth century.

The *Hanfu* movement demonstrates very clearly a selective borrowing from the past to create a new modern Chinese identity, and is definitely not a revival of traditional or ancient norms. The same dynamic unfolds in other material

Figure 13.3 *Hanfu* fans in Singapore. Photograph used with permission from Mr. Michael Jow.

dimensions, as in the case of Liushen soaps and body wash. The rise in national-ethnic pride in China around the turn of the twenty-first century offered an opportunity for products to address the cultural contradiction felt by Chinese consumers. It is a situation that Liushen successfully addressed and benefited from to defeat the Lux brand.

First launched in 1995, Liushen incorporated many traditional Chinese herbal and medicinal ingredients such as green tea, aloe vera, wheat bran, chrysanthemum, clove and lily, with which consumers can identify. These ingredients are used as part of their 'secret recipes' and/or 'traditional formulations', mentioned on the product packaging (《青囊立效秘方》,《青囊立效秘方》,《千金月令》, 《温病条辨》,《太平圣惠方》). At the same time, the company stressed the use of traditional herbal knowledge combined with modern technology (中草药经现代工艺精心研制而成). This traditional/modern interlink is also reflected in the dual approach of their advertisements, using both very traditional settings and modern Chinese settings.

The fragrances used in Liushen products have an association with traditional raw materials but with modern twist. The fragrances signal the 'cultural content' (Chua 2003) of their bath products and invest them with an identity and a means to establish communication with consumers.

Liushen's positioning as 'Chinese' and 'modern', which is reflected in the different designs of its advertisements, resonates with Chinese consumers who have described the scent as modern Chinese fragrances. Liushen's popularity also indicates the acceptance of traditional Chinese medicinal knowledge and its efficacy in beauty bath products. These sentiments have converged within Liushen's slogan, 'Way of the East' (东方之道).

Liushen was able to benefit from the cultural shift, as Shanghai Jiahua traced its corporate founding to the period after the Opium war, and its aim was to establish 'a national enterprise to invigorate China through industry'.[14] This aspiration fits neatly with Fong's concept of 'filial nationalism' (Fong 2004). The ascent of Liushen is thus driven by the rise in cultural pride among Chinese consumers and marks their transition from the 'loss of confidence' (Croll 2006) during the reform period to the current time where they embrace cultural heritage and appropriate it in the construction of modern Chinese cultural identity.

Conclusion

I have used the rise of Liushen soap and body wash to explore the relationship between fragrance preference and social change in China. Similar to Oakley's

(Oakley, this volume) unpacking of gold into its four facets (elemental, noble, transcendent and gold-as-money), fragrances have both chemical and social facets as well. In fact, it is the social facets of fragrance that shape consumer preference in the Deng and post-Deng era.

Unlike the physical properties of gold, fragrances exist in various forms and are often invisible when the scent is released. As a material incorporated in soap and body wash, it is invisible but detectable though the sense of smell, and it lingers on the skin after washing. Most people can only describe scents through metaphors or references to other senses, and while people can identify a fragrance they like, most cannot account for why they like it. However, fragrances are informed materials (Barry, this volume), as fragrance houses rely on consumer insight, market trends and customer briefs to create new fragrances.

Liushen's success has been explained in terms of good marketing strategy or consumers' familiarity, but neither adequately explains its popularity. Foster (2008) has noted the inadequacy of crediting marketers for success of a brand, while familiarity with Liushen did not give it the top ranking during the Deng reform era. With the Deng reform era and post-Deng era as backdrops, we see that while fragrances are materials whose properties remain unchanged, as in one way they smell consistently the same, the social aspirations of each period have influenced fragrance preferences, from Lux as a symbol of modernity to Liushen as a modern Chinese fragrance.

Appreciating fragrances from this perspective, they are loaded with social meanings and historical memories, and definitely mean different things to different groups of people at different historical periods. As such, they become barometers of social change. This dynamic, if understood and appropriated by marketers, can have a profound effect on brands and makes a strong case for the move towards a parallel histories of fragrances as opposed to the current linear history of fragrances. We interact with fragrance materials through our sense of smell but our fragrance preferences are probably more social than biological.

Notes

1. These figures are publicized by Leffingwell and Associates: see online at <http://www.leffin-gwell.com/top_10.htm> (accessed 2012). This chapter engages with the flow of information from the professional fragrance industry, much of which circulates in various market reports, market research reports and online information.
2. See <http://www.thisismanufacturing.co.uk/sites/bmit/files/pzcuzzons-videotranscript.pdf> (accessed 2012).

3. For a discussion and explanation of major terms of fragrance raw materials, see <http://www.cosmeticsandtoiletries.com/formulating/ingredient/fragrance/136099708.html?page=1> (accessed October 2012).

4. A natural identical synthetic fragrance raw material has the same chemical structure as a natural fragrance, but is created chemically and not derived from botanicals. For example, a natural identical synthetic rose fragrance material will smell similar to a rose but is not derived from the rose plant. A non-natural identical synthetic fragrance raw material has a chemical structure that is not found in nature, and its fragrance profile has no natural equivalent.

5. A version of Michael Edwards' fragrance wheel is reproduced, with permission, in this book in black and white. The wheel is much more rich if viewed in colour, and a version can be found at Michael Edwards' website: <http://www.fragrancesoftheworld.com/index.aspx> (accessed November 2014).

6. Another example is the history of fragrance as presented by the Fragrance Foundation. The Foundation represents major players in the fragrance industry, and their fragrance history again reflects the Western orientation that I have described as a linear history. The Foundation describes itself as 'a non-profit making educational trust founded in New York in 1949 by Chanel, Coty, Elizabeth Arden, Guerlain, Helena Rubinstein and Parfums Weil. It has become a substantial organization in the United States and is well known internationally as the forum for the fragrance industry'. See <http://www.fragrancefoundation.org.uk/history-of-fragrance.htm> (accessed October 2012).

7. The industry has two main categories, beauty and anti-bacterial, for soap and body washes. Beauty soaps and body washes offer customers real or imagined benefits, such smooth skin or a more fair complexion, from regular use. Anti-bacterial soaps and body washes promise the ability to kill germs and bacteria. This chapter examines beauty soap and body wash products in China.

8. Safeguard brand, by Procter & Gamble, has the largest share by retail value. However, Safeguard is a 'health' bath product, offering antibacterial benefits. Liushen has the second-largest share by retail value in the bath product category and is the top beauty soap brand. Source: Euromonitor International, *Country Sector Briefing 'Bath and Shower Products - China'*, May 2009.

9. Exceptions do happen, as in the case of whitening soaps in Indonesia and Papaya whitening soaps in the Philippines. However, in both instances, the local brands are still unable to surpass the global brands in sales.

10. These various quotations are taken from the Liushen brand section of the website of Jahwa, the manufacturer. The site was accessed in 2012 but no longer easily accessible by 2014: http://www.jahwa.com.cn/en/brand/liushen.php.

11. One young lady explained her choice of foreign brand as a form of social mobility, and cited the Chinese idiom of humans aspiring for social mobility (人往高处爬).

12. It must be mentioned that this feeling of revival is not confined to Chinese nationals in China but also felt by Overseas Chinese, especially the elderly and the Chinese-educated diaspora, as evidenced by the purchase of stolen antiques and the recent Hong Kong activist visit to disputed islands in the East China Sea. The Chinese in China and the diasporas may have different political views and different nationalities, but there is still a sense of filial ethnicity, to borrow Fong's concept. In the context of this chapter, filial ethnicity has implications for global fragrance trends.

13. See for example the Hanfu movement's Facebook group in Singapore <https://www.facebook.com/groups/2204561358/?ref=ts>.

14. See Jiahua Chinese website: <http://www.jahwa.com.cn> (accessed October 2012).

References

Barme, G. R. (1995), 'To Screw Foreigners Is Patriotic: China's Avant-Garde Nationalist', *The China Journal*, 34: 209–234.

BBC (2009), 'China Condemns Christie's Auction', published online 26 February 2009, available online at: <http://news.bbc.co.uk/2/hi/asia-pacific/7911091.stm> (accessed November 2014).

Benn, C. (2004), *China's Golden Age: Everyday Life in the Tang Dynasty*. Oxford: Oxford University Press.

Chua, B. H. (2003), *Life Is Not Complete without Shopping: Consumption Culture in Singapore*. Singapore: Singapore University Press.

Classen, C. (1992), 'The Odor of the Other: Olfactory Symbolism and Cultural Categories', *Ethnos*, 20(2): 133–166.

Classen, C. (1993), 'The Odour of the Rose: Floral Symbolism and the Olfactory Decline of the West', *Worlds of Sense: Exploring the Senses in History and across Cultures*, pp. 15–27. New York: Routledge.

Classen, C. and D. Howes (1996), 'Making Sense of Culture: Anthropology as a Sensual Experience', *Ethnofoor*, 9(2): 86–96.

Clunas, C. (2007), *Empire of Great Brightness: Visual and Material Culture of Ming China*, pp. 1368–1644. London: Reaktion Books Ltd.

Croll, E. (2006), 'Conjuring Goods, Identities and Cultures', in K. Latham, S. Thompson and J. Klein (eds), *Consuming China: Approaches to Cultural Change in Contemporary China*. New York: Routledge.

Curtis, T. and D. Williams (2001), *Introduction to Perfumery*. Weymouth: Micelle Press.

Euromonitor International (2011a), *Country Sector Briefing 'Bath and Shower Products – China'*, June 2011, Euromonitor International.

Euromonitor International (2011b), *Country Sector Briefing 'Bath and Shower Products – Japan'*, August 2009, Euromonitor International.

Euromonitor International (2011c), *Country Sector Briefing 'Bath and Shower Products – South Korea'*, June 2009, Euromonitor International.

Fong, V. (2004), 'Filial Nationalism among Chinese Teenagers with Global Identities', *American Ethnologist*, 31(4): 631–648.

Foster, R. J. (2008), 'Commodities, Brands, Love and Kula: Comparative Notes on Value Creation in Honor of Nancy Munn', *Anthropological Theory*, 8(1): 9–25.

Gernet, J. (1996), *A History of Chinese Civilization*. Cambridge: Cambridge University Press.

Gernet, J. (1962), *Daily Life in China, on the Eve of the Mongol Invasion, 1250–1276*. Stanford: Stanford University Press.

Guldin, G. E. (1996), 'Desakotas and Beyond: Urbanization in Southern China', *Ethnology*, 35(4): 265–283.

Harris, M. (1974), *Cows, Pigs, Wars, and Witches: The Riddles of Culture*. New York: Random House.

Holt, D. (2004), *How Brands Become Icons: The Principles of Cultural Branding*. Harvard: Harvard Business Review Press.

Holt, D. (2010), *Cultural Strategy: Using Innovative Ideologies to Build Breakthrough Brands*. Oxford: Oxford University Press.

Iris, C. (1998), *The Rape of Nanking: The Forgotten Holocaust of World War II*. Harmondsworth: Penguin.

Lardy, N. R. (1984), 'Consumption and Living Standards in China, 1978–83', *The China Quarterly Review*, 100: 849–865.

Lim, He-Min (2007), 'Stanley Ho Pays $ 8.9m for Looted Bronze Horse', Bloomberg 20 September 2007, available online at <http://www.bloomberg.com/apps/news?pid=newsa rchive&sid=aEN5JJVQuuXo> (accessed November 2014).

Michaelson, C. (1999), *Gilded Dragon. Buried Treasures from China's Golden Ages*. London: British Museum Press.

Miyazaki, I. (1976), *China's Examination Hell. The Civil Service Examinations of Imperial China*. New Haven, CT: Yale University Press.

Moeran, B. (2005), 'Japanese Fragrance Descriptives and Gender Constructions: Preliminary Steps towards an Anthropology of Olfaction', *Etnofoor SENSES*, 18(1): 97–123.

Pan, J. X. (1986), 'An Analysis of the Lifestyle of the Single Child Family', *Sociology*, 1: 111–216.

Roberts, J. (2003), *The Complete History of China*. Charleston: The History Press.

Stoller, P. (1990), 'The Taste of Ethnographic Thing: The Senses in Anthropology', *American Ethnologist*, 17(4): 800.

Synnott, A. (1991), 'A Sociology of Smell', *Canadian Review of Sociology and Anthropology,* 28(1): 437–459.

Tsui, M. (1989), 'Changes in Chinese Urban Family Structure', *Journal of Marriage and Family*, 51(3): 737–747.

Turin, L. (2006), *The Secret of Scent: Adventures in Perfume and the Science of Smell*. London: Faber and Faber.

Wong, S. (2006), 'Han Follow Suit in Cultural Rennaissance', *Asia Times,* 26 August 2006, available online at <http://www.atimes.com/atimes/China/HH26Ad01.html> (accessed November 2014).

Yan, Y. X. (1997), 'MacDonalds in Beijing: Golden Arches East', in J. L. Watson (ed.), *McDonalds in East Asia*, pp. 39–76. Stanford: Stanford University Press.

Yingzi, T. (2008), 'Call for Return of Stolen Treasures', *China Daily,* 25 October 2008, avail-able online at <http://www.chinadaily.com.cn/china/2008-10/25/content_7140673.htm> (accessed November 2014).

Young, D. (2005), 'The Smell of Greenness: Cultural Synaesthesia in the Western Desert', *Etnofoor*, 18(1): 61–77.

Zhang, Q. (2005), 'A Chinese Yuppie in Beijing: Phonological Variation and the Construction of a New Professional Identity', *Language in Society*, 34(3): 431–466.

Chapter 14

The woollen blanket and its imagined values: Material transformations of woollen blankets in contemporary art

Fiona P. McDonald

Woollen blankets have been numerous things to many people. The mutability of this single object is captured in the ever-shifting symbolic and mnemonic values that emerge in diverse social and cultural contexts of use. From the original manufacture of woollen blankets of raw wool in the United Kingdom and France around the seventeenth century, to the transformation of woollen blankets as a ready-made medium for contemporary artists in Canada, the United States, and Aotearoa New Zealand, the unpredictable values and previous meaning(s) of this single material object make visible its involvement in larger histories, its presence within distinct social contexts, and its participation between cultures at specific historical junctures. This chapter presents, in relation to theories of value concerning material culture, how the nuanced meanings of woollen blankets become visible when artists transform them from serviceable or discarded objects into sculptural works of art.[1] As David Graeber notes, 'to understand the meaning (value) of an object, then one must understand its place in a larger system' (Graeber 2011: 14). Therefore, this chapter contributes to this volume by considering larger issues and systems around the conceptualization of materials through aesthetics, in relation to the agency given to objects by creative makers, and to the sensory experience of our material world.

Concerns with the ever-shifting values of materials, when coupled with an interest in the materiality of things and their social lives, in particular the sensory effects of materials on each of us, have recently occupied the discourse of anthropology. First, by understanding relevant values and associated cultural meanings of objects such as woollen blankets, we gain insight into what motivates cultural producers, craftspeople, and artists within distinct cosmological frames to consciously transform materials for aesthetic, visual, sensual, and tangible outcomes. And second, by looking specifically at the material transformation and transfiguration of woollen blankets as a material case study allows actions upon materials more broadly, and related social responses, to become visible once things and objects are moved within and through various contexts.

A woollen blanket is a compelling and complex thing, one whose intangible content (meanings and values) and tangible context when brought in to a new form within a work of art rely heavily on understanding the cosmological perspectives of those who transform the woollen blanket, and those who experience it within an art gallery. The plurality and historicity of things and objects like woollen blankets is central to questions such as: What is a thing versus an object? Who gives an object its bounded or unbounded meanings? And how does a single object attract varied experiences and values? Material culture discourse that engages with art often looks specifically at the work of art as an object that conveys meaning or the potency and potential of agency, but how does the materiality *of* that object as an art form inform a larger understanding of our engagement with our material world?

In this discussion, the presentation of the varied understandings, meanings and values ascribed to woollen blankets will be approached with circumspection in order to present *how* two contemporary artists interpret and present the ontological status of woollen blankets in our material world, both historically and today, and how their physical engagement with woollen blankets represents one way in which we come to interact with the meaning and value of objects by way of the aesthetic transformation of materials.

The use of a woollen blanket in a work of art placed inside a contemporary art gallery validates the blanket beyond just being read as a textile or a thing (Brown 2001, 2010; McDonald 2014). Fred Myers notes, '"Art" has been situated in the West as a category of redemptive value, distinct from money and discrete from other sociocultural values' (Myers 1997: 7). The monetary value and meaning of a woollen blanket, however, are re-contextualized within the 'system' of art determined by the institutions, as well as by the artists who use them, and by those who privilege these objects beyond their homes as domestic necessities or 'biographic objects' (Burren 1971). Placement of blankets by an artist resituates their value and meaning, and their material transformation foregrounds other significant meanings and values.

Several artists participate in this process of transforming the woollen blanket through their artwork. Independently they assert particular values and meanings of the woollen blanket that reflect their own embodied experience and cultural references. But taken collectively they represent a distinct social phenomenon

within the art world that captures the way that art and objects enable an anthropological understanding of the social and aesthetic transformation of material
culture. Each case study presented in this chapter is extracted from a larger
material ethnography on woollen blankets within distinct social and geographic
contexts: North America and Aotearoa New Zealand (McDonald 2014). The
data from each visual case study (specifically how artists and curators speak
about their engagement with woollen blankets) illuminates how qualitative
(and mnemonic) values have come to be associated with woollen blankets
and their material properties. In advance of unpacking each work, the parallel values between the two examples include, but are not limited to: use-value,
economic-value, historical-value, labour-value, sentimental-value, and the larger
understanding of the mnemonic-value of woollen blankets. According to Arthur
Danto, 'transformation [of materials] in the practice of art in recent decades has
made . . . meanings available to artists in realizing works that draw on the meanings fabric possesses in vernacular forms of life' (Danto 2002: 84).[2]

The theoretical frames that buttress this chapter owe a debt to the work of
many scholars, including those in this volume. First, a basic understanding of
material objects is informed by the writing of Arjun Appadurai, Igor Kopytoff,
Bill Brown and Fred R. Myers. Their foundational work concerning 'regimes of
values and material culture' enables more nuanced readings of objects across
time. For example, Bill Brown notes that:

> [A] given object culture entails the practical and symbolic use of objects. It
> thus entails both the ways that inanimate objects mediate human relations
> and the ways that humans mediate object relations (generating differences of
> value, significance, and permanence among them), thus the system (mater-
> ial, economic, symbolic) through which objects become meaningful or fail to.
> (Brown 2010: 188)

Second, Alfred Gell's propositions concerning dynamic social relations that
coalesce around art objects are used to undergird how values are ascribed and
circulate within the contemporary art world. Gell, by way of taking up Simmel's
central thoughts on value and money, notes:

> The idea that valued objects present themselves to us surrounded by a kind of
> halo-effect of resistance, and that it is this resistance to us which is the source
> of their value. Simmel's theory, as it stands, implies that it is in the difficulty of
> access to an object which makes it valuable. (Gell 1998: 48)

Gell goes beyond this idea around restrained access as the sole reason an
object acquires value to posit that the power of the object 'resides in the *symbolic*

processes they provoke in the beholder' (Gell 1998: 48). This returns to the idea of values placed on woollen blankets so as to reflect more on the personal experience that each person brings to bear on experiencing a woollen blankets in the social context of contemporary art, and how the symbolic values of a woollen blanket can vary depending upon the experience one brings to their sensory (seeing, touching, smelling) encounter.[3]

The essentialized materiality of woollen blankets and their manufacture

When looking critically at the larger values associated with woollen blankets, one needs to consider the essentialized materiality of this object (Figure 14.1). What is a woollen blanket? A blanket, in this case a woollen blanket, is something with which many of us have had a visceral, corporeal and embodied experience. There is a shared sensorial experience most human beings have with blankets no matter what their material make up. All taxonomies of blankets (hide, wool, cotton, synthetic fibres, etc.) are generally associated with a sense of survival (primal instinct) that evokes a common sensorial experience of warmth and protection. Woollen blankets are no exception. They are comprised of raw wool that has been systematically washed, dyed, carded and fulled and have been produced in the United Kingdom and France since shortly before the seventeenth century.

Figure 14.1 'Queen's Coronation Hudson's Bay Point Blanket'. Royal Alberta Museum – H89.220.169 (Ethnology Collection). Photograph taken with permission by Fiona P. McDonald.

Woollen blankets in this study may vary in size, colour and patterning, but historically they have always had the same essentialized woollen material-ity. The material essence of manufactured woollen blankets is that they are: thick, warm, itchy, impenetrable, durable, robust. They have been employed in varied contexts because of these very characteristics. The imagined poten-tial of a woollen blanket ranges from bedding to sails on small boats, and coverings on doors, and they have been employed in the form of shelter to protect from the elements. These basic essentialized characteristics are what have allowed the woollen blanket to be introduced and adopted into various contexts around the globe. Buttressing the material characteristics of woollen blankets are their aesthetic qualities.

While the woollen blankets discussed here have tended to have monochro-matic fields (the larger background colour) (see Figure 14.1) that feature dark bands at the top and bottom, and some with point markings along one side to designate their size and value (up to a maximum of six points), they have tended to vary in colour ever since their original manufacture at weaving mills in the United Kingdom. The colour and pattern range is vast and is generally reflective of the weaving mills that have produced them around the globe. For example, grey blankets have commonly been issued for naval and military services even though they have been produced at various different mills.

The type of woollen blanket considered in this discussion was originally produced at the Witney Mills in Oxfordshire, England, until it officially closed down in 2002. Specifically, Witney Mills is the starting point for many of the woollen blankets that have appeared around the globe and in settler states. Beyond Witney Mills, however, the colour of the woollen blanket's field and any additional patterns or markings have always been dependent upon the mill that manufactured them. Since the late-nineteenth and early-twentieth century, for example, the presence of blankets in different colours, patterns, and quality increased as weaving mills were technologically revolutionized in England and globally. Eventually, many mills were set up across Canada, the United States, and Aotearoa New Zealand, and with this flourished new communities.[4] While the blankets were and are signature products of their mill, generally speaking, the mills in both North America and in the Antipodes operated on technology that emerged during the mechanization of the blanket industry in the United Kingdom, which was spurred on by the Industrial Revolution (see McDonald 2013: 108). The distribution of woollen blankets manufactured in Canada, the United States, and Aotearoa New Zealand have tended to have more of a regional character when compared to the global reach that Witney blankets originally had.

The consistency of manufacture to produce the basic essential qualities of the woollen blanket is what has enabled it to be legible to numerous audiences. Its legibility as an object – a blanket – is where we begin when looking further into a critical material assessment of the meanings and values that have saturated the woollen blanket within various social contexts and at distinct historical moments.

The woollen blanket in art

Ruth Phillips wrote that 'because we are material beings inhabiting a material world, artefacts can uniquely serve as trans-temporal and trans-spatial witnesses to alternative modes of cross-cultural historical interaction' (Phillips 2011: 135). This observation is perhaps the most accurate way to encapsulate the diversity of researching the mutability of woollen blankets within contemporary art from an anthropological perspective.

The presence of woollen blankets in contemporary art stands in a poetic relationship to the historical visibility of this serviceable object found in numerous visual representations from the colonial trade era that discretely document the woollen blanket and its subtle movement into different landscapes and cultures.[5] In North America for example, in paintings done by Paul Kane (1810–1871) and Cornelius Kreighoff (1815–1872) that romanticize distinct landscapes in North America, woollen blankets appear naturalized in scenes of trade and exchange, as well as critical objects in outerwear such as jackets. Similarly, in Aotearoa New Zealand, artists aboard ships captained by James Cook (1728–1779) rendered similar scenes of men and women wrapped in blankets, and later William Strutt (1825–1915), Gottfried Lindauer (1839–1926) and Charles Frederick Goldie (1870–1947) painted varied portraits with Māori men and women wrapped in plaid woollen blankets that are now treasured items in national art and archive collections. These stereotyped representations of Indigenous individuals wrapped in woollen blankets persisted beyond the canvas throughout the nineteenth and twentieth centuries and are also well evidenced in ethnographic and studio photography.

From these colonial images and constructions, more recent works by contemporary artists either challenge, or are positioned in relation to, historical metanarratives and visualizations that incorporate the woollen blanket. As Arthur Danto once observed, 'by bringing into their works objects and materials with often powerful meanings in lived forms of life, artists have been able to appropriate those meanings for their art, and even to communicate with audiences in ways considerable beyond what pictorial representation would allow' (Danto

2002: 84). Therefore, through the literal incorporation of woollen blankets into their works of art, how does such a material engagement within the context of an art gallery allow audience access to other values, meanings and histories of woollen blankets beyond their own lived experiences?

Since the mid-1980s, woollen blankets started to appear both literally and figuratively in works of art by several practicing artists in Canada, the United States, and Aotearoa New Zealand. In the context of this discussion, only two examples are presented to reflect upon how artists have *literally* transformed one or more woollen blankets in their sculptural installations. This does not mean that pictorial or figurative representations of woollen blankets by other artists carry any less effect upon a viewer, but Danto's argument in relation to the communicative power material objects possess suggests that works of art where woollen blankets are used by artists can clarify some of the meanings that have been appropriated and represented. In the context of this discussion, the simple fact that a woollen blanket appears in a sculptural work that has been exhibited in a gallery context and been called art by the maker has qualified it for inclusion. Nicholas Thomas argues that 'the anthropologist is not obliged to define the art object' (Thomas 1998: 7).

The list of artists who have used the woollen blanket as a ready-made object in their works is formidable. In the United States, for example, Bob Boyer created a series of works titled 'Blanket Statements' starting in 1985, where his works functioned on one level as an act of resistance toward dishonoured treaty agreements. Bob Boyer's 'Blanket Statement' series conveyed many meanings associated with the woollen trade blanket. Interestingly, Boyer worked on cotton blankets but referenced the woollen trade blankets distributed by traders, government officials and also at ceremonies. Wendy Winter wrote that 'Boyer's paintings in Blankets, and their proactive titles, often contrasted the historical and cultural symbolism of a blanket (security, warmth, generosity) with difficult issues related to the colonization of North America' (2009: 16). However, his later works, in series such as 'Smallpox Issue', 'address the deliberate and horrific impregnation of the smallpox virus into government-issued blankets distributed to aboriginal populations during the nineteenth century' (15).

One of the first examples I have identified where an artist directly *transformed* a woollen blanket was in a site-specific installation titled 'Up Biblum God' (1987) by Mohawk artist Alan Michelson. Michelson used a Hudson's Bay Company multicoloured striped Point blanket as a canvas that he transformed with an encaustic paint to render a beaver pelt and trap upon it. Here the woollen blanket gets transformed into a canvas, and is installed in the gallery in relation to other material objects that speak to and of colonial histories, trade interactions and assimilation practices between settlers and Indigenous communities. The title of this work references *Mamusse Wunneetupanatamwe Up-Biblum God,* also known as the Algonquin bible.

In 1991, Ron Noganosh also reconfigured the multicoloured woollen striped blanket into a traditional Native American drum with the title 'That's All it Costs', a title that invites a reading of the role of blankets in trade and treaty agreements.[6] Seneca artist Marie Watt's comprehensive body of work since 2003 meanwhile represents one of the largest series of sculptural works made from woollen blankets, which are either folded and stacked into totem-like structures within the gallery or take the form of large-scale wall-piece installations that speak to histories of tapestry and wall hangings.

Turning to Canada, in 2010, Liz Magor created eight sculptural works from blankets that she installed in a self-entitled exhibition in Toronto, Ontario. Sonny Assu's engagement with the woollen blankets has taken many forms, in particular his 'Silenced' series, which consists of stacked hide drums painted to look like piles of trade blankets. Assu also incorporates the blanket as a material is his sculptural work '*1884/1951*' (2010), where he uses the blanket unchanged as a plinth upon which he places 67 copper cast Starbucks cups to commemorate each year that the traditional potlatch ceremonies were banned in Canada (McDonald 2013). Other notable works that work directly with the Hudson's Bay Company Point blanket are Leah Decter's 'Trade Value' (2011–present) and Teresa Burrows' 'Rupert land Regalia: The (Sul)fur Queen' (2008).

In Aotearoa New Zealand, the incorporation of woollen blankets produced both in the United Kingdom and in Aoteaora New Zealand is equally distinctive. In 2009, Tracey Williams created the site-specific installation 'My Ship | Tēnei Wakahēra' where she clad a model ship with woollen blankets. Also since 2009, textile designer and sculptor Jo Torr has created a series of Victorian gown sculptures made from woollen blankets and tapa cloth. And Rona Ngahuia Osborne, who has worked with woollen blankets since the late 1990s, recently collaborated with Alexis Neal for a site-specific installation entitled, 'Whare Taonga' (2012) at the Sargent Gallery in Whanganui (A/NZ).

These works offer a snapshot, if only a partial one, of the larger global phenomenon of the aesthetic transformation of woollen blankets in art, craft and Indigenous regalia.

Case study 1: United States

One prominent artist whose larger artistic practice is centred on transforming woollen blankets is contemporary artist Marie Watt. Since 2003, Watt's work with woollen blankets has ranged from towering totem pole-like structures made of stacked woollen blankets, to large-scale stitched installations that hang upon the wall like a tapestry when installed in the gallery, to her small intimate 'sampler' works. In particular, Watt's 'Blanket' series (Figure 14.2), started in 2003, is a strong example of how the blanket, what Watt calls a 'humble yet loaded object',[7] is transformed from a serviceable object into a work of art.[8] Her most recent and largest work, a welcome pole, was created from hundreds of donated blankets from people across North America. They were accompanied by stories of love, loss, birth, travel, home, youth, and life. This site-specific work, *'Blanket Stories: Seven Generations, Adawe, and Hearth'* (2013), was installed at the National Gallery of Canada as a key work in the first *quinquennial* exhibition, *Sakahàn: International Indigenous Art* (May–September 2013). Watt, who is from the Turtle Clan of the Seneca Nation (Iroquois/Haudenosaunee), is fully aware of the history of woollen blankets as a trade item between Indigenous and non-Indigenous communities in the United States. She speaks about the blanket as what Bill Brown might call a storied object. Watt notes:

> Blankets hang around in our lives and families – they gain meaning through
> use. My work is about social and cultural histories imbedded in commonplace

Figure 14.2 Marie Watt 'Blanket Stories – Blanket Stories: Three Sisters, Cousin Rose, Four Pelts, and Sky Woman', 2005. Each approximately 20'×20'×180'. Stacked and folded wool blankets, salvaged cedar. Installation view, Hoffman Gallery, Lewis & Clark College, Portland, Oregon. Image courtesy the artist.

objects. I consciously draw from Indigenous design principles, oral traditions, and personal experience to shape the inner logic of the work I make. These wool blankets come from family, friends, acquaintances and secondhand stores (I'll buy anything under $5). As friends come over and witness my blanket project in progress, I am struck by how the blankets function as markers for their memories and stories.[9]

It is hard to write about Watt's work without referencing her most heavily cited statement on her work. Watt writes:

We are received in blankets, and we leave in blankets . . . I am interested in human stories and rituals implicit in everyday objects . . . I find myself attracted to the blanket's two- and three-dimensional qualities: On a wall, a blanket functions as a tapestry, but on a body it functions as a robe and living art object. Blankets also serve a utilitarian function. As I fold and stack blankets, they begin to form columns that have references to linen closets, architectural braces, memorials (The Trojan Column), sculpture (Brancusi, for one), the great totem poles of the Northwest and the conifer trees around which I grew up. In Native American communities, blankets are given away to honor people for being witnesses to important life events – births and comings-of-age, graduations and marriages, namings and honorings. For this reason, it is considered as great a privilege to give a blanket away as it is to receive one.

In this statement on her website, Watt touches upon several personal values and meanings that she brings to her interpretation of the woollen blanket. According to curator and anthropologist Rebecca J. Dobkins, who curated Watt's work in an exhibition entitled *Lodge* at the Hallie Ford Museum of Art (2012), 'Watt began to use woollen blankets as a form and material as well as conceptual vehicles. The blankets carry associations not only with an array of life experiences but specifically with tribal communities, which have a long history of exchanging blankets for resources and other goods with settlers and traders as well as marking life transitions with the giving and receiving of blankets' (Dobkins 2012: 35). While Dobkins addresses the way woollen blankets have been engaged with historically, from exchange value to gift value (which begs a Marxist reading from a commodity fetish perspective, or a Maussian one informed by the notion of the gift), art historian Janet Catherine Berlo unpacks Watt's work to suggest that her use of woollen blankets 'evoke[s] a 500-year saga of inter-cultural relations' (Berlo 2005: 112). Watt's own statements regarding her work with the blanket, however, favour a reading of woollen blankets in relation to their (e)valuation as an heirloom. As Watt states: 'My work explores human stories and rituals implicit in everyday objects.

I am interested in wool blankets and their heirloom-like quality. Freud considered blankets as "transitional" objects, but I like to consider how these humble pieces of cloth are *transformational'* (Watt cited in Dobkins 2012: 72).

This transformational dimension is also the transformation of blankets from serviceable object to artistic medium. It is the infinite transformational possibilities of the woollen blanket that have allowed Watt to use this object's histories, values and meanings to engage diverse experiences. Her works demonstrate the unpredictability of the permutations and combinations mapping the meanings and values of woollen blankets and the unpredictability of the reactions of people who experience her work. Dobkins has suggested that Watt's works have the sensibility of Joseph Beuys' 'social sculptures', in that 'art should be participatory and has the power to affect transformations in the self and society' (Dobkins 2012: 11). When works from Watt's *Blanket Series* are installed in a gallery setting, a book is left in the gallery to allow others to record their responses to her work, and their sentiments when interacting with woollen blankets in a non-domestic setting. From conversations with Watt, I have learned these statements tend to address personal memories evoked by the materiality of the work.[10] While Watt's work articulates multiple meanings and values at once, her work engenders the mutability of the blanket through 'recontextualization' (Thomas 1998: 18). The *Blanket Series* offers a number of iterations, transformations, and experiences through which Watt's personal experience with blankets, as well as the viewer's own material and sensory experience, can play out.

Case study 2: Aotearoa New Zealand

In the second example in this discussion, contemporary multimedia artist Tracey Williams takes up the malleability of woollen blankets through her site-specific installation entitled, 'My Ship | Tēnei Wakahēra' (Figure 14.3), exhibited at the Tauranga Art Gallery, Toi Tauranga, in 2009.[11] It is composed of several components: a two-channel video projection of still images of 67 constellations, a looped video work of a model boat that floated in and out of the frame, a sculptural ship clad in woollen blankets and 'renewed' textiles, as well as site-specific elements mounted to walls. The larger context of this work speaks to Williams' exhaustive research into the region's local histories, so as to move past 'master' narratives by looking for 'specifically a little history or a forgotten history or some kind of tangential history'.[12] In the creation of this work, Williams noted:

> I went looking for sub-texts of Tauranga Moana's multifarious written history. I wanted to spotlight the points that meta narratives unravel, rupture and split.

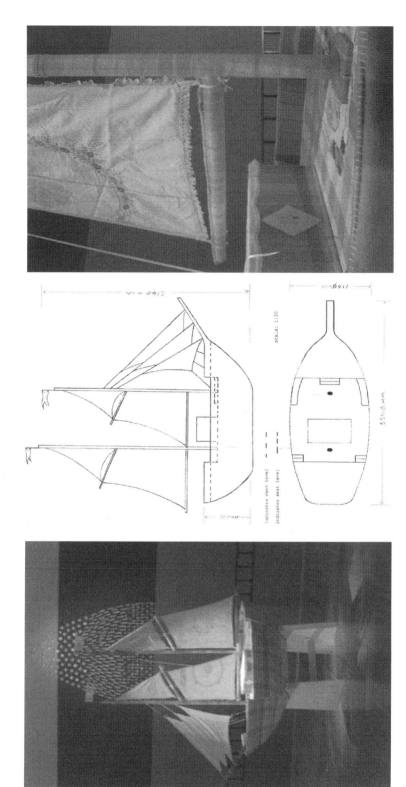

Figure 14.3 Tracey Williams. 'MY SHIP | Tēnei Wakahēra', 2009. Recycled woollen blankets, wood, cotton. Image courtesy the artist and the Tauranga Art Gallery, New Zealand.

> This was an amnesiac experience. Smaller narratives still interlace popular history, concealing private stories . . . Unexpectedly, the information I sought was lyrically embedded in old textiles and craftwork. The[se] objects inherently cite Otherness, holding implicit narratives. They are containers of ephemeral and intangible aspects of identity; and preservers of oblique cultural tales. They also signify protection and labour. (Williams and Jackson 2009: 1)

This mention of the history of labour illuminates yet another value associated with woollen blankets, their manufacture and their transportation to settler states.

Regarding Aotearoa New Zealand, more expansionist historical interpretations of Captain James Cook have argued that his 1779 mission aboard *HM Endeavour* might have been the first moment when woollen blankets were gifted or traded with Māori communities. I cannot confirm this. After Cook's first explorative mission, which followed the travels of Abel Tasman, it was the South Pacific Trading Company that likely played a vital role in moving woollen blankets to Aotearoa New Zealand, just as both the Hudson's Bay Company and Northwest Trading Company did in Canada and the United States respectively. A century after Cook's first voyage, as documented in historical text, *The Authentic and Genuine History of the Signing of the Treaty of Waitangi* (1840), woollen blankets are noted in the attire of 'principle Native chiefs of several tribes' (Colenso 1890:15) during the signing of the Treaty of Waitangi. Colenso notes that:

> Some [are] clothed with dogskin mats made of alternate longitudinal stripes of black and white hair; others habited in splendid-looking new woollen (sic) cloaks of foreign manufacture, of crimson, blue, brown, and plain, and indeed, of every shade of striking colour . . . while some were dressed in plain European and some in common Native dresses. (Colenso 1890: 15)

The appearance of woollen blankets at this moment in the colonial history of Aotearoa New Zealand points to the value of the woollen blanket as a new material in trade and treaty relations. Shortly after their introduction to Aotearoa New Zealand many settler communities began to appear, and with them mills were set up across both the North and South islands. These mills were modelled on the post-Industrial Revolution technology where mechanized manufacture replaced the previous hand- and steam-powered looms that started the blanket making industry in Europe. By the eighteenth and nineteenth centuries, the dynamic system of supply and demand that Adam Smith devoted much of his life to understanding was visible in the blanket-making industry not only in England but in Aotearoa New Zealand. Consequently, the import of wool from various settler colonies across the British Empire from India to Aotearoa New Zealand and elsewhere in the British Isles was well underway (Smith, 1776; MacKay 1935:

45–49; Rex 1958: 33).[13] Aotearoa New Zealand, however, was able to not only produce the raw wool needed to manufacture the blankets in England, but they were able to produce enough wool to manufacture these much-coveted blankets whose essentialized materiality bodes well in the cool winter months in the South Pacific. Petone Woollen Mills, Mosgiel, Omaru and Robinswurl are just a few examples of key mills that supported communities across both the North and South Islands (McDonald 2014). Today, Williams uses blankets manufactured by these mills as a ready-made material on her sculptural ship.

Looking to the designs of the aforementioned ships captained by Tasman and Cook, Williams collaborated with a local ship builder to design her own ship, one that fuses together elements from a variety of historical vessels but doesn't represent a single one.[14] According to Williams, the ship is an 'allegory of hope and desire'. In preparation of her sculptural ship, Williams sought out textiles similar to those aboard these original ships, which she would subsequently transform as cladding of the ship's hull, deck and masts. In appropriating and transforming a blanket into her art as a ready-made material, Williams makes visible the material qualities that seem impractical for a ship and the labour involved in this transformation. By literally wrapping the hull and masts of the ship in woollen blankets, Williams unwraps the history of labour associated with the woollen blanket in Aoteaora New Zealand, and the labour involved in articulating the 'conceptual framework' and 'historical content' of 'My Ship | Tēnei Wakahēra'. Gathering together a community of sewers, she employed the skills of several women to blanket-stitch this project together. In response to the woollen blanket materials on the boat, Williams noted that visitors, mostly women, said, 'Oh I know this stuff. I made this stuff.'

'This stuff', for Williams, is 'a way of materially talking to some of the other ideas', such as the complexity of colonial histories and 'some of the darker politics of trading between European and Māori'.[15] But in talking to these histories through the use of a specific object, Williams felt she was also:

> talking to ideas of woman's histories [that] are never mentioned in the histories like in those mainstream narratives. Those culture-defining narratives are always by men for men and they are linear . . . We don't hold onto those histories of labour, and the histories of love which is what sort of underpins that. The people that stitched and made the blankets, and not just the blankets but made the meals and made the clothes.[16]

Conscious of the symbols she uses – ships, birds, land, sea, and storied textiles – Williams notes that through her larger methodology (if we refer back to Danto's comment earlier about using objects and materials laden with meaning), 'You are maybe taking something and you are reprocessing it and representing it; but it is all to do with and all tied up with these histories and the distribution of knowledge'.[17]

Conclusion

From these two examples, it is palpable how complex the woollen blanket is within a contemporary work of art. The varied values and meanings of a woollen blanket have accumulated to illuminate the way material culture is used, consumed, read or mis-read, collected, distributed and ultimately transformed in our multiplex material world, so as to make political statements, articulate identity and engage with history. When woollen blankets are considered within the larger system of contemporary art, they give us access to new perspectives on how cultures come to form values and meanings that reflect past historical happenings and personal narratives transferred into the materials by artists. Not only are artists active agents in reiterating and even recontextualizing such values as birth, death, warmth, disease and reconciliation but also the transformation of a woollen blanket into an artist's work also brings additional economic and cultural value to this object. By consciously using a woollen blanket in their art, the artists presented in this chapter have placed this 'humble', 'potent', 'utilitarian', 'serviceable', 'trade', and 'gifted' object into another complex context. This consequently increases its monetary value and exclusivity because it becomes, in a way, at a distance, within a new system of commerce and value (Gell 1998).

Bill Brown notes, 'These days, history can unabashedly begin with things and with the sense by which we apprehend them' (Brown 2001: 2). The woollen blankets in the two works of art presented in this discussion fundamentally evoke a sensory relationship with objects for the artist, an experience that in turn enhances the mnemonic value of such objects and reminds us, the viewer, of the passage of mundane objects through our own lives and into the system of the art world. In Canada, the United States, and Aotearoa New Zealand, the presence of a woollen blanket in a work of art provokes a reading of this material object not only as a ready-made object and artistic medium but also one that is laden with social and cultural meanings and values independent of, and sometimes at odds with, the historical narrative of an artefact with exchange-value that is traced back to the seventeenth century. The manifold and mutable uses of the woollen blanket enable a more in-depth understanding of how things become objects that possess value and meanings that are simultaneously mnemonic, poetic and potent.

In conclusion, what these two examples show is a synoptic glimpse into how artists have the agency to make us aware of the materials that are present yet obscure in our everyday lives. By taking an item as mundane as a woollen blanket, an artist's intervention and transformation bring awareness of its meanings and values and allow a distinct reading of how we come to experience the materiality of our current historical moment. By placing the woollen blanket within the conceptual category of contemporary art, artists evoke synesthetic experiences that confront the way we experience woollen blankets beyond their essentialized materiality and come to more deeply understand their values and meaning within and across cultures.

Notes

1. For the sole purpose of this publication, Bloomsbury has full permission to reproduce the images provided to accompany my written contribution. I have secured full-permission from each artist to use the images provided for publication. All images have been provided by the artists and galleries where exhibitions have been displayed. In accordance with the wishes of each contributor, I have labelled the images accordingly with title, date, medium, photographer, etc.This chapter is an extraction from a larger material ethnography that not only looks at contemporary art but also considers how blankets have been used in contemporary craft in Aotearoa New Zealand, as well as their past and present use in traditional ceremonial regalia along the Pacific Northwest Coast. See McDonald (2014).
2. Annie E. Coombes writes of Benjamin's essay: 'The essay describes translation as an art of exchange that has the potential to transform both the object (the subject of translation) and the very tools that effect this transformation. Understood as a thesis about exchange and transformation, his suggestive essay has fundamental implications for the way we think about the relations between cultural value, historical narrative, and agency' (Coombes 1997: 237).
3. With these theoretical frames in place, the geographically expansive nature of this discussion may not then seem so unwieldy. For it is only through showing the movement and uses of the blankets more broadly (and historically) that the unique transformations, values and meanings associated with woollen blankets today emerges.
4. Other blanket field colours included, but were not limited to, red, blue, pale green and navy. Historically, they were more prevalent during the height of the fur trade in North America, whereas the purple woollen blanket with the white band and markings (Figure 14.1) was created by Whitney Mills in England to commemorate the coronation of Queen Elizabeth II. In '"Making Sense Out/Of the Visual": Aboriginal Presentations and Representations in Nineteenth-Century Canada', Ruth B. Phillips comments that 'throughout the fur trade era, red woollen cloth was preferred because of its analogic relationship to red ochre and Indigenous scarlet dyes' (Phillips 2004: 606). The red colour that Phillips mentions is 'Turke Red.' According to 'Textiles from the Fur Trade: A Textiles Glossary for the York Factory Indents, 1801 to 1860', turke red was 'a bright durable red dye for cotton and wool cloth originally made from madder and later from alizarian in connection with an aluminium mordant and fatty matter'. The earliest date cited in the Oxford English Dictionary is 1784. The 1830 York Factory indent listed '1032 yds. Turked red and Blue stripe cotton Druggets' ('Textiles From the Fur Trade: A Textiles Glossary for the York Factory Indents, 1801 to 1860', found at the Royal Alberta Museum Archives Search File: Fur Trade Textiles).

5. Such extensive visibility through various media has overshadowed the participation of numerous other trading companies intimately involved in the Canadian fur trade throughout the last three centuries. For example, the North West Company, with its home base in Montréal, competed with the Hudson's Bay Company for access through Hudson Bay until they officially merged in 1821.

6. In the chapter, in terms of the economic value of blankets, the giving and gifting of woollen blankets for land in treaty agreements with the British Crown was common practice in many settler states such as Canada, the United States and Aotearoa New Zealand.

7. In *The System of Objects*, Jean Baudrillard also refers to 'objects as humble' (Baudrillard 1996: 26).

8. Marie Watt is a multidisciplinary artist currently based in Portland, OR (US). 'Born in 1967 to the son of Wyoming ranchers and a daughter of the Turtle Clan of the Seneca Nation (Iroquois / Haudenosaunee), Watt identifies herself as "half Cowboy and half Indian". Formally, her work draws from [I]ndigenous design principles, oral tradition, personal experience, and Western art history. Her approach to art-making is shaped by the proto-feminism of Iroquois matrilineal custom, political work by Native artists in the 1960s, a discourse on multiculturalism, as well as Abstract Expressionism and Pop Art. Like Jasper Johns, she is interested in "things that the mind already knows". Unlike the Pop Artists, she uses a vocabulary of natural materials (stone, cornhusks, wool, cedar) and forms (blankets, pillows, bridges) that are universal to human experience (though not uniquely American) and noncommercial in character' (from her own website: http://www.mkwatt.com/).

9. See: http://mkwatt.com/index.php/content/work_detail/category/blanket_stories_objects/.

10. Marie Watt, personal communications, 2012–2014.

11. Tracey Williams is a multidisciplinary artist based in Auckland, Aotearoa New Zealand. She obtained her MFA with Honours from the University of Auckland (Elam School of Fine Arts). She has exhibited widely in Aotearoa New Zealand, Australia, and the United States and her work takes up the notion of 'little narratives' nested in larger metanarratives. Williams is a founding member of the community-based artistic group, The Friendly Girls Society, and a founding member of the research-based group, Paper Does Not Refuse Ink.

12. Tracey Williams, personal communication, 20 July 2011.

13. Douglas MacKay addresses the history of the woollen blanket examined from the perspective of the Hudson's Bay Company. He comments that '"Point" blankets are made from selected wools from England, Wales, Aotearoa New Zealand and India, each bringing a definite quality which contributes to the water resistance, the warmth, the softness, and the strength of the final article' (MacKay 1935: 45–49). This summary on wool corresponds with a letter dated 4 July 1923 from C. V. Sale to C. W. Veysey (General Manager, Hudson's Bay Company, Winnipeg), however, it is noted: 'Australia is not one of the sources from which the particular type of wool used in these blankets originated' (p. 1). Kay Rex also notes that South America and South Africa also supplied wool used in the blankets (Rex 1958: 33; McDonald 2006).

14. Tracey Williams, personal communication, 20 July 2011: 'I like the way the work becomes ambiguous. I like that ambiguity. That's why with the ship itself I made sure it didn't look like a specific ship so that people couldn't go "oh that it's the such-and-such" or "it's this ship". I took a whole lot of ships from the periods I was interested in and I kind of extrapolated bits of them and made my own ship. In the end that is why it is called 'My Ship'. Because that is the only position I can really speak from with authority . . . You can take on the whole of these histories and go out looking for these histories where you find some little narrative that will hold a spotlight to you [for] you [to] know history in another way'.

15. Tracey Williams, personal communication, 20 July 2011.
16. Ibid.
17. Ibid.

References

Appadurai, A. (1986), 'Introduction: Commodities and the Politics of Value', in A. Appadurai
    (ed.), *The Social Life of Things: Commodities in Cultural Perspective,* pp. 3–63. Cambridge:
    Cambridge University Press.
Baudrillard, J. (2005), *The System of Objects*. New York and London: Verso.
Bell, L. (1982), 'Artists and Empire: Victorian Representations of Subject People', *Art History
    (U.K),* 5(1): 73–87.
Bennett, J. (2010), *Vibrant Matter: A Political Ecology of Things*. Durham, NC and London:
    Duke University Press.
Berlo, J. C. (2005), 'Back to the Blanket: Marie Watt and the Visual Language of Intercultural
    Encounter', in J. Nottage (ed.), *Into the Fray*. Indianapolis: Eitlejorg Museum.
Bloch, M. (2005), *Essays on Cultural Transmission*. Oxford: Berg.
Brown, B. (2001), 'Thing Theory', *Critical Inquiry,* 28(1): 1–22.
Brown, B. (2010), 'Objects, Others, and Us (The Refabrication of Things)', *Critical Inquiry,*
    36(2): 183–217.
Buren, D. (2010 [1971]), 'The Function of the Studio', in M. Jacob and M. Grabner (eds),
    The Studio Reader, pp. 156–162. London and Chicago: The School of the Art Institute of
    Chicago.
Coole, D. and S. Frost (eds) (2010), *New Materialisms: Ontology, Agency, and Politics*.
    London: Duke University Press.
Coombes, A. E. (2001), 'The Object of Translation: Notes on "Art" and Autonomy in a
    Postcolonial Context', in F. Myers (ed.), *The Empire of Things: Regimes of Value and
    Material Culture*. Santa Fe, New Mexico: School of American Research Press.
Danto, A. C. (2002), 'Reflections on Fabric and Meaning: The Tapestry and the Loin Cloth',
    in M. B. Stroud (ed.), *New Material as New Media: The Fabric Workshop and Museum*.
    Cambridge, MA: MIT Press.
Decter, L. (2012), *Homepage. (Official Denial): Trade Value in Progress*, her website, available
    at: <http://www.leahdecter.com/official_denial/home.html> (accessed 10 December 2012).
Decter, L. and J. Isaac (2012), '(Official Denial) Trade Value in Progress: Unsettling Narratives',
    West Coast Line (Summer 2012): 162–178.
Dobkins, R. J. (2012), *Marie Watt: Lodge*. Seattle, WA: The Hallie Ford Museum of Art at
    Willamette University and the University of Washington Press.
Duffek, K. (1988), 'Bob Boyer: A Blanket Statement', *UBC Museum of Anthropology Museum
    Note,* 23.
Fabian, J. (2002), *Time and the Other: How Anthropology Makes Its Object*. New York:
    Columbia University Press.
Fowler, C. (2010), 'Materiality and Collective Experience: Sewing as Artistic Practice in Works
    by Marie Watt, Nadia Myre, and Bonnie Devine', *American Indian Quarterly,* 34(3): 344–364.
Frevelyan, J. (2011), 'Jo Torr', *Nga Kakahu: Change and Exchange, Exhibition Catalogue*.
    Poirua. New Zealand: Pataka Museum.
Gell, A. (1996), 'Vogel's Net: Traps as Artworks and Artworks and Traps', *Journal of Material
    Culture,* 1(1): 15–38.
Gell, A. (1998), *Art and Agency: An Anthropological Theory*. Oxford: Clarendon Press.

Gell, A. (1999), *The Art of Anthropology: Essays and Diagrams*, edited posthumously by E. Hirsch. Oxford: Berg.

Graeber, D. (2001), *Toward An Anthropological Theory of Value: The False Coin of Our Own Dreams*. New York: Palgrave.

Hanson, C. E. (ed.), (1973), 'Noted Blanket Manufacturer Visits Museum', *The Museum of the Fur Trade Quarterly,* 9(2): 3.

Humphrey, C. and S. Hugh-Jones (eds) (1992), 'Introduction: Barter, Exchange and Value', in *Barter, Exchange and Value: An Anthropological Approach*, pp. 1–20. Cambridge: Cambridge University Press.

Jessup, L. and S. Bagg (eds) (2002), *On Aboriginal Representation in the Gallery*. Hull, QC: Canadian Museum of Civilization.

Kemal, S. and I. Gaskell (eds) (1993), *Explanation and Value in the Arts*. Cambridge: Cambridge University Press.

Kopytoff, I. (1985), 'The Cultural Biography of Things: Commoditization as Process', in A. Appadurai (ed.), *The Social Life of Things*, pp. 64–91. Cambridge: Cambridge University Press.

Küchler, S. and A. Eimke (2009), *Tivaivai: The Social Fabric of the Cook Islands*. London: The British Museum Press.

MacKay, D. (1935), 'Blanket Coverage', *The Beaver* (June): 45–49.

Marx, K. and F. Engels (2004 [1848]), *The Communist Manifesto*. London: Penguin Books.

Mauss, M. (2001 [1954]), *The Gift: The Form and Reason for Exchange in Archaic Societies*. London: Routledge.

McDonald, F. P. (2006), 'Blanketing a Nation: Tracing the Social Life of the Hudson's Bay Company Point Blankets through Canadian Visual Culture', MA Thesis, Alberta: University of Alberta.

McDonald, F. P. (2013), 'Woollen Blankets in Contemporary Art: Mutable and Mobile Materials in the Work of Sonny Assu', *Material Culture Review*, 76: 108–116.

McDonald, F. P. (2014), 'Charting Material Memories: An Ethnography of Visual and Material Transformations of Woollen Blankets in Canada, Aotearoa New Zealand, and the United States', PhD Dissertation. London: University College London.

Miller, D. (ed.) (2005a), *Materiality.* Durham, NC: Duke University Press.

Miller, D. (2005b), 'Consumption', in V. Buchli (ed.), *The Material Culture Reader*, pp. 237–263. Oxford: Berg.

Mintz, S. (1985), *Sweetness and Power: The Place of Sugar in Modern History*. New York: Penguin Books.

Myers, F. (2001), 'Introduction: The Empire of Things', in *The Empire of Things: Regimes of Value and Material Culture*, pp. 3–64. Santa Fe, New Mexico: School of American Research Press.

Newman, P. C. (1989), *Empire of the Bay: An Illustrated History of the Hudson's Bay Company*. Toronto, ON: Madison Press Ltd.

Phillips, R. B. (2004), '"Making Sense Out/Of the Visual": Aboriginal Presentations and Representations in Nineteenth-Century Canada', *Art History,* 27(4): 593–615.

Pinney, C. and N. Thomas (eds) (2001), *Beyond Aesthetics: Art and the Technologies of Enchantment*. Oxford: Berg.

Rex, K. (1958), 'The Weavers of Witney', *Canadian Geographical Journal* (July) 33.

Richardson, L. (1980), 'Mackinaws Came from St. Joes's', in *The Sault Daily Star* (5 April 1980).

Ryan, A. (1999), *Trickster Shift: Humour and Irony in Contemporary Canadian Art*. Vancouver: UBC Press.

Smith, A. (1776), *An Inquiry into the Nature and Causes of the Wealth of Nations*, accessed through: Penn. State Electronic Classics Series. <http://i-ahrens.de/schule/bvw/Wealth-Nations.pdf> (accessed 10 March 2012).

Susan Hobbs Gallery (2012), *Homepage,* http://www.susanhobbs.com/exhibition_2011_
    magor.html (accessed 11 March 2012).
Swagerty, W. R. (2002), 'Indian Trade Blankets in the Pacific Northwest: History and
    Symbolism of a Unique North American Tradition', *Columbia: The Magazine of Northwest
    History,* 16(2) (Summer): 6.
Thomas, N. (1998), 'Foreword', in A. Gell, *Art and Agency: An Anthropological Theory*. Oxford:
    Clarendon Press.
Thomas, N. (2001), 'Appropriation/Appreciation: Settler Modernism in Australia and New
    Zealand', in F. Myers (ed.), *The Empire of Things: Regimes of Value and Material Culture*.
    Santa Fe, New Mexico: School of American Research Press.
Tichenor, H. (2002), *The Blanket: An Illustrated History of the Hudson's Bay Point Blankets*,
    Toronto: Madison Press Books.
Tichenor, H. (2003), *The Collector's Guide to Point Blankets of the Hudson's Bay Company and
    Other Companies Trading in North America*. Bowen Island: Cinetel Press.
Ulrich, L. (2011), *The Age of Homespun: Objects and Stories in the Creation of an American
    Myth*. New York: Random House.
Unknown (1938), 'Hudson's Bay Company: Its 'Point' Blankets Have Survived the Rigid Test of
    159 Frigid Northern Winters', *Textile Age* (October 1938): 30.
Vervoort, P. (2004), 'Edward S. Curtis's "Representations": Then and Now', *American Review
    of Canadian Studies,* 34(3): 463–484.
Vogel, S. (1988), 'Introduction', in *Art/Artifact*, exhibition catalogue. New York: The Center for
    African Art and Prestel-Verlag.
Watt, M. Artist's Website. http://www.mkwatt.com/ (accessed 2 April 2012).
Williams, T. and P. Jackson (2009), *My Ship | Tēnei Wakahēra*, exhibition catalogue. Tauranga,
    NZ: Tauranga Art Gallery – Toi Tauranga.
Willmott, C. (2005), 'From Shroud to Strouds: The Hidden History of a British Fur Trade Textile',
    Textile History, 36(2): 196–234.
Winter, W. (2009), *The Legacy of Bob Boyer: A Teacher's Guide*. Regina, Saskatchewan: The
    MacKenzie Art Gallery.
Wooley, H. J. L. (1928), 'The Origin of the Mackinaw Coat', *The Canadian Magazine* (January):
    28.

Part 6

Conclusion

Chapter 15

Materials: The story of use

Susanne Küchler

While the twentieth century is known for its unprecedented growth in population and the expansion of the global economy (Krausmann et al. 2009), the twenty-first century is fast becoming characterized by the flourishing of a materials economy. This economy is being driven by a flood of engineered materials that are highly mobile, moving from institution to institution as they are adopted, transformed and manufactured into products to suit a number of distinct object functions (Ashby and Johnson 2002; Ball 1997; Bensaude-Vincente 2004). The increase in materials productivity, and its heightened significance as a general feature of economic development, have led some to speculate about a fundamental shift in the fabric of capitalism away from industry, as the distinction between production and consumption gives way to a socially informed material production via the co-creation of commodities with consumers (Barry 2005; Bennett 2010; Küchler 2008; Thrift 2006). It is, however, not production alone that is notable for the changes that have put societal forces into the driving seat but also the nature and scale of use itself.

The 2009 report on the growth in global materials use by Fridolin Krausmann and others deploys the image of metabolism to assess the efficiency with which materials, and energy, are used, and this metabolism of use they see as having increased eight-fold over the twentieth century. This accompanies the shift from a dominance in use of renewable biomass towards mineral materials, a well-known by-product of the transition from an organic to a mineral economy that defined the industrial revolution in the United Kingdom (Wrigley 2008). It is no secret that this increase in the societal use of materials has had a massive impact, transforming natural systems and society-nature-relations alike in unprecedented ways (McNeill 2000: 3).

The understanding of materials *use* has so far only ever figured in research as a by-product of a concern with forecasting trends to inform the research and the co-production of materials, in anticipation of their eventual designation to a specific commodity function. By reducing use to patterns of consumption, global policy makers have been able to fully embrace the potential of cutting-edge scientific research that takes the societal benefit of newly invented materials as axiomatic and unproblematic. A bifurcated picture emerges against this background that pitches science against social science. In science, innovation for its own sake is privileged, with a trajectory that goes from invention to successful initial application on a case-by-case basis; failures are not highlighted or even acknowledged. From this perspective, new technology looks entirely positive and tends to be adopted by policy makers without a broad evidence base as to its potential consequences. From the perspective of social science, which focuses on the societal use of new materials *after* initial application, over a prolonged period of time, the view is very different. From this perspective, production quickly segues into overproduction, and use often into misuse. Reduced to a critical voice that resonates with debates reflecting on matters that lie outside of and independent of materials, from sustainable resources and climate change to the environment, social science has lost its perspective on materials. This chapter will review the reasons behind the neglect of the study of materials use in social science research, and reflect on the methodological challenges involved in filling this gap, richly demonstrated in the chapters assembled in this book.

A short history of materials in social science research

One hundred years ago, the art historian Alois Riegl published his now classic piece, 'The Modern Cult of Monuments: its Character and its Origin' (1903 [1982]), originally written in German as a document on the restoration of public architecture. His observation of a decisive change in early twentieth-century attitudes towards materials, shifting from a valuation of the old to a valuation of the new, reflected on the rapid diversification of new materials and new commodity forms and functions that had dominated the previous century. Riegl's note on the preoccupation with newness at the start of the twentieth century is reflected in research by historians on the role of materials in commerce and politics in early modern Europe (Schiebinger and Swan 2005; Smith and Findlen 2002) and in the rise of institutions devoted to the archiving of materials whose properties promised the creation of new worlds.

London's Museum of Economic Botany at Kew documents that at the close of the nineteenth century botanical specimens were no longer of interest for consumption alone but as a knowledge resource able to convert new materials into political power and economic capital for the industrial world system

(Brockway 2002; Desmond 2007). The Museum collection (now known as the Economic Botany Collection) contains many thousands of biomaterials, dominated by rubber, gutta percha and other exudates, textiles and fibres, papers, timbers, adhesives and dyes. Following Gottfried Semper's (1854/2004) foundational text on the technical uses of materials for an emerging field of architecture, materials were now of explicit scientific interest, inspiring the search for ways to imitate and substitute for more expensive materials, and to innovate new material properties and object forms and functions. The purchase of materials and their properties for envisioning new forms of living and being was thus well-established at the time of Riegl's publication. What, we might ask, went wrong, leaving social science materials research out of step with the rapidly accelerating innovations in materials science that came to shape much of the lived in social world of the twentieth century?

A glimpse into the popular imagination that attached itself to all things material during the early industrial revolution has come down to us in Johann Wolfgang von Goethe's novel *Elective Affinities,* which, published in 1809, captured the prevailing use of chemical and alchemic analogies in debates about the nature of familial relationships (Adler 1990; Kim 2003). Chemical substances were said to unite 'like friends and acquaintances' or stay as 'strangers side by side' depending on their different reaction to one another, projecting a covert and 'inner' connection, hidden from view, that could validate new forms of contractual relations where previously overt relations sanctioned by marriage had prevailed (Raistrick 1950, 1953). A whole array of moral lessons were drawn from the behaviour of chemical substances and their human analogues, making chemistry 'an authentic discipline' with prestige and public visibility well before the onset of the Chemical Revolution and nearly a century earlier than modern physics. The affective qualities of materials, apparent in their mutability and their capacity to be turned into something completely new, were increasingly harnessed in the nineteenth century, pivotally leading to the controlling of the properties of iron in the production of steel, and of rubber in the production of the precursor of modern plastics, Bakelite (Mossmann and Smith 2008). The manifold uses to which these materials were put are still visible in the staircase banisters, doors and balcony railings of Victorian townhouses built to house an industrial class. The literature of the time offers a less-known trace of a conscious appreciation of materials (Wolff et al. 2005), used to create and authenticate new ways of living and fuelling the consumption of a seemingly irrepressible stream of commodities in ways that have not substantially changed until today (Forty 1986; Phillip 1998).

The diversification of commodities at the close of the nineteenth century, however, masqued a fundamental change in the conception of materials, laying the foundation for the relentless search for new material properties and functions and their eventual synthetic replication, which came to dominate the twentieth century. Drawing on Gottfried Semper's notion of a 'truth to materials', the art historian Monika Wagner (nd.) has argued that before the middle of the nineteenth century, both the form and the style of an object were inseparable from its materials, on account of the constraint the material exercises on tools and on the manufacturing processes. This is described well by Michael Baxandall (2008) in his narration of the consequences for the technique of carving, and the resulting style of religious sculptures, when switching from oak to limewood at the onset of the Renaissance in Germany, a change itself resonant of complex transformations in the social fabric at the time.

The discovery of new malleable materials in the nineteenth century, promising liberation from manual labour and the capacity for machinic transformation, led to the separation both conceptually and concretely of the design of an object, its form and function, from its material, which in turn became secondary and passive in relation to the chosen form. Design itself, in turn, now was no longer thought to have an inherent materiality and could be transferred to many different materials. Monica Wagner cites the example of the unveiling of a victory column made from one single piece of vulcanized *caoutchouc*, or natural rubber, at the 1873 World Fair in Vienna as a historical moment that galvanized a new imaginary both around the potential of design and the potential of materials that offer themselves up to an infinite range of forms. The 'shock of *caoutchouc*', as she calls it, resulted from the fact that although the form of this victory column was conventional, and greatly resembled a similar triumphal column inaugurated in Berlin that same year, it was produced from a single 'inauspicious vegetable material', soon found in numerous other commodities. Since rubber could be transformed to resemble many other materials, both hard and soft, and could take on many different forms, it sparked the invention of new object functions, such as fire hoses, bouncing balls and diving suits. Semper was therefore at a loss as to how to classify this material, which could be used for inflatable boats, victory columns and waterproof building coating, into his system of style-generating materials, signalling an ending that arguably provoked him to write a manual for style in the techtonic arts.

Malleable materials had in fact existed long before the 'shock of *caoutchouc*', for example, in the form of bronze or *papier mâché,* but rubber was incomparable in its manifold applications as it could be changed chemically at the microstructural level and with no physical effort through a small pinch of sulphur. The 'shock of *caoutchouc*' therefore had brought to light a new way of conceiving of the nature of a prototype, as functionality and form were no longer thought to be linked to the material, but instead relied exclusively on design.

This idea of design as both preceding and independent of the material within which it is taking on form has given way to new technical ways of creating form so that today prototypes may exist virtually on a computer, to be materialized in many different materials. As Monika Wagner shows in her work on the history of twentieth century art, an intimate relationship with and knowledge of materials remained active only in the world of fine art, chemistry and physics, a world away from commodity manufacture and consumption, which had become the playground for design and the experiential domain open to introspection by social and historical sciences (Wagner 2001). Today, the materials industry in the United Kingdom has an annual turnover of around £200 billion, contributing 15 per cent of GDP to the economy and employing 1.5 million people directly and supporting a further 4 million jobs. Yet we could be forgiven for being entirely oblivious to it as it is largely invisible. The twentieth century, as well as the twenty-first, have inherited the legacy of the nineteenth-century separation of the noumenal from the phenomenal, leaving materials to the peculiar concrescence of science, inaccessible to all but the expert and rendering all other acquaintance with materials subject to the experience of design.

Global policy makers today have embraced the potential of cutting-edge scientific research that takes the societal benefit of newly-invented materials as axiomatic. The development of advanced materials is being posited by governments in the United States, Germany, China, Japan and South Korea as crucial to global competitiveness and national security and essential for addressing the broader challenges of clean energy, food security and human health and well-being. As a result, the early twenty-first century is being defined by a new materials economy driven by a flood of engineered technological materials whose capacities offer far-reaching promises.

Consequently, in science, innovation for its own sake is privileged, with a trajectory that goes from invention to successful application on the basis of individual materials. From this perspective, the discovery and deployment of ever-new materials looks entirely positive. From the perspective of social science, which focuses on the use of materials after invention and first application, the view is very different. On-the-ground research shows that a staggering percentage of materials invented and manufactured at great cost fail within the first five months to establish a secure market, often for social rather than scientific reasons. For every lasting 'success', many materials come into circulation and then fail, exacerbating the very problems that new materials are supposedly developed to solve. At the same time, the privileging of innovation drives the development of yet more new materials, instead of fully exploring the potential and qualities of recent inventions, leading to waste, overproduction, increased risk and uncertainty, and an increasingly-felt lack of knowledge about the materials that surround us. Indeed, there is a general resistance to thinking about materials at all.

The precedent for this was set in the 1950s with the commercialization of the first mass-market new material – plastic. The consequences unleashed by the unbridled development of plastics is one of the greatest environmental challenges of our times, and yet people are still hypnotized by what some have called the 'exuberant proliferation' of design and new materials. In our obsession with novelty, we overlook the fact that materials are not inert, they leak, transform and interact with what is around them in ways that are invisible and unsuspected.

There are at present two competing approaches to how best to mitigate the uncertainty and risk that surround the discovery, deployment and disposal of materials. One calls for increased governance, the other for deregulation and global connectivity, but both are hampered by existing economic and management systems set up for commodity production, that either unnecessarily restrict movements of materials or are totally unaware of the possibilities. But on closer inspection both have the potential to make the problems worse.

The governance model directs attention almost exclusively to identifying and securing materials resources, driven by narratives of risk, volatility, scarcity, frontiers, resilience and governance. It calls for a holistic approach that includes: (a) strategic diplomatic efforts in the international arena to boost supply through trade agreements and knowledge exchange; (b) increasing the efficiency of resource use; and (c) improving the husbandry of resources through reuse, remanufacture and recycling in secondary markets. The governance model argues that it is de facto resource politics, not 'environmental preservation or sound economics' that is set to dominate the global agenda, played out through trade disputes, climate negotiations, market manipulation strategies, aggressive industrial policies and the scramble to control frontier areas.

The global connectivity model, however, is all about finding innovative advanced alternatives, with narratives of opportunity, experimentation and collaboration. It advocates speeding up the movement of materials from discovery through to deployment, on un-precedented scales. This typically involves public-private partnerships granting open access to generic materials databases within an evolving IP framework. Examples of its implementation include the United States's Materials Genome Initiative, launched in 2011, which aims to double the speed of new materials innovation and deployment through computational research and develop a national infrastructure to integrate data generated in materials science and engineering, based upon a public-private open access model. The computational research uses algorithms to generate millions of potential new materials and model their physical properties, without their ever having been manufactured, and it models spatially and temporally the new materials' behaviours and properties, building supposedly accurate predictive algorithms into product design tools.

In another example, supercomputing clusters at Berkeley have been harnessed for the Materials Project, which aims to compute the properties of all known materials and make them available to researchers. This will improve software's predictive capacities for new material combinations and allow for targeted screening of the potentially most useful materials before they have been synthesized in a lab. It is claimed that such advanced combinatorial techniques accelerate tenfold the transition from new materials discoveries to practical applications. Another project seeking a clearly defined advanced material solution to a practical problem is Harvard's open access Clean Energy Project, currently the world's largest computational chemistry experiment, which aims to develop high-performance organic photovoltaic candidates for solar cell materials. Using IBM's World Community Grid, the general public can participate by donating idle computer time for computational research. This has so far generated 2.3 million candidate materials, whose properties have been made available in online databases, allowing other materials scientists and engineers to design experimental new products.

The screening and selection of suitable virtual candidates results in what Andrew Barry (2005; this volume) has termed 'informed materials', whose properties are simulated by computers and whose proposed use is built into their very existence if they are selected for actual manufacture, yet whose real social use cannot be predicted or imagined. The emergence of 'informed' materials interestingly is bringing us back to an acknowledgement of the capacity of materials to both resist and attract potential transformation, modalities of manufacture and functionality, reasserting an active element in the project of design that had been lost to western thought since the height of the industrial revolution (Bennett 2010). The problem of recapturing what we have lost sight of is fundamentally an anthropological one: How do people from very different and overlapping cultures interact with, use and understand materials in their changing environments? With theoretical traditions that balance cultural relativism with universalist principles, and a foundation in fine-grained ethnography as a methodology, anthropological studies of cultural perceptions of materials in use have never been more urgently needed.

Ironically, in a world in which potentially millions of materials compete to be turned into objects with rather more limited forms and functions than they are technically capable of, we are now generally ignorant of the properties, levels of sustainability and future impact of the material objects that surround us. And this is precisely at a moment when materials are beginning to take over the technical functions we once associated exclusively with object forms. The step-change in both the quantity and inherent qualities of materials is swift, and largely unrecognized outside of the laboratory environment, arriving in the marketplace as a fait accompli apparently undifferentiated from previous materials. This leaves existing structures of training, monitoring and planning for materials' long-term impact hopelessly behind and unable to respond intelligibly. Without a deep understanding of the role of the social in materials development and use, how can we define criteria of success and understand how and why some materials fail? How are we to evaluate the 'usefulness' of materials and, by the same token, avoid wasting their potential and simply creating more waste? Understanding the value of materials through a deeper understanding of social and cultural values associated with them is a core contribution that social science ought to be making, and this volume presents the starting point for such work.

Materials use has today a hollow ring, conjuring up images of desperation, standing in front of do-it-yourself shelves searching for the right glue or in the supermarket searching for the right ingredient among dozens all seemingly alike, all made with use already designed into the fabric of the good. Armies of advisors, from the nutritionist to the new job type of the materials librarian, are standing by to broker the bewildering manifold of materials choices now available to decision makers in the kitchen and in design, all equally ill-equipped to handle each other's specialist knowledge: that of materials properties and that of use (cf. Küchler 2010). The lack of interest in understanding of materials' use beyond potential for the market, and the disconnect of interest from the lived-in social world in which people are desiring to make informed decisions, is suddenly no longer surprising. Yet these are crucial problems for a twenty-first century eager to rectify the fall-out from the excesses of the previous centuries.

Between invention and innovation

The conceptual separation of material from design paradoxically gave way to one of the most astonishing innovations of the twentieth century: the advent of materials by design. In her work on the history of materials innovation, the historian of science Bernadette Bensaude-Vincent (2004) discusses the cultural and epistemic impact of advancements in materials science, such as the development of high-performance materials, biomimetic materials and nano-biomaterials, outlining three 'generations' of materials designed to offer optimal solutions to specific problems or requirements of an end product. The social and political context of the first generation of high performance materials emerged as a result of the military space programmes of the 1970s with their strong demand for materials with never-seen-before properties for rockets and missiles. In the aftermath of World War II and the Cold War, the invention of new materials was further encouraged by science policy, leading to the innovation of composites that had several advantages over more traditional materials: they were especially strong as a result of the reinforcing carbon or aramid fibres they contained. They were able to combine the properties of various families of materials, such as the lightness of plastics, toughness of metals and heat resistance of ceramics. And, they could be designed to specification.

As a result of the substitution of these new materials-by-design for conventional materials, whole pieces of machinery, like the helicopter, were redesigned to be much more efficient and lighter. The production of composites used for parts of machines, such as aircraft wings or engines, required a complete departure from industrial machine mass production and a shift of manufacture to artisanal activity in that each piece is unique, produced for a specific task, with a customized design. As well as a change in the manufacturing process, the development of performance materials also saw a change in the traditional linear model of materials production. Whereas traditionally, production would begin with a raw material that is processed and used to manufacture the end product, which then reaches the consumer, with materials-by-design, the application or requirements often come first, and the material is then concocted to meet those needs. Materials development now no longer follows a linear model, but requires a 'systems approach', with continuous feedback from end users and design specialists into the production and ongoing modification of materials.

Materials by design have thus shifted the concern with innovation to what Barry (2002, 2005) has called 'invention'; that is, to a practice of iterative improvement, with the iterative process itself providing added value. Co-creation, the direct involvement of the concept of the ideal consumer in the design of a commodity, once happening at the consumption stage, has now moved to the process of materials manufacturing, pervading and structuring into sequences the entire process of production, from primary research into materials manufacture through to the purposing of the material for commodity function.

A notable recent example of an ethnography that inquires into the way ideal use informs manufacture and production is De Monchaux's (2011) detailed reconstruction of the selection of materials used in the construction of the Apollo spacesuits, whose image came to shape the way we think of the world we inhabit today and future worlds beyond. Rather than hard materials engineered for the purpose of space exploration, which projected the image and mind set of the mastery of nature through technology, soft materials originally designed with very different uses in mind were chosen. De Monchaux shows that the membrane-like quality of this material, comprised of layered, additive composition rather than external reinforcement, embodied and perpetuated an accommodation between nature and technology, representing a literal extension of the astronaut's body, and setting the precedent for new ways of thinking about materials and their transformations.

Another ethnography, by Kaori O'Connor (2011), of the invention and commercialization of Lycra, reveals how social forces and cultural factors inform what new materials are developed and how sometimes actual take-up and use can be very different. There can be very different consequences for production and for society than originally envisioned when the material was designed and put to market.

This new understanding of innovation as an iterative process of inventive discovery and deployment has come to blur not just the distinction between production, distribution and consumption, but also has shifted, as Nigel Thrift (2006) has argued, the entire fabric of capitalism. The world, according to Thrift, has 'become a continuous and inexhaustible process of inventions', creating new interactive senses of causality. This is a world of indirect but continuous expression, a new epistemic ecology, with commodities made persuasively empathetic by bringing them literally close to hand and appealing via the senses as the 'undertow of thought and decision' (Thrift 2006: 286). Reminiscent of Jane Bennett's (2010) theory of an emergent conception of an agentive vital materialism, cut loose from its moorings in materials that offer real constraints, the work of design has effaced the very basis from which it once arose as made plain in the work of Bensaude-Vincent and Thrift. This requires in turn new forms of marketing through the medium of websites, known as honey traps, that serve to increase the stickiness of commodities by engaging sensory registers, conjuring up future consumers from the scaffold of an idealized image of what it is to be human. With the hope of true innovation long past, invention now is not just referring to new commodities, but the capture and configuration of new worlds via materials that are discovered and deployed from within laboratory environments (cf. Barry 2005; Ingold 2010; Thrift 2006: 288).

Light, flexible, multifunctional, optimized and responsive materials-by-design, invented in laboratories appear as the new 'natural' when compared to 'old' materials that are rigid, uni-functional, inert, heavy and limited in their performance and also take on much of their seemingly pre-hermeneutic properties.

Bernadette Bensaude-Vincent and Michael Newmann (2007) point to a collaps-ing of the categories of the artificial and the natural, as there are no longer any limitations to control the properties and performance of materials, allowing the material scientist to assume the role of the demiurge. Writing about the *Inhuman* in the late 1980s, Lyotard reflected on the potential realization of a dream of mankind to overcome the constraints of matter in its entirety, suffusing it with mind, and allowing for what Theodore Adorno (1970) had called the irreducible materiality of things to be overcome in a world in which immaterial information takes precedent.

Philip Ball's (2014) book on the invisible and the lure of the unseen draws out this history, of the dream of mankind to evade material constraints and aspire to giving concrete expression to an idea of transcendence. The tragic human quality of this idea was famously captured by the anthropologist Claude Levi-Strauss, who argued that humankind dreams of 'that fleeting moment when it [is] permissible to believe that the law of exchange could be evaded, that one could give without losing, enjoy without sharing' (Levi-Strauss 1969: 496). Science and design have triumphed in giving texture to the dream of escaping the shackles of nature, by creating an artificial one in their own image.

Nature, in the words of Bensaude-Vincent (2004), has become a model for the ability of materials to act as complete materials systems that self-assemble at low temperatures, are smart and responsive and are easily produced and recycled with no low energy costs. We now know however that this hoped-for capacity of engineered materials will likely remain a dream, as it was soon real-ized that, while nature was an insuperable engineer, using it as model was not as simple as adapting nature's elegant solutions to our human technology. Bensaude-Vincente demonstrates convincingly that the principles underlying natural technologies diverge quite considerably from those underlying human technologies, as nature uses predominantly soft, organic materials behind which there is no grand design. The reference to the human element in production, assumed to be generic and 'natural' rather than culturally specific and socially motivated, is thus steeped in misconception, requiring us to look closely at how materials are used outside of the laboratory, where materials are perceived as indexes of complex intentions that are embedded in complex relations.

Materials use beyond laboratory life

The art historian Hans Belting (1995) famously once stated that art is for those who 'do not feel at home'. Arguably indeed, a world of consociates who share a lived-in social world, as captured by the Austrian sociologist and philosopher Alfred Schütz (1932), do not require the aid of an image or performance to recognize ways of thinking and being that bind people together in the myriads of actions in the everyday. Schütz's manifesto for a phenomenology of the social world described a world of consociates in which empathy and intersubjective understanding rest on the unmediated experience of the everyday, a world whose unquestionable existence was, at the time of the original publication of the work, about to end. The idea of a shared social world may have ended while it was being extended into a myriad of social networks through war, exile and migration; yet empathy and inter-subjective understanding grew even stronger when carried, refracted as index of what is relational about actions, in the form of poetry, literature and art, to the far reaches of the world. The question is how the lessons of art, and its capacity to unleash empathetic understanding and lasting intersubjective attachment, can be learnt by those keen to address the lack of indexicality built into materials by design; materials which paradoxically, in-spite of or perhaps because of their aspiration to speak to a generic human element, have effectively disabled understanding, evaluation and lasting attachment with materials in general and their use.

In their recent essay on the use of mundane materials as interfaces, Michael Barany and Donald MacKenzie (2014) discuss the role of chalk, blackboards and scrap paper in the development of theoretical approaches and developments in mathematics. Chalk here is introduced as material surrogate for the practices that constitute mathematicians as community, as it is the very material properties of chalk that enable abstract thought. Chalk serves both as metaphor and as device in the construction and circulation of new concepts, presenting a potent resource in its implicit relation to other materials and serving as constraint that combine to shape mathematical research in innumerable ways. Chalk writing and its relation to tracing out mathematical thought verbally and manually, fashion the intrinsic necessity of the unfolding of the argument in mathematical exposition.

Barany and McKenzie challenge Bruno Latour's argument that preparatory practices such as paper and pen materialize and stabilize unruly natural phenomena in the form of data, plots and other representations (Latour 1990). They show instead that while mathematicians expend a remarkable amount of labour to materialize their concepts of study, they do that with the goal of coaxing those thought objects to behave in some new way rather than disciplining them to hold some stable and circulatable form. Mathematical thinking, therefore, is markedly dependent on material media, an insight that recalls Alfred Gell's (1998) theorization of the cognitive stickiness of certain artefacts embedded in an artefact's indexical, internally held relations.

Science and Technology Studies has long pointed out that the take-up of material technologies of all kinds is a social process par excellence (Bijker 1997; Latour 1992). Latour (1993) in his work on the Pasteurization of France points out that Pasteur neither discovered nor invented microbes, but that the invention was the result of the interactions between Pasteur and resources and allies such as politicians, hygienists, laboratories, experiments, cattle, and bacilli, that worked to transform microbes from entities to qualified things with definite and stable attributes. In the same way as a mathematician's intuition and imagination spring forth from the properties of the chalk, the worlds of potential that pasteurization came to conjure up similarly sprang from the recognition of the material properties of microbes and their capacity to manifest sequences of processes and relations in ways that propelled attention to new understanding and vocabulary.

The quasi-magical capacity of materials to conjure up associations and attach vocabularies and modalities of attention to its aesthetic qualities is born out in a number of case studies brought together in this volume. Fiona P. McDonald shows how the multiple resonances of woollen blankets, industrially produced and distributed as the signature piece of colonial intervention, provoke their transformations into art, craft and indigenous cultural property. Rather than eliciting a uniform response, the chapter shows how the perception of blankets as indexical of complex relations and complex histories provokes distinct and diverse actions upon the material, whose 'mattering' pervades a social and cultural imagination that is both radical and mainstream.

In contrast to the response invited by an already-transformed material whose resonances call up forms of labour and loyalty rooted in industrial and colonial worlds, Laurence Douny takes us to the space of imagination and social action afforded by a material whose own futurity attracts other transformational materials, with a logic that relations between materials act as a site of cultural imagination. Wild silk, collected and laboriously prepared for threading and weaving, almost invites indigo dye as the substance that, reminiscent of Semper, is 'true to the material'. Indigo dye resonates as index of transformation with the futurity of 'becoming', that is so subtly made tangible by the cocoons whose discarded shells offer up the resource for silk. Relations that are seen in or are built out of materials, are in both cases the vital ingredients for understanding relations between persons and between persons and things. They enable people to make informed decisions about what to do or what to think about seemingly completely removed domains of social, political and economic life.

At the other end of the spectrum, we have chapters that discuss the problems that occur when materials no longer offer up an understanding of relations. Sarah

Wilkes takes us through the minefield of what is sustainable about materials, revealing the open-ended and uncertain nature of this question when directed to engineered materials, whose relations, once so wonderfully grasped via classificatory regimes, have long ceased to function. Mark A. Miodownik outlines the slippage of these regimes, and speaks from the engineering perspective on the need to understand once again the relations that materials harbour and offer up for our engagement.

These and other chapters in this volume bring together perspectives both on the indexicality of materials and associated problems of classification and analysis as well as on the methodological challenges of conducting ethnographies of materials use. Together they seek to address the blind spot that materials occupy in social and historical sciences in the hope of paving the way for a new vocabulary and a new intellectual engagement, with what the anthropologist Claude Levi Strauss has long ago identified as 'the science of the concrete', to build bridges across the divide between the noumenal and the phenomenal that has remained a lasting shadow cast by the industrial world onto the twenty-first century.

References

Adorno, T. (1970), *Ästhetische Theorie*, edited by G. Adorno and R. Tielmann. Frankfurt am Main: Suhrkamp Verlag.

Ball, P. (1999), *Made to Measure*. Oxford: Oxford University Press.

Ball, P. (2014), *Invisible: The dangerous allure of the Unseen*. London: Random House.

Barany, M. and D. MacKenzie (2014), 'Chalk: Materials and Concepts in Mathematics Research', in C. Coopmans, J. Vertesi, M. Lynch and S. Woolgar (eds), *Representation in Scientific Practice Revisited*, pp. 107–131. Cambridge, MA: MIT Press.

Barry, A. (2005), 'Pharmaceutical Matters: The Invention of Informed Materials', *Theory, Culture and Society,* 22 (1): 51–69.

Barry, A. and N. Thrift (2007), 'Gabriel Tarde: Imitation, Invention, and Economy', *Economy and Society,* 36(4): 509–525.

Baxandall, M. (1980), *Limewood Sculpture in Renaissance Germany*. Berkeley: California University Press.

Belting, H. (1995), 'Global Art and Minorities: A New Geography of Art History', in *Art History After Modernism*, pp. 62–74. Chicago: University of Chicago Press.

Bennett, J. (2010), *Vibrant Matter : A Political Ecology of Things*. Amherst: Duke University Press.

Bensaude-Vincent, B. (2004), *Se libérer de la matière? Fantasmes autour de la nouvelles technologies*. Versailles Cedex: Editions Quae.

Bensaude-Vincent, B. and M. Newmann (eds) (2007), *The Artificial and the Natural: An Evolving Polarity*. Cambridge, MA: MIT Press.

Bijker, W. (1997), *Of Bicycles, Bakelites and Bulbs: Toward a Theory of Socio-Technical Change*. Cambridge, MA: MIT Press.

Brockway, L. H. (2002), *Science and Colonial Expansion: The Role of the British Royal Botanical Gardens*. Yale: Yale University Press.

Clark, A. (2001), *Mindware: An Introduction to the Philosophy of Cognitive Science*. Oxford: Oxford University Press.

Colchester, C. (2003), *Clothing the Pacific*. Oxford: Berg.

Cordeschi, R. (2002), *The Discovery of the Artificial: Behaviour, Mind and Machine before and beyond Cybernetics*. Dordrecht: Kluwer Academic Publishers.

Desmond, R. (2007), *The History of the Royal Botanic Gardens Kew*. London: Kew Publishing.

Forty, A. (1986*), Objects of Desire: Design and Society since 1750*. London: Thames & Hudson.

Gell, A. (1998), *Art and Agency*. Oxford: Clarendon Press.

Goethe, J. W. von (2008 [1809]), *Elective Affinities: A Novel*, translated by David Constantin. Oxford: Oxford Paperbacks.

Ingold, T. (2010), 'The Textility of Making', *Cambridge Journal of Economics*, 34(1): 91–102.

Kim, M. G (2003), *Affinity, That Elusive Dream: A Genealogy of the Chemical Revolution*. Cambridge, MA: MIT Press.

Küchler, S. (2008), 'Technological Materiality: Beyond the Dualist Paradigm', *Theory, Culture and Society*, 25(1): 101–120.

Küchler, S. (2010), 'Materials and Design', in A. Clarke (ed.), *Design Anthropology*, pp. 130–145. Vienna: Springer.

Küchler, S. and G. Were (2005), *Pacific Pattern*, with Photographer G. Jowitt. London: Thames & Hudson.

Küchler, S. and A. Eimke (2009), *Tivaivai: The Social Fabric of the Cook Islands*. London: British Museum Press and Te Papa Museum Press.

Latour, B. (1990), 'Drawing Things Together', in M. Lynch and S. Woolgar (eds), *Representation in Scientific Practice*, pp. 19–69. Cambridge, MA: MIT Press.

Latour, B. (1992), 'Where Are the Missing Masses: The Sociology of a Few Mundane Artifacts', in W. Bijker and J. Law (eds), *Shaping Technology/Building Society: Studies in Socio-Technical Change*, pp. 225–258. Cambridge, MA: MIT Press.

Latour, B. (1993), *The Pasteurization of France*, translated by A. Sheridan. Boston, MA: Harvard University Press.

Levi-Strauss, C. (1966), *The Savage Mind*. Paris: Librarie Plon.

Levi-Strauss, C. (1969), *The Elementary Structures of Kinship*. Boston, MA: Beacon Press.

Lyotard, J.-F. (1991), *The Inhuman: Reflections on Time*. New York: Polity Press.

Moncheaux, N. (2011), *Spacesuit: Fashioning Apollo*. Cambridge, MA: MIT Press.

Mossmann, S. and R. Smith (2008), *Fantastic Plastic: Product Design and Consumer Culture*. London: Black Dog.

O'Connor, K. (2011), *Lycra: How a Fiber shaped America*. New York and London: Routledge.

Phillips, R. (1998), *Trading Identities: Souvenir in Native North American Art from the Northeast, 1700–1900*. Seattle: University of Washington Press.

Raistrick, A. (1950), *Quakers in Science and Industry*. New York: Philosophical Library

Ralstrick, A. (1953), *Dynasty of Iron Founders: The Darbys and Coalbrookdale*. London: Longmans, Green.

Schiebinger, L. and C. Swan (eds) (2005), *Colonial Botany, Science, Commerce and Politics in Early Modern Europe*. Philadelphia: University of Pennsylvania Press.

Schütz, A. (1932), *Der sinnhafte Aufbau der sozialen Welt: eine Einleitung in die verstehende Soziologie*. Wien: J. Springer.

Schütz, A. (1967), *The Phenomenology of the Social World*, (a translation of Schütz 1932, above). Evanston, IL: Northwestern University Press.

Semper, G. (2004[1854]), *Style in the Technical and Tectonic Arts; Or, Practical Aesthetics*. Santa Monica: The Getty Publications.

Smith, P. and P. Findlen (eds) (2002), *Merchants and Marvels: Commerce, Science and Art in Early Modern Europe*. New York: Routledge.

Uberoi, J. P. S. (2002), *The European Modernity: Science, Truth & Method*. Delhi: Cambridge University Press.

Wagner, M. (2001), *Das Material der Kunst: Eine andere Geschichte der Moderne*. Munich: C. H. Beck.

Wagner, M. (nd.), 'New Materials and the End of Rigid Form'. Unpublished paper delivered to the workshop on The Social History of the Prototype, 8 February 2008 as part of the ESR funded seminar series New Materials and New Technologies: Innovation, Future and Society.

Wallace, A. (1972), *Rockdale: The Growth of an American Village in the Early Industrial Revolution*. Lincoln: University of Nebraska Press.

Wallace, A. (1982), *The Social Context of Innovation*. Princeton, NJ: Princeton University Press.

Wolff, V., M. Wagner and D. Rübel (2005), *Materialästhetik*. Hamburg: Reimer Verlag.

Index